MYSTICISM IN
THE REFORMATION
(1500–1650)

A multi-volume series

THE PRESENCE OF GOD:
A HISTORY OF WESTERN CHRISTIAN MYSTICISM

MYSTICISM IN THE REFORMATION (1500–1650)

Vol. VI, Part 1 of
The Presence of God:
A History of Western Christian Mysticism

by
Bernard McGinn

A Herder & Herder Book
The Crossroad Publishing Company
New York

A Herder & Herder Book
The Crossroad Publishing Company
www.CrossroadPublishing.com

In continuation of our 200-year tradition of independent publishing, The Crossroad Publishing Company proudly offers a variety of books with strong, original voices and diverse perspectives. The viewpoints expressed in our books are not necessarily those of The Crossroad Publishing Company, any of its imprints or of its employees, executives, or owners. Although the author and publisher have made every effort to ensure that the information in this book was correct at press time, the author and publisher do not assume and hereby disclaim any liability to any party for any loss, damage, or disruption caused by errors or omissions, whether such errors or omissions result from negligence, accident, or any other cause. No claims are made or responsibility assumed for any health or other benefits.

Book design by The HK Scriptorium

Library of Congress Cataloging-in-Publication Data
available from the Library of Congress.

ISBN 978-0-8245-0171-6

Books published by The Crossroad Publishing Company may be purchased at special quantity discount rates for classes and institutional use. For information, please e-mail sales@CrossroadPublishing.com.

Contents

Preface

An oft-told, if not historically verifiable tale has the Augustinian monk Martin Luther nailing ninety-five theses on indulgences he wished to dispute to the door of the castle church at Wittenberg on October 31, 1517. Everybody loves an easily remembered date, like Columbus's discovery of America in 1492, the Norman Conquest of England in 1066. Great historical transitions, though, are usually prepared for over many decades, or longer, and their real effects are rarely seen immediately. Luther's Ninety-Five theses of 1517, however, remain one of the iconic dates of Western history, and not just for religion and theology. The contested meaning of what we have come to call "The Reformation," begun back in 1517, continues to be debated today five hundred years later, even when the polemical fires that pitted Christian against Christian have, for the most part, subsided. One thing seems certain among these debates: 1517, at least as a symbol, marks a turning point.

The "Divided Christianity" that resulted from the actions of Luther and the other Reformers was real. Although serious divisions had always been found in Christianity, both between East and West, and even within Western Christendom, what happened in the sixteenth century was of a different order of magnitude—a division that fragmented the "seamless body of Christ" into many violently contending parts. It has only been within the last century that the ecumenical movement among Christian denominations has begun to foster the kinds of discussion and cooperation that have started to turn the corner on the divisions of the last five centuries.

If, as Friedrich von Hügel argued more than a century ago, a good way of considering the inner dynamism of Christianity is to see it in terms of the interaction between three elements—the institutional element represented by Peter, the intellectual element figured in Paul, and the mystical element of John—it stands to reason that the sixteenth-century division of Christendom had serious effects on all three of these elements. I mention von Hügel's tripartite model here not to pursue it in detail but only to note that the split in religion had repercussions on the mystical aspect of Christendom. All would admit that mysticism, however defined, was powerful in the Late Middle Ages. Did it remain so after the division, especially among those who broke with Rome? One influential school of Protestant theologians strong from the late nineteenth through the mid-twentieth centuries claimed that the evangelical faith of the Reformers jettisoned the mysticism of the corrupt Catholicism of the Middle Ages to return to the pure gospel faith that knew nothing of the Hellenic mystical tendencies that had begun to infect Christianity from the second century C.E. on. This book is written to counter this argument, and it does so with considerable support from many Protestant scholars over the past century.

The case that I will try to present in what follows is that the Reformation was not the end, but rather a recalibration of the mystical element that had been present in Christianity from the time of the writing of the New Testament. Protestantism, at least in its formative first century or more, did not lack for mystics, and evangelical theology, even in its fountainhead, Martin Luther, had an important relation to the mystical aspects of faith. The extent to which the mysticism found in many denominations of Protestant Christianity was something new, or more properly a reevaluation and redirection of inherited themes about the need for a religion based on the experience of God within, is a complex topic that is open to many interpretations. My own view is that there is more continuity than break between inherited mystical traditions and what we find in the Protestant mystics studied here. Many may think this view is overly optimistic, and I can appreciate some of the particular arguments to the contrary. My main point, however, is different. It is the claim that, unless we recognize the importance of Protestant mysticism for the broader story of Western mysticism, both Protestants and Catholics will be the poorer, and less able to profit from the mutual understanding that the ecumenical age has opened up.

This book, like its predecessors in *The Presence of God: A History of Western Christian Mysticism*, has had a long and complicated development. The general title of this, the sixth volume of the series, is *Mysticism in Divided Christianity, 1500–1650*. It is intended to embrace the effects of the religious division of Europe on both the Protestant and the Catholic mystics of the sixteenth and much of the seventeenth centuries. So rich is the material, so striking the thought of these mystics, so powerful their impact, that it gradually became clear to me that it would be best to split the Protestant and the Catholic sections into three parts, of which this is the first. Much of part II is already written, at least in draft; but it will be some time before part III is finished, so I decided to publish part I in the fortuitous year of 2017, the five-hundredth anniversary of Luther's epochal protest.

I want to thank Gwendolin Herder, the publisher of Crossroad-Herder, for her encouragement and for agreeing with this new plan. Warm thanks are also due to the staff at the press, especially Chris Myers, the editor, for their invaluable assistance in the editing, production, and publication process. I am not a Reformation scholar by training, so I am particularly grateful to four friends and colleagues of great expertise in Reformation studies who agreed to read individual chapters and make comments, critiques, and suggestions. They will be appropriately thanked below in the respective chapters. Naturally, any errors, problems, or dubious views that remain are fully my own. Finally, I want to thank, as ever, my wife Patricia Ferris McGinn, who with her discerning editorial eye and knowledge of the Christian tradition read the whole manuscript as it developed, correcting, amending, and often clarifying what was ill-formulated, or just plain confusing. I hope that the final product will be a clear expression of my views on this subject, and, above all, that it may provoke further discussion about the nature and importance of Protestant mysticism.

CHICAGO
JULY, 2016

Abbreviations

CO	Calvini Opera
DS	*Dictionnaire de spiritualité: Ascétique et mystique, doctrine et histoire.* Edited by Marcel Viller et al. 17 vols. Paris: Beauchesne, 1937–97.
The Dionysian Corpus	The writings ascribed to Dionysius the Areopagite are in the critical edition of Beate Regina Suchla, Günter Heil, and Adolf Martin Ritter, *Corpus Dionysiacum*, 2 vols. Berlin: Walter de Gruyter, 1990–91. The following abbreviations will be used here:
CH	*De caelesti hierarchia (The Celestial Hierarchy)*
DN	*De divinis nominibus (The Divine Names)*
EH	*De ecclesiastica hierarchia (The Ecclesiastical Hierarchy)*
Ep	*Epistulae (Letters)*
MT	*De mystica theologia (The Mystical Theology)*
Eckhart	The critical edition of the writings of Meister Eckhart is: *Meister Eckhart: Die deutschen und lateinischen Werke herausgegeben im Auftrag der deutschen Forschungsgemeinschaft.* Stuttgart and Berlin: Kohlhammer, 1937–. The two sections of this edition are *Die lateinischen Werke* (LW, cited by volume, page, and line where necessary) and *Die deutschen Werke* (DW, cited in the same manner).
Martin Luther	The critical edition of the writings of Luther is *D. Martin Luthers Werke: Kritische Gesamtausgabe.* 120 vols. Weimar: Hermann Böhlau,

	1883–2009. The volumes in the main collection, known as the Weimarer-Ausgabe, will be cited here under the abbreviation WA by volume, page, and line number where necessary (e.g., WA 1:112.12–26).
McGinn	Bernard McGinn, *The Presence of God: A History of Western Christian Mysticism*. New York: Crossroad Herder, 1991–. The five previous volumes of this series will be abbreviated as follows:
Foundations	*The Foundations of Mysticism: Origins to the Fifth Century* (1991)
Growth	*The Growth of Mysticism: Gregory the Great through the Twelfth Century* (1994)
Flowering	*The Flowering of Mysticism: Men and Women in the New Mysticism, 1200–1350* (1998)
Harvest	*The Harvest of Mysticism in Medieval Germany, 1300–1500* (2007)
Varieties	*Varieties of Vernacular Mysticism, 1350–1550* (2012)
Oxford Encyclopedia	*The Oxford Encyclopedia of the Reformation*. Edited by Hans J. Hillerbrand. 4 vols. New York and Oxford: Oxford University Press, 1996
PL	*Patrologia cursus completus: Series Latina*. Edited by J.-P. Migne. 221 vols. Paris: J.-P. Migne, 1844–64
STh	Thomas Aquinas, *Summa theologiae* (cited by part, question, and article; e.g., Ia, q. 3, a. 1)
TRE	*Theologische Realenzyklopädie: Studienausgabe*. Edited by Gerhard Krause and Gerhard Müller. 36 vols. Berlin: Walter de Gruyter, 1993–2006.
Vg	Vulgate Bible

MYSTICISM IN
THE REFORMATION
(1500–1650)

The Dividing of Western Christianity

HE DIVISION OF WESTERN CHRISTIANITY into Catholic and Protestant camps in the first half of the sixteenth century is one of the salient markers of early modern history, but the causes, extent, significance, and effects of the division continue to be debated. The disputes over the significance of the Reformation, the term traditionally used for this split,[1] cannot be settled here; but in order to understand the impact of this religious divide on the history of the mystical element in Christianity during the period 1500 to 1650, the focus of this book, some remarks about the issues at stake need to be presented at the outset.

Martin Luther (1483–1546) may not have actually nailed a copy of his ninety-five theses on indulgences and other ecclesiastical abuses on the church doors at Wittenberg on October 31, 1517; but events, like people, need birthdays, and so in later years this date became celebrated as "Reformation Day." It has also often been seen as the beginning of a new epoch in history. But did Luther's protest against some practices of the medieval church really mark the end of the Middle Ages and the beginnings of the modern world, or should his actions rather be seen as the culmination of movements for church reform stretching back for centuries? To put it another way, were the events of 1517 and afterwards the onset of *the* Reformation or just another, if more powerful, example of *a* medieval effort at church reform? One can also ask about the relation of *the*

1

Reformation to *the* Renaissance, often seen as another intellectual and cultural challenge to medieval culture and society. Were Renaissance and Reformation allied in bringing an end to the Middle Ages, or were the two movements separate, even opposed, phenomena? Confronting such issues, historical investigation tends to merge into philosophical speculation, something evident in the considerable literature on the meaning of the Reformation.[2]

A tradition in German thought going back at least as far as Georg W. F. Hegel's *Vorlesungen über die Philosophie der Geschichte* [*The Philosophy of History*], lectures originally given in 1830–31, emphasized a strong distinction between Protestantism and Catholicism and saw the Reformation as the start of modern history.[3] This view received support in Leopold van Ranke's classic *Deutsche Geschichte im Zeitalter der Reformation* first published in six volumes (1839–47). It has had powerful adherents, such as the church historian Karl Holl (1866–1926) and his students.[4] An alternative proposal had its beginnings with Ernst Troeltsch (1865–1923) in a paper of 1906 and later in his *Protestantism and Progress: The Significance of Protestantism for the Rise of the Modern World* (German original 1910). As Troeltsch put it, "The genuine early Protestantism of Lutheranism and Calvinism is, as an organic whole, in spite of its anti-Catholic doctrine of salvation, entirely a Church civilization like that of the Middle Ages." Somewhat later he summarized, "Protestantism—especially at the outset in Luther's reform of the Church—was, in the first place, simply a modification of Catholicism, in which the Catholic formulation of the problems was retained, while a different answer was given to them."[5] Troeltsch's distinction between the "Old Protestantism" (*Altprotestantismus*) and the "New Protestantism" (*Neuprotestantismus*) has been echoed by many over the past century. Beginning in the 1960s, Heiko A. Oberman (1930–2001) expanded on Troeltsch's alternative in a series of books and essays analyzing Luther, Calvin, and the early Reformation from the perspective of the late Middle Ages.[6] Oberman's students and others have developed this line of argument over the past half century.[7] This option has not prevented reformulations and expansions of the view of the Reformation as a decisive break, such as Brad S. Gregory's *The Unintended Reformation*, which sees the doctrinal split of the sixteenth century as the beginning of a process that led to contemporary secularism and hyperpluralism characterized by political polarization, rampant consumerism, and intellectual relativism.[8] Alternative projects have also emerged, such as Constantin Fasolt's proposal to see the Reformation as "part and parcel of a single process of social development that began around the turn of the millennium, that was European-wide, and that was carried forward by Protestants and Catholics alike."[9] Some historians of Christianity, like John Bossy, consider the very term "Reformation" misleading and try to do without it.[10] Clearly, consensus about *the* meaning of *the* Reformation is hard to find.

That said, few would want to deny that something significant happened in the early sixteenth century. Western Christianity fractured into opposed camps whose mutual suspicions and hatred led to attempts to destroy each other that lasted for centuries. Martin Luther, whether we wish to consider him a medieval or a modern figure, or neither,[11] was a major catalyst of the changes. If the components of the forms of European Christianity of the sixteenth and seventeenth centuries—Catholic, Lutheran, Reformed, Radical, Anglican—were in some part continuations of aspects of late medieval religion, their arrangement and relations had shifted in important ways that made the new confessions increasingly alien to each other. The mystical element, broadly conceived of as the aspect of religious life that seeks a deep and transformative sense of the direct presence of God, was certainly affected by these shifts. Nevertheless, the changes in mysticism, as I shall argue, were not so much *within* the traditions of mystical teaching themselves, where one can detect considerable continuity between sixteenth-century mysticism and the forms of mysticism characteristic of the "New Mysticism" that emerged in the thirteenth century, but rather in the *relation* of mysticism to the other elements of religion in the complicated world of 1500–1650.

The ways in which mysticism came to expression amid the religious quarrels that erupted in the first half of the sixteenth century already show significant variations that became more pronounced with the growth of "confessionalization," that is, the creation of communities with fixed religious identities based on explicit statements of belief that emerged in the second half of the century.[12] Just as the Tridentine Roman Catholicism created in the wake of the Council of Trent (1547–1563) differed from late medieval Catholic Christianity in important ways, so too the role that the mystical element played within the new Catholicism took on new hues during the sixteenth and seventeenth centuries. More radical developments occurred within Protestantism, although, contrary to the claims of some nineteenth-century Protestant theologians, mysticism was by no means absent from the developing Protestant confessions.[13] Mysticism did, however, have a different place in the varieties of Protestantism: Lutheranism, the Reformed tradition initiated by Zwingli and Calvin, the Spiritual/Radical reformers, and the distinctive form of the Reformation that developed in England in the second half of the sixteenth century.

The Protestant historian of doctrine Adolph von Harnack (1851–1930) summed up modern Protestant opposition to mysticism in his *Lehrbuch der Dogmengeschichte (History of Dogma)* published between 1885 and 1890, by claiming, "Mysticism as a rule is rationalism worked out in a fantastic way, and rationalism is faded mysticism." Hence his famous remark that "a Mystic that does not become a Catholic is a dilettante."[14] This form of Protestant opposition to mysticism, however, was based on an inadequate view of the mystical element of Christianity, taking it as a monolithic phenomenon based on "mystical union" (*unio mystica*) conceived of as a mingling of God and the human creature. In the twentieth century, a number of major Protestant thinkers, beginning with Ernst Troeltsch, Albert Schweitzer, and Paul Tillich, argued, albeit in different ways, that there was indeed a place for mysticism, or at least some forms of mysticism, in Protestantism. Today we can say that to deny a mystical dimension to Protestant Christianity is much like saying there is no reforming tradition in Catholicism.[15]

Historical Background[16]

Calls for reform of the church "in head and members," originating as early as the fourteenth century, persisted throughout the fifteenth. Even after the revival of the papacy following the Council of Constance (1414–1418) and the victory of popes Martin V, Eugene IV, and their successors over the proponents of the conciliar option for reform appeals to constitutional conciliarism as the best way of getting rid of corrupt practices and rejuvenating the church continued.[17] Early in his career, Luther himself called for a general council to judge between himself and his Roman opponents. It would be incorrect to suppose that all the popes of the period ca. 1450–1520 were opposed to reform, but what good intentions did exist produced little fruit. A large part of the resistance to reform came not only from the entrenched power of the curial officials anxious to hold on to their perquisites but also from the fact that the popes after Constance tended to concentrate on their role as Renaissance princes, rulers of the papal states in the rough-and-tumble world of fifteenth- and early sixteenth-century Italian power politics. Thus, it is no surprise that the reforming council convened by Julius II known as Lateran V (1512–1517) may have been a rhetorical success (everybody gave great speeches), but was a reform failure. The fact that the first papally approved council for a century achieved so little was a judgment on how ineffective Rome had become in the face of mounting dissatisfaction with the current state of the church.

What were the complaints of contemporary Christians about church structures and practices? Obviously, these are hard to summarize and differed from area to area and from group to group. Some involved personal morality, such as concubinage among the clergy and nepotism on the part of influential clerics (i.e., favoring relatives for ecclesiastical appointments). Many concerned the financial abuses and exactions of the ecclesiastical establishment, such as the accumulation of multiple salaried positions (benefices) on the part of clerics, and the consequent nonresidency of these officeholders, who farmed out their pastoral duties to an often-negligent clerical underclass. Various forms of papal taxation were also resented, as well as the misuse of ecclesiastical censures. The sale of indulgences, that is, remissions of the temporal punishment remaining after the sacramental forgiveness of sins, also disturbed many. Other complaints were more specifically doctrinal and liturgical, such as the Hussite insistence on the reception of the Eucharist under both the forms, bread and wine. Some objected to devotional practices, such as the cult of relics, that seem to have gotten out of hand.

The failure of reform in the late medieval church has led to a widespread view that the pastoral ineffectiveness of the late medieval church was an important part of the success of Luther and others who offered a different model of access to salvation. Assertions of the pastoral deficiencies of late medieval Christianity became a part of "the myth of the Reformation," the story that came to be told and accepted about why Luther, Calvin, and the other "protestors" were so successful. This traditional view has come under attack over the past generation, both in regional studies, such as those of Eamon Duffy concerning England,[18] and in wider historiography.[19] Was the late medieval church a pastoral failure? Was the sacrament of penance, for example, an onerous burden on the faithful, or a consoling ritual that made people feel closer to God? Were the veneration of relics and the use of indulgences scams that people saw through, or expressions of a deeply felt popular piety that, despite abuses, fulfilled a real need? There are no satisfactory general answers to these questions, though regional variations about how believers felt about these and other aspects of late medieval religious life have something important to say about the success or failure of Luther and his followers. It seems, for example, that complaints about selected church practices were more widespread in Germany than in southern Europe, especially in Spain, where some reforms had already been undertaken. Late medieval Christianity was vibrant and effective in some of its practices—and more in some areas than others. It was viewed with suspicion, even resentment, in others. Otherwise, it would be impossible to understand how the originally conservative call of one German monk had the success it did.

It is important, nonetheless, not to exaggerate the significance of ecclesiastical abuses as the cause of the Reformation. As Lucien Febvre noted long ago, it is difficult to think "that such a positive and complex movement of religious revival as the Reformation could have been engendered by abuses 'alone.'" Rather, important doctrines, especially justification by faith alone, and practices such as reading the Bible in the vernacular, should be given the central role in the success of the Reformation, which Febvre saw as "a profound revolution in religious sentiment."[20] So much has been written about the doctrinal disputes of the sixteenth century that it has been easy to forget the significance of the disputes over the correct way to live the Christian life. As Scott Hendrix has reminded us, "One can even say that the Reformation . . . was a reformation in spirituality, since the unresolved issues that led to the permanent separation of Protestant confessions from obedience to the pope were mainly matters of worship and piety."[21]

Martin Luther has had as much written about him as almost anyone in the history of Christianity.[22] It is evident that Luther was a typical late-medieval figure in his education, his religious world, and his growing desire to correct abuses in the church, both doctrinal and practical.[23] Luther never meant to divide the church, but only to bring it back to its true self. Again to cite Scott Hendrix, Luther "did not intend to create a new theology, any more than he intended to create a new church."[24] Nevertheless, that is exactly what Luther effected: an "accidental revolution" that involved a new church/churches and a new theology.[25]

What strikes one immediately about Luther's theology in comparison with that of the Scholastics, some of whom he knew well, is the deeply personal, we might even say existential, mode of his approach.[26] Luther eschews dry, objective attempts to understand Christian faith as he wrestles with the personal import of the biblical message for his life and the lives of his audience. The existential character of Luther's theology helps explain its impact on his hearers and readers; it also casts light on why Luther felt an affinity for a number of medieval mystics (more on this in chapter 1). The course of the development of Luther's theology between 1512 and 1522, and even earlier, has been much studied.[27] The details and disputes about this evolution cannot be presented here, but it is important to see that Luther's dissatisfaction with aspects of contemporary religious practices, such as the sale of indulgences, was rooted in his deepening grasp of how God makes salvation available to sinful humanity. Luther's problems about indulgences and later about papal authority formed the edge of a wedge that inexorably began to split medieval Christianity apart.

Luther was willing to accept pious practices that did not conflict with what he read in the Bible, but he refused to countenance those he judged were contradictory to evangelical faith. At the beginning of his career, he felt that all he needed to do was to call attention to these problems to begin the process of overcoming them. As he met with more and more opposition from the defenders of the papacy, especially after his debate with Cardinal Cajetan at Augsburg in 1518, he began to realize that it was not just the current pope (Leo X) and his spokesmen who were in error, but that the whole apparatus of the papacy was acting contrary to Christ and therefore was to be identified with the Antichrist, whom Paul predicted would resist Christ and his followers in the last days (2 Thessalonians 2). (Luther was profoundly apocalyptic in outlook in the sense of living in the shadow of the second coming, though he wisely made no predictions about the date of the end.) It was no surprise that Leo X excommunicated the intransigent monk in the bull "Exsurge Domine" of 1520, or that Luther promptly burned the papal document.

A key event in Luther's development was what has often been called his "Reformation Breakthrough" to the sense of God's sole initiative in justifying humans despite their sins and therefore our need for total trust in God's promise and distrust of self and our own works. Luther later spoke of this realization as coming to him in the tower of his Augustinian convent, hence the term "tower experience" (*Turmerlebnis*). He said that this happened in 1519, but it seems to have actually taken place a year or two earlier. The insight, doubtless building up over some time, involved a new understanding of the relationship between righteousness and faith. Luther realized that "the righteousness of God revealed through faith for faith, as it is written, 'The one who is righteous will live by faith'" (Rom. 1:17) refers not to the active righteousness by which God judges sinners but to the passive righteousness by which we are justified through the gift of faith. We are not justified because we do righteous works; we are able to perform righteous works because we have faith in the God who justifies. Thus, in ourselves we always remain sinners, but at the same time we are also

justified through faith (*simul justus et peccator*).[28] Salvation by faith in
God's grace (*sola fide, sola gratia*), along with insistence that the Bible
alone, not human tradition, is the basis of belief (*sola scriptura*), forms
the foundation of Luther's theology.

Passive righteousness and evangelical faith are fundamentally
Christocentric, involving what Luther by 1518 began to speak of as
"the theology of the cross" (*theologia crucis*). Salvation becomes available to us only through Christ's suffering on the cross. Our response
must be willingness to fulfill our baptismal vocation of suffering with
him. This theological program was deeply biblical, based on Luther's
readings of the books of both the Old Testament (e.g., Psalms, Genesis) and the New (especially the Pauline Epistles and John). On this
basis Luther advanced a broad vision of a distinctive evangelical
Christianity, as can be seen in the three "Reformation treatises" of
1520 (*Address to the Christian Nobility*, *The Babylonian Captivity of the
Church*, and *The Freedom of the Christian*), as well as in such works as
The Papacy in Rome, and *On Good Works*. These popular writings elic-
ited a broad response in many parts of Germany and elsewhere in
Europe, a response cemented by Luther's groundbreaking translation
of the Bible into German.

Luther was the first off the mark, but the circle of German evangelical leaders, such as Philip Melanchthon, Andreas Karlstadt, and
Martin Bucer, rallied around his call. The appearance of other reforming centers in German-speaking lands within a few years of 1517 demonstrated the breadth of the dissatisfaction with many aspects of late
medieval belief and practice in Germany and the emergence of new
forms of evangelical teaching and spirituality. These other outbreaks
of reforming zeal also show the emergence of disagreements and fis-
sures among the reformers from the start. By late 1521, Luther was
already attacking the activities of popular preachers whom he felt were
taking his call for the freedom of the gospel too far. Luther remained
a social moderate throughout his life, so it is not surprising that in
1524–25 he turned against the German peasants who revolted against
their feudal overlords, partly under the inspiration of one of his former disciples, Thomas Müntzer (1489–1525). These early appearances
of more radical voices, people whom Luther called "enthusiasts," or
"fanatics," marked the beginnings of what is often called the "Radical
Reformation," whose mystical aspects will be treated in chapter 2.

Among the other early evangelical voices was the Swiss priest
Huldrych Zwingli (1484–1531), active in Zürich, who insisted that he

had discovered the biblical message of salvation by faith alone independently of Luther. By 1519, Zwingli was already attacking popular beliefs and practices like purgatory and the cult of the saints. By 1522, he was preaching against ecclesiastical regulations that he felt departed from the divine law revealed in the Bible, which he contended should be the only norm for the church. The iconoclasm of Zwingli and his followers, and especially his arguments for a symbolic understanding of the Eucharist, soon brought him into conflict with Luther. A 1529 attempt at Marburg to work out a compromise between the two parties came to nothing, and by the 1530s two major, differing forms of evangelical protest against Rome were evident: Luther and his supporters, and the originally Swiss and soon international wave of what eventually became Reformed Protestantism. The Reformed strand of Protestantism found its greatest exponent in the French humanist and theologian John Calvin (1509–1564), whose career was spent mostly at Geneva.

The complicated political situation of German-speaking lands helps explain why the papal reaction, even with the support of the emperor Charles V, was not able to put an end to the growing division in Christendom. An important political shift occurred in the decade that saw Luther's initial protest. Three new rulers with new concerns and agendas succeeded to the major thrones of Europe: the Tudor Henry VIII in England (1509); the Valois Francis I in France (1515); and the Hapsburg Charles V (1519), who ruled both the German Empire and Spain. Although the Hapsburg was the most powerful ruler in Europe, the opposition of the other leaders and the sheer extent of Charles's realms put limits to his power. The structure of the German Empire, where Charles's authority was balanced against that of various princes and independent cities, especially the imperial Electors, also limited his effectiveness. Charles summoned Luther to appear at an Imperial Diet held at Worms in 1521. Luther refused to retract his positions and is famously said to have proclaimed, "My conscience is captive to the Word of God. Thus I cannot and will not recant, for going against my conscience is neither safe nor salutary. I can do no other, here I stand, God help me. Amen."[29] Charles had given Luther a safe-conduct, and the monk had the support of his local ruler, Frederick the Wise of Saxony, so he was allowed to leave the Diet unharmed.

In 1529, at another Imperial Diet held at Speyer, the princes and cities who supported Luther and Zwingli, led by Philip of Hesse, issued a minority report called a *Protestatio* affirming their belief in reform, thus giving rise to the term "Protestant."[30] In 1530, at the Imperial Diet of Augsburg, Melanchthon drew up a statement of faith that he hoped could be a starting point for discussions between Luther's followers and reform-minded Catholics, but Charles V heeded the papal delegate and rejected the "Augsburg Confession," which was to become the foundation document for confessional Lutheranism. The Protestant princes, knowing that the emperor was strongly opposed to them, drew up a defensive alliance of Lutheran and Zwinglian princes in 1531 known as the Schmalkaldic League. Armed struggle ensued. Although Charles eventually defeated the League in 1547, Protestantism was by then too well established to be eliminated. Charles recognized the fact by issuing an attempt at religious compromise in 1548 (the *Interim* of Augsburg). Some Protestants accepted it; most did not and continued their resistance. Charles's enemies, within and without the empire, combined against him and war dragged on. In 1555, the exhausted Charles abdicated, leaving to his brother and heir Ferdinand I (ruled 1558–64) the task of working out the political settlement known as the Peace of Augsburg, which recognized the existence of both Catholic and Lutheran realms in the empire according to the principle of "the ruler determines the religion" (*cuius regio eius religio*). Ominously, both for the permanence of peace and the spread of the Reformation, the princes and cities that had adopted Reformed Protestantism were not given political recognition.

The reaction to these movements of reform on the part of Rome and its political allies was fragmented and ineffective for two decades.[31] The popes recognized the danger evident in Luther but had no clear policy about addressing the necessary reforms that would have removed at least some of the appeal of the Wittenberg theologian. Rome was also reluctant to summon a general council. The history of the Catholic reaction to Luther and the other evangelicals, not unlike the debates over the meaning of *the* Reformation, reflects changing currents in historiography, involving both religious and philosophical commitments.[32] Leopold von Ranke's *History of the Popes (Geschichte des Pappstums)*, first published 1834–36, popularized the term "Counter Reformation,"[33] characterizing sixteenth-century Catholicism as essentially a reaction to Luther's protest. In the late nineteenth century, historians both Catholic (Ludwig von Pastor) and Protestant (Wilhelm Maurenbecher) noted the existence of important currents of reform in Catholicism before and after 1517, and the term "Catholic Reform/ Reformation" began to be widely used. In 1946, the historian of the Council of Trent Hubert Jedin (1900–1980) published a short book entitled *Catholic Reform or Counter Reformation?*, in which he tried to show the inner connection of two currents of reform in Roman Catholicism in the sixteenth and seventeenth centuries.[34] As he put it, "The Catholic Reform is the church's remembrance of the Catholic ideal of life through inner renewal, [and] the Counter Reformation is the self-assertion of the church in the struggle against Protestantism."[35] More recently, historians like John O'Malley and Robert Bireley have opted for a more neutral characterization, "Early Modern Catholicism," as a nomenclature for incorporating both Catholic Reform and Counter Reformation within a wider perspective.[36] Other scholars have sought to show the inner connections between Catholicism and Protestantism in the sixteenth and seventeenth centuries. Jean Delumeau, for example, treated the role of the two reformations (Luther's and the papacy's) in what he judged to be the ultimately unsuccessful evangelization of Europe's peasant population.[37] Ernst Zeeden, Heinz Schilling, Wolfgang Reinhard, R. Po-chia Hsia, and others have emphasized the importance of the formation of confessional churches, both Protestant and Catholic, as responses to broad social and political developments in the early modern period.

Given the hierarchical nature of Catholicism as compared with more localized and looser forms of church order found in the Protestant denominations, it is helpful to distinguish between "bottom-up" and "top-down" Catholic reform movements, though the two cannot be separated. Most of the movements associated with what has been called Catholic Reform were bottom-up, feeding off religious developments that began in the fifteenth century, such as the Modern Devotion (*devotio moderna*) and various renewals of the religious orders. In the sixteenth century, Catholic Reform is especially evident in the genesis of new forms of religious life designed both to correct the abuses found in established religious orders (e.g., the Capuchin reform of the Franciscans) and also to initiate new ways of living the gospel in the world.[38] The most important of the latter was the formation of the Jesuit Order between the time of the conversion of Ignatius Loyola in 1522 and the order's gaining papal approval in 1540. The later apologetical and polemical role of the Jesuits in post-Tridentine Catholicism should not obscure the fact that Ignatius's original aims were apostolic and spiritual, even mystical in nature.[39] The Jesuits were later to play an important role in mystical piety, especially in Italy and France.

Many other religious orders and groups made notable contributions. The Capuchin reform was begun by Matteo da Bascio in 1528 as a renewal of the life of poverty and contemplative prayer that had been the ideal of Francis. The departure of the third Capuchin general Bernardino Ochino to the Protestant camp in 1539 created difficulties for the order, but it surmounted these to become a major force in post-Tridentine Catholicism with such figures as the Italian Lawrence of Brindisi (1559–1619) and the French Joseph du Tremblay (1577–1638), Cardinal Richelieu's righthand man. New male and female orders emerged in early modern Catholicism. The Theatines, founded in 1524, evolved from reform circles in Italy, such as the Oratory of Divine Love connected with the mystic Catherine of Genoa, and included members who worked in reforming circles of the Roman curia in the mid-sixteenth century. The Theatines did not have a great interest in mysticism, but a member of the order, Lorenzo Scupoli (1530–1610), wrote the ascetical classic *The Spiritual Combat* (1st edition, 1589), which became one of the all-time best-sellers of spiritual literature among both Catholics and Protestants (and even Orthodox).[40] Other new orders, such as the Barnabites (Milan, 1533) and the Oratorians (Rome, not approved until 1575), played roles in revivifying Catholicism. The Oratorians were later significant in seventeenth-century French mysticism. The Carmelite Discalced Reform initiated by Teresa of Avila in 1562 and finally approved in 1593 had the most pronounced impact on the history of mysticism. The Ursulines were begun by an unmarried laywoman, Angela Merici (1474–1560), whose intention was to form a noncloistered group of dedicated women. The order, which achieved papal recognition in 1544, was oriented toward charitable activity and education of the poor. The French Ursuline Mary of the Incarnation (d. 1672) was their major mystical author

Bottom-up reform, however, involved more than just new religious orders, though in this context it is not possible to give a detailed treatment of such important developments as the revival of preaching, the spread of catechisms, the continuing role of the medieval confraternities, and, of course, the hunger for spiritual and mystical literature on the part of the laity, a phenomenon that began in the fifteenth century and continued to grow in the sixteenth and seventeenth centuries.

Older Catholic historiography tended to emphasize "top-down" reform, although recent writers have worked to correct a rigidly hierarchical view of post-Tridentine Catholicism. Even at the top, that is, within the papacy and the Roman curia, there was no single point of view or program, as the ongoing struggles between intransigents and reformers shows. One group of reformers, often called "Spiritu-als" (*spirituali*), or Catholic Evangelicals, such as the English cardinal Reginald Pole, the Venetian aristocrat Gasparo Contarini, and Cardinal Giovanni Marone, the hero of Trent, had significant influence but had to struggle against strong opposition. The process that led to the Council of Trent (1545–1563) demonstrates that contemporary Catholicism, far from being a monolithic structure, was characterized by internal debates and competing parties.[41] Charles V wanted a council, but he wished it held in his domains. A succession of popes temporized, fearing a too-independent gathering that might reach a compromise with the Protestants and/or dictate a reform agenda to the curia.

The papacy's attitude toward reform had a slow evolution. Luther's opponent Leo X (1513–21) was succeeded by the Dutch reformer who took the name Adrian VI, but he was not up to the task and his reign was brief (1522–23). The new pope, Clement VII (1523–34), was another Medici with little interest in confronting abuses. Clement also opposed Charles V's ambitions in Italy. The result was the savage sack of Rome by unpaid soldiers of the emperor in 1527, when Clement barely escaped with his life. Clement's refusal to recognize Henry VIII's divorce from his first wife, Catherine of Aragon, in 1534, however justified, began the loss of England to Catholicism. The next pope, the Farnese Paul III (1534–49), announced three goals upon his election: to establish peace among the Christian rulers, especially Charles V and Francis I; to summon a council to deal with religious problems; and to organize a crusade against the Turkish menace. Paul was a reformer of sorts, but his blatant nepotism showed his involvement in some of the worst abuses of the time. In 1542, he issued a bull calling for a council to assemble in Trent, a city within the emperor's domain, although on the Italian side of the Alps. It was not until December of 1545 that the council actually convened.

Trent was an on-again, off-again affair of three periods (1545–47, 1551–52, 1562–63), twenty-five sessions, and a changing number of participants. Though ostensibly convened to deal with the split in Christendom, it was a Catholic affair (a few Protestants did attend during the second period). The complicated internal history of the council and its response to external political pressures have recently been well described by John W. O'Malley. Paul III's successors, Julius III (1550–55) and Pius IV (1559–65), generally supported Trent, but the intransigent Paul IV (1555–59), though himself a reformer, was deeply opposed to the Hapsburgs and threatened to sabotage the council, which he judged too independent, by summoning a new council in Rome under his presidency. Fortunately, he died before he could bring this to pass. Trent was never really a universal affair—most of the attendees were Italian, because Charles kept the majority of the German bishops out, as did Francis I the French, at least until the final period. Different theological schools—Thomists (usually Dominicans), Scotists (mostly Franciscans), Augustinians, and others—fought with each other, although the final doctrinal decrees were content with establishing Catholic truth against Protestant error in language that could be interpreted by the various Catholic schools of thought to suit their own theological approaches. Luther and the reformers set the doctrinal agenda in the sense that the questions taken up, such as the authority of scripture in relation to tradition, the meaning of justification, the role of original sin, the nature and number of the sacraments, the sacrifice of the Mass, indulgences, relics, and purgatory, were largely responses to Protestant challenges. The declarations issued by Trent became formative for Catholic teaching down to the mid-twentieth century. Among the most signal theological achievements of the council was the Decree on Justification in Session VI (January 13, 1547), where the fathers set out a carefully honed middle course that affirmed the universality of sin and the need for the gift of faith as "the foundation and root of all justification," but also left room for human cooperation in the process of salvation.

Trent was also a pastoral and reform council, though one limited in important ways, especially because the popes forbade the council from taking up questions relating to the reform of the curia and the papacy itself, relegating these to its own decisions. Nevertheless, Trent issued important reform decrees relating to laity, clergy, religious, and especially bishops. For example, it stressed the importance of preaching (Session V), made reforms in the practice of marriage (Session XXIV), and strongly advised residency for bishops (Session VII). Some of the questions that were debated, such as whether the office of bishop was established by divine law, the issue of clerical celibacy, and the administration of the cup to the laity, were left undecided. Curiously, the council said nothing about missionization, which was rapidly becoming the most significant new dimension of early modern Catholicism as it spread across the globe. One of the council's most far-reaching mandates seems to have been almost an afterthought. Canon 18 of Session XXIII (July 15, 1563) ordered that all dioceses should set up "colleges" (i.e., seminaries) for the proper training of the young men preparing for the priesthood. The subsequent implementation of this decree was decisive in producing the better-trained clergy of early modern Catholicism.

It is important to distinguish between the Council of Trent and Tridentine Catholicism. The council and its decrees were a major initiative, the beginnings of pastoral reform and a careful statement of Roman Catholic faith against Protestant "errors." Tridentine Catholicism, however, was a confessionalization process by which the popes, Catholic rulers, reforming bishops, reenergized religious orders, and, of course, the Catholic laity cemented their religious identity in the early modern period. Much that has been called "Tridentine," such as the "Tridentine Mass," was not actually discussed by the council. In the final decades of the sixteenth century, however, the revived papacy under the leadership of reformers who were at times even willing to correct some of the more egregious abuses of the curia led a newly confident Roman Catholic communion that kept the religious allegiance of much of Western Europe, even regaining some territories, despite the considerable inroads of the reformers and the rulers who supported them.

The protests of Luther and the other reformers, as well as the attempts by Catholic reformers and counter-reformers to answer them, involved issues central to all Christian belief and practice. A number of these touched on mysticism, directly or indirectly. One foundational theme that shows the continuity between medieval and early modern Christianity was the question of salvation—existentially: How am I to be saved? The insistence by Luther and the other Protestants that salvation depends on God, not on human efforts, was deeply Augustinian and not that far removed from the views of many medieval and sixteenth-century Catholic theologians, as various modern attempts at ecumenical cooperation have indicated. Allied with this concern for salvation was the need for religious certitude shared by almost all thinkers of the age. How can one be sure not only about the best way to be saved but also about how to read the Bible and locate the true church? As Susan Schreiner has observed, "the concern with certitude determined the theology, polemics, and literature of the age."[42] Not least among the ways in which the hunger for certainty expressed itself was in the realm of inner religious experience, or, as I prefer to call it, consciousness of the presence of God.[43] The stress on the quest for certainty about the experience of God highlights an important connection between the doctrinal quarrels of the sixteenth century and the role of mysticism, not only among Catholics but also in the varieties of Protestantism.

Notes

1. *Reformatio* was a term with broad ecclesiastical, political, and legal applications in the Middle Ages and the sixteenth and seventeenth centuries. Martin Luther, however, used the word rarely about his attempt to correct abuses in ecclesiastical beliefs and practices. It was not until the late eighteenth century that the term "the Reformation" came to be applied to the movements that divided Christendom in the sixteenth century. See Konrad Repgen, "Reform," in *Oxford Encyclopedia*, 3:392–95; and Gerald Strauss, "Ideas of *Reformatio* and *Renovatio* from the Middle Ages to the Reformation," in *Handbook of European History, 1400–1600: Late Middle Ages, Renaissance, and Reformation*, ed. Thomas A. Brady Jr., Heiko A. Oberman, and James D. Tracy, 2 vols. (Grand Rapids: Eerdmans, 1996), 2:1–30. More broadly, see Giuseppe Alberigo, "'Réforme' en tant critère de l'Histoire de l'Église," *Revue d'Histoire Ecclésiastique* 76 (1981): 72–81.

2. Some helpful essays on these issues include William J. Bouwsma, "Renaissance and Reformation: An Essay in Their Affinities and Connections," in *Luther and the Dawn of the Modern Era: Papers for the Fourth International Congress for Luther Research*, ed. Heiko A. Oberman, Studies in the History of Christian Thought 8 (Leiden: Brill, 1974), 127–49; Gerhard Ebeling, "Luther and the Beginning of the Modern Age," in ibid., 11–39; Thomas Nipperday, "The Reformation and the Modern World," in *Politics and Society in Reformation Europe: Essays for Sir Geoffrey Elton on His Sixty-fifth Birthday*, ed. E. I. Kouri and Tom Scott (London: Macmillan, 1987), 535–52; Heinz Schilling, "Reformation—Umbruch oder Gipfelpunkt eines Temps des Réformes?," in *Die frühe Reformation in Deutschland als Umbruch*, ed. Bernd Moeller (Heidelberg: Gütersloh, 1998), 13–34; Thomas A. Brady, "The German Reformation between Late Middle Ages and Early Modernity," in *Die deutsche Reformation zwischen Spätmittelalter und Früher Neuzeit*, ed. Thomas A. Brady and Elisabeth Müller-Luckner (Munich: R. Oldenbourg, 2001), VII–XX; Berndt Hamm, "How Innovative Was the Reformation?," in *The Reformation of Faith in the Context of Late Medieval Theology and Piety: Essays by Berndt Hamm*, ed. Robert J. Bast, Studies in the History of Christian Thought 110 (Leiden: Brill, 2004), 254–72; and Constantin Fasolt, "Hegel's Ghost: Europe, the Reformation, and the Middle Ages," *Viator* 39 (2008): 345–86.

3. G. W. F. Hegel, *The Philosophy of History* (New York: Dover, 1956), 412–27.

4. Karl Holl, *Gesammelte Aufsätze zur Kirchengeschichte*, 3 vols. (Tübingen: Mohr, 1923–63).

5. Ernst Troeltsch, *Protestantism and Progress: A Historical Study of the Relation of Protestantism to the Modern World* (Boston: Beacon Press, 1958), 44–45, 59. Troeltsch's 1906 essay was "Die Bedeutung des Protestantismus für die Entstehung der modernen Welt," *Historische Zeitschrift* 97 (1906): 1–66.

6. Heiko A. Oberman, *The Harvest of Medieval Theology: Gabriel Biel and Late Medieval Nominalism* (Cambridge, MA: Harvard University Press, 1963); and idem, *The Reformation: Roots and Ramifications* (Grand Rapids: Eerdmans, 1994). See also his essay "The Long Fifteenth Century: In Search of Its Profile," in Brady and Müller-Luckner, *Die deutsche Reformation zwischen Spätmittelalter und Früher Neuzeit*, 1–18.

7. For example, Steven Ozment, *The Age of Reform (1250–1550): An Intellectual and Religious History of Late Medieval and Reformation Europe* (New Haven and

London: Yale University Press, 1980); and the essays in Steven Ozment, ed., *The Reformation in Medieval Perspective* (Chicago: Quadrangle Books, 1971).

8. Brad S. Gregory, *The Unintended Reformation: How a Religious Reformation Secularized Society* (Cambridge, MA: Belknap Press of Harvard University Press, 2012), "Introduction." See the debate on Gregory's claims in the "Forum Essay" in *Catholic Historical Review* 98 (2012): 503–16.

9. Fasolt, "Hegel's Ghost," 379.

10. John Bossy, *Christianity in the West 1400–1700* (Oxford and New York: Oxford University Press, 1987), 91.

11. For Gerhard Ebeling ("Luther and the Beginning of the Modern Age, 28–30), Luther was neither medieval nor modern.

12. For an introduction to the phenomenon of "confessionalization," see Heinz Schilling, "Confessional Europe," in Oberman and Tracy, *Handbook of European History, 1400–1600*, 2:641–81.

13. The theological tradition of Albrecht Ritschl (1822–1889) and his followers was strongly opposed to seeing any relation between evangelical faith and mysticism, as is clear from his 1881 essay "Theologie und Metaphysik." The dialectical theology of Karl Barth (1886–1968) and his followers, such as Emil Brunner, was also critical of mysticism.

14. Adolph Harnack, *History of Dogma*, 8 vols. (New York: Dover, 1961). The first quotation is found in 4:271n3, while the second comes in 6:99.

15. For an overview of the relation between Protestantism and mysticism, see Markus Wriedt, "Mystik und Protestantismus—ein Widerspruch?," in *Mystik: Religion der Zukunft – Zukunft der Religion?* (Leipzig: Evangelische Verlagsanstalt, 2003), 67–87.

16. Two collections provide broad treatments of the period in question: the twenty-one papers in Brady and Müller-Luckner, *Handbook of European History, 1400–1600*, vol. 2; and the thirty essays in R. Po-chia Hsia, ed., *The Cambridge History of Christianity*, vol. 6, *Christianity: Reform and Expansion, 1500–1660* (Cambridge: Cambridge University Press, 2007). In addition, see Diarmaid MacCulloch, *The Reformation: A History* (New York: Penguin Books, 2003).

17. See Francis Oakley, *The Conciliarist Tradition: Constitutionalism in the Catholic Church* (Oxford: Oxford University Press, 2003).

18. Eamon Duffy, *The Stripping of the Altars: Traditional Religion in England, 1400–1580* (New Haven and London: Yale University Press, 1992).

19. See, e.g., Bernd Moeller, *Die Reformation und das Mittelalter: Kirchenhistorische Aufsätze*, ed. Joannes Schilling (Göttingen: Vandenhoeck & Ruprecht, 1991).

20. Lucien Febvre's "The Origins of the French Reformation: A Badly-Put Question?" originally appeared in 1929 and can be found in English in *A New Kind of History from the Writings of Lucien Febvre*, ed. Peter Burke (New York: Harper & Row, 1973), 44–107 (quotations from 56 and 59). Febvre recognized the importance of mystical literature in the religious sensibility that fostered the Reformation (see 67–68, 79).

21. Scott H. Hendrix, ed. and trans., *Early Protestant Spirituality*, Classics of Western Spirituality (New York: Paulist Press, 2009), 5. Later in this collection Hendrix declares, "Protestant spirituality, as the reformers envisaged it, was more about action than contemplation, or, more accurately stated, it was the new theology in practice" (141).

22. For a brief biography, see Martin Marty, *Martin Luther* (New York: Viking Penguin, 2004). For an overview of Luther's theology, see Scott Hendrix, "Luther," in *The Cambridge Companion to Reformation Theology*, ed. David Bagchi and David C. Steinmetz (Cambridge: Cambridge University Press, 2004), 39–56.

23. The medieval aspects of Luther's person and program are emphasized in Heiko A. Oberman, *Luther: Man between God and the Devil* (New Haven: Yale University Press, 1989; German original 1982).

24. Hendrix, "Luther," 56.

25. On the Reformation as an accidental revolution, see MacCulloch, *Reformation*, 123–32.

26. On Luther's theology as experiential, see Hermann Otto Pesch, "Existential and Sapiential Theology—the Theological Confrontation between Luther and Thomas Aquinas," in *Catholic Scholars Dialogue with Luther*, ed. Jared Wicks (Chicago: Loyola University Press, 1970), 59–81.

27. For a sketch down to 1517, see Jared Wicks, *Man Yearning for Grace: Luther's Early Spiritual Teaching* (Washington, DC: Corpus Books, 1968). More recently, Bernd Hamm has insisted that only a study of Luther's development between 1505 and 1520 reveals the full progress to his mature evangelical position; see Hamm, *The Early Luther: Stages in a Reformation Reorientation* (Grand Rapids: Eerdmans, 2014).

28. For a brief presentation, see Hamm, *Early Luther*, chapter 9, "Justification by Faith Alone: A Profile of the Reformation Doctrine of Justification."

29. Quoted from Oberman, *Luther*, 203. On this event, see also Marty, *Martin Luther*, 66–69.

30. Although Catholics began to use the term "Protestant" in polemical writings as early as the 1560s, the Evangelical Reformers did not identify themselves as "Protestants" until the eighteenth century. From the time of Friedrich Schleiermacher in the early nineteenth century there has been a theological debate among Protestants over the essential nature of "Protestantism." See Hermann Fischer, "Protestantismus," *TRE* 27:542–51; and Wriedt, "Mystik und Protestantismus—ein Widerspruch?"

31. Two works that provide an overview of early modern Catholicism are Michael A. Mullett, *The Catholic Reformation* (London and New York: Routledge, 1999); and Robert Bireley, *The Refashioning of Catholicism, 1450–1700: A Reassessment of the Counter-Reformation*, European History in Perspective (Washington, DC: Catholic University of America Press, 1999). Older accounts include Pierre Jannell, *The Catholic Reformation* (Milwaukee: Bruce, 1949); John C. Olin, *The Catholic Reformation: Savonarola to Ignatius Loyola* (New York: Harper & Row, 1969); and H. Outram Evennett, *The Spirit of the Counter-Reformation* (Cambridge: Cambridge University Press, 1968).

32. For the historiography, see John W. O'Malley, *Trent and All That: Renaming Catholicism in the Early Modern Era* (Cambridge, MA: Harvard University Press, 2000).

33. The designation "Counter Reformation" (*Gegenreformation*) appears to have been invented by the Lutheran historian Johann Stephan Pütter in 1776.

34. Hubert Jedin, *Katholische Reformation oder Gegenreformation? Ein Versuch zur Klärung der Begriffe nebst einer Jubiläumbetrachtung über das Trienter Konzil* (Lucerne: Josef Stocker, 1946).

35. Jedin, *Katholische Reformation oder Gegenreformation?*, 38, as cited and translated in O'Malley, *Trent and All That*, 55.

36. See O'Malley's summary of the advantages and disadvantages of four keys terms: Counter Reformation; Catholic Reform/Reformation; Tridentine Reform/Tridentine Age; and Early Modern Catholicism (*Trent and All That*, 119–43).

37. Jean Delumeau, *Catholicism between Luther and Voltaire: A New View of the Counter-Reformation* (London: Burns & Oates, 1977). For an evaluation of Delumeau's attempt to change the nature of the debate, see O'Malley, *Trent and All That*, 101–3.

38. For an overview of the new orders, see Richard DeMolen, ed., *Religious Orders of the Catholic Reformation: In Honor of John C. Olin on His Seventy-Fifth Birthday* (New York: Fordham University Press, 1994).

39. John W. O'Malley, *The First Jesuits* (Cambridge, MA: Harvard University Press, 1993).

40. On the history of the Theatines and a selection of sources, see William V. Hudon, ed. and trans., *Theatine Spirituality: Selected Writings*, Classics of Western Spirituality (New York: Paulist Press, 1996).

41. On Trent, see John W. O'Malley, *Trent: What Happened at the Council* (Cambridge, MA: Harvard University Press, 2013). O'Malley pays tribute to the classic four-volume history of Hubert Jedin, *Geschichte des Konzils von Trient*, 4 vols. (Freiburg im B.: Herder, 1949–75), the first two volumes of which were translated into English.

42. Susan E. Schreiner, *Are You Alone Wise? The Search for Certainty in the Early Modern Era* (New York: Oxford University Press, 2011), viii, 13–15.

43. Schreiner devotes two chapters to themes allied with mysticism: chapter 5, "Experientia: The Great Age of the Spirit," (ibid., 209–60); and chapter 6, "Unmasking the Angel of Light: The Discernment of Spirits" (ibid., 261–321).

CHAPTER 1

Mysticism and the Magisterial Reformers

A TRADITIONAL NOMENCLATURE regarding the first decades of evangelical Christianity distinguishes between the "Magisterial Reformers," such as Luther, his companions, and the founders of the Reformed churches, and the "Spiritual," or "Radical Reformers," including the Anabaptists, the "Spiritualists," and all those who felt that neither Luther, Zwingli, Calvin, nor their associates had gone far enough in advancing the inner religion of the Holy Spirit. This distinction appears less used today, but it does reflect the difference between those critics of Rome who founded what were to become established confessional churches and the more radical leaders who led groups that did not win state support. This chapter will look at the attitudes to mysticism among the early magisterial leaders of the Lutheran and Reformed traditions.

Martin Luther

Luther's relation to the mystical element in Christianity is complicated. His criticism of the Dionysian writings and traditional mystical theology is well known. He also became scornful and dismissive of the monastic life he had led, but which he felt had blinded him to the true understanding of the path to God.

I want to thank my colleague Susan Schreiner of the Divinity School of the University of Chicago for her generous and very helpful comments for the revision of this chapter.

Nonetheless, much of Luther's preaching and teaching can be characterized as presenting a spiritual message.[1] But can Luther be called a mystic, at least in some way? As noted in the introduction, significant Protestant voices of the nineteenth and twentieth centuries denied that Luther was in any way a mystic. Nonetheless, a body of scholarly literature produced over the past half-century and more has shown that Luther's theology had important connections to the writings of the mystics and made use of many mystical themes.[2] Some have even contended that Luther should be considered a mystic, though one who effected a major transformation of late medieval mysticism.[3]

The following treatment will argue for a middle ground. Luther's vast output of writings, mostly scriptural commentaries and sermons, certainly make use of many mystical themes, though these are more frequent early in his career. Works such as the *First Commentary on the Psalms (Dictata super Psalterium)* of 1513–15, the *Commentary on the Penitential Psalms* (1518), the treatise on *The Freedom of the Christian* (1520), and the *Commentary on the Magnificat* (1521–22), all feature mystical elements.[4] But Luther never wrote a work that was primarily mystical, that is, something devoted to guiding the soul through the stages of contemplation to reach loving union with God. Rather, he embedded aspects of mysticism within the context of his new evangelical theology of the cross. Even those scholars who argue that Luther was a mystic admit that his way of using mysticism constituted a major transformation of inherited mystical traditions. Whether such a transformation can be said to remain a mystical theology is the question. In that sense, I prefer a line of argument similar to that of the late Heiko A. Oberman, who argued that Luther had a *sic et non* relationship to mysticism: one characterized by both appropriation and rejection.[5] Luther's transformation of aspects of mysticism in the context of his new theology, however, did allow some of his followers in the later Lutheran tradition, such as Johann Arndt and the Pietists, to emphasize these aspects of the Reformer's thought and thus create distinctive Protestant forms of mysticism.

Luther's years as an Augustinian monk, as well as his training as a theologian at Erfurt between 1501 and 1512, gave him a good acquaintance with patristic and medieval theology and a number of the classic mystical works. As Luther turned against the Occamist scholastic theology in which he was trained, he found a natural ally in the nonscholastic theology of patristic and medieval authors, especially those medieval mystics who expressed criticism of scholasticism.[6] His friend, mentor, and confessor, Johannes von Staupitz (ca. 1469–1525), the vicar-general of the Observant Augustinians, seems to have played an important role in furthering Luther's acquaintance with the mystics.[7] Luther thanked him for enlightening him about key aspects of evangelical faith, such as the nature of divine mercy and the meaning of true penance.[8] Insofar as mysticism is rooted in the Bible, Luther's study of scripture brought him face-to-face with biblical themes that were central to mysticism, such as union with God (1 Cor. 6:17; John 17:21), divinization (e.g., 2 Pet. 1:4), and the "happy exchange" (*sacrum commercium*; e.g., Phil. 2:5ff.) between God and humanity effected by the incarnation. The presence of these and other mystical aspects in Luther's message guaranteed a continuing, if not necessarily central, role for mysticism in his thought. In what follows I will first look at Luther's relation to mystical authors, and then turn to the task of evaluating the significance of the mystical aspects of his theology.

Luther and the Mystics

Perhaps no figure exercised greater influence on Luther than Augustine.[9] In a conversation (*Tischreden*, i.e., "Table-Talk") recorded in 1532, Luther said, "In the beginning I did not read Augustine; I devoured him. He opened the door into Paul for me, so that I could know what the justification of faith was."[10] Marginal comments recorded as early as 1509 in an edition of Augustine's writings show how diligently the young monk was reading the father of his order, including the *Confessions*, the *Literal Commentary on Genesis*, and the *City of God*.[11] Luther's *First Commentary on the Psalms (Dictata super Psalterium)* reveals him often turning to Augustine for understanding the message of saving grace found in the Bible. Luther was familiar with the *Confessions*, especially books 8 and 9, though his focus was not so much on the moments of ecstatic contact with God found therein as on Augustine's story of his conversion as an illustration of how salvation depends not on human efforts but on the grace freely given by God on the basis of his predestinating will.[12] Luther never abandoned his devotion to Augustine, but he cites him less frequently in his later years. As his theology of justification developed, he often employed the bishop's anti-Pelagian writings in support of his views. The issue of the role of Augustine in Luther is a large topic; for our purposes, it is enough to say that it was not so much Augustine the mystic as Augustine the authority on grace and justification who was essential to Luther.

Luther was also aware of the other major patristic source of Western mysticism: the Dionysian corpus, especially the DN and the MT.[13]

These works, which were accorded quasi-apostolic authority throughout the Middle Ages, were important for their insistence on the radical unknowability of God and their treatment of the various kinds of theology culminating in the mystical theology beyond all speech and knowing, both positive and negative. The young Luther was well acquainted with Dionysius's teaching, as he mentions in several places. For example, in the *First Commentary on the Psalms*, discussing the darkness that hides God in Psalm 18:11, he gives five possible readings, including, "Second, because he dwells in an unapproachable light [1 Tim. 6:16], so that no mind can penetrate to him, unless it has given up its own light and has been lifted up higher. Therefore, blessed Dionysius teaches that someone must enter into anagogical darkness and ascend by negations, because God is hidden and incomprehensible."[14] Later, commenting on the silence mentioned in Psalm 64:2, he also recalls Dionysius by identifying one meaning of the text as the divine inexpressibility "according to ecstatic and negative theology." He goes on: "This is the true Cabala which is very rare. For just as the affirmative way about God is imperfect, both in understanding and in speaking, so the negative is most perfect. Hence Dionysius often uses the word 'hyper,' because it is necessary simply to enter into the darkness above all thought."[15] In his *Lectures on Hebrews* (1517–18) he cites approvingly the three Dionysian modes of theology: symbolic, proper (i.e., rational), and mystical.[16] While Luther was not a Dionysian, he seems to have regarded Dionysius with respect up to about 1518/19.

As the Reformer's view of justification by faith and his theology of the cross developed, however, he turned against Dionysius. Luther discovered two fundamental problems in Dionysius: first, the absence of any focus on Christ, especially Christ crucified; and, second, a false understanding of divine darkness. The hiddenness of God, as Luther came to see it, was not a speculative mystery of unknowing, but rather the darkness of affliction and suffering (*Anfechtung*) caused by the God who hides himself *sub contrariis*, that is, under contrary appearances, such as temptation, suffering, even despair and human reason itself.[17] Luther put Dionysius's errors down to his Platonism. In a passage in the *Babylonian Captivity of the Church* of 1520, speaking of Dionysius, he says, "But in his *Theology*, which is rightly called *Mystical*, of which certain very ignorant theologians make so much, he is downright dangerous, for he is more of a Platonist than a Christian. So if I had my way, no believing soul would give the least attention to these books."[18]

Luther also expressed opposition to Dionysius's incorrect understanding of apophaticism in a *Commentary on Psalm 90* written in 1534:

> Therefore Dionysius, who wrote about negative theology and affirmative theology, deserves to be ridiculed. In the latter part of his work he defines affirmative theology as "God is being." Negative theology he defines as "God is non-being." But if we wish to give a true definition of negative theology, we should say that it is the holy cross and the temptations in which we do not, it is true, discern God, but in which nevertheless that groaning is present of which I have already spoken.[19]

This about-face regarding Dionysius seems to have taken place in 1519, because it already appears in his *Second Commentary on the Psalms (Operationes in Psalmos)* of 1519/20, where he highlights the fundamental difference between Dionysian speculative apophaticism and his own experience of God's terrifying hiddenness. Commenting on Psalm 5:2, he dismisses Dionysian mystical theology: "This is a mere provocation of a self-inflating and show-off theology, that someone could believe himself a 'mystical theologian' if he were to read, understand, and teach this stuff, or rather seem to himself to understand and teach it. By living, yet more, by dying and being damned you become a theologian, not by understanding, reading, and speculating."[20]

Luther's attitude toward other mystics of the medieval monastic and mendicant traditions was not so negative. The Reformer knew and respected Gregory the Great, both as a spiritual writer and as a representative of a good occupant of the chair of Peter. He also was familiar with some of the spiritual writings of Bonaventure, such as the *Mind's Journey into God*. It has been suggested that the use of a six-fold structure of the soul's relation to God in Luther's *Commentary on the Magnificat* may reflect knowledge of Bonaventure's treatise.[21] Later in life, Luther criticized Bonaventure for the scholastic aspects of his theology. In his *Table Talk* he puts Bonaventure in the same camp as Dionysius:

> The speculative theology of the theologians is simply empty. I read Bonaventure on this, but he made me quite crazy in that I wanted to feel God's union with my soul by a union of intellect and will, which is useless talk. These are bizarre ideas. This is the true speculative theology, which is actually more practical: Believe in Christ and do what you are supposed to do. Thus, Dionysius's *Mystical Theology* contains total fictions.[22]

Still, the aging Luther continued to pay tribute to Bonaventure for his presentation of the importance of Christ crucified. Another piece in the *Table Talk* says, "Bonaventure is the best among the scholastic doctors."[23] (Not high praise for Luther.)

Jean Gerson (d. 1426) was neither a monk nor a mendicant, but his mystical writings, especially the popular treatises on *Speculative and Practical Mystical Theology* (1402–8), represent the broad medieval mystical tradition well and were widely read in the fifteenth and sixteenth centuries.[24] Luther used Gerson, especially in his early works, such as the *First Commentary on the Psalms*,[25] but he soon broke with the Paris teacher's theology of justification and view of union with God. Three other medieval mystics played a more substantive role in Luther's theology and help us understand the mystical dimension of his thought. Throughout his career Luther praised the Cistercian Bernard of Clairvaux, the Dominican John Tauler, and the anonymous author of the late fourteenth-century *Theologia Deutsch* (Luther once thought Tauler was the author but later retracted this). Older views of Luther's relation to mysticism,[26] influenced by his praise for Tauler and the *Theologia* author as good "German theologians," emphasized his relation to "German mysticism," but this needs to be qualified by noting that it was content, not language, that was uppermost in Luther's mind. What is clear is that Luther read these mystics selectively for his own purposes, although his respect for them demonstrates the impact of mystical traditions on the Reformer.

Luther greatly admired Bernard.[27] He used Bernard's sermons, especially those on the Song of Songs and for the Liturgical Year, but expressed reservations about what he called Bernard's "disputations" (*disputationes*), presumably his treatises on the monastic life. Interestingly enough, Luther appears not to have known Bernard's key mystical treatise, *On Loving God*, though he probably would not have liked its emphasis on love as uniting us with God. Bernard was nonscholastic and deeply Augustinian in his theology of grace. Furthermore, he was experiential, insisting that knowledge of our sinfulness, the gift of grace, and the call to inner transformation in Christ cannot be mere intellectual convictions but need to become living inner realities. Thus, we can understand why Luther continued to praise Bernard "as above all the teachers in the church."[28] Luther also appreciated Bernard's emphasis on Christ crucified. In the treatise *Against the Antinomians* (1539) he says:

> To be sure, I did teach, and still teach that sinners shall be stirred
> to repentance through the preaching or the contemplation of the

passion of Christ, so that they might see the enormity of God's wrath over sin and learn that there is no other remedy for this than the death of God's Son. This doctrine is not mine, but Saint Bernard's. What, Saint Bernard? It is the preaching of all Christianity, of all the prophets and apostles.[29]

Thus, Bernard's interpretation of the "little bundle of myrrh" between the bride's breasts in Song of Songs 1:12 as the memory of Christ's wounds attracted Luther's praise on several occasions.[30]

Luther used Bernard as an authority in his polemics against his Catholic opponents, such as Cardinal Cajetan,[31] but what especially drew him to "Saint Bernard" (*divus Bernhardus*) was the Cistercian's emphasis on the necessity of faith for justification and the ongoing life of the Christian. Commenting on Romans 8:16, he selectively cites Bernard's *First Sermon on the Annunciation* to show that Paul's reference to "the testimony the Spirit gives to our spirit" is "nothing else but the trusting faith of our heart in God" (*fiducia cordis in Deum*).[32] Bernard certainly taught that we are justified by faith and not by our own works, though he probably would not have shared Luther's formula of justification *sola fide*. A second aspect of faith where Luther made use of Bernard concerns the need for experience of faith in the heart. In his *Third Sermon for Christmas Eve* Bernard says that the Word's assumption of human nature reveals three "singular miracles"—the joining of God and man, of a mother and a virgin, and of faith and the human heart.[33] Luther referenced this text in a Christmas sermon of 1520, saying that the greatest of the three miracles is that "even the human heart and faith in such matters could come together and become one."[34] He returned to the theme several times in his career.[35] This shows that there is a place for the birth of the Word in the heart in Luther's thought, but it is always conceived of as the wondrous birth of faith by the gift of the Holy Spirit, following the example of Mary.[36]

A third Bernardine theme Luther utilized was the notion that the life of faith can never be content with standing still—not to progress toward God is really to begin to regress. Luther speaks of this and of Bernard's role in helping him understand it in his *First Commentary on the Psalms* in relation to Psalm 118:122: "Thus, . . . we who are righteous are always in movement, always to be made righteous. Hence it follows that all righteousness for the present moment is sin [in relation] to that which is to be added to the following moment. Saint Bernard rightly says: 'When you begin to be disinclined toward becoming better, you cease to be good. For there is no standing still in the way of God; that delay is sin.'" Thus, Bernard became a support for Luther's development of the central hinge of his theology of justification: that even the justified person always remains *simul justus et peccator*.[37]

Luther's rejection of monasticism and his conflict with the papacy led to some cooling of his views about Bernard's teaching.[38] The Reformer worked out a strategy for continuing to use the "good Bernard" and rejecting the "bad Bernard" on the basis of a distinction between the abbot's spiritual *sapientia* and his fleshly *scientia*. Bernard, says Luther, frequently erred in his fleshly judgments about the papacy, "but he is not to be condemned for that" (*sed propter hoc non damnandus Bernhardus*). Luther summarized: "Bernard did not err in the spirit; he knew that Christ is the Redeemer and he felt that in his heart. But the flesh erred and that condemned him when he drew back from the spirit."[39] For all Luther's respect for Bernard, as well as the way some Bernardine texts helped him clarify his evangelical theology, we must remember that there were real differences in their views, not least on the central issue that for Bernard love is what brings about full union with Christ, while for Luther it is faith. Bernhard Lohse aptly summarizes the relation between the two: "Therefore, one can say that Bernard mediated a line of important thoughts to Luther representing the best tradition, but that these were not necessarily Reformation thoughts; Luther, however, interpreted these thoughts in a Reformation sense."[40]

The Dominican mystical preacher John Tauler (ca. 1300–1361) was famous in his own time and remained so over the centuries, not least because Luther was so enthusiastic a supporter.[41] Unlike Meister Eckhart and Henry Suso, Tauler left only vernacular works, specifically about eighty sermons, though other sermons, including some of Eckhart's, were often mingled with his in manuscripts and early editions.[42] Tauler's popularity is indicated by the fact that his sermons were printed first in 1498, and again in 1508 and 1521/22.[43] Luther's friend Johann Lang brought the 1508 edition to his attention and the Augustinian devoted himself to reading and studying Tauler's sermons at a critical point in the evolution of his theology. (This edition included a few sermons by Eckhart mistakenly attributed to Tauler.)[44] Luther wrote marginal comments on his copy of the book in 1515/16.[45] He also mentioned Tauler twenty-six times in his later writings—always with praise. In introducing the *Marginalia*, he says, "I have found more solid and true theology in him, even though all written in the German vernacular, than is found in all the scholastic teachers of all the universities—or than could be found in their opinions."[46] Later he declared, "since the time of the Apostles, there has scarcely been a writer who is his equal."[47] Tauler, along with Bernard, is the most important mystical source of Luther's theology.[48] But what did Luther learn from Tauler? Was Tauler the source for important elements of Luther's evangelical breakthrough, or only a useful ally and an authority for citation?

As in the case of Bernard and his other mystical sources, Luther read Tauler selectively and for his own purposes. The Reformer was happy to find support in theological tradition—especially that of "good German theology"—for his break with late medieval scholasticism. But his selective approach to these texts qualifies, once again, overly strong views of Luther the mystic. Among the things that Luther praises the Dominican for is his emphasis on the need for humility and total passivity in the face of God's action. We cannot save ourselves by our good works; we must be content to wait on God's saving grace to break into our lives. In the margin of Sermon 1 on Christ's three births in the 1508 edition,[49] remarking on a phrase about attaining union with God, Luther says, "Note that one ought to undergo divine things rather than to act; indeed, sense and intellect are naturally passive powers."[50] At this early stage Luther seems to understand the teaching on the mystical birth of the Word in the soul found in this sermon in Dionysian terms:

> It is true that God is born in us according to the state of the contemplative life by spiritual lifting up [*anagogia*]. But morally he is born not in silence, but in the working of the virtues according to the state of the active life. This belongs to Martha; the former to Mary; this is easy, the other difficult; this happens often, the other is rare. Everyone understands this easily; the other only the experienced grasp. Hence the whole of this sermon comes from mystical theology, which is experimental and not doctrinal wisdom. . . . He is speaking about the spiritual birth of the Uncreated Word.[51]

Both Tauler and Luther emphasized the necessity for experience and not just book-knowledge, but, in Luther, experience soon came to be identified with inner experience of saving faith, not that of the birth of the Uncreated Word in the soul. This is already evident in Luther's comments on other Tauler sermons. For example, a gloss on Sermon 45 (= Vetter 41) talks about God working on us *sub contrario* and the need for patient faith, stating, "Therefore, the whole of salvation is resignation of the will in all things, whether spiritual or temporal, as he teaches. And naked faith in God."[52]

Also important for Luther was his discovery of Tauler's "mysticism of dereliction," that is, the way that the preacher explained how experiencing abandonment by God is a necessary part of spiritual progress. This theme was not new in medieval mysticism, but Tauler brought it to a height of expressive power.[53] Several of the dereliction sermons found in the 1508 edition drew comments from the Reformer. Sermon 4 (= Vetter 3) on the Feast of the Epiphany analyzes three kinds of myrrh: the myrrh of detachment from the world; the myrrh of inner and outer suffering; and "the very bitter myrrh that God gives, inner anguish and inner darkness." Luther was taken with this passage and offered comments on all three kinds of myrrh, describing the third form as "the suspension of grace and the spirit," which we must "accept with patience," when, as Job says, 'the Lord gives and the Lord takes away' (Job 1:21)."[54] Tauler's influence on Luther in this matter can be seen in the roughly contemporary *Lectures on Romans*, where the Reformer notes, "Concerning this patience of God and suffering, see Tauler, who beyond others clearly brought this matter to light in the German language."[55] Another link between Tauler and Luther can be seen in Luther's comments on the last sermon, Sermon 78 (= Vetter 65), where the Reformer found support in Tauler for his evolving view of penance as primarily interior sorrow for sin and not the reception of the sacrament, which is useless without true repentance: "Confession often is harmful," says Luther, "while loving trust [*fiducia*] produces the forgiveness of sin, where nonetheless a true pledge of not doing something in the future was not from the heart."[56]

For all Luther's praise of Tauler, however, there were real differences between the two preachers. Although Luther preferred to pass over these in silence, those who have analyzed the relation between the two have been quick to point them out.[57] First of all, it seems that Tauler, unlike Bernard, was only influential on Luther in a restricted period of time (ca. 1515–20), though this was obviously a time of great importance. On a deeper level there was an essential divide between the Dominican and the Augustinian on human nature and how humans can attain union with God. Following Eckhart, Tauler maintained that, despite sin, God remained present in the ground of the soul, so that the mystical path with its three fundamental stages of loving enjoyment, dereliction, followed by deep union fulfills the essential nature of the human. Although in his earliest years Luther did talk about the *synteresis*, or the inner core of the soul, as always directed to God and a ground for judgment against sin, his breakthrough during the period ca. 1515–18 to a sense of the utter estrangement between God and sinful humans rejected the high anthropology of the fourteenth-century

German mystics. This also meant that Luther's conception of union was different from theirs—no union of mutual love, let alone a deep uniting in some form of identification, or a constant birth of the Word in the soul—Luther admitted only a dark union marked by the inner troubles (*Anfechtungen*) found in naked faith in the crucified Christ. Thus, for all that Luther used Tauler and Bernard and agreed with them on significant issues, there were points where his theology was quite different.

There was one final text from the medieval mystical tradition that Luther read and praised during his formative period. This was the anonymous *Theologia Deutsch*, which he discovered in 1516.[58] Luther rushed a copy into print in December of that year, along with a brief preface. It was his first publication. When he came upon a more complete manuscript of the work, he was equally energetic in getting it published in 1518 with a longer introduction.[59] Other editions appeared during Luther's life, and his praise for the work guaranteed it an extensive history in Protestantism (Catholics remained suspicious for centuries). All together, some 190 editions and translations are said to have appeared by 1960, making it one of the most popular of medieval mystical texts.

Luther's preface is enlightening for the way he viewed the book. He begins with the scriptural topos of God choosing children and simple speech to overturn the wisdom of the world, so that "this noble little book, poor and unadorned as it is," comes after only the Bible and Augustine as the best way to learn about "God, Christ, man, and what all things are." He then rebuts attacks against "Wittenberg theology" as a novelty. "Let anyone read this booklet," he says, "and determine for yourself whether our theology is new or old, for this book is not new. Some will perhaps say, as they have done already, that we are German theologians, as we are. I thank God that I can hear and find my God in the German tongue." He concludes even more boldly, "God grant that this booklet will be more known, so that we will find that the German theologians are without doubt the best theologians. Amen."[60]

There is much in the book that appealed to Luther, although he does not appear to have cited the work often in his own writings. Despite its ontology of the essential goodness of the divine nature, the *Theologia Deutsch* is fundamentally concerned with humanity's existential situation and its practical consequences. The book reconfigures many of the themes of late medieval German mysticism within the perspective of a biblical view of radical obedience and discipleship. The work is full of sharp contrasts between good and evil, old and new, perfect and imperfect, self will and divine will. Perhaps the most fundamental polarity is that between Adam's disobedience and the obedience of Christ, the God-man. The essence of sin is disobedience; hence, human nature since Adam is a totally fallen nature (Luther loved this). It is only by surrendering our self-reliance and the pretensions of reason, taking up the cross, and following the example set by the humility and obedience of Christ that God can begin to redirect the will from within. The book says little about the sacraments and external practices, though, of course, it does not deny them. Like Tauler, the *Theologia Deutsch* also has a role for the experience of dereliction and even the feeling of being damned on the path to God. Another fundamental theme is divinization, which, as we shall see below, was something at least the early Luther appreciated. All this shows why Luther praised the book so much. Nevertheless, there was much in the *Theologia Deutsch* that Luther overlooked because it did not conform to his evangelical theology. Most notably, although its account of the path to God is always christological, the book teaches a deep union based on love that was different from Luther's understanding of union by faith.

This brief sketch of how Luther used some medieval mystical authors in the crucial second decade of the sixteenth century as he developed his new theology of justification shows both the contributions and the limits of his attitude toward mysticism and mystical authors. Luther's evangelical breakthrough led to his abandonment of medieval conceptions of mystical theology rooted in Dionysius. Nevertheless, the Christocentric and Augustinian elements of Bernard of Clairvaux, Tauler's emphasis on passivity and dereliction as a part of the path of faith, and the role of obedience in the *Theologia Deutsch* were vital for Luther as he struggled to discern the meaning of justifying faith. These authors helped him on his path, but the journey was his own.

Mystical Themes in Luther's Theology

A variety of terms have been used to characterize Luther's mysticism by those who argue that Luther was a mystic: Christ-Mysticism, Cross-Mysticism, Word-Mysticism, Faith-Mysticism, Evangelical-Mysticism. All these descriptions touch on themes that were central to the Reformer and help us understand how mystical elements affected the major headings of his teaching. Nevertheless, one can wonder why any single description should be considered more appropriate than the others, especially if, as I am arguing, Luther's theology is more than just its mystical elements. Luther's groundbreaking theology was not really a "mystical theology," at least in the medieval sense, just as his descriptions of his decisive religious experiences are different from traditional accounts of mystical consciousness. The Reformer maintains a *sic et non* attitude toward mysticism, as suggested above.

Luther's theology centers on justification: "The proper subject of theology is the man accused for his sin and lost, and the God who justifies and saves the sinner. Whatever is researched or disputed outside this subject in theology is error and poison."[61] Justification through the reception of God's saving activity (*iustitia dei passiva*) ties together the major themes of the early Luther's evangelical breakthrough: the centrality of faith; the christological reading of scripture; the relation of law and gospel; the cross as both God's judgment and the revelation of God's mercy; God's working *sub contrariis* and the role of *Anfechtung*; the status of believers as both justified and sinners (*simul iustus et peccator*); and many others. For Luther, faith in the word of God replaces love as the location of our immediate relation to God,[62] so that, as Scott Hendrix put it, we move from the medieval church centered on *caritas* (*caritas-ecclesia*) to a church based on faith (*fides-ecclesia*).[63]

The importance of Luther's theology of faith can scarcely be overestimated. If we take Thomas Aquinas as a representative of the medieval view of faith (*STh* IIaIIae, qq. 1–16), we can see a basic shift from the Thomistic view of salvation centering on charity to Luther's view of the all-importance of faith. For Thomas, faith is an essential foundation as the theological virtue of the intellect directed to God, the First Truth. Faith, or thinking with assent, is an act that is properly in the intellect, although "inasmuch as the will moves it to assent" (q. 2, aa. 1–2). Because faith is directed to the Divine Goodness as its end, "charity [not any other virtue such as obedience] is called the form of faith insofar as the act of faith is perfected and formed by charity" (q. 2, a. 3). Luther reacted against this view, although his evolving doctrine of faith made use of elements taken from late medieval discussions, as Berndt Hamm has shown.[64] Luther found the emphasis on *human* love for God in danger of overemphasizing human activity at God's expense and overlooking the remaining power of sin. Hence, he concluded that it is only by faith conceived of as a pure reception of the righteousness of Jesus Christ that we are justified and saved. Luther did not deny the intellectual component of faith as knowing the truth of the Bible, but faith is not so much thinking with assent as the consoling certainty in humility and hope that one has been forgiven by God. Thus, nothing is more important than faith: "Indeed, faith, which is given by God's grace to the ungodly and by which they are justified, is the substance, foundation, fountain, source, chief, and firstborn of all spiritual graces, gifts, virtues, merits, and works."[65] As for faith formed by love (*fides caritate formata*), he would have none of it. As Hamm summarizes, "Love no longer forms faith; faith itself has become the form of a life guided by love."[66]

The short treatise Luther sent to Pope Leo X in 1520 entitled *The Freedom of the Christian*, which he described as containing "the whole of the Christian life in a brief form," makes Luther's new theology clear. "The Word of God," says Luther, "cannot be received and cherished by any works whatever, but only by faith. Therefore it is clear that, as the soul needs only the Word of God for its life and righteousness, so it is justified by faith alone [*sola fide*] and not any works."[67] Luther goes on to employ a traditional mystical motif related to loving union with God to the life of faith: "Just as the heated iron glows like fire because of the union of fire with it, so the Word imparts its qualities to the soul. It is clear, then, that a Christian has all he needs in faith and needs no work to justify him."[68] The first power of faith, therefore, is justification. The second power is trust in God's promises because he is supremely truthful and righteous. Finally, "The third incomparable benefit of faith is that it unites the soul with Christ as a bride is united with her bridegroom. By this mystery, as the Apostle teaches, Christ and the soul become one flesh" (Eph. 5:31–32). And if they are one flesh, a true wedding is consummated between them; indeed, the most perfect of all."[69] This marriage is the expression of the "happy exchange" (*sacrum commercium/fröhliche Wechsel*) that took place at the incarnation. "Accordingly, the believing soul can boast of and glory in whatever Christ has as though it were its own, and whatever the soul has Christ claims as his own." Luther expresses this exchange forcefully: "By the wedding ring of faith he shares in the sins, death, and pain of hell which are his bride's." But since Christ and his righteousness are more powerful than sin, death, and hell, they cannot overcome him and the soul united with him. "Thus the believing soul by means of the pledge of his faith is free in Christ, its bridegroom, free from all sins, secure against death and hell, and is endowed with the eternal righteousness, life, and salvation of Christ its bridegroom."[70] It is not that there is no role for love, but for Luther love is subsequent to faith and is directed primarily to the neighbor, not to God. According to Luther, "The Christian lives not in himself, but in Christ and his neighbor. . . . He lives in Christ through faith, in his neighbor through love. By faith he is caught up beyond himself into God. By love he descends beneath himself into his neighbor. Yet he always remains in God and in his love, as Christ says in John 1" (see John 1:51).[71]

The mystical resonance of these texts is evident, but so too is how the mystical themes have been transformed in the service of Luther's view of justifying faith. Similar transformations can be seen in other aspects of Luther's theological program. For example, like many medieval mystics, Luther insisted on the necessity of lived experience for faith and the theology based on it.[72] "Only experience makes a theologian," as he said in his *Table Talk*.[73] Purely academic theology, for Luther, was no theology at all. The need for personal experience is much to the fore in Luther's *Commentary on the Magnificat*.[74] One of the most attractive of Luther's spiritual treatises, the *Commentary* presents Mary's humility and dependence on God as a model for all Christians. Mary's prayer testifies to her deep experience of God's action in her life. Luther begins by saying, "In order to properly understand this song of praise, one must recognize that the Blessed Virgin Mary is speaking from her own experience, for no one can understand God or God's word without receiving it directly from the Holy Spirit."[75] Throughout the treatise Luther often returns to the need for experience of God, as when, commenting on the first verse, "My soul magnifies the Lord," he says, "Thus it happens to all in whom godly sweetness and God's spirit has poured, that they experience more than they can describe. It is not a human work to praise God with joy. It is a joyful suffering and God's work alone and cannot be taught with words but only by personal experience." The emphasis on the sweetness of God's gift, as well as the passivity of the soul, once again shows the mystical background to such comments. Luther insists that receiving the experience of such sweetness depends on "trusting God with one's whole heart in the depths and the distresses of life."[76]

We may ask at this stage if Luther, at least the young Luther, had what might be called mystical experiences, or moments of immediate consciousness of union with God. Some Luther scholars have affirmed this; others question it.[77] The remarks on reading Bonaventure cited above (i.e., "Bonaventure . . . made me quite crazy in that I wanted to feel God's union with my soul") show that he at least had tried to attain the kind of unitive experiences described in mystical treatises. Furthermore, in a text from 1523 Luther says, "once I was carried away to the third heaven" (2 Cor. 12:2).[78] Whatever kind of experiences the young monk may have had, he soon decisively moved away from mystical states of consciousness in the usual sense as he discovered the true meaning of faith and justification. One of the Reformer's most famous accounts of his religious experience, recorded years later, demonstrates the difference between the first-person narratives found in medieval and early modern mystics and Luther's self-understanding of God's action in his life. In 1545, Luther recalled his discovery of the truth of God's passive justice as revealed in Romans 1:17. He says:

> I had begun to understand that the justice of God is that by which the just person lives by the gift of God, that is to say, by faith. This means that the gospel reveals to us the justice of God, that is to say the passive justice by which God, in his mercy, justifies us by faith, as it is written: "The just one lives by faith." I felt then reborn and I entered into the wide-open gates of paradise itself. Then the whole Bible immediately showed me another face. . . . As much as I had previously hated the expression "God's Justice," so now I prized it with a corresponding greater love as the sweetest word for me. So this text in Paul truly became for me the gate of paradise.[79]

The language of sweetness and love, the evocation of the "door of paradise," the feeling of being reborn, and the illumination regarding the meaning of the Bible all recall mystical themes, but Luther is fundamentally describing an experience related to justifying faith.

Like a number of late medieval mystics, Luther had a negative attitude toward mystical gifts and charisms, such as visions and claims of paranormal experiences. He went further than the mystics, however, in insisting that in this life there is no seeing of God but only the hearing and obeying of God's word.[80] Luther expresses opposition to any face-to-face vision of God on earth, and even to the notion of dwelling in God's being, in a scholion on Psalm 90:1: "Don't wish to dwell immediately in God; don't abandon his protection, because in this life there is no face-to-face vision. You are not able to dwell in God, but in his protection; your dwelling place will be in his shadow."[81]

One mystical theme that Luther did use, perhaps because of its presence in the Bible (e.g., Ps. 115:11; 2 Cor. 12:2–4), was that of rapture (*ecstasis/excessus/raptus*).[82] Here too the Reformer transformed the usual meaning of rapture as being swept above the mind and the self to God through ecstatic love (*amor ecstaticus*) in order to redirect rapture to the realm of faith. In his early *Commentary on the Psalms* he exegetes the text from Psalm 115:11, "I said in my 'excess': every human is a liar" (*Ego dixi in excessu meo: omnis homo mendax*). What can this odd expression mean? Luther wrestles with the meaning of *excessus* in this text, finding in it both the fear and disturbance during persecution that

Augustine had identified as one meaning of the verse in his *Expositions on the Psalms*, as well as "the being lifted up [*excessus*] by which one is lifted above self through faith, so that one can see the things to come [i.e., in heaven]."[83] The interpretation of *excessus/raptus* in terms of faith lifting one up to God and the knowledge of our own misery before God was enforced in Luther's later works. For example, in the late *Commentary on Genesis*, speaking of Genesis 28:12–14, he states, "We are raptured through faith and are made one flesh with him, as Christ says in John 17:21: 'That they all may be one, even as You Father are in me and I in you, that they may be one in us.'"[84] Rapture is an experience of faith, not ecstatic love.

Luther thus distinguishes between rapture and the "access" we have through Christ first into grace and eventually into glory, as mentioned by Paul in Romans 5:2. In his *Commentary on Romans*, Luther argues that both faith and the mediating activity of Christ are necessary, so that those who follow "mystical theology" and try to leave aside the "pictures of the sufferings of Christ . . . to ascend in rapture through the Incarnate Word to the Uncreated Word" will fail unless they are purified within and carried away by God as Paul was (2 Cor. 12:2). Hence, he concludes, "this rapture cannot be called an 'access.'"[85] In speaking of rapture, therefore, Luther adopts a mystical vocabulary that had been used with reference to the transcending of human modes of knowing and loving into a state of union and applies it to the life of faith and our reliance on Christ alone. The Christ who is outside us (*extra nos*) lifts us up in *raptus* through the gift of faith. This transformation of mystical discourse is summarized by Karl-Heinz Zur Mühlen: "Luther made use of mystical terminology to present his understanding of justification, but interpreted it in a new way in relation to the word and to faith. In the process of clarifying his thought he remained open to mystical resources in themselves."[86]

Given his new understanding of rapture, it is not surprising that Luther criticized another major motif of traditional mystical theology, the notion of ascending to heaven through a series of contemplative stages. For Luther, there is an ascent to heaven in this life, but it is the ascent of Christ by means of faith. In the preface to *The Babylonian Captivity of the Church* of 1520, he says, "I do not speak as one who knows; let us rather hear Paul, who says that we should learn 'Jesus Christ and him crucified' (1 Cor. 2:2). This is our 'way, truth, and life' (John 14:6); this is the ladder by which we come to the Father, as it says, 'No one comes to the Father except through me.'"[87] Luther attacks the usual mystical understandings of ascent to heaven in a number of places.[88]

Not unlike Bernard of Clairvaux, for Luther the most important thing was Christ's *descent* in taking on flesh for our salvation. "He descended and prepared a ladder," as he put it in a Christmas sermon.[89] Luther's most important treatment of the ladder-to-heaven motif comes in his exegesis of the ladder that the patriarch Jacob saw stretching between heaven and earth in Genesis 28:12–14.[90] Jacob received the vision in the midst of exile and troubles, which is where we too encounter the Savior. "God painted that picture of the ladder to comfort and console Jacob in faith in the future blessing." According to the literal sense, the ladder represents the union of God and man in the person of Christ—"the inexpressible union and association of the divine and human natures." "Later," says Luther, "there is another union, a union between us and Christ, as St. John expresses it in a very beautiful manner: 'I am in the Father and the Father is in me,' says Christ (John 14:10). This comes first. Later he says, 'You in me and I in you' (John 14:20). This is the allegorical meaning of the ladder." This meaning is meant to nourish faith, not to teach works. The significance of the ladder is to recognize our unity with Christ in faith. Luther concludes:

> In this way we ascend to him and are carried along through the word and the Holy Spirit. And through faith we cling to him, since we become one body with him and he with us. He is the head; we are the members. On the other hand, he descends to us through the word and the sacraments by teaching and by exercising us in knowledge of him. The first union, then, is that of the Father and the Son in divinity. The second is that of the divinity and the humanity in Christ. The third is that of the church and Christ.[91]

For Luther, both are equally necessary: the Christ *extra nos* who lifts us up in faith and the Christ *in nobis* who comes down to unite himself with us in the "happy exchange" of marriage. As Berndt Hamm puts it, "Instead of a person going upward to become ever holier, Christ moved downward to the unholy sinner in a radical mysticism of descent."[92]

One form of traditional mystical consciousness that Luther had much to say about was the experience of suffering, turmoil, dereliction, even the feeling of being abandoned by God and condemned to hell: *Anfechtung*.[93] Luther was a troubled man. Without resorting to psychohistory for a possible explanation of his anxieties,[94] any extensive reading of the Reformer reveals his fears, inner turmoil, and sense of anguish in the face of divine judgment and the possibility of damnation. Luther dealt with his troubles not by trying to forget or dismiss them but by making them a key aspect of his theology. He found an ally for this move in Tauler and his reflections on the role of the experience of God's abandoning the faithful soul, what the Dominican once called "night work." Luther's sufferings, however, were not learned from books; they were part of his life. His views on the importance of *Anfechtung* has attracted a large literature, some of which deals with its relation to dereliction themes in medieval mysticism.[95] The role of *Anfechtung* allowed Luther to make use of another of the forms of mystical language common in the late Middle Ages, that of annihilation, or being reduced to nothing in the face of our unworthiness before God. As early as the Heidelberg Disputation of April 1518, Luther condemned those who had not learned to be totally reduced to nothing by Christ's cross and passion, noting, "Someone emptied out through sufferings, no longer works, but knows that God works in him and does everything. Therefore, whether he works or not, it is all the same to him. . . . He himself knows that it is enough if he suffers and dies through the cross, so as to be the more reduced to nothing [*ut magis annihiletur*]."[96] Once again, however, Luther's view of annihilation was christological and passion-centered, rather different from the more speculative forms of annihilation of much late medieval mystical thought.

Luther's sense of trial and tribulation was closely linked with another important theme in his writings, that of the hidden God.[97] God hides himself both *sub contrariis*, that is, under contrary signs, and also within the dark mystery of his predestinating will. The two are distinct, although their experiential effect, in terms of confusion, trouble, even terror, is often similar. A good example of hiddenness *sub contrariis* is found in Luther's exegesis of the trials of the patriarchs recounted in Genesis. Speaking of Joseph, Luther says, "Therefore, we should know that God hides himself under the form of the worst devil. This teaches us that the goodness, power, and mercy of God cannot be grasped by speculation, but must be understood on the basis of experience."[98] The foremost example of God's hiding *sub contrariis* is Christ dying on the cross. The paradox of this central truth of Luther's *theologia crucis* is found again and again in his writings. Commenting on Genesis 25:22 Luther states, "Thus when Christ himself is about to enter into the glory of the Father, he dies and descends into hell. There all glory disappears. He says to his disciples, 'I go to the Father' (John 14:12), and he goes to the grave. Let us constantly meditate on such examples and place them before our eyes."[99] Jesus had the experience of being confronted by the mystery of God's hidden predestination. Interpreting Christ's tears over Jerusalem (Matt. 23:37), Luther says,

"It is likewise the part of this incarnate God to weep, wail, and groan over the perdition of the ungodly, when the will of the Divine Majesty purposely abandons and reprobates some to perish. We should not ask why he acts this way, but revere the God who is both able and willing to do such things."[100]

The Psalms, which Luther loved, were full of expressions of the *Anfechtung* that the devout Christian should make his or her own in prayer. An example is found in Psalm 6, the first of the so-called Penitential Psalms, on which Luther commented several times.[101] Luther claims that "this psalm and others like it will never be fully understood and prayed unless disaster stares a person in the face as it does in death and at the final departure." Such a time of affliction "seems especially and immeasurably long to those who have that inner hurt of the soul, the feeling of being forsaken and rejected by God." The fourth verse ("Turn, O Lord, save my life") presupposes that God has turned away from us: "A turning away on the part of God implies an inner rejecting and forsaking. Then a horrible terror and, as it were, the beginning of damnation is felt." The saints in the midst "of their crosses," he says, "are in every way like the damned." Luther continues, "The difference is this, that the saints retain a good will toward God, and that they are more concerned about losing God's gracious will, praise, and honor than about being damned."[102] In his *Second Commentary on the Psalms*, exegeting Psalm 6:2, Luther calls to mind the suffering of Job: "The conscience that has been rebuked and convicted soon feels that it has been threatened with its eternal damnation. Only one who has tasted it understands this supreme feeling, and therefore we are not worthy to treat it. Job suffered it more than others and suffered it often."[103] Job, David, Ezechias, and Christ in the Garden of Gethsemane all suffered this "dread and horror of conscience before the face of God's judgment." "All other temptations," says Luther, "are little exercises and preludes of this consummate one. In them we get used to fleeing to God against God."[104]

There is some debate about what Luther meant by "fleeing to God against God," an issue that casts light on the role of *Anfechtung* in his theology. Is Luther fleeing from the hidden, predestinating God toward the saving God revealed *sub contrario* in Jesus on the cross, or is he is fleeing from the God of appearances to the true God? In any case, this distinction, which is not found in medieval mystical ideas of dereliction, shows once again Luther's innovative sense of turmoil and terror before God. While Luther's *Anfechtung* was nourished by mystics like Tauler, it sprang from his own experience and reflection.

Luther was convinced that God is present to and works on our behalf under the contrary sign (*sub contrario*). As his *Commentary on Romans* 9:3–5 summarizes:

> For our good is hidden and that so deeply that it is hidden under its opposite. Thus our life is hidden under death, self-love under self-hatred, glory under shame, salvation under perdition, the kingdom under banishment, heaven under hell, wisdom under foolishness, righteousness under sin, strength under weakness. And generally, every yes we say to any good under a no, in order that our faith may be anchored in God.[105]

The fundamental realization of this general law is the contrary sign of Christ dying on the cross as the source of our salvation. Thus, Luther's theology is always a *theologia crucis*: it is only through Christ that we can hope to have access to saving grace and to heaven. Luther was happy to find a similar christological emphasis in his mystical sources, especially in Bernard, but his theology of the cross is his own creation. Key aspects of this theology, such as his view of the imitation of Christ (*imitatio Christi*), of our divinization as sharers in Christ's Sonship, and of our union with Christ as bride with Bridegroom, display, once again, an affinity with mystical themes, as well as evidence of how he transmuted mystical language in the context of his new theology.[106]

Christ works outside us to justify us (*extra nos*), as well as dwelling within us (*in nobis*). Luther does not confuse the two. The importance of the theme of "Christ in us" meant that both early and late the Reformer spoke about the union of the believer with Christ.[107] In his treatise *The Freedom of the Christian*, as noted above, there are strong formulations of the marriage union between Christ and the believer.[108] In the *Second Commentary on the Psalms*, he discusses union in terms of God's justice: "It is called God's justice and ours, because it has been given to us by his grace as a work of God that works in us, so that God and we may be just by the same justice, just as by the same Word God creates and we are what he is, so that we are in him and his existence may be our existence" (*suum esse nostrum esse sit*).[109] Other forms of union language Luther uses speak of becoming "one thing with Christ,"[110] "being baked into one cake with Christ,"[111] and even "becoming one with Christ's substance."[112] Commenting on Galatians 2:20, he speaks about becoming one person with Christ: "By faith you must be taught correctly, namely, that by it you are so glued together to Christ that he and you are one person, which cannot be separated but remains attached to him forever and declares, 'I am as Christ,' and he in turn says, 'I am as that sinner who is attached to me and I to him.'"[113] At times Luther appeals to 1 Corinthians 6:17 ("Becoming one spirit with God"), the foremost biblical prooftext for union in medieval mysticism. For example, in the *Commentary on Hebrews*, speaking of the righteousness by which we are made just, he says, "faith so exalts a person's heart and transfers it to God that the heart and God become one spirit and thus in a way are the divine righteousness."[114]

It would be easy to cite a larger group of union texts in Luther. It is clear, however, that the Reformer was quite willing to use strong language about our uniting with God; but is it equally clear that, in the context of his whole theology, such expressions need to be qualified by Luther's insistence on the great gap between God and humans, as well as his teaching that uniting with Christ is something given at baptism to all Christians and realized in faith. Thus, Luther's view of union is not the loving union of wills found in Bernard of Clairvaux and many medieval mystics,[115] let alone the supra-cognitive union of indistinction of Eckhart and his followers.[116] Furthermore, Luther's notion of mystical union is not a gradual process attained through prayer and contemplation but is an immediate gift to all believers given in faith. Again to quote Hamm: "One can say that Luther transferred the typical focus on immediacy and directness . . . to an immediacy of the word. The unmediated relationship of the soul to God became for him the immediate relationship to the living word of God."[117]

Two aspects of our faith-union with Christ keep recurring in Luther's writings. The first is his use of the language of erotic union between the bride-soul and Christ the Divine Bridegroom, though he bases this less on passages from the Song of Songs rather than on texts like Psalm 44:10, Matthew 22:1ff., 2 Corinthians 11:2, and Ephesians 5:22.[118] The second theme might be called the signature of Luther's view of mysticism: his appeal to the "happy exchange" between God and humanity.

Although he sometimes speaks about Christ as "our Brother,"[119] Luther's most frequently used language about our personal relationship with Christ is that of bride to Bridegroom, which, as in the medieval tradition, he uses both for the church's relation to Christ and for that of the individual and the Redeemer.[120] For example, in a sermon from November of 1522, he speaks about how Christ wants his bride to be totally pure, chaste, and not involved with anyone else. "In this parable [Matt. 22] he [Christ] discloses his wonderful love to us, for it is not possible to give a better example of true union and love than a marriage in which bride and groom are most closely joined." In language echoing Bernard of Clairvaux, he stresses the mutuality and devotion of the two spouses: "It is enough for her that she neither wishes nor is able to be satisfied in the Bridegroom alone unless she totally possesses him."[121] There can be no mediation in such a union—bride and Bridegroom are immediately joined and share "wine, bread, and whatever is in the house."[122] A sermon on the Parable of the Wedding Banquet in Matthew 22 preached in 1537 presents the mystical marriage in detail, speaking of "the bride taking the Bridegroom's heart as her own . . . so that he does not consider you in any way different from the way your own heart does."[123] Marital union is nothing else but the "happy exchange" between God and human effected at the incarnation.[124] Based on Pauline texts, especially Philippians 2:5–7, earlier Christian writers, such as Augustine,[125] had explored this biblical motif, but Luther made it central to his theology, at least as early as *The Freedom of the Christian*. In a sermon preached in Erfurt in October of 1522, Luther once again praises "the wonderful exchange, namely, that Christ gives the believer himself and all his possessions and takes to himself the heart and what belongs to it. . . . Christ's innocence becomes his innocence; Christ's own piety, holiness, blessedness, and whatever is in Christ, is all in the believer's heart along with Christ."[126]

Although Christ dwells within the believer in a marital union, human beings always remain both sinners and justified. Within this paradox Luther locates another theme of traditional Christian mysticism, the notion of *imitatio Christi*, the imitation of Christ.[127] To be sure, the Reformer was at pains to avoid any sense that our pious works in following Christ give us any claim to salvation. Taking over a formula from Augustine,[128] Luther says, "The crucifixion of Christ is a sacrament and an example [*sacramentum et exemplum*], because it thus signifies the cross of penance and truly exhorts that the body be offered up or crucified to the death in which the soul died to sin." The Redeemer is first of all a sacrament for us in his death on the cross, and only then can he become an exemplar for how we are to deliver ourselves over to dying in imitation of him. "The death of Christ," he continues, "makes the soul die to sin, so that we are thus crucified to the world and the world to us."[129] Therefore, there can be no literal attempt to imitate Christ and thus come closer to God; rather, Christ's death mediates salvation to us so that we can live as he did. In his *Lectures on Hebrews*, Luther puts this clearly:

> In this way works issue spontaneously from faith. Thus, our patience
> comes from Christ's patience, our humility from his humility, and his
> other gifts in the same way. . . . Therefore, if anyone wants to imitate
> Christ as an example, he must firmly believe that Christ suffered and
> died for him as a sacrament. Therefore, they make a huge mistake
> who try first to blot out their sins by penitential works, beginning
> with Christ's example, when they ought to begin with the sacrament
> [i.e., the passion].[130]

Another important aspect of Luther's theology also has a connection with late medieval mysticism. Luther challenged the medieval
conception of the hierarchy of the church in many ways, not least by
his emphasis on the priesthood of all believers. Already in the *Freedom
of the Christian* Luther proclaimed this to Leo X and his readers: "We
are priests, which is far more than being a king or a queen, because the
priesthood makes us worthy to stand before God and to intercede for
others. . . . Christ has redeemed us in order that we might spiritually
represent and intercede for one another, just as a priest represents the
people bodily and prays for them."[131] The priesthood of all believers
has a scriptural foundation (e.g., 1 Pet. 2:5–9) but had not been much
stressed in medieval theology. Still, a significant aspect of the "New
Mysticism" of the late Middle Ages had democratized and secularized
the mystical ideal in the sense of no longer relegating mystical union to
the spiritual elite of the cloisters but rather insisting that all believers
are called to deep experience of God, even in the world and worldly
professions.[132] Luther's favorite mystic, Tauler, said that any inner man
can function as a priest and enter into the Holy of Holies.[133] Thus,
Luther's doctrine of the universal priesthood of believers can be seen
as in line with the universalizing tendencies in some late medieval mystics regarding spiritual authority. Once again, however, Luther effected
a transformation of this tendency in the context of the requirement of
all Christians to preach the gospel message.[134]

   Theōsis, or deification, is one of the oldest themes of Christian mysticism. For many Protestants it represented all that was bad and counter-
evangelical in mysticism. Even figures like Albert Schweitzer, who was
willing to admit that a Pauline "Christ-Mysticism" was integral to the
gospel, thought that the Johannine "God-Mysticism" with its overtones
of deification formed the first departure from the evangelical message.[135] In many accounts, deification is seen as a hallmark of Greek
theology, patristic and Byzantine, but deification themes were important in Augustine, Bernard, and a number of the German mystics dear
to Luther, and, indeed, in Western mysticism in general.[136] One of the

major developments of recent Luther scholarship came when Finnish Lutheran scholars, influenced by their dialogue with Orthodox theologians, discovered that Luther (at least the early Luther) had employed the language of deification.[137] Comparing Luther to medieval Orthodox theologians like Gregory Palamas, whom Luther could not have known, is a generous ecumenical gesture, although the Reformer's contact with Western patristic and medieval uses of deification is more important as a possible source of his teaching.

It is not surprising that Luther, with his teaching on the "happy exchange," his emphasis on Christ "in us," and his many expressions of union, was willing to talk about how we are "deified by Christ," though he seems to have used this language mostly in his early writings. In one place he says, "God empties out his beloved Son over us and pours him into us and engenders him in us so that he is entirely made man and we are wholly deified [*gantz und gar vergottet werden*] . . . and all is one thing [*ein ding*] with each other—God, Christ, and you."[138] In the *First Commentary on the Psalms,* there are a number of passages on deification. For example, "God gives me faith and truth by means of which I am true before him, as if I am no longer a human being, but God and God's son and an offspring similar to the Father."[139] According to Luther, the believing Christian as "a part of Christ and Christ's inheritance is a 'god on earth,' though partially."[140] There are also later appearances, as in a sermon for Pentecost on the Gospel text from John 14, where Luther references 1 Peter 2, saying, "We also shall share in the divine nature and be so highly ennobled that we shall not only be loved by God through Christ, and have his favor and grace as the highest holiness, but we shall have our dwelling wholly in him, the Lord himself (John 14:10)."[141] A sermon of 1536 on John 20:21–23 says, "Christ becomes I and I become Christ." Another sermon from the same year claims, "If I believe in him, I partake in all his goods and not just part. I gain eternal justice."[142] There is no question that deification has emerged as an important theme in recent Luther studies. How important it was for Luther remains under discussion, although some Luther scholars, like Ulrich Asendorf, are willing to claim that "for Luther deification belongs to the core of his Christology."[143]

The issue regarding Luther's use of deification is not whether it gives us a "different Luther," once again a "mystical Luther," this time more Eastern Orthodox than Western German, but rather whether Luther's use of this mystical theme changes our view of his fundamental theology. What those who have stressed Luther's bond to Bernard and German mystics, as well as the scholars who have tried to show

that deification has an important role in the Reformer, have demonstrated is that his theology was more complex in its use of sources and
in its developing patterns than has been admitted in the past, both by
the Lutheran tradition, which ossified his often paradoxical views into
a confessional system, and by the Catholics, who, until the ecumenical
era, vilified him as a confused heretic. The real Luther, and his view
of mysticism, was complex, ambiguous, and still open to investigation
and interpretation.

   In conclusion, I reiterate that my treatment has not pretended to
answer all the questions about Luther's relation to mysticism, but rather
has sought to show how indebted the Reformer was to aspects of the
mystical teaching of his predecessors, as well as to reveal how deeply
mystical elements were embedded in his evangelical theology, though
in ways often different from what is found in patristic and medieval
mystics. Luther's view of fallen human nature broke with the anthropology of the mystics—not only the German mystics who emphasized
the ground of the soul but even Bernard of Clairvaux with his teaching on humans as made in the image and likeness of God.[144] Luther
replaced the intellectual darkness of Dionysian apophatic mysticism
with the darkness of faith in the crucified Christ. Finally, Luther had
a different view of the role of faith and love in relation to God. In this
life, insisted Luther, everything begins and ends with faith, through
which alone we can be saved. Our union with Christ is given to us in
the faith received in baptism; it is this gift that allows us to love our
neighbor. Toward God, however, our attitude must remain primarily
one of humility and receptivity. Earlier mystics often made use of the
text of Philippians 3:13 about "forgetting the things that are behind
and stretching myself forth to those that are ahead" to indicate the
mystic's unending progress in loving unknowing toward the divine
mystery. It is characteristic of Luther that he interpreted this text in
terms of faith: "So too as we do not attain righteousness in this life but
always stretch out to it, so we always ask to be justified, always ask for
our sins to be forgiven."[145]

   The position advanced here argues that Luther's theology was not
a mystical theology as such. I have not tried to evaluate Luther's own
inner consciousness of God and how "mystical" it might have been.
Regarding evaluations of Luther as mystic, much depends on what one
means by mysticism and mystical theology. Luther certainly rejected
the traditional "mystical theology" as a characterization of his efforts
to preach and teach the gospel, however much he learned from those
we today call mystics. The importance of transformed elements of

mysticism in Luther's evangelical teaching is not sufficient, in my mind, for calling Luther a mystic. In the last analysis, we are faced with the choice of either describing Luther's theology as a radically *new* form of mysticism, or of adopting the view that, as in so much else, Luther's theology has a *sic et non* relation to previous theologies, including the mystical, adapting and altering aspects he found helpful, rejecting others in the formation of his own understanding of the gospel.

Mysticism in Reformed Protestantism

The second major branch of evangelical Christianity that appeared in the early sixteenth century began in Switzerland and soon spread across northern Europe. Initially these reformers, spearheaded by the Zurich priest Hyldrich Zwingli (1484–1531), allied themselves with Luther and his followers. What was to become the Reformed wing of Protestantism agreed with Luther on such fundamental issues as justification by faith alone and *sola scriptura*, but soon serious differences emerged over how much of the structure and ceremony of the medieval church should be maintained, the form of organization of the new evangelical communities, the understanding of Christ's presence in the Lord's Supper, as well as the role of the law. Luther and Zwingli soon fell out, and the divergence between the Lutheran and the Reformed traditions has continued down to the present. As with Luther and the Lutheranism that emerged by the mid-sixteenth century, it has become customary now to speak of a "Reformed Spirituality," though the term is of recent origin.[146] Is there a Reformed mysticism?

The major voice of Reformed Protestantism, John Calvin (1509–1564), never met Luther or Zwingli.[147] Calvin was born a Catholic in France. Trained as a lawyer and imbued with Renaissance humanism, he came under the influence of evangelical currents in his twenties. Sometime around 1530–33 Calvin experienced a conversion that he later described in a rare personal passage in the "Preface" to his *Commentary on the Psalms* (1557). Calvin avers that he was "obstinately devoted to the superstitions of Popery" until "God by a sudden conversion subdued and brought to a teachable frame my mind." He continues, "Having thus received some taste and knowledge of true piety, I was immediately inflamed with such intense a desire to make progress therein, that, although I did not altogether leave off other studies, I yet pursued them with less ardor."[148] Like Luther, Calvin did not see himself as establishing a new religion or denomination, but as returning the church to its true form based on scripture by getting rid of the abuses introduced by the papacy. Thus, he argued that his teaching was in line with the best patristic authors, especially Augustine, and he approved of some medieval authors, such as Bernard of Clairvaux. He was, however, strongly opposed to scholastic theology, often denouncing even those he called "the saner Schoolmen."[149]

In 1534, attacks on French Protestants convinced Calvin to flee Paris and go to Basel, a center of the reform. He moved on to Strassburg, and then to Geneva in 1536, an independent city-state that had turned to the evangelical faith in 1532 under the leadership of the French preacher William Farel. Calvin longed for a life of scholarly leisure, but Farel convinced him to become a lecturer and preacher to help reform the church of Geneva. Disagreements between Calvin and the powerful city council over reform made this a difficult task. From 1538 to 1541 he lived in exile in Strassburg. Eventually he was called back, and from 1541 until his death in 1564 he was the religious leader of the fractious Geneva community and increasingly the spokesman for Reformed Christianity through his numerous writings. Like Luther, Calvin was a prodigious preacher, biblical commentator, and liturgical and spiritual writer, one who also penned many polemical treatises.[150] Unlike Luther, he also wrote a full presentation of evangelical theology, *The Institutes of the Christian Religion*, whose first brief Latin form appeared in 1536 but which was published in an expanded version in 1539, translated into French in 1541, and revised and expanded throughout his life.[151] Calvin's *Institutes* has long been received as the classic theological work of the evangelical Christianity of the sixteenth century.[152]

Calvin's connections with the world of late medieval theology, while not totally lacking, were not as strong as Luther's. His background was in the world of humanist and legal scholarship. His attacks on the papacy and the contemporary abuses of the Roman church are as powerful as those of the Wittenberg theologian, but they come from a more systematic perspective. The same traditional Protestant antipathy to spirituality and mysticism that long denied any mysticism in Luther also considered spirituality and mysticism anathema to Calvin's views.[153] Although Calvin never spoke of "spirituality," "piety" (*pietas*) is a key theme in his writing and preaching, and what he has to say about piety overlaps quite well with the way spirituality is often used today. Hence, during the past half-century, there has been growing discussion about what Heiko A. Oberman called "that elusive entity best called the spirituality of Calvin."[154] The view of Calvin as a dry-as-dust systematic theologian has been recognized as more a function of the Calvinist tradition than of the Geneva reformer himself, who saw his *Institutes* as a *summa pietatis* ("Summa of Piety").[155] Calvin thought of himself as a pastor, one called to teach, to preach, and to shepherd his flock. Emphasizing the pastoral dimension of Calvin's life and thought has opened the door to analyzing Calvin's distinctive form of Reformed piety (and/or spirituality).[156] Since Calvin also makes use of the themes and language found in some medieval mystics, such as Bernard of Clairvaux, the question has recently emerged as to whether Calvin might be called a mystic. A few scholars have begun to make this claim,[157] but it seems to me that Calvin should not be termed a mystic in the sense of a Bernard, Bonaventure, or other major figures in the mystical tradition. Nevertheless, the relation of Calvin to mysticism and the investigation of how he used mystical themes are of some significance for appreciating the meaning of his Reformed theology and piety.

Calvin's strictures against some mystical authors go beyond Luther. Like the Wittenberger, he was dismissive of the Dionysian writings. Early in the *Institutes*, speaking of knowledge of the angels, he says, "No one will deny that Dionysius, whoever he was, subtly and skillfully discussed many matters in his *Celestial Hierarchy*. But if anyone examine it more closely, he will find it for the most part nothing but talk" (*Institutes* 1.14.4).[158] He contrasts the blabbermouth Dionysius with Paul, who testified that it was unlawful to speak the secret things he had seen (2 Cor. 12:4). In a 1559 letter to the Reformed congregation at Frankfurt, Calvin forcefully attacks Luther's beloved "Frankfurter," the unknown author of the *Theologia Deutsch*, saying, "in the name of God flee like a plague all those who try to infect you with such trash."[159] Calvin never refers to Tauler, and the language of late medieval German mysticism is notably absent from his works. Calvin was like Luther, however, in his respect for Augustine and in his admiration for Bernard of Clairvaux.[160] It would be too much to say that Calvin merely took over themes like mystical union and deification from these sources, but insofar as we can speak of mystical aspects of his thought, Calvin was doubtless encouraged by finding some of them in acceptable authors like Bernard. I will not attempt to give an account of Calvin's theology here, but it is necessary to mention a few essential themes in order to see where the mystical elements fit.

We can start with *pietas* itself.[161] At the outset of the *Institutes*, Calvin says that all true and sound wisdom consists in the knowledge of God and of ourselves (1.1.1), but there can be no true knowledge of self without knowledge of God. Real knowledge of God, however, is not just knowing that God exists, but it is grasping what is fitting for us and proper to his glory, both with regard to his fashioning of the universe and his redeeming action in Christ (1.2.1). The knowledge that we totally depend on God for all things is the source of piety: "For this sense of the powers of God is for us a fit teacher of piety, from which religion is born. I call 'piety' that reverence joined with love of God which the knowledge of his benefits induces" (1.2.1). More briefly, he later says that "the first step toward piety [is] to recognize that God is our Father to watch over us, govern and nourish us" (2.6.4). Piety therefore is a loving knowledge of God and his benefits, a knowledge realized in doing what belongs to us as creatures created and redeemed by God. Piety is rooted in the faith in Christ that alone brings salvation to fallen humanity. It also produces union with Christ (what Calvin at times called a "mystical union," *unio mystica*). This union is realized through the distinct, but inseparable, two forms of grace that Calvin spoke of as the grace of justification and the grace of sanctification or regeneration.

Piety has a twofold root in Calvin's thought. The first root is in the doctrine of creation.[162] Adam was created by the beneficence of the heavenly Father through the eternal mediation of the Word and the action of the Holy Spirit in order to share in God's own life, that is, to enter into communion with the Trinitarian God (1.13.14). The key element in Calvin's anthropology, as in patristic and medieval thought, is his understanding of the statement in Genesis 1:26 about humanity being made in God's image and likeness. Calvin's exposition of this, as laid out in *Institutes* 1.15 and in his commentaries, especially that on Genesis, breaks with traditional teaching. First of all, Calvin did not distinguish between *imago* and *similitudo*, correctly seeing them as a dual formula of emphasis. Even more important was Calvin's move away from analyzing the passage in terms of the ontological structure of the soul and its powers. He rather adopted what Heiko Oberman called a psychological approach; that is, what is fundamental to humanity is its relationship toward God, which is one of proper orientation before the Fall, but of alienation after.[163] Calvin conceived of humanity's creation as developmental: first, humans were created from the dust of the earth; then, they were given a soul; and finally, they were gifted with the image of God designed to grow toward God by participating in Christ, the true and perfect Image of the Father. Adam fell of his own free will (1.15.8); as a consequence, human beings now cannot avoid sin. Calvin says that "God's image was not totally annihilated and destroyed in him [Adam], yet it was so corrupted that whatever remains is frightful deformity" (1.15.4). Since the image can no longer fulfill its purpose by growing toward God, its effectiveness is lost (e.g., 2.2.12). What does remain in corrupt human nature after the Fall is what Calvin calls the "sense of divinity" (*sensus divinitatis*), or "seed of religion," as well as the "conscience" (*conscientia*) by which the distinction between good and evil can be recognized even if the will cannot follow the good. In fallen humanity, therefore, the corruption of our nature means that neither of these remnants has any power to give rise to good action in the sense of something directed to God.

The second and more powerful root of piety is found in God's work of justification and regeneration effected through the Incarnate Word and the continuing action of the Holy Spirit. In *Institutes* 3.11.1 Calvin sums up:

> Christ was given us by God's generosity to be grasped and possessed by us in faith. By partaking of him, we principally receive a double grace: namely, that of being reconciled to God through Christ's blamelessness, so that we may have in heaven instead of a Judge a gracious Father; and secondly, that sanctified by Christ's Spirit we may cultivate blamelessness and purity of life. . . . For unless you first of all grasp what your relationship to God is, and the nature of his judgment concerning you, you have neither a foundation on which to establish your salvation nor one on which to build your piety toward God.

Both justification and sanctification are equally necessary and given to us simultaneously in Christ. "By faith we grasp Christ's righteousness, by which alone we are reconciled to God. Yet you could not grasp this without at the same time grasping sanctification also. . . . Although we may distinguish them, Christ contains them both inseparably in himself" (3.16.1). Justification is given in its fullness by faith in Christ, while sanctification is a gradual process by which the Holy Spirit draws us nearer and nearer to God, a task never complete in this life (3.6.2, 4). The whole of the important section of *Institutes* 3.6–10, devoted to "The Life of the Christian," may be described as a treatise on piety in action, that is, the process of sanctification.[164]

Calvin's teaching on justification and sanctification is far from any form of abstract theoretical knowledge. The "right definition of faith" is "firm and certain knowledge of God's benevolence toward us, founded on the truth of the freely given promise in Christ, revealed to our minds and sealed upon our hearts through the Holy Spirit"

(3.2.7). Faith is a form of "knowledge," but not anything similar to how we know created things; even when the mind attains it, "it does not comprehend what it feels" (3.2.14). Thus, the affective and experiential dimensions of faith are central for Calvin (see 3.2.33),[165] that is, faith as "a matter of the heart," as he argues in *Institutes* 3.2.36. Faith is the mode of knowing appropriate to believers, one taught by the Holy Spirit and involving a partaking in Christ himself (3.2.24). Faith does not exclude love (remember that love of God is included in the definition of piety cited above), but Calvin insists that "as our freedom must be subordinated to love, so in turn ought love itself be under the purity of faith" (3.9.13). Calvin teaches that the soul must first be filled with love of God before it can flow out into a true love of neighbor (2.8.51, 54). So, there is place for both knowledge and love in Calvin's thinking, although these are understood within the confines of justification by faith alone.[166]

That Calvin's notion of piety is thoroughly Christocentric cannot be doubted, but it is often overlooked that the Genevan reformer is just as pneumatological in his emphasis on the role of the Spirit in making Christ accessible to us and in drawing us up to God. *Institutes* 1.9.3 is devoted to explaining how the Word and the Spirit always work together, one of the texts where Calvin also speaks of contemplation: "For by a kind of mutual bond the Lord has joined together the certainty of his Word and of his Spirit so that the perfect religion of the Word may abide in our hearts when the Spirit, who causes us to contemplate God's face, shines." What Calvin means by this contemplation is revealed in a passage in *Institutes* 3.2.19, where, in dependence on Plato's Myth of the Cave in the *Republic*, he speaks about how "the least drop of faith" begins the process of the contemplation of God's face, like being gradually released from a dark prison. At the outset, "We see him afar off." "Then," he continues, "the more we advance as we ought continually to advance with steady progress, as it were, the nearer and thus surer sight of him we obtain; and by the very continuance he is made more familiar to us." This contemplation, however, is not any conceptual knowing, or even unknowing, of the divine nature itself, but is rather a "clear knowledge of the divine will towards itself . . . the first and principal parts of faith."[167] Contemplation is thus tied decisively to faith, as is also evident in Calvin's comment on Paul's ascent to the third heaven in 2 Corinthians 12:1–4, where he emphasizes that it was an ascent of faith, one of which Paul revealed nothing except the fact that it had happened.[168]

Calvin was not interested in contemplation in the traditional mystical sense, nor in the mysteries about the divine nature that may or may not have been shown to the biblical heroes of the Old and the New Testament. He was also aware of the dangers of the mystically inclined pantheistic identification with God he found in the contemporary sectarians he denounced as "Libertines."[169] His interest rather focused on what Christ has gained for all the saved who have become one with him in his body the church. Hence, he has much to say about some of the traditional christological themes of redemption theology, such as adoption after the model of the firstborn Christ,[170] as well as the happy exchange between God and humanity effected through the incarnation.[171] One theme of Calvin's Christology that has often been overlooked, as Julie Canlis has reminded us, is the importance of Christ's ascent as both the source and the exemplar of our return to God.[172] Christ's descent in taking on flesh is the beginning of our ascent: "For this reason Christ descended to us, to bear us up to the Father, and at the same time to bear us up to himself inasmuch as he is one with the Father" (1.13.26). Ascent to God was a major theme of patristic and medieval mysticism, but one most often expressed in terms of describing the stages of contemplative ascent and the respective roles of love and knowledge in the process. There is little of this in Calvin.

The area of mystical terminology that plays the largest role in Calvin is that of union with Christ and the deification attendant upon this uniting. The noted Calvin scholar Wilhelm Niesel went so far as to say, "For Calvin . . . that joining together of Head and members, that indwelling of Christ in our hearts—in short, that mystical union—is fundamental."[173] Union with Christ is a frequent theme in Calvin's writings and is expressed in a variety of ways.[174] Among these expressions (*insero, communio/communico, societas, coniugium, coniunctio, coalesco, participatio*, etc.) Calvin found place for the phrase *unio mystica*, though only twice. More frequently found are equivalent expressions, such as *coniunctio spiritualis* (nine times), *communio cum Christo* (nineteen times), and *insitio in Christo* (thirty-three times). These and like phrases occur throughout the *Institutes* and Calvin's commentaries on Paul and John.

It may be surprising to those unfamiliar with the history of Christian mysticism to learn that *unio mystica* was not a common expression in patristic or medieval mysticism. Although found a few times in the Dionysian writings, it was rarely used for the next millennium, although there were many other forms of union-language employed by the mystics. In Calvin, *unio mystica* keeps its etymological sense of "hidden union," as can be seen from the fact that he sometimes substitutes *arcana*, *incomprehensibilis*, or the French *secret*. One of the first writers to use *unio mystica* extensively was a French Catholic mystic almost exactly contemporary with Calvin, the Benedictine abbot Louis de Blois (1506–1566), who employs the expression nine times in his *Spiritual Institution*, first published in 1553.[175] Louis and Calvin were pioneers, if on different sides of the religious divide of the sixteenth century.

Calvin's most extensive discussion of *unio mystica* comes in *Institutes* 3.11.10. The context is largely polemical, because this section occurs in the midst of an attack (3.11.5–12) on the dissident Lutheran pastor Andreas Osiander (ca. 1496–1552) and his view of "essential righteousness," that is, that justification by faith is an infusion of Christ's divine nature into human beings.[176] Calvin wants to make it clear that his attack on Osiander's "strange monster of essential righteousness" (3.11.5) does not mean that he does not have a place for union with Christ. On the contrary:

> That joining together of Head and members, that indwelling of Christ in our hearts—in short, that mystical union—are accorded by us the highest degree of importance, so that Christ, having been made ours, makes us sharers with him in the gifts with which he has been endowed. We do not therefore contemplate him outside ourselves from afar in order that his righteousness may be imputed to us, but because we put on Christ and are engrafted into his body—in short, because he deigns to make us one with him.[177]

This real, but spiritual union, says Calvin, is far from the "gross mixture" of human and divine proposed by Osiander. The scriptural proofs that Osiander brings forward concerning deification (2 Pet. 1:4; 1 John 3:2) will be fully realized only at Christ's second coming, not in the present. Calvin's eschatological interpretation of deification texts (e.g., *Institutes* 3.25.10, and the *Commentary on 2 Peter* 1:4) shows a significantly cooler attitude toward this mystical theme than that found in Luther.

Calvin's teaching on our union with Christ conforms to his doctrine of twofold grace. We are, on the one hand, fully made one with Christ through our justification by faith alone (3.1.1), so that only the elect can be said to be united to God (3.22.10). On the other hand, the grace of sanctification means that there is a progressive character to union as well. In *Institutes* 3.2.24, Calvin says, "Christ is not outside us but dwells within us. Not only does he cleave to us by an indivisible bond of fellowship, but with a wonderful communion, day by day, he grows more and more into one body with us, until he becomes completely one with us" (see also 3.6.2, 4). The twofold aspect of mystical union is clear in a letter Calvin wrote to his friend Peter Martyr Vermigli (1499–1562) on August 8, 1555.[178] The first part of the letter deals with "the hidden communication with Christ" (*de arcana cum Christo communicatione*) that Calvin says "is of great moment." He continues, "I say that at the same time we receive Christ in faith as he offers himself in the Gospel, he truly makes us his members and life flows down from him into us in no other way than from the Head. The only way he reconciles us to God by the sacrifice of his death is because he is ours and we are one with him." Calvin says that the words "association" (*consortium*) and "society" (*societas*) are insufficient for designating "that sacred union by which the Son of God inserts us into his body so that he can share everything he has with us." He goes on to insist on the Holy Spirit's role in this union and to clarify that the union has nothing to do with becoming one essence with Christ. In the second part of the letter, he turns to union as the source for our sanctification, mentioning many of the practices that help "the pursuit of justice and piety" (*iustitiae et pietatis studium*) to grow strong.

Following oft-cited biblical texts about the spousal relation of God and his people, Calvin speaks of this union as a spiritual marriage: "God very commonly takes on the character of a husband to us. Indeed, the union by which he binds us to himself when he receives us into the church is like sacred marriage, which must rest upon mutual faithfulness [Eph. 5:29-32]" (*Institutes* 2.8.18; see also 4.19.35). The union is realized primarily between Christ and the church, and then derivatively in us as members of the body of the church. Although it is a marriage with Christ, the incarnate second person of the Trinity, the three persons are at work in its production. "The Holy Spirit is the bond by which Christ effectually unites us to himself" (3.1.1; see 4.17.31), and the "Life-Giving Spirit enables us to participate in Christ and to enjoy the Father's Fatherhood" (3.1.2).

Without touching on all aspects of Calvin's view of our union with Christ, especially its relation to the sacraments, it should be clear that union/mystical union is deeply embedded in his outlook and piety. Calvin's view of union shows both strong similarities to and real differences from the main line of Western medieval monastic mysticism represented by Bernard of Clairvaux, who also emphasized Christ's spousal union with the church as the ground for striving to attain union of wills (*unitas spiritus*, 1 Cor. 6:17) between Christ and individual believers.[179] Like Calvin, Bernard and the monastic mystics eschewed any substantial merging of God and humans, and they also held that full union was only to be attained in heaven. Calvin, however, emphasized faith as the essential ground of union. Bernard would not have denied faith's role, but he gave greater attention to the progression of stages of love that led to brief direct encounters with the Word in this life. Bernard and other medieval mystics also gave a greater role to analyzing contemplation and the process of deification that accompanied the path of loving union. From this perspective, it appears that Calvin was not really a mystic, either in the sense of the medieval monastic mysticism he knew through Bernard, or in that of the late medieval German mysticism that influenced Luther and some other reformers. Despite these important differences, Calvin had enough in common with Bernard to help us understand why he could speak of the abbot as being among the "devout witnesses" to the understanding of true righteousness (*Institutes* 3.12.3).

Notes

1. On Luther's spirituality, see Jared Wicks, "Luther (Martin)," *DS* 9:1206–43; Marc Lienhard, "Luther and the Beginnings of the Reformation," in *Christian Spirituality II: High Middle Ages and Reformation*, ed. Jill Raitt, in collaboration with Bernard McGinn and John Meyendorff, World Spirituality 17 (New York: Crossroad, 1987), 268–99, as well as the collection of texts in *Luther's Spirituality*, ed. and trans. Philip D. W. Krey, and Peter D. S. Krey, Classics of Western Spirituality (New York: Paulist Press, 2007).

2. On Luther's relation to mysticism, along with Wicks, *Man Yearning for God*, and Hamm, *Early Luther*, mentioned in the introduction, see Steven E. Ozment, *Homo Spiritualis: A Comparative Study of the Anthropology of Johannes Tauler, Jean Gerson, and Martin Luther (1509–16) in the Context of Their Theological Thought*, Studies in Medieval and Reformation Thought 6 (Leiden: Brill, 1969); and Karl-Heinz Zur Mühlen, *Nos extra nos: Luthers Theologie zwischen Mystik und Scholastik*, Beiträge zur historischen Theologie 46 (Tübingen: Mohr Siebeck, 1972). Many essays treat Luther's mysticism; see, e.g., Erich Vogelsang, "Luther und die Mystik," *Luther Jahrbuch* (1937): 32–53; Erwin Iserloh, "Luther's Christ-Mysticism," in Wicks, *Catholic Scholars Dialogue with Luther* (Chicago: Loyola University Press, 1970), 37–58; Heiko A. Oberman, "*Simul Gemitus et Raptus:* Luther and Mysticism," in Ozment, *Reformation in Medieval Perspective*, 219–51; Alois M. Haas, "Luther und die Mystik," *Deutsche Vierteljahrsschrift für Literaturwissenschaft und Geistesgeschichte* 60 (1986): 177–207; Wriedt, "Mystik und Protestantismus—ein Widerspuch?," 79–82; Volker Leppin, "Transformationen spätmittelalterliche Mystik bei Luther," in *Gottes Nähe unmittelbar erfahren: Mystik im Mittelalter und bei Martin Luther*, ed. Berndt Hamm and Volker Leppin (Tübingen: Mohr Siebeck,

2007), 165–85; and the overview of Leppin, "Mystik," in *Luther Handbuch*, ed. Albrecht Beutel (Tübingen: Mohr Siebeck, 2003), 57–61.

3. See, e.g., Reinhold Schwarz, "Martin Luther (1483–1546)," in *Grosse Mystiker: Leben und Wirken*, ed. Gerhard Ruhbach and Josef Sudbrack (Munich: C. H. Beck, 1984), 185–201; Sven Grosse, "Der junge Luther und die Mystik: Ein Beitrag zur Frage nach dem Werden der reformatorischen Theologie," and Berndt Hamm, "Wie mystisch war der Glaube Luthers?," both in Hamm and Leppin, *Gottes Nähe unmittelbar erfahren* (Tübingen: Mohr Siebeck, 2007), 187–235 and 237–87, as well as Hamm's *Early Luther*, esp. chapter 8, "How Mystical Was Luther's Faith?"

4. I will make use of the standard edition of Luther's writings: *D. Martin Luthers Werke Kritische Gesamtausgabe*, 120 vols. (Weimar: Hermann Böhlau, 1883–2009). The volumes in the main collection, known as the "Weimarer-Ausgabe (WA)," will be cited by volume, page, and line number (e.g., WA 1:112.12–26). There is a translation of much of the WA in the sixty volumes of *Luther's Works* (Saint Louis: Concordia, 1955–86), but I will make my own translations unless otherwise noted and I will generally not cite the Latin and German original texts unless needed.

5. Oberman, *"Simul Gemitus et Raptus,"* 224–30.

6. Luther's growing rejection of scholasticism reached its climax in his September 1517 treatise *Disputation against Scholastic Theology* (WA 1:221–28). On Luther's campaign against scholastic theology, see Wicks, *Man Yearning for Grace*, 178–99.

7. Hamm ("Wie mystisch war der Glaube Luthers?, 255–61) argues for a strong influence of Staupitz on Luther's mysticism. For more on Staupitz, see David C. Steinmetz, *Misericordia Dei: The Theology of Johannes von Staupitz in Its Late Medieval Setting*, Studies in Medieval and Reformation Thought 4 (Leiden: Brill, 1968); and idem, *Luther and Staupitz: An Essay in the Intellectual Origins of the Protestant Reformation*, Duke Monographs in Medieval and Renaissance Studies 4 (Durham, NC: Duke University Press, 1980).

8. See the dedicatory letter to Staupitz of May 30, 1518, in WA 1:525–27.

9. The role of Augustine in the young Luther was discussed by Adolf Hamel, *Der junge Luther und Augustin*, 2 vols. (Gütersloh: C. Bertelsmann, 1934), and there are many other studies. A brief overview can be found in Léon Cristiani, "Luther et saint Augustin," in *Augustinus Magister*, 3 vols. (Paris: Études Augustiniennes, 1954–55) 2:1029–38. See also Erik L. Saak, "Luther, Martin," in *The Oxford Guide to the Historical Reception of Augustine*, ed. Karla Pohlmann et al., 3 vols. (Oxford: Oxford University Press, 2013), 3:1341–45.

10. Luther's *Table Talk* (*Tischreden*) is edited in six separate volumes in the Weimar edition and is abbreviated WATr. This passage is no. 347 (WATr 1:140.5–7).

11. For the context of Luther's use of Augustine, see Heiko A. Oberman, "The Augustinian Renaissance of the Later Middle Ages," in Oberman, *Masters of the Reformation: The Emergence of a New Intellectual Climate in Europe* (Cambridge: Cambridge University Press, 1981), 64–110.

12. Luther's use of the *Confessions* has been studied by Pierre Courcelle, *Les Confessions de Saint Augustin dans la tradition littéraire: Antécedents et postérité* (Paris: Études Augustiniennes, 1963), 353–70.

13. On the role of the Dionysian writings in the Reformation, see Karlfried Froehlich, "Pseudo-Dionysius and the Reformation of the Sixteenth Century," in the "Introduction" to *Pseudo-Dionysius: The Complete Works*, ed. and trans. Colm Luibhead, Classics of Western Spirituality (New York: Paulist Press, 1987), 33–46. On

Dionysius and Luther, see Paul Rorem, "Martin Luther's Christocentric Critique of Pseudo-Dionysian Spirituality," *Lutheran Quarterly* 11 (1997): 291–307; see also Iserloh, "Luther's Christ-Mysticism," 41–45; and Haas, "Luther und die Mystik," 182–85. Recently Piotr Malysz has argued that, despite Luther's negative comments about Dionysius, there are points of continuity regarding divine hiddenness and soteriology between the two theologians; see "Luther and Dionysius: Beyond Mere Negations," in *Re-Thinking Dionysius the Areopagite*, ed. Sarah Coakley and Charles M. Stang, Directions in Modern Theology (Oxford: Wiley-Blackwell, 2009), 149–62.

14. *Dictata super Psalterium* (WA 3:124.30–33).

15. *Dictata super Psalterium* (WA 3:372.13–19).

16. *Lectura super Epistolam ad Hebraeos* (WA 57/III:179.6–9, 197.18–20).

17. The theme of divine hiddenness and its relation to *Anfechtung* is central to Luther's theology and will be studied in more detail below. For a brief presentation in relation to the medieval mystics, see Bernard McGinn, "*Vere tu es Deus absconditus*: The Hidden God in Luther and Some Mystics," in *Silence and the Word of God: Negative Theology and Incarnation*, ed. Oliver Davies and Denys Turner (Cambridge: Cambridge University Press, 2002), 94–114.

18. *The Babylonian Captivity of the Church* (WA 6:562.8–14). A similar passage can be found in the *Disputation of December 18, 1537* (WA 39/I:389.21–390.5).

19. *In Psalmum 90* (WA 40/III:543.8–13).

20. *Operationes in Psalmos* (WA 5:163.26–29).

21. George Tavard, "Medieval Piety in Luther's *Commentary on the Magnificat*," in *Ad fontes Lutheri: Toward the Recovery of the Real Luther; Essays in Honor of Kenneth Hagen's Sixty-Fifth Birthday*, ed. Timothy Maschke, Franz Posset, and Joan Skocir (Milwaukee: Marquette University Press, 2001), 281–301, esp. 292–94, 299–300.

22. *Table Talk* no. 644 (WATr 1:302.30ff.).

23. *Table Talk* no. 683 (WATr 1:330.1).

24. For an introduction to Gerson's role in Western mysticism, see McGinn, *Varieties*, 86–95, and the literature cited there. On Gerson and Luther, see Ozment, *Homo Spiritualis*, part 2, and chapter 11 (205–9).

25. See, e.g., the *Scholion to Psalm 26:9* (WA 3:151.5ff.). A reference to Gerson's *De mystica theologia* is found in Luther's *Marginal Comments on Tauler's Sermons* (WA 9:99.36–40).

26. An example can be found in Vogelsang, "Luther und die Mystik."

27. The most detailed study of Luther's use of Bernard is Theo Bell, *DIVUS BERNHARDUS: Bernard von Clairvaux in Martin Luthers Schriften* (Mainz: Philipp von Zabern, 1993). Bell also contains a review of the earlier literature discussing Bernard and Luther (1–17). Other treatments of Bernard and Luther include Erich Kleinedam, "Ursprung und Gegenstand der Theologie bei Bernhard von Clairvaux und Martin Luther," in *Dienst der Vermittlung: Festschrift zum 25-jährigen Bestehen d. Philosoph.-Theol. Studiums in Priesterseminar Erfurt*, ed. Wilhelm Ernst, Konrad Feiereis, and Fritz Hoffmann, Erfurter theologische Studien 37 (Leipzig: St. Benno, 1977), 221–47; Franz Posset, "*Divus Bernhardus*: Saint Bernard as Spiritual and Theological Mentor of the Reformer Martin Luther," in *Bernardus Magister: Papers Presented at the Nonacentenary Celebration of the Birth of Saint Bernard of Clairvaux, Kalamazoo, Michigan, Sponsored by the Institute of Cistercian Studies*, ed. John R. Sommerfeldt, Cistercian Studies 135 (Kalamazoo, MI: Cistercian Publications, 1992), 517–32; and Bernhard Lohse, "Luther und Bernard von Clairvaux," in *Bernhard von Clairvaux: Rezeption und Wirkung im*

Mittelalter und in der Neuzeit, ed. Kaspar Elm, Wolfenbütteler Mittelalter-Studien 6 (Wiesbaden: Harrassowitz, 1994), 271–303.

28. *Table Talk* no. 584 (WATr 1:272.4–8); see also no. 5439a (WATr 5:154.6).

29. *Against the Antinomians* (WA 50:471.1–6). Posset (*"Divus Bernhardus,"* 530–31) lists eleven passages of Luther's praise for Bernard.

30. E.g., *First Commentary on the Psalms* on Ps. 84:4 (WA 3:640.40–43; 645.31–646.20); *Table Talk* no. 5898 (WATr 5:395.1–2). In these passages Luther conflates the "little bundle of myrrh" mentioned in Bernard's *Sermo super Cantica* 43.1–4 (*Sancti Bernardi Opera,* 2:41–43) with the notion of Christ's wounds as a nest for the soul in *Sermo super Cantica* 61.6–8 (*Sancti Bernardi Opera,* 2:151–53).

31. Luther appeals to Bernard in his 1518 debate with Cajetan, e.g., WA 2:13.6–10 and 15.35–16.5.

32. *Lectures on Romans* 8:16 (WA 56:369.28–370.23). Luther quoted this passage from Bernard's *Sermo 1 de Annunciatione* (*Sancti Bernardi Opera,* 5:13.9–15) in several places. See Posset, *"Divus Bernhardus,"* 519–23.

33. *Sermo 3 in Vigilia Nativitas* 7 (*Sancti Bernardi Opera,* 4:216–17).

34. *Christmas Sermon* (WA 7:188.18–189.30).

35. Five such texts are cited by Posset, *"Divus Bernhardus,"* 526–27.

36. In one early text Luther even speaks of the *nativitas dei in anima;* see *Luthers Werke im Auswahl: V, Der junge Luther,* ed. Erich Vogelsang (Berlin, 1933), 307.

37. *Dictata super Psalterium, Scholion to Psalm 118:122* (WA 4:364.54ff.). On the importance of this text, see Ozment, *Homo Spiritualis,* 132–38. On the theme of constant progress in Luther and its relation to Bernard, see Wicks, *Man Yearning for Grace,* 88–94, 111–14, and 139–40. My thanks to Susan Schreiner for bringing this to my attention.

38. For an analysis of Luther's critical remarks about Bernard, see Lohse, "Luther und Bernard von Clairvaux," 296–300.

39. WA 20:753.22–25. For this and similar texts, see Bell, *DIVUS BERNHARDUS,* 296–98.

40. Lohse, "Luther und Bernard von Clairvaux," 292.

41. For a sketch of Tauler's mysticism, see McGinn, *Harvest,* chapter 6.

42. The most cited, but inadequate, modern edition of Tauler is Fernand Vetter, ed., *Die Predigten Taulers* (Berlin: Weidmann, 1910; reprint, 1968).

43. On Tauler's influence on Luther and the early Reformation, see Henrik Otto, *Vor- und frühreformatorische Tauler-Rezeption: Annotationen in Drucken des späten 15. und frühen 16. Jahrhunderts,* Quellen und Forschungen zur Reformationsgeschichte 75 (Gütersloh: Gütersloher Verlagshaus, 2003).

44. For a comparison of Luther and Eckhart, see Steven E. Ozment, "Eckhart and Luther: German Mysticism and Protestantism," *The Thomist* 42 (1978): 259–80.

45. These *Marginalia on Tauler's Sermons* have been edited both in WA 1:95–104, and in an improved form in WA 9:97–104. See Steven E. Ozment, "An Aid to Luther's Marginal Comments on Johannes Tauler's Sermons," *Harvard Theological Review* 63 (1970): 305–11.

46. *Marginalia on Tauler's Sermons* (WA 9:95.20–23).

47. WA 10/II:329.25ff.

48. All who have written on Luther's mysticism discuss Tauler. See esp. Ozment, *Homo Spiritualis,* part 1, and 197–205, as well as Bernd Moeller, "Tauler und Luther," in *La mystique rhénane: Colloque de Strasbourg, 16–19 mai 1961* (Paris: Presses universitaires

de France, 1963), 157–67, who lists Luther's citations of Tauler (158n3). Also useful are Haas, "Luther und die Mystik," 187–95; and Hamm, "Wie mystisch war der Glaube Luthers?," 277–84, and *Early Luther*, 100–101 and 224–29.

49. V1 (ed. Vetter, 7–12) is most likely a compilation of passages from Eckhart sermons.

50. *Marginalia on Tauler* (WA 9:97.12–14).

51. *Marginalia on Tauler* (WA 9:98.14–23).

52. *Marginalia on Tauler* (WA 9:103.34–36).

53. For an introduction to Tauler on dereliction, see McGinn, *Harvest*, 285–89. On the relation between Tauler and Luther on *Anfechtungen*, see Hamm, "Wie mystisch war der Glaube Luthers?," 277–82.

54. Luther's comments on the three kinds of myrrh can be found in *Marginalia on Tauler* (WA 9:99.1–34).

55. *Lectures on Romans* 8:26–27 (WA 56:378.13ff).

56. *Marginalia on Tauler* (WA 9:104.12–14). On the influence of Tauler on Luther's changing notion of repentance and indulgences, see Volker Leppin, "'omnem vitam fidelium penitentiam esse voluit': Zur Aufnahme mystischer Traditionen in Luthers erster Ablassthese," *Archiv für Reformationsgeschichte* 93 (2002): 7–25.

57. See Moeller, "Tauler und Luther," 166–69; Ozment, *Homo Spiritualis*, 214–16; Otto, *Vor- und frühreformatorische Tauler-Rezeption*, 213–14; and Hamm, "Wie mystisch war der Glaube Luthers?," 282–84.

58. For a sketch of the mysticism of the *Theologia Deutsch*, see McGinn, *Harvest*, 392–404. On the role of the book in early Protestantism, see Steven E. Ozment, *Mysticism and Dissent: Religious Ideology and Social Protest in the Sixteenth Century* (New Haven: Yale University Press, 1973), chapter 2.

59. Luther's two prefaces are edited in WA 1:375–79. There is an English translation of the 1518 edition in *The Theologica Germanica of Martin Luther*, ed. and trans. Bengt Hoffman, Classics of Western Spirituality (New York: Paulist Press, 1980). Luther's edition of fifty-six chapters is somewhat different from the modern critical editions of fifty-three chapters.

60. *Preface to 1518 Edition* (WA 1:379.5–12).

61. WA 40/II:328.17–20.

62. This is well set out by Hamm, "Wie mystisch war der Glaube Luthers?," 265–69; idem, *Early Luther*, 59–60, 77–79, and 217–23.

63. Scott H. Hendrix, *Ecclesia in via: Ecclesiological Developments in the Medieval Psalms Exegesis and the Dictata super Psalterium (1513–1515) of Martin Luther*, Studies in Medieval and Reformation Thought 8 (Leiden: Brill, 1974), 185, 194–95, 198.

64. Hamm, *Early Luther*, chapter 3, "Why Did Luther Turn Faith into the Central Concept of the Christian Life?" (59–84). Hamm sees Luther's new understanding of faith appearing as early as the *Dictata* (1513–15). See also Wicks, *Man Yearning for Grace*, 73–83, 106–11, 131–43, 270–71.

65. *Dictata super Psalterium* (WA 3:649.17–20).

66. Hamm, *Early Luther*, 79.

67. *The Freedom of the Christian* is found in WA 7:49–79, but I have used the newer edition in *Martin Luther: Lateinisch-Deutsche Studienausgabe*, ed. Johannes Schilling, 3 vols. (Leipzig: Evangelische Verlagsanstalt, 2006) 2:101–85. I will generally cite the translation of W. A. Lambert in *Martin Luther, Three Treatises*, 2nd rev. ed. (Philadel-

phia: Fortress, 1970), 265–316. The passage cited is at *Studienausgabe* 2:124.25–27 (trans., 280).

68. *The Freedom of the Christian* (*Studienausgabe* 2:130.25–28; trans., 284). See Bernard, *De diligendo deo* 10.28 (*Sancti Bernardi Opera*, 3:143.17–18), but many mystics have used the analogy of iron melting in fire for loving union.

69. *The Freedom of the Christian* (*Studienausgabe* 2:134.14–18; trans., 286). Since this is one of Luther's key texts on marital union, I cite the Latin: Tertia fidei gratia, incomparabilis est haec, Quod animam copulat cum Christo, sicut sponsam cum sponso, Quo sacramento (ut Apostolus docet) Christus et anima efficitur una caro, Quod si una caro sunt, verumque inter eos matrimonium, immo omnium longe perfectissimum consummatur.

70. *The Freedom of the Christian* (*Studienausgabe* 2:136.11–14; trans., 286–87).

71. *The Freedom of the Christian* (*Studienausgabe* 2:174.3–7; trans., 309).

72. On the importance of experience in Luther, see Haas, "Luther und die Mystik," 195–201.

73. "Sola experientia facit theologum" (WATr 1:16.13, no. 46).

74. The German translation and commentary on Mary's prayer were written in 1521 for the young prince John Frederick of Saxony (1503–1554) and are found in WA 7:545–604. I will use the partial English translation found in Krey, *Luther's Spirituality*, 91–103.

75. *Commentary on the Magnificat* (WA 7:546.21–24; trans., 94).

76. *Commentary on the Magnificat* (WA 7:550.2–25; trans., 97–98). See also the further comment on this initial verse, as well as several later places in the full text. On sweetness in Luther, see Hamm, *Early Luther*, 52–55.

77. Leppin affirms that Luther had such experiences ("Transformationen spätmittelalterliche Mystik bei Luther," 166–67).

78. Sermon for Pentecost Monday (WA 11:117.35–36): "Multos vidi monachos et clericos, qui incerti sunt, et ego semel raptus fui in 3um celum."

79. WA 54:186.5–9. On this passage and its difference from mystical accounts, see Schwarz, "Martin Luther," 187–88; and Wriedt, "Mystik und Protestantismus—ein Widerspruch?," 79–81.

80. See, e.g., the remarks on Psalm 17:18 (WA 3:124.129), the exegesis of Hebrews 10:5 (WA 3:225.10ff), and the commentary on Genesis 26:9 (WA 43:458).

81. *Scholion to Psalm 90:1* (WA 4:65.1–3).

82. On *raptus* in Luther, see Hamel, *Der junge Luther und Augustin* 1:73–77; Oberman, "*Simul Gemitus et Raptus*," 234–37; Zur Mühlen, *Nos extra nos*, esp. 51–66, 114–16, 273–75; and Hamm, "Wie mystisch war der Glaube Luthers?," 271–75; and idem, *Early Luther*, 217–23.

83. *Commentary on Psalm 115* (WA 4:266–73). Luther comments on the verse three times (WA 4:267.16–33; 268.29–269.2; and 273.14–22, the passage cited here). For a treatment of this passage in relation to the history of its exegesis, see Zur Mühlen, *Nos extra nos*, 54–66.

84. *Commentary on Genesis* (WA 43:582.21ff.). For other texts on faith as rapture, see the *Commentary on Hebrews* (WA 57/III:144.10–12), and the *Dictata super Psalterium* (WA 3:372.13–27).

85. *Commentary on Romans* (WA 56:299.17–300.8). See also WA 57:168.18–22.

86. Zur Mühlen, *Nos extra nos*, 108.

87. *The Babylonian Captivity of the Church* (WA 6:562.12–14).

88. E.g., Sermon of 1525 (WA 17/I:438.22-25); Christmas Sermon of 1527 (WA 23:732.5ff.); and *Table Talk* no. 5658 (WATr 5:295.21-25).

89. Christmas Sermon on Exodus (WA 16:144.3-5). See also WA 9:494.24ff.; WA 40/III:657.37ff. See the discussion in Hamm, "Wie mystisch war der Glaube Luthers?," 249-55.

90. *Commentary on Genesis* (WA 43:575-83). There is a partial translation in *Luther's Spirituality*, 172-81.

91. *Commentary on Genesis* (WA 43:582.18-29).

92. Hamm, *Early Luther*, 205.

93. The debate over the role of suffering, especially the difference between true and false suffering, was an important theme of the first reformers, such as Luther, Karlstadt, and Müntzer. See Vincent M. Evener, "'Enemies of the Cross': Suffering, Salvation, and Truth in Sixteenth-Century Religious Controversy" (PhD dissertation, University of Chicago, 2014).

94. A noted psychohistorical investigation of Luther is Erik Erikson, *Young Man Luther: A Study in Psychoanalysis and History* (New York: W. W. Norton, 1958).

95. See Schwarz, "Martin Luther," 195-97; Haas, "Luther und die Mystik," 192-93; Hamm, "Wie mystisch war der Glaube Luthers?," 266-68, 277-84; idem, *Early Luther*, esp. 32-34, 41-50, 55-58, 226-29; Grosse, "Der junge Luther und die Mystik," 222-29; and McGinn, "*Vere tu es Deus absconditus*," 94-100. The work of Helmut Appel, *Anfechtung und Trost im Spätmittelalter und bei Luther* (Leipzig: M. Heinsius, 1938) deals more with Luther's relation to late medieval consolation literature than mysticism.

96. *Heidelberg Disputation*, Thesis 24 (WA 1:363.25-37). There are a number of later references to annihilation in the *Lectures on Isaiah* (1527-30); e.g., on Isa. 40:29 (WA 31.2:284.21-285.6), and on Isaiah 40 in general (WA 31.2:265.15-30). I owe these references to Vincent Evener with gratitude.

97. For an introduction to the literature on the hidden God in Luther, see B. A. Gerrish, "'To the Unknown God': Luther and Calvin on the Hiddenness of God," *Journal of Religion* 53 (1973): 263-92.

98. *Commentary on Genesis* 41:40 (WA 44:429.24-26).

99. *Commentary on Genesis* 25:22 (WA 43:393.24-27; trans. *Luther's Works* 4:357).

100. *The Bondage of the Will* (WA 18:689.32-690.3).

101. Luther commented on Psalm 6 both in his *Dictata super Psalterium* and in his *Operationes in Psalmos*, as well as in his special *Commentary on the Seven Penitential Psalms*, composed in 1517 and revised in 1525 (WA 18:480-84).

102. *Commentary on the Seven Penitential Psalms* (WA 18:481-82; trans., *Luther's Works* 14:141-43).

103. *Operationes in Psalmos* 6:2 (WA 5:203.10-14).

104. *Operationes in Psalmos* 6:2 (WA 5:204.25-27).

105. *Commentary on Romans* (WA 56:392.28-393.3).

106. On the relation between Luther's theology of the cross and mysticism, see the historiographical review in Hubertus Blaumeiser, *Martin Luthers Kreuzestheologie: Schlüssel zu seiner Deutung von Mensch und Wirklichkeit; Eine Untersuchung anhand der Operationes in Psalmos, 1519-1521*, Konfessionskundliche und kontroverstheologische Studien 60 (Paderborn: Bonifatius, 1995), 64-72.

107. Luther's notion of union has attracted considerable study; see, e.g., Erich Vogelsang, "Die Unio mystica bei Luther," *Archiv für Reformationsgeschichte* 35 (1938): 63-80; Iserloh, "Luther's Christ-Mysticism," 47-51; Haas, "Luther und die Mystik,"

202–7; Schwarz, "Martin Luther," 192–200; and Hamm, "Wie mystisch war der Glaube Luthers?," 247–52; and idem, *Early Luther*, 203–5.

108. E.g., *The Freedom of the Christian* (*Studienausgabe* 2:132–36).

109. *Operationes in Psalmos 5* (WA 5:144.19–22). The notion of God's justice becoming our justice bears comparison with Meister Eckhart's view of the identity of *justitia* and *justus*. On Eckhart on justice, see Julie Casteigt, *Connaissance et verité chez Maître Eckhart: Seul le juste connaît la justice* (Paris: Vrin, 2006). For more on the Bridegroom giving all that is his to the bride, especially his justice, see WA 41:554–58.

110. On becoming one thing with Christ, see, e.g., WA 10/I:319.16ff; WA 20:230.10ff.; and WA 28:184.15ff.

111. On being baked as one cake with Christ, see, e.g., WA 2:748.18ff., WA 10/III:271.31ff., WA 12:583.17ff.

112. On uniting in substance, see, e.g., WA 28:489.9ff., WA 33.225.18ff., and 227.10ff.

113. *Commentary on Galatians* (WA 40/I:285.5–23; trans., *Luther's Works* 26:168). The comments on Gal. 2:20 ("I live, yet not I, but Christ lives in me") is one of the most important exegetical sources for Luther's view of union (see WA 40/I:280–300). See the discussion in Schwarz, "Martin Luther," 196.

114. *Commentary on Hebrews* 7:1 (WA 57/III:187.15–188.3; trans., *Luther's Works* 29:188).

115. A few texts in Luther's writings suggest something like Bernard's notion of loving union (e.g., WA 4:263.35–39, WA 5:35.4–8, WA 56:369.3–5), but this does not represent his general mode of speaking.

116. Luther criticized Andreas Karlstadt, Thomas Müntzer, and others for trying to seek direct contact with God without the mediation of the word of God and the church; e.g., WA 18:136–37; WA 21:468–71; WA 34/II:487–88; WA 36:491 and 499; WA 50:245 and 646; and WA 54:173. As Ozment puts it, "For Luther, man's union with God *in via* both presupposes and confirms the *maximum dissimilarity* between man and God: he who is 'unlike' God is one with God" (*Homo Spiritualis*, 180).

117. Hamm, *Early Luther*, 213.

118. Reinhard Schwarz, "Mystische Glaube: Die Brautmystik Martin Luthers," in *Von Eckhart bis Luther: Über mystischen Glauben*, ed. Heiko A. Oberman and Wolfgang Böhme (Karlsruhe: Evangelische Akademie Baden, 1981), 20–32.

119. On Christ as our Brother, see WA 10/II:214.32ff., and WA 32:89.1ff.

120. Luther frequently interprets Psalm 45 in terms of the union between Christ and the church; see, e.g., the long 1532 reading found in WA 40/II:472ff., esp. 555–58.

121. WA 10/III:415.8–15. This passage can be compared with Bernard, *Sermones super Cantica* 83.5 (*Sancti Bernardi Opera*, 2:301.18–22).

122. Sermon of October 21, 1522 (WA 10/III.357.28–34). See also WA 21:152.19–36.

123. WA 22:337.30–34.

124. On the "happy exchange" in Luther, see Hamm, "Wie mystisch war der Glaube Luthers?," 249–52; and idem, *Early Luther*, 200–203, 240–41, and 253–55.

125. For Augustine's view of Christ as the Divine Merchant who makes the "happy exchange," see *Sermo* 130.2 (*PL* 38:726). The notion of the "sweet, or happy, exchange" goes back as far as the second-century *Epistle to Diognetus* 9.3–5. It also appears in Luther's mentor Johann von Staupitz's treatise *Eternal Predestination* IX (see Heiko A.

Oberman, *Forerunners of the Reformation* [New York: Holt, Reinhart & Winston, 1966], 188).

126. WA 10/III:356.21–30.

127. On the imitation of Christ in Luther, see Iserloh, "Luther's Christ-Mysticism," 51–57; and Hamm, "Wie mystisch war der Glaube Luthers?," 252–55.

128. Augustine, *De Trinitate* 4.3.6 (*PL* 42:891).

129. *Marginalia on Augustine* (WA 9:18.19–30).

130. *Lectures on Hebrews* (WA 57/III:114.7–19).

131. The priesthood of all believers is a major theme of *The Freedom of the Christian* (*Studienausgabe*: 2:140–46, trans., 288–94).

132. McGinn, *Flowering*, 12–14.

133. John Tauler, V 40 (Vetter ed., 164.35–165.2).

134. See further Leppin, "Transformationen spätmittelalterliche Mystik bei Luther," 183–85; and Lienhard, "Luther and the Beginnings of the Reformation," 278–79.

135. Albert Schweitzer, *The Mysticism of Paul the Apostle* (London: A. & C. Black, 1931), 5, 378–79.

136. The patristic doctrine of *theōsis* has been well studied; see, e.g., Jules Gross, *The Divinization of the Christian according to the Greek Fathers* (Anaheim, CA: A & C Press, 2002; French original 1938); and the multiauthor "Divinisation," in *DS* 3:1370–1459, which, unfortunately, neglects Protestant authors. Less has been written on medieval deification.

137. On deification in Luther, see Simo Peura and Antti Raunio, eds., *Luther und Theosis: Vergöttlichung als Thema der abendländische Theologie* (Erlangen: Martin-Luther-Verlag, 1990); Simo Peura, *Mehr als ein Mensch? Der Vergöttlichung als Thema der Theologie Martin Luthers von 1513 bis 1519* (Mainz: Institut für Europäische Geschichte, 1994); Reinhard Flogaus, *Theosis bei Palamas und Luther: Ein Beitrag zum ökumenischen Gespräch*, Forschungen zur systematischen und ökumenischen Theologie 78 (Göttingen: Vandenhoeck & Ruprecht, 1997); and Carl E. Braaten and Robert W. Jensen, eds., *Union with Christ: The New Finnish Interpretation of Luther* (Grand Rapids: Eerdmans, 1998).

138. WA 20:229.30–230.10.

139. WA 4:269.28–30. See also WA 4:280.2–5.

140. WA 3:106.13–14.

141. WA 21:458.11–22.

142. As found in two Sermons of 1536 (WA 17/I:187.8–188.3; 93.6–7).

143. Ulrich Asendorf, "Die Einbettung der Theosis in die Theologie Martin Luthers," in Peura and Raunio, *Luther und Theosis*, 99.

144. See Ozment, *Homo Spiritualis*.

145. *Scholia on Psalm 5* in the *Archiv zur Weimarer Ausgabe der Werke Martin Luthers*, ed. Gerhard Hammer, 2 vols. (Cologne: Böhlau, 1981–), 1:548.7–10.

146. Howard G. Hageman, "Reformed Spirituality," in *Protestant Spiritual Traditions*, ed. Frank C. Senn (New York: Paulist Press, 1986), 55–79.

147. For a life of Calvin, see William J. Bouwsma, *John Calvin: A Sixteenth-Century Portrait* (Oxford and New York: Oxford University Press, 1988). A brief account of his theology can be found in David C. Steinmetz, "The Theology of John Calvin," in Bagchi and Steinmetz, *Cambridge Companion to Reformation Theology*, 113–29.

148. I cite from the translation by Elsie Anne McKee, *John Calvin: Writings on Pastoral Piety*, Classics of Western Spirituality (New York: Paulist Press, 2001), 59.

149. Alexandre Ganoczy shows that Calvin's knowledge of scholastic theology was pretty much restricted to Peter Lombard and Gratian (*The Young Calvin* [Philadelphia: Westminster, 1987], 168–78).

150. Calvin's writings are available in *Ioannis Calvini opera quae supersunt omnia* (abbreviated CO), ed. Wilhelm Baum et al., 59 vols. (Brunswick: C. A. Schwetschke, 1863–1900). There are numerous translations; those used here will be cited as necessary.

151. For an introduction, see Bruce Gordon, *John Calvin's "Institutes of the Christian Religion": A Biography* (Princeton: Princeton University Press, 2016).

152. The most convenient English version, with a good apparatus, is that of John T. McNeill and Ford Lewis Battles, eds. and trans., *Institutes of the Christian Religion*, 2 vols., Library of Christian Classics 20–21 (Philadelphia: Westminster, 1959). I will use this translation unless otherwise noted, referencing it by book, chapter, and section (e.g., *Institutes* 2.2.6).

153. An example of denial that Calvin had anything to do with mysticism can be found in the classic study of Wolfgang Kolfhaus, *Christusgemeinschaft bei Johannes Calvin* (Neukirchen: Buchhandlung des Erziehungsverein, 1938), 125–47.

154. Heiko A. Oberman, "Calvin's Critique of Calvinism," in Oberman, *The Dawn of the Reformation: Essays in Late Medieval and Early Reformation Thought* (Edinburgh: T&T Clark, 1986), 265.

155. On the *Institutes* as a *summa pietatis*, see Brian A. Gerrish, *Grace and Gratitude: The Eucharistic Theology of John Calvin* (Minneapolis: Fortress Press, 1993), 14–20.

156. See Lucien Joseph Richard, *The Spirituality of John Calvin* (Atlanta: John Knox, 1974); Otto Gründler, "John Calvin: Ingrafting in Christ," in *The Spirituality of Western Christendom,* ed. E. Rozanne Elder, Cistercian Studies 30 (Kalamazoo, MI: Cistercian Publications, 1976), 169–87; William J. Bouwsma, "The Spirituality of John Calvin," in Raitt et al., *Christian Spirituality II,* 318–33; McKee, *John Calvin: Writings on Pastoral Piety*; and Julie Canlis, *Calvin's Ladder: A Spiritual Theology of Ascent and Ascension* (Grand Rapids: Eerdmans, 2010).

157. See, e.g., Carl-A. Keller, *Calvin Mystique: Au coeur de la pensée du Réformateur* (Geneva: Labor et Fides, 2001). More nuanced in discussing Calvin's relation to mysticism is Dennis E. Tamburello, *Union with Christ: John Calvin and the Mysticism of St. Bernard* (Louisville: Westminster John Knox, 1994).

158. Calvin also dismisses Dionysius in his commentary on 2 Cor. 12:4.

159. CO 47:442, as cited in Tamburello, *Union with Christ,* 1.

160. Tamburello, *Union with Christ;* see chapter 1, "Calvin and Mysticism: The State of the Question" (1–22). The chapter includes an overview of the previous literature on Calvin and Bernard.

161. For a brief survey, see Ford Lewis Battles, "True Piety according to Calvin," in Battles, *Interpreting John Calvin* (Grand Rapids: Baker, 1996), 289–306.

162. See Canlis, *Calvin's Ladder,* chapter 3, "Creation: The Ground and Grammar of Ascent" (53–88).

163. Heiko A. Oberman, "The Pursuit of Happiness: Calvin between Humanism and Reformation," in *Humanity and Divinity in Renaissance and Reformation: Essays in Honor of Charles Trinkaus,* ed. John W. O'Malley, Thomas M. Izbicki, and Gerald Christianson, Studies in the History of Christian Thought 51 (Leiden: Brill, 1993), 262–66. See also Canlis, *Calvin's Ladder,* 76–83; Tamburello, *Union with Christ,* 29–40; and Luke Anderson, "The *Imago Dei* Theme in John Calvin and Bernard of Clairvaux,"

in *Calvinus Sacrae Scripturae Professor: Calvin as Confessor of Holy Scripture*, ed. Wilhelm H. Neuser (Grand Rapids: Eerdmans, 1994), 178–98.

164. On the significance of this section for Calvin's spirituality, see Battles, "True Piety according to Calvin," 295–300; and Gründler, "John Calvin: Ingrafting in Christ," 182–85.

165. On the importance of experience in Calvin, see Bouwsma, "Spirituality of John Calvin," 322–24.

166. Calvin's prayers sometimes speak about being "ravished with ardent love." See McKee, *John Calvin: Writings on Pastoral Piety*, 227 and 231.

167. Oddly enough, the "Subject Index" in the McNeill-Battles translation of the *Institutes* (2:1652) misses both of these references to contemplation, only noting passages on "Contemplation of God in his works" (1.5.9) and to monasticism as a form of contemplative life (4.13.10). See also the reference to "contemplating Christ," rather than contemplating self, in 3.2.24.

168. For an English translation, see John Pringle, *John Calvin, Commentary on the Epistles of Paul the Apostle to the Corinthians*, 2 vols. (Grand Rapids: Baker Book House, 1984) 1:365–71.

169. Calvin attacked the Libertines in a treatise of 1545, *Against the Libertines*. The French original can found in CO 7:149–248, and there is a translation and study by Benjamin Wirt Farley, *John Calvin, Treatises against the Anabaptists and against the Libertines* (Grand Rapids: Baker, 1982), 161–326.

170. On adoption in the *Institutes*, see, e.g., 2.14.5, and 3.6.3. There is a discussion in Canlis, *Calvin's Ladder*, 130–59.

171. On the "happy exchange," see, e.g., *Institutes (1536)* 4.24, and *Institutes (1539)* 4.17.2 and 9.

172. See Canlis, *Calvin's Ladder*, esp. chapters 3, 4, and 6.

173. Wilhelm Niesel, *Reformed Symbolics* (Edinburgh: Oliver & Boyd, 1962), 182.

174. For a study, see Tamburello, *Union with Christ*, chapter 5, "John Calvin on Mystical Union" (84–101), as well as his chapter 6, "Conclusions" (102–10). Tamburello also has a helpful appendix (111–13) listing the appearances of terms relating to union with Christ in the *Institutes* and other writings of Calvin. See also D. Willis-Watkins, "The Unio Mystica and the Assurance of Faith according to Calvin," in *Calvin: Erbe und Auftrag; Festschrift für Wilhelm Heinrich Neuser* (Kampen: Kok, 1991), 77–84. Also useful, despite its denial of any mystical aspects in Calvin, is Kolfhaus, *Christusgemeinschaft bei Johannes Calvin*.

175. For more on Louis de Blois (often referenced under his Latin name, Ludovicus Blosius), see the treatment of Louis in the coming *Presence of God*, vol. VI, part 3.

176. See Gottfried Seebass, "Osiander, Andreas," in *Oxford Encyclopedia*, 3:183–85. On the dispute with Calvin, see Schreiner, *Are You Alone Wise?*, 124–29.

177. Because of the importance of this passage, I will supply the Latin from CO 2:540: "Porro ne suis cavillis decipiat imperitos, fateor hoc tam incomparabili bono nos privari donec Christus noster fiat. Coniunctio igitur illa capitis et membrorum, habitatio Christi in cordibus nostris, mystica denique unio a nobis in summu gradu statuitur, ut Christus noster factus, donorum quibus praeditus est nos faciat consortes. Non ergo eum extra nos procul speculamur, ut nobis imputetur eius iustitia, sed quia ipsum induimus, et insiti sumus in eius corpus, unum denique nos secum efficere dignatus est." The other place in the *Institutes* that mentions *unio mystica* is in another

attack on Osiander, that found in 2.12.7, where Calvin says that Matt. 19:4-6, contrary to what Osiander claims, "is not discussing the mystical union with which he [Christ] graced the church, but only fidelity in marriage."

178. The letter (no. 2266) can be found in CO 15:722-25.

179. For a comparison of Bernard and Calvin on union, see Tamburello, *Union with Christ*, 105-7.

CHAPTER 2

Mysticism in the Radical Reformation

Development of the Radical Reformation

THE TERM "RADICAL REFORMATION" is recent, beginning to be used in the 1950s and given wide distribution in English-language scholarship by the appearance of the first edition of George Huntston Williams's *The Radical Reformation* in 1962.[1] Although the figures previously described as Anabaptists, Spiritualists, Fanatics, and the like, are also spoken of as the "Left Wing of the Reformation," the term "Radicals" seems fitting as an umbrella to cover a variety of thinkers, groups, and movements who sought to go back to the roots of "real" Christianity, and who rejected the alliance between religious belief and worldly government that helped guarantee the continuity of the established Protestant denominations. Nevertheless, serious questions remain about the meaning of the Radical Reformation and how to describe its characteristics and contours.[2]

Much of the scholarship on the Radical Reformation has sought to place it within the theological world of the sixteenth century; but another approach, initiated by German Marxists and now continued by some historians, has insisted that the Radicals need to be investigated from the perspective of the major social transformations of the time, especially the shift from feudalism to an early form of bourgeois capitalism.

I wish to thank Prof. Andrew Weeks of the University of Illinois at Champaign-Urbana for many helpful suggestions regarding this chapter.

Nowadays, historians of the Radical Reformation recognize that both theological and social concerns are important for a fuller understanding of the phenomenon.[3] Here, however, I will concentrate on the theology and spirituality of these reformers, specifically how far some at least can be spoken of as mystics.[4]

Along with weighing the respective roles of theological and social-historical approaches to the Radical Reformation, a second important issue concerns how far the Radicals might be said to represent the "real" Reformation, that is, the inherently revolutionary character of the challenge set by Luther to late medieval church and society. Was Luther's protest, as reflected, for example, in the three famous Reformation Treatises of 1520, a call to do away with the whole fabric of the medieval church, to empower the laity to take control of Christian faith, and to challenge the basic structures of medieval society? The later Luther did not think so. But did Luther know his own mind? Did Radicals like Thomas Müntzer understand Luther better than he understood himself?[5] Was Luther a radical who became a moderate? These remain disputed issues. One of the ironies of the history of the Reformation is to show how malleable a term like "radical" really is. Who is a radical, and from what perspective? The word "radical" is radically contextual and highly ambiguous. Nevertheless, I will consider the thinkers treated here as "radical" in the sense that they challenged church and society more deeply than Luther, Calvin, and the Magisterial Reformers did.

A third neuralgic issue is how to describe the types of Radical Reform and plot the story of its leaders and groups over the period ca. 1520 to ca. 1560. George H. Williams proposed a typology of four main groups: Revolutionaries, who sought to foster the arrival of the kingdom of God by force (Müntzer and the Radicals of Münster); Anabaptists, who stressed committed communities of those who had been rebaptized (the original Swiss Anabaptists, Balthasar Hubmaier, Hans Denck, and others); Spiritualists, who rejected outer religious forms to emphasize the inner working of the Holy Spirit (Sebastian Franck, Caspar Schwenkfeld, and others); and finally the Evangelical Rationalists, who argued that reason should govern religious beliefs and practices (Michael Servetus, Sebastian Castellio). This typology, however, has proved cumbersome, if only because the characteristics of the various groups were often shared by figures in other categories. Recent investigators have generally dropped the category of Rationalists, since these were mostly figures from Italy and Spain who had little direct role in the communities of Radicals who developed in European Germanic-speaking lands (Germany, Switzerland, and the Low Countries). Ongoing historical investigation of the spread of radical thinkers and their followers conducted over the past four decades tends to stress two main tendencies—Anabaptism and Spiritualism—and recognizes many complicating crossovers and changes within leaders and groups.

It may be helpful to identify four intellectual strands in the two main tendencies among the early Radicals—the Anabaptist, the Spiritual, the Apocalyptic, and the Mystical. First, Anabaptism, that is, the insistence on adult baptism as the only valid form of the sacrament, a view that expresses a biblical literalism and a desire to form small cohesive groups of true believers living according to a rigorous code of conduct. Second, Spiritualism, which reduces or even eliminates the role of the Bible and the church, emphasizing the inner illumination of the Holy Spirit as the criterion of true Christianity. Spiritualists by definition have difficulty forming communities, sometimes resorting to outward conformity to ecclesiastical structures and practices while concealing their true beliefs (often called "Nicodemism" after Nicodemus in John 3). Third, Apocalypticism, that is, the conviction of the imminence of the end of time, which existed as a volatile leaven among many groups of Radicals.[6] Nonetheless, not all the Radicals believed that the end of the present age and the establishment of Christ's millennial rule on earth were near. Among those who did, some, like Melchior Hoffman, adhered to the tradition of nonviolent apocalypticism prevalent in the Middle Ages, according to which the role of the justified was to wait and suffer until their impending vindication when Christ returns to earth. In other cases, notably those of Müntzer and Hoffman's followers who took over the city of Münster in 1534–35, apocalypticists took up arms to fight for the establishment of the kingdom. Finally, there is the Mystical Dimension. Many, though by no means all, the Radicals had contact with late medieval German mysticism, mostly through reading John Tauler sermons and the *Theologia Deutsch*. Like Luther, they found these texts to be powerful sources for their own convictions about the experiential role of faith, as well as the union between Christ and the soul. They also believed that this union could be described as a form of deification. The Radicals who were influenced by late medieval mysticism, however, went beyond Luther in a number of ways, notably by their teaching concerning the divine spark or ground of the soul, as well as such issues as the need for poverty of spirit, the role of mystical "releasement" (*Gelassenheit*), and in some cases an insistence on strong views of union, even involving a return to one's pre-creational identity with God.

Many intellectual factors were at work in the agenda of the Radicals, not all held in common. The Radicals did not deny the role of the grace brought by Christ to fallen humans, but they put greater stress on free will and the need for holy living by the redeemed than did Luther and the Magisterial Reformers. Most stressed the superiority of "believers' baptism," and a spiritual interpretation of the Lord's Supper, but they differed over the role of the Bible and the proper way to interpret it. Anabaptists tended to be New Testament literalists who stressed lay interpretation; Spiritualists held, to a greater or lesser degree, that the outer letter of the Bible was dispensable. Many Spiritual groups, but not all, made the community of goods found in the Jerusalem church (Acts 2 and 4) the touchstone of the true church. The Anabaptists and others insisted on the visible church of the few, one that would be characterized by strict discipline and holy living. The most extreme Radicals, on the other hand, believed in an invisible church open to all, whether or not they had ever heard of the gospel. Most Radical groups stressed separation from the world and refused to have anything to do with secular power, though a few were willing to compromise, as long as the state did not coerce belief. Most Radicals adopted a policy of nonresistance in the face of persecution and martyrdom, but there were striking apocalyptic exceptions that attempted violent overthrow of the evil world. Opting out of the sociopolitical structure of the sixteenth-century world, however, was almost as radical as the revolutionary uprisings of Radicals like Müntzer. Both approaches earned the Radicals the bitter enmity of Catholics and mainline Protestants.

The Radical movement began in the period 1520–30. It has been customary to distinguish between two main foci of the protest: one in Southern Germany, and the second in Switzerland, but the relation between the two is still under discussion.[7] In Southern Germany, followers of Luther, like Andreas Karlstadt (1486–1541) and Thomas Müntzer (ca. 1490–1525), who became disillusioned with Luther's refusal to follow through on what they saw as the implications of his initial radical agenda of 1517–20, are the best-known names. The social and political implications of their views became evident when Müntzer allied himself with the protests of the peasants against the feudal social order and welcomed being identified as an apocalyptic prophet proclaiming the need for violence to usher in the kingdom of God. The defeat of the peasants and Müntzer's execution in 1525 scattered the dissidents and served as an object lesson across Europe about the dangers of radicalism. A second focus of early radicalism was in Switzerland ca. 1523–25, where a group of followers of Zwingli (Conrad Grebel, Felix Mantz, George Blaurock, and others) questioned the practice of infant baptism (pedobaptism) because it did not appear in the New Testament. After some hesitation, Zwingli turned against these Swiss Brethren, or Anabaptists. When they proceeded to engage in rebaptizing in early 1525, some were rounded up and executed.[8] The horrors of the Peasants' War and Anabaptist martyrdoms added fuel to the fire rather than stamped it out. Wandering radical preachers, like Hans Denck (1500–1527), Balthasar Hubmaier (ca. 1480–1528), and Hans Hut (ca. 1490–1527),[9] spread the message of the new radical Christianity, although it may not have always been quite the same message. In February of 1527 Michael Sattler (himself soon to be martyred) wrote the Schleichtheim Confession that gave shape to Anabaptism as a movement. Many Anabaptists migrated to Moravia, where they found a political situation that allowed them to spread their message without persecution.[10]

Most of the early leaders of Anabaptism were dead by 1529, but a new generation arose of whom the most important figures were Pilgram Marpeck (ca. 1495–1556) and Melchior Hoffman (ca. 1500–ca. 1543). Once again, these two by no means preached the same message, but they did agree on important issues, like the necessity for believers' baptism to belong to the true church. Both were active in Strassburg ca. 1528–33, where a lenient attitude on the part of civic and ecclesiastic leaders allowed room for religious dissent.[11] Hoffman spread Anabaptism to the Rhineland and the Low Countries, where it speedily took root, while Marpeck consolidated Anabaptism by breaking with Spiritualist conceptions of inner religion, such as those of Caspar Schwenkfeld (1489–1561) and Sebastian Franck (ca. 1499–1542), emphasizing instead a strict biblicism and adopting a more positive, if not uncritical, attitude toward the state. Hoffman was an apocalypticist who announced that the present world order would end in 1533 and that Strassburg would become the New Jerusalem. When these events failed to materialize, some Anabaptists took up a dangerous course. The Dutch baker Jan Mathijs and his accomplice, Jan Beukelsz, or Bokelson (known as John of Leiden), announced that God had chosen the city of Münster in Westphalia as the New Jerusalem. Anabaptists flocked there. Mathijs took control of the Lutheranizing reform movement in the city and expelled all those who refused to be rebaptized. He established a community of goods modeled on the Acts picture of the original Jerusalem believers. The Catholic bishop of the city soon led a combined Catholic-Protestant army against the Radicals. Jan was killed in a sortie in 1534, and the stresses of the siege led the Anabaptists within Münster, now led by John of Leiden, in bizarre directions. John declared himself messianic king and instituted polygamy as a way of solving the imbalance in numbers between men and women in the desperate city. Eventually, in June of 1535, Münster fell to the besiegers. John of Leiden and the other leaders were tortured and executed. Once again, the Radical Reform had led to bloodshed and savage repression.[12] Both Catholics and Protestants continued to shiver at the thought of such radicalism, although the great majority of the Radicals were peaceful "dropouts," as we might say today.

The Radical Reformation did not die out. After the debacle of Münster, leaders arose, especially the former Catholic priest Menno Simons (ca. 1496–1561), who set the movement on a more permanent course. Simons was anti-Spiritualist and also anti-apocalyptic. From about 1539 on he reorganized the remnants of the Melchiorites into biblically faithful and pacifist communities, which exercised strict control over their members through the use of the ban and shunning, still a part of the Mennonite communities today. Other Dutch Anabaptists, such as David Joris (ca. 1501–1556) turned in a more Spiritualist direction. David and his followers adopted a Nicodemite position, hiding their true religious beliefs and outwardly conforming to whatever ecclesiastical situation in which they found themselves—Catholic, Lutheran, or Reformed. Joris fled Holland and lived in Basel for years under an assumed name, writing lengthy Spiritualist tracts. Perhaps the most notable Nicodemite was the Lutheran pastor Valentin Weigel (1533–1588), who was also among the most mystically inclined of the Radicals. Another Nicodemite was the Dutch Spiritualist Dirck Coornhert (1522–1590), who agreed with Franck and Schwenkfeld about the inferiority of external religion but who never formally gave up Catholicism.

To what extent can some of these Radical thinkers be called mystics? It has long been known that mysticism, at least late medieval German and Dutch mysticism, played an important role in the religious thinking of the Radicals. According to R. Emmet McLaughlin, "In reappropriating the Catholic element, they [the Radicals] drew upon their general religious formation, since all the first generation reformers were, after all, Catholics. However, the radicals also made use of certain identifiable sources. Mysticism, Erasmus, and monasticism were the most important."[13] Not all the Radicals were influenced by mystical themes, but we will investigate some whose mystical credentials have often been proposed to see to what extent it is useful to speak of a mysticism of the Radical Reformation. I will examine five sixteenth-century Radicals in this chapter. The first two, Andreas Karlstadt and Thomas Müntzer, were early followers of Luther ("Martinians"), who soon turned against him.[14] Hans Denck was among the early Anabaptists. Finally, I will look at two figures classified as Spiritualists: Sebastian Franck and Valentin Weigel. This selection is not meant to exclude a role for mysticism in other radical reformers, such as Hans Hut, Caspar Schwenckfeld, Melchior Hoffman, and David Joris, but I think these five are good representatives of the links between mysticism and the Radical Reformation.

Andreas Karlstadt (1486–1541)

Luther's evangelical breakthrough galvanized a generation. From the end of the second decade of the sixteenth century a group of preachers and theologians rallied to the Wittenberger's view of the gospel. Quite soon, however, a number of Luther's associates began to express their own ideas about evangelical faith, sometimes at odds with Luther. These differences had become evident by 1522, and between 1522 and 1525 Luther wrote a number of attacks on his former associates, decrying them as "fanatics," "false prophets," and worse. The issues under dispute often concerned sacramental theology, as well as the social implications of the gospel message. The fundamental difference, however, was how much reliance should be given to the inner witness of the Holy Spirit in relation to the external word of scripture. A good illustration of this parting of the ways can be found in Luther's former admirer, Andreas Bodenstein von Karlstadt (1486–1541). Our main concern will be to investigate how far Karlstadt's use of medieval mystical literature may have shaped his break with Luther and contributed to the formation of his own theology.

Andreas Karlstadt was second only to Luther among the German Reformers in the number of his writings (between eighty and ninety) and the proliferation of editions of his works.[15] A difficult person, Karlstadt antagonized most of his friends and, not surprisingly, led a life of exile and hardship for many years.[16] Originally a secular priest, Karlstadt received his doctorate at Wittenberg in 1510 and became a colleague and defender of Luther in the early days of the evangelical protest, such as at the Leipzig Disputation of 1519. Although Karlstadt was originally a Thomist, intensive study of Augustine and the Bible moved him in an evangelical direction, not only with regard to justification by faith and an insistence on *sola scriptura*, but also on practical issues such as attacking clerical celibacy, monastic vows, the cult of images, and the Latin Mass. When Luther went into hiding at the Wartburg, Karlstadt became the leader of the Wittenberg movement that reformed the city's religious practices, most notably by the city council's approval of the "New Order for the City of Wittenberg" on January 24, 1522. Frederick III of Saxony and others were not pleased with the radical aspects of the "New Order" and the public upheavals it provoked; nor was Luther, who hurried back to the city in March and preached a series of sermons vindicating his leadership of the Wittenberg reform and breaking with Karlstadt, who was increasingly marginalized.

Karlstadt then grew more radical, rejecting his academic career and speaking of himself as a layman.[17] In the spring of 1523 he became the minister of the Thuringian parish at Orlamünde, where he was able to realize his model of a true reformed congregation and where he produced some of his most important writings. The gap between Luther and Karlstadt continued to widen, especially over the question of the place of images and the nature of the Lord's Supper, as well as the underlying issue of the relation of the word of God in the Bible and the inner reception of the Holy Spirit. An attempted reconciliation between the two men in August of 1524 failed and the Elector exiled Karlstadt from his domains.[18] Karlstadt's continuing publications, especially on the Lord's Supper, provoked Luther's attack on him and others who shared his views in two pamphlets published in late 1524 and early 1525 entitled *Against the Heavenly Prophets in the Matter of Images and Sacraments.*[19] Karlstadt wandered through Germany and Switzerland for a number of years, continuing to spread his ideas and to engage in the kind of disputations that marked the growing divisions in the evangelical camp. In 1534 he became professor of Old Testament at Basel, where he remained until his death on December 24, 1541.

Karlstadt's connections with all three wings of the Continental Reformation make him difficult to locate.[20] With regard to Lutheranism, he started out as a defender of Luther, but the decisive break between the two made him a *bête noire* to Lutheran orthodoxy. (His writings, however, continued to influence later Lutheran mystics, like Johann Arndt and the Pietists.)[21] Karlstadt also had an apocalyptic side. He had contact with the "Zwickau prophets," the three visionaries who visited Wittenberg in late 1521 and early 1522, as well as with Thomas Müntzer. Nevertheless, Karlstadt broke with Müntzer over the latter's appeal to violence at the time of the Peasants' War. Finally, Karlstadt also shared some issues with the early Anabaptists.[22] He is said to have suspended infant baptisms while at Orlamünd and later wrote against the practice. His treatise *On the Priesthood and Sacrifice of Christ* of December 1523 is one of the earliest witnesses to a spiritual interpretation of the presence of Christ in the Lord's Supper. This work and later tracts endeared him to Zwingli, who found him a position at Zurich in the early 1530s. Nonetheless, Karlstadt does not feature in the usual genealogical line of the Reformed tradition of Protestantism. Gordon Rupp saw Karlstadt's moralizing insistence on inner religion as an anticipation of Puritanism, but concluded, "In the Karlstadt pattern of Reformation we see something equally important [to Luther, Zwingli, and Calvin] . . . : how second-rate minds and 'awkward squads' may also have insights, penetrate new truth, rank therefore also among the pioneers."[23]

I will not attempt to give a full picture of the complex figure of Karlstadt, or to trace the development of his theology,[24] but rather I only wish to investigate the extent to which mystical themes shaped his writings. Like Luther, Karlstadt began reading mystical authors about 1517–18 as he moved away from his early Thomism. He studied Tauler and, again like Luther, wrote marginal comments in his edition of the Dominican's sermons.[25] He was also influenced by the *Theologia Deutsch* and paraphrased passages from it in some of his treatises.[26] Karlstadt knew the *De imitatione Christi* and may have read Henry Suso's *Little Book of Eternal Wisdom*, but this needs more investigation. The fruit of his mystical reading appeared as early as October 1520, when he published a brief *Tract on the Supreme Virtue of Gelassenheit*.[27] It was during his transition from Wittenberg to Orlamünde in the spring of 1523, however, that his most significant mystical works were published. These were (to give them their full titles): *What Is Said: Letting Go of Self, and What the Word Releasement Means, and Where It Is Found in Scripture;*[28] and *The Manifold, Singular Will of God, The Nature of Sin.*[29]

Gelassen, "to let go, or release," and the words connected with it, especially *Gelassenheit* (releasement, abandonment, and so on), are among the characteristic terms of late medieval German mysticism, being often used in conjunction with "detachment" (*Abgeschiedenheit*). This vocabulary goes back to Meister Eckhart, and it was found in texts known to Karlstadt, such as Tauler's sermons and the *Theologia Deutsch.*[30] Different authors used the terms in somewhat different ways in the context of their forms of mysticism, but there is a semantic continuity to *Gelassenheit* as signifying radical abandonment of self and all created things. Karlstadt's understanding is an important contribution to the history of this mystical theme.

Luther never wrote a mystical treatise. It is hard, however, to deny that title to Karlstadt's work on *Gelassenheit*, though this is not to say that his teaching on releasement, the ground of the soul, union with God, deification, and the like, are the same as those of Eckhart, Tauler, or the *Theologia Deutsch*. A brief analysis of the tract will help set out its understanding of these mystical themes. Karlstadt describes himself as "A New Layperson" at the beginning of the work, a mark of his abandonment of his academic and clerical career to live as a common farmer and to address a lay audience. Noting that his addressee, Jörg Schenk, was familiar with the *Theologia Deutsch*, he says he is writing to explain the origin and meaning of the terms *sich gelassen* and *Gelassenheit* found there. He begins with reflections on the possible origin of the words but admits he does not know for sure. "*Gelassen*," he says, "means about the same as *verlassen*—abandoned, forsaken. . . . There is no difference whether we use 'detached,' or 'forsaken,' 'detachment,' or 'abandonment.'"[31] Releasement has both active and passive aspects—we can turn away from something but being detached or released also signifies someone who has been left behind (he cites the Latin *relinquere* of Matt. 19:5 and 29). Later in the work he gives a fuller definition: "This *Gelassenheit* is a cutting off of love, pleasure, worry, trust, and fear, which we may have in and for ourselves and the things that are ours. In short, such letting go is to destroy all we are and a turning away from everything that we might covet, so that God alone is our love, pleasure, worry, trust, help, fear, and everything to which we must cling."[32]

Karlstadt sees releasement as part of a complex of mystical themes, as is evident from two subsections following the initial discussion, the first on "Spiritual Marriage between God and the created soul," the second dealing with "Why God unites himself with our soul." Citing the usual biblical prooftexts about marital union with God, as well as 1 Corinthians 6:17 on becoming "one spirit" with God, he states, "God enters into marriage with human beings so that we may discern and know how we are united with God, and that we must leave father, mother, house, and possessions for the sake of God's will."[33] The major task of releasement, then, is to utterly abandon everything that is not God and to cling to him alone as our "universal delight."

There follows a detailed exposition of the central importance of releasement, which, toward the end of the treatise, Karlstadt calls "the most supreme virtue." In language reminiscent of earlier German mystics, he says,

> Everything to which "I" and "I-ness" (*icheit*), "me" and "myself," may cling must leave me and fall off, if I am to be released. For releasement [*gelassenheit*] penetrates and flows through every created thing and comes into its uncreated nothingness [*ungeschaffen nicht*]—where it is uncreated and has no being, that is, its Origin and Creator. Wherefore, when you were nothing, you stood wholly in God's knowledge and will, and there was nothing at all in heaven and on earth which you could rightfully have claimed. So, I and everybody should do the same today.[34]

A similar text about returning to our uncreated state occurs later in the treatise, where Karlstadt says, "just as a true and released service of God swings the soul's eyes up into God's abyssal will, and creeps into the abyssal Good which is God himself, [so] there is no 'self' or 'I' there. . . . Yes, the soul presses on and is lifted up, and sinks itself in God's will, and dies there right from its ground." This total giving up of self is the fundamental pattern of the Christian life, as expressed by Paul in Galatians 2:20, a text also favored by Luther. Karlstadt, however, presses this point home in ways that Luther would not have, especially with regard to the return to the pre-creational state:

> Do not let "I," "selfness," and "I-ness" trouble you, because you know that they are frequently found in the *Theologia Deutsch*. . . . A released "I" or "I-ness" occurs when I despise myself and give over and grant all good to Him, for "the little streams must flow back and return into their source and water" [Ecclus. 1:7], when it wants to return in an orderly way. This "I" and "Self'" is then usefully released when self-will is released, when self-will is melted [*verschmiltzt*] and God receives his work in the creature, and nothing else is willed but what God wills and how God wills.[35]

Given such texts, it is difficult to see how some scholars can deny that Karlstadt, like the German mystics he read, did not hold that on some level at least *Gelassenheit* allows a return to the pre-creational state, however different his conception of this might be from Tauler and the *Theologia Deutsch*.[36]

Much of the rest of Karlstadt's treatise consists of further reflections on the meaning of releasement, contrasts drawn between releasement and the opposed state of the "devilish vice of agreeableness and lack of releasement" (*ungelassenheit*), and, as the title suggests, scriptural proofs for the necessity of releasement in the Christian life. Releasement is required because of the power of human sinfulness, whose essence Karlstadt finds (as did many mystics before him) in the selfishness of the "I" and "I-ness" that grasps at everything to make it "mine" and therefore not God's.[37] Letting go of created goods is necessary, but even more important is releasing the self (*sich gelassen*). Karlstadt puts this so strongly that he insists that acts that proceed from a lack of releasement are *all* mortal sins.[38] In terms that echo Eckhart (Karlstadt would have read some Eckhart sermons in his edition of Tauler), he says, "Releasement loves and desires God purely without any mediation. It does not love God as this or that, but as an essential Good. Unreleasement loves and desires that which has been created; it loves this or that good as its own."[39] In biblical terms, Karlstadt often appeals to the practice of circumcision as a model for the spiritual "cutting away of the heart from all creatures."[40] As the title indicates, the treatise is replete with biblical texts supporting his analysis of *Gelassenheit*, some of them used by other writers (e.g., Gal. 2:20, Luke 9:23, John 12:24–26, etc.); others rather unusual, as when he gives a long exegesis of the story of King Assur (Isa. 10:5–19) as an example of someone who, although God's instrument in punishing Israel, himself was overthrown because he did not let go of his "I-ness" and "selfhood" (*seinheit*).

Given the innate mortal sinfulness of fallen humanity, Karlstadt makes it clear that the releasement God asks of us is not our own work, something we can achieve by our efforts. Christ knows that leaving all things is not within human power, so he consoles us with the message, "What is impossible with human beings is possible with God" (Matt. 19:26). God alone, therefore, can bestow *Gelassenheit*.[41] It is equally obvious that releasement is not a stable, completed state in this life; it is a process whereby grace gradually regenerates the sinner, leading him or her into deeper union with God.[42] Karlstadt was well aware of the deceptive power of human selfishness, even in the lives of those being regenerated. Thus, he insists on the necessity of maintaining "releasement in releasement" (*Gelassenheit in Gelassenheit*), that is, avoiding undue attention either to our suffering or to our good works, lest we begin to take credit for them. "All that is ours," he says, "must be fused in God's eternal will and become nothing."[43]

What is the relation of releasement to the other virtues and practices of the Christian life, especially faith and love? Karlstadt says that "releasement is the beginning of the Christian life and must maintain all divine virtue,"[44] so all the virtues are contained within it. In one place he talks about faith as what circumcises the heart, and love as the glue by which God binds himself to us; another passage identifies releasement with faith, hope, and love.[45] Karlstadt was not concerned about working out a theoretical account of the relationship of *Gelassenheit* and the other virtues but rather with their practical effect in the life of the believer. In other words, releasement simplifies religion and religious practice. Unlike Luther, he puts faith and love on the same level; his treatises often speak of "faith rich in love and love rich in faith." As he put it in the tract *Regarding the two Greatest Commandments: The Love of God and Neighbor*, written a year after the work on *Gelassenheit*: "Faith without love is worthless; love without faith does not satisfy. Therefore, the right work is loving faith or faithful love."[46]

Karlstadt's view of releasement is christological. Like Tauler and the *Theologia Deutsch*, he finds a central role for Christ in the practice of releasement, especially as the teacher and exemplar of giving up self and all things. As he says, "Note that Christ was right in saying, 'Whoever does not carry his cross cannot be my disciple' [Luke 14:27]. Christ said this before he began his general farewell speech. There Christ teaches that the releasement which surrenders everything is the daily cross we must carry without standing still. Rather, we must follow Christ and be where Christ is in will, thought, love, desire, and suffering at the right hand of God."[47] There are numerous other references to Christ's role within the treatise, especially in its later sections.[48] Exemplary Christology does not exhaust Karlstadt's view of the Redeemer's role in our salvation,[49] but it is to the fore in this treatise.

Did Karlstadt so emphasize the inner witness of the Holy Spirit that the necessary mediation of the word of scripture and Christ's presence in the Lord's Supper were slighted? This was the brunt of Luther's polemical attack on him as "false prophet," "enthusiast," and an "agent of Satan" in *Against the Heavenly Prophets*. According to Luther, Karlstadt destroys the freedom given to the Christian, restores a form of works' righteousness, and misunderstands the work of the Spirit. Luther says that God deals with us "first outwardly, then inwardly." The outward dealing is by the oral word of the gospel and the material signs of the sacraments. "Inwardly he deals with us through the Holy Spirit, faith and other gifts," says Luther; "but whatever their measure or order, the outward factors should and must precede. The inward experience follows and is effected by the outward." The problem with Karlstadt and the other "enthusiasts" is that they have reversed this order, subordinating God's outward order to an inner spiritual one.[50] Luther takes the opportunity to poke fun at Karlstadt's mystical terminology. "But should you ask how one gains access to this same lofty spirit, they do not refer you to the outward gospel but to some imaginary realm, saying, 'Remain in slowness [*stehe ynn der lange weyle*], where I now am and you will have the same experience. A heavenly voice will come and God himself will speak to you.'"[51] Earlier in the tract Luther had memorably criticized "Dr. Karlstadt" for considering himself "the greatest spirit of all, he who had devoured the Holy Spirit feathers and all."[52]

How fair was Luther to Karlstadt? In the treatise on *Gelassenheit*, as noted above, Karlstadt was at pains to show that releasement is taught throughout the Bible. One section, however, is devoted to "letting go of scripture." Karlstadt says, "Here I must also state how a truly released person must let go of Holy Scripture and not know its letters, but enter into the might of the Lord (as David says) and ceaselessly pray to God for true understanding." The succeeding discussion indicates that Luther was correct, at least here, in saying that Karlstadt reverses the order from outer to inner, because the passage counsels beginning from within with the released person hearing what God has to say to him in his soul and then turning outside to "recall and then verify and justify it with Holy Scripture."[53] Other passages in the work and elsewhere in his writings indicate that Karlstadt thought that outer realities and works were necessary but not sufficient for salvation without the inner activity of the Spirit. There are also some texts that seem to say that external things are unnecessary and sometimes even deceptive.[54]

From the point of view of the mystical tradition, *The Meaning of Gelassenheit* is significant as a thoroughgoing evangelical consideration of releasement, along with related mystical themes such as union and divinization. Releasement–union–deification were major elements in the doctrine of inner regeneration in Christ that has been identified as the core of Karlstadt's theology.[55] Regeneration and inner sanctification, of course, were not absent from late medieval mysticism, and their proper understanding was much debated during the Reformation. Karlstadt put them at the center of the Christian message, as his constant motif of "loving faith and faithful love" demonstrates. Luther did not shy away from speaking of union with God and deification, but Karlstadt's insistence on union through releasement as the purpose of the gospel teaching on the regeneration of believers shows a deeper engagement with mysticism.

A central passage in *The Meaning of Gelassenheit*, partly excerpted above, begins with lifting up the soul's eyes into "the abyssal will of God" (*in den abgründigen willen Gottes*) and creeping into "the abyssal Good which is God himself" (*in dass grundloss gütt*). It goes on to emphasize the necessity for total releasement in order to let go of all "I-ness," and finally to become "one with the eternal divine will" (*mit dem götlichen ewigen willen ayns werden*). This state is one of total conformity to Christ, "a divine life, in which a person does not live, but Christ lives in him" (*ain Christförmigs ich oder sich, . . . ain götlich leben, und er nitt lebet, sonder Christus in ime Gala. 2*).[56] Using a formula dear to Cistercian mystics such as William of Saint-Thierry, a passage from *The Manifold, Singular Will* says, "God is a spirit, therefore the created creature must unite [*vereynen*] with God's Uncreated Spirit in and through the spirit."[57] Releasement and union with God are inseparable for Karlstadt.

Karlstadt's *The Manifold, Singular Will of God, The Nature of Sin* is less explicitly mystical, dealing as it does with the distinctions in the divine will (the scholastic categories of God's eternal and permissive will), as well as with sin, grace, faith, and love. Nevertheless, the work contains discussions of what it means to become one with God[58] and also uses the late medieval mystical category of the regenerated person as a "true friend of God."[59] Other treatises, such as *Regarding the Two Greatest Commandments*, which argues how only the loving knowledge of faith can bring us to oneness with God and allow us to truly love our neighbor, occasionally feature releasement language. Karlstadt's reading of the German mystics seems to have continued to affect his later writings, but *The Meaning of Gelassenheit* is the best expression of his form of Radical Evangelical mysticism.

Karlstadt integrated late medieval mysticism into his theology more systematically than did Luther. Some scholars who have recognized his debt to mysticism, however, have sought to distance his thought from "mysticism," often by appealing to a constrictive model of late medieval German mysticism as "ontological," while Karlstadt is said to be "practical" and "ethical," as if late medieval mystics had no interest in the application of their speculation about God and the soul to human action. There are, to be sure, differences between Karlstadt and the German mystics, even on the issue of releasement.[60] The medieval mystics indulged in investigations of the divine nature not found in Karlstadt's treatise. They also say more about the "ground of the soul" and its relation to the powers of knowing and loving than did Karlstadt.[61] In that sense, Karlstadt and the Radical Reformers who came in his wake generally did not share the speculative and epistemological concerns of the late medieval German mystics. Their lack of interest in these issues can be viewed as loss or gain, depending on one's perspective. What it should *not* do, however, is to exclude Karlstadt and some other Radical Reformers from being considered as a new chapter in the history of Western mysticism.

Thomas Müntzer (ca. 1490–1525)

Thomas Müntzer's short life (ca. 1490–1525) has been the subject of many treatments over the past century.[62] His role as the main spokesman for the radical farmers during the Peasant's War of 1524–25 made him a favorite of Marxist historians.[63] Müntzer was certainly a social radical, and also an apocalyptic revolutionary who believed that taking up arms against oppression was part of a cosmic war in which the divinely inspired forces of God's justice would triumph against satanic evil—scarcely a class-determined project. (Indeed, he first appealed to the German princes to defend God's justice.) Among the issues that have dominated studies of Müntzer in modern times two stand out: What was his relation to Luther?[64] What was the connection between his radical apocalyptic agenda and medieval mysticism?

Thomas Müntzer was born about 1490 at Stollberg in the Hartz mountains of Saxony. He received a good theological education, matriculating at Leipzig in 1506, and then studying at Frankfurt an der Oder. Müntzer became a follower of Luther between 1517 and 1519. Luther recommended him to a pastorate first at Jüterbog and then at Zwickau (1519–21), where he attacked the Catholic clergy and the Erasmian humanist pastor John Egranus. At this stage Müntzer was still one of Luther's men, but his theological views were already evolving away from Luther. In any case, it was from Zwickau that three lay charismatics came to Wittenberg toward the end of 1521, preaching a message of the superiority of the inner inspiration of the Holy Spirit as displayed in visions and prophecies to the external witness of the word of God in the Bible. These "Zwickau prophets" have affinities with late medieval visionary and apocalyptic groups, but the connections remain obscure. Luther interviewed and denounced the prophets. Müntzer later claimed to have had nothing to do with them, but historians have wondered if this is the whole truth.

During his time at Zwickau, Müntzer began distinguishing himself from Luther and his concept of reform, especially by his emphasis on the inner action of the Spirit and by his growing conviction that the current crisis of religion showed that the end of the world and God's final incursion into history were near. Müntzer was taking a step anathema to Luther and to most medieval thinkers by recombining the mystical impetus for direct contact with God with the conviction that the approaching end of history would introduce a messianic age in which, after the destruction of the ungodly, the just remnant would live in a form of perfect church.[65]

In Second Temple Judaism, visionaries who received divine messages about the approaching end of history were sometimes raised up to the heavenly realm to experience contact with God and/or angelic beings. In early Christianity, the conviction that God had become man in Jesus allowed new forms of experiencing a direct presence of God. Thus, Paul can be characterized as an apocalyptic mystic or a mystical apocalypticist, because of his conviction about the imminent return of the risen Christ and his first-person accounts of direct contact with Jesus (1 Cor. 9:1; 15:8), as well as being raised up to the divine realm, that is, the third heaven (2 Cor. 12:1–4). In subsequent Christian history it became increasingly difficult to hold the nascent mystical and the apocalyptic dimensions together. The separation between the two was the result of many factors, not least the rejection of literal apocalypticism on the part of many Christians and the attack on esoteric knowledge during the Gnostic controversy. Nonetheless, the birth connection of the separated twins allowed for recombinations, especially when hopes for a better church on earth involved the realization of a fuller form of God-consciousness in the age to come: a mystical-contemplative kingdom of God. Thomas Müntzer was one of the most striking examples of this form of collective mystical-apocalyptic hope, even though he said little about what he thought this new church would look like.[66]

Müntzer's increasing radicalism, especially in its appeal to the common folk, was anathema to Luther. However radical the Wittenberger's message about the priority of scripture and faith over the structures of late medieval papal religion may have been, Luther remained a social conservative: the political status quo, whatever its injustices, was ordained by God. Any violence against established social institutions was a grave sin. Müntzer disagreed. The clash of views soon turned ugly. Müntzer was forced out of Zwickau and went to Prague (June–December 1521), where he could consult with the descendants of Hus's revolt against the medieval church and develop his ideas. His first radical pronouncement was the "Prague Manifesto" of November 1521, in which he began to take on the role of an apocalyptic prophet predicting the end of times and a new outpouring of the Holy Spirit. The use of medieval mystical themes in this document indicates that Müntzer had begun to fuse the mystical and apocalyptic aspects of the Christian tradition. By the time Müntzer returned to Germany in early 1522, he had become more openly critical of Luther and the "Wittenbergers." He had not, however, completely broken with the "Martinians." With some help from Luther he was made a pastor at Allstedt, where he served from Easter of 1523 to August of 1524. Here, Müntzer's break with Luther became fully evident. He introduced a new vernacular liturgy and gave scriptural arguments for his reliance on visions and revelations. Müntzer's letters and treatises show that justification by faith had begun to take a diminished role in his thought, being replaced by an emphasis on the contrast between Luther's comfortable "sweet Christ" and his own teaching that the path to salvation is based on being willing to suffer with the "bitter Christ." As he put it in his 1524 treatise written against Luther, *On Contrived Faith*:

> The sheep are poisoned by a toxic meadow but nourished by the salt. To preach a sweet Christ to a carnal world is the most dangerous poison that has ever been given to the lambs of Christ. For a person who preached this wants to be in conformity with God, but he never desires, and certainly does not clamor, to be conformed to Christ. . . . He who does not want to accept the bitter Christ will eat himself to death on honey.[67]

Müntzer's radicalism reached a culmination in the sermon he preached to the assembled princes of Saxony (the "Fürstenpredigt") on July 13, 1524. This extraordinary document (what did the princes think?) is one of the more extreme apocalyptic pronouncements in the history of Christianity, an announcement of the imminence of the end and a call on the princes to wipe the wicked from the face of the earth. It is hard not to think that Müntzer had become somewhat delusional, which is exactly what Luther said in his attacks on his former disciple, whom he now spoke of as "Satan in Allstedt."

Müntzer had to flee Allstedt in August 1524. He then began to issue apocalyptic pamphlets proclaiming himself "Thomas Müntzer with the hammer" to destroy the wicked. The princes had failed, so he turned to a more likely instrument of divine vengeance, the disaffected peasants and artisans of Southern Germany who had heeded the call for a new society promised by the reformers and were attempting to wring political concessions from the nobility, who controlled the late medieval feudal world. The Peasants' Revolt would have happened without Müntzer, but his fiery preaching and effective pamphleteering made him the intellectual voice of the increasingly violent attempts of the peasants to overthrow the old order through late 1524 and early

1525. Luther was horrified and attacked Müntzer with constant vitriol; Müntzer responded in kind. The prophet was present with the peasant army at Frankenhausen on May 15, 1525, as they faced the professional forces of the princes, still predicting divine intervention and victory. The peasant army was cut down, thousands perished. Müntzer was captured, tortured, and executed.

Müntzer was certainly a "Radical Reformer," if anyone ever was. Although he preferred adult baptism, he did not forbid baptizing infants, so he was not really an Anabaptist. Some aspects of his thought, such as his insistence on the inner voice of the Spirit, as well as his reliance on dreams and visions, were shared by the later Spiritualist Reformers, but they rejected his violent apocalypticism. For our purposes the main issue is to determine in what sense Müntzer can be said to figure in the history of Christian mysticism. It is doubtful that anyone today would want to read Müntzer as a guide to finding deeper contact with God. Unlike Karlstadt, Müntzer never wrote a treatise on a particular mystical theme, however much some of his works incorporate mystical elements, taken especially from Tauler and the *Theologia Deutsch*.[68] He also had been influenced by late medieval pseudo-Joachite literature, such as the *Commentary on Jeremiah* ascribed to the Calabrian abbot Joachim of Fiore.[69] On this basis, he created a form of radical apocalyptic thought with strong mystical elements. Although both Joachim of Fiore and his follower the Franciscan Peter John Olivi (d. 1297) had also recombined the mystical and the apocalyptic dimensions of Christianity, these mystics never incited violence. Müntzer did so without hesitation.

The "Prague Manifesto" that Müntzer issued in late 1521 at the end of his stay in the city is the best place to start in investigating his thought. It exists in four versions: a fairly mild Latin form, probably delivered to clerics: two longer and stronger German texts; and a Czech version.[70] Although inchoate, all the elements of Müntzer's later program can be found here: (1) violent condemnation of the clerical order (this was later to include secular authority); (2) a conviction that all Christians can find the sources for moral and social transformation within themselves by listening to the voice of the Spirit; (3) emphasis on inner experience of God through suffering with Christ as the means of access to the depth ("abyss") of the human soul where true transformation occurs; and (4) the sense that inner transformation is part of a broader process in which God is establishing his millennial kingdom on earth. In the Manifesto, Müntzer had not yet fully embraced physical violence, though the germs of his later views are already present.

What did mysticism and mystical themes contribute to the Manifesto? First and perhaps foremost is Müntzer's insistence that it is only common believers, not the proud clergy, who can experience the inner fear of God in the depths of the soul that will enable them to grasp his message, what he called (note the mystical accents), "the beneficial tribulations and useful abyss that the providential spirit meets as it empties itself."[71] Such a spirit of the fear of God never possessed the clergy, but only the elect, who "are submerged and drowned in an outpouring of this spirit," so that "each person must receive the Holy Spirit in a sevenfold way." This reference to the traditional seven gifts of the Holy Spirit leads on to other mystical topoi, including an invocation of the nuptial relation between Christ and the believer. Treacherous priests, says Müntzer, have never heard "the voice of the Bridegroom" (*dye stimme des brutgams*), which, however, he equates not with an inner message about Christ's love for the soul, as most medieval mystics did, but with "revelations" to be communicated to the community, as the Zwickau prophets had received.[72] Mysticism in the late Middle Ages had been much concerned with discerning between true and false revelations, mystical and prophetic. Müntzer marks a break with clerical control of this visionary ferment by seemingly insisting that all revelations are good and that no rules for discernment are needed.[73] The basis for this prophetic program is found in what follows, a section that shows Müntzer to be one of the forerunners of the later Spiritualists. He says, "Where the seed falls on good ground [Matt. 13:15], that is, in hearts that are full of God, this is then the paper and the parchment on which God does not write with ink, but rather writes the true Holy Scripture with his living finger, about which the external Bible truly testifies. . . . All of the elected people can read this Scripture, for they increase their talent [Luke 19:12-27]."[74] The external word has yielded to the internal voice of spiritual inspiration, a message that only the elect can read. The office of a "true shepherd" is to lead the flock to such revelations, something that is impossible for the "inexperienced faith" of the current clergy, "which is not worth a louse."[75] Like Luther, Müntzer stresses the necessary role of "fear of God" in breaking down the fallen soul's resistance to God, but he places this experiential theme in a different theological context, that of the dawning millennial kingdom which he has been appointed to usher in: "The time of the harvest is at hand! Thus God himself has appointed me for his harvest! I have made my sickle sharp, for my thoughts are zealous for the truth and my lips, skin, hands, hair, soul, body, and my life all damn the unbelievers."[76] Müntzer's sense of the approaching apocalyptic transformation grew stronger in the months to come. It is summarized in a letter he wrote to his friend Hans Zeiss on July 22, 1524, in which he advises him, "Think about the transformation of the world that is now imminent, Dan. 2."[77] Shortly before the battle at Frankenhausen, this conviction of imminence of the end was no less strong, and even more violent, as in the famous call to arms in a letter written to the League at Allstedt: "You must go at them! The time is here! . . . At them, at them, while the fire is hot! Do not let your sword get cold, do not let your arms go lame! Strike—cling, clang!—on the anvils of Nimrod. Throw their towers to the ground!"[78]

The anticlericalism and apocalyptic violence of the Manifesto are its dominant themes, but Müntzer seasoned these with mystical language. We may ask if the mystical elements become more prominent in his later writings. This is not the case with some of his more political pieces, like the famous "Sermon to the Princes," in which Müntzer, despite some references to the "abyss of the heart," is fixated on apocalyptic violence, putting himself forward as the new Daniel with a message from God about the need for his noble audience to take up the sword to slaughter God's foes, that is, clergy and rulers who oppose his program.[79] By this stage, with violence in full flood, Müntzer proclaimed that if the rulers did not support his message, "may they be strangled without mercy," and asserted that the "whole of divine law" teaches "that godless rulers, especially priests and monks, should be killed."[80] There are, however, some letters and treatises that give a sense of how deeply Müntzer's apocalypticism was intertwined with a sense of the need for the mystical transformation of the elect.

An example of such a more mystical text is a brief letter written to unknown associates at Halle on April 19, 1523, counseling them not to be concerned about his rejection by that city.[81] "I beg you," says Müntzer, "not to get angry on account of my expulsion, for, in such tribulation the abyss of the soul [*der selen abgrunt*] is cleansed, so that it is increasingly enlightened and recognized as worthy of obtaining the insuperable witness of the Holy Spirit. In order to discover God's mercy, one must be forsaken, as Isaiah clearly testifies in 28[:19] and 54[:7]." The theme of the "abyss" (*abgrunt*) had a long history in late medieval mysticism, especially in Germanic lands.[82] As another way of speaking about the Eckhartian "ground of the soul,"[83] or "spark of the soul," mystics like Tauler had used the Psalm text about "the abyss calling out to the abyss" (Ps. 41:8 Vg.) to indicate the union of indistinction between God's unknowable nature and the soul made to God's image and likeness. Karlstadt, as we have seen, used *abgrund*, though sparingly, to refer to both God and the soul, but never correlatively, as Tauler did. Müntzer speaks of "the ground of the soul" and "the ground of the heart" about fifteen times, thus showing an affinity with German mystical anthropology; but he never used the term in relation to God, as far as I can see. In the context of his appropriation of mysticism, Müntzer often views the abyss of the soul as the "location" where the tribulation induced by fear of the Lord brings about the purgation by which the elect are made ready to receive the illumination of the Holy Spirit. At times, however, he invokes a wider range of mystical terminology reminiscent of Eckhart and Tauler when speaking about God's action in the soul's abyss, such as the language of "breaking-through." An example can be found in a passage from the *Special Exposure of False Faith*, written in 1524:

> The power of the All-Highest (which Luke describes in the first and last chapters) rejects all false, secret unbelief in the most radical way. This unbelief will be discovered through the putting on or the breaking through of the Divine Spirit in the abyss of the soul, as Paul says, "You should put on Christ" [Rom. 13:14]. Then false faith can have absolutely no place. But whoever has not experienced this breakthrough knows absolutely and utterly nothing of faith.[84]

A second mystical text is the "Open Letter to the Brothers at Stolberg," dated July 18, 1523. The first of Müntzer's published works, this missive advises his followers to be cautious of too hasty a rebellion against repressive authority.[85] In the preface, Müntzer invokes German mystical vocabulary, including the term *Gelassenheit* dear to Karlstadt: "In the weakness that the outward person has in releasement [*gelassenheyt*] the Lord gives him an attraction with the strength that goes forth from Him."[86] In both the preface and the body of the letter, Müntzer addresses his audience in a term favored in German mysticism, as "elect friends of God" (*ausserwelten freunden Gots*), a designation he uses more than a dozen times in his writings. The gist of his message is also taken from the vocabulary of German mysticism, the need to attain true poverty of spirit (Matt. 5:3). Poverty of spirit (*armuth des geysts*) must be put to the test, that is, the poor in spirit must give up all solace in created things and seem like they have been abandoned by God.[87] A third mystical theme also appears, the notion of the poor soul becoming "the true kingdom of God," and later "the throne of God" and "the house of God." "The true kingdom of God," he says, "begins with genuine pleasure when the elect first see what God lets them discover in themselves, through his action, in the experience of the spirit.

People who have not experienced the bitter opposite of faith do not know this, for they have not believed against belief, or hoped against hope, or hated against the love of God."[88] This *sub contrario* experience of God is not far from Luther's notion of *Anfechtung*. It is not, however, based on the "dead letter of Scripture" but is the work of "the living finger of God, which writes in the heart" (2 Cor. 3:2). Such a tested faith will allow the elect to overcome in the end. Like Luther, then, Müntzer agreed with the emphasis on the necessity for real experience of God as the foundation for true faith.[89]

Another example of a mystical text is a letter written to a certain "dear brother George" (*Jeori*), which lacks place and date.[90] George had come to Müntzer for spiritual counsel, but the preacher did not have time and so later sent this letter. Müntzer says that instruction "is not the work of a day." The renewal of the inner man needs to be total and should begin with instruction about "contrived faith" (*getichten glauben*), whose evident falseness drives "the mountain of our selfishness into the bottom of the sea." Only when this abasement and affliction have been deeply experienced, does Christ come to rescue us. "For Christ, the true Son of God, climbs down to those who are almost completely drowned and who no longer have any consolation. Christ comes to them in the night, when the affliction is at its greatest, and the elect think that he is a devil, or a ghost. Then he says, 'Oh, you most beloved, do not be afraid. It is I, and I cannot enlighten you differently. I have no other way of pouring my grace into you.'"[91] Those who are not willing to experience such tribulation have no patience for the God who writes not in external letters but "with the pen of his spirit in the abyss of the soul, where a person recognizes that he is a son of God and that Christ is the highest among the sons of God. What the elect are on account of grace, Christ is through his divine nature."[92] Once again Müntzer's similarity to Luther's notion of *Anfechtung* is evident, but also clear is his knowledge of an important mystical topos concerning deification, namely, that we become sons of God by grace, while Christ is Son by nature. The letter goes on to discuss other mystical themes: submerging our will in the water of suffering and losing the self; attaining true poverty of spirit; and rooting out contrived and imperfect faith. The transformation is liturgical, being nourished by Müntzer's new German liturgy. It is also christological— "Take heed that Christ is your stone, and that in a wind storm your will is grounded on the same cliffs."[93]

Müntzer's treatise *The Special Exposure of False Faith*, mentioned above, employs many of his mystical themes in the context of an attack on "the libelous writings of Luther."[94] Although the work is rambling, perhaps hastily assembled from sermon materials, the numbering of the sections enables the reader to follow it fairly easily. True faith, as contrasted with Luther's false form, can only be taught to the "common man" (*gemeyner man*) by the correct interpretation of scripture contained in the "teachings of the spirit of Christ." Therefore, Müntzer begins (section 1) with an "Explanation of the First Chapter of Luke," because the story of Zechariah and Mary found there shows that true faith starts from the experience of fearful terror before God— "the fear of God at the beginning of faith is an unbearable thing to human nature."[95] No theme is more prevalent in Müntzer's theology than the need for experiencing (not just imagining or appreciating from a distance) fear and terror in order to break down our pride and self-sufficiency. The human sense of faith is really "unbelief" and hence needs to be destroyed through the pure fear of God that breaks through into the abyss of the soul and reveals true faith, as seen in the passage quoted above. Müntzer rails at Luther and his followers, "who have made a shameful cloak out of Scripture" and thus hidden the true message of faith. The supremacy of the inner revelation of truth by the Holy Spirit acting within the soul is a fundamental difference between the two reformers and shows why Müntzer has sometimes been seen as a forerunner of the Spiritualist Radicals. After citing a string of biblical passages about the need for inner instruction from God, he summarizes: "These and many other passages of Scripture force all of us to the conclusion that we need to be taught by God alone."[96]

Section 2 reiterates this message. Zechariah, Elizabeth, and Mary found faith to be something impossible to human nature. "And all of us," Müntzer avers, "must have just this experience of impossibility at the beginning of faith. And we must hold to it that we carnal, earthly men shall become gods through the incarnation of Christ as man." We will be taught and deified by God. "Yes, even more, we should be completely and totally transformed into him, so that earthly life turns around into the heavenly, Philippians 3[:20–21]."[97] Such transformation is impossible for the godless and hesitant, so Müntzer launches into an attack on the rulers of the world who block this evangelical understanding, as well as the "defenders of the godless" (read Luther) who collude with them and attack him as a "fanatic." The third section of the treatise opens with a revealing passage in which Müntzer says that the revelation of the Spirit through fear prepares the heart for the reception of the divine gift. This state of utter passivity, much like Eckhart's view of detachment, is one that "compels" God to act:

"For God cannot despise the repentant heart that has become humble. He must yield to it [*er muos es erhoeren*] because such a good sacrifice is made from it."[98] This section then discusses how the experience of holy fear enables a person to delve into himself and discover that he is "a temple of God," a theme noted above. The fourth section emphasizes another aspect of belief in which Müntzer broke with Luther—his insistence that such inner teaching necessarily involves revelations and visions, which are no less vital and real today than they were in the time of the Old and New Testaments.

The fifth and sixth sections of the *Special Exposure of False Faith* come to the heart of Müntzer's mystical teaching. He does not exactly construct a mystical itinerary, but he does provide an exposition of central aspects of how he understands the process of deification, though he is silent about many traditional mystical themes concerning transformation, especially union with God. He begins by repeating that the servants of God (read Müntzer and followers) must be willing to cleanse Christendom of its godless rulers and also to reprimand the faithful. Such teachers should propound the most rigorous interpretation of the first movement of faith, but often cannot due to circumstances. In his attempt to explain this, Müntzer utilizes a terminology that may have been clear to him but is perhaps opaque to the modern reader:

> Yes, this initial movement is so distasteful to them that they have not even endured the suspension [*langweil*] through which alone God's action is to be found, Psalm 40[:2]. In the first place God's action is experienced through sprinkling, Numbers 19[:19], where the waters of divine wisdom stir, Ecclesiastes 15[:3]. Then the sad person perceives that God has begun a most rapturous thing in him. Thus, for the first time, he is terrified by God's name, which is revealed to him in the divine action.[99]

Müntzer is obviously trying to coordinate his experience of the overwhelming fear of God with passages in scripture, but it is not easy to see exactly how. Section 5 continues with a description of how this "first sprinkling" that is "the breath of the Holy Spirit" forces a person to repent and return to God. This leads to a state of "complete liberation," where "exuberant faith" triumphs. Müntzer then takes off on a long polemic against those who do not recognize how true faith works, that is, how to lay bare "the abyss of the soul." In section 6 he again picks up on the language of German mysticism, saying that "the totally abandoned person must be awakened by God from the desert of the heart" to "call out in the miserable deserts of erring hearts" to put them on the path to right faith.[100] Here, as elsewhere in Müntzer, we are left with some uncertainty about the goal of the process. The section seems to argue that the goal is the separation of the Christian community into the elect and those who refuse election and are therefore to be exterminated:

> The elected friend of God discovers a rapturous joy when his brother has also come to faith through the same process as he. Therefore, the mother of God gives testimony to Elizabeth, and she in turn to Mary. We must do this as well. . . . In a short time, each will have to give an account of how he has come to the faith. The separation of the godless from the elect would indeed bring about a true Christian church. What can the godless know of true faith . . . ?[101]

The final two sections of the treatise return to the importance of the fear of God as revealed in the story of Mary in Luke 1, underlining that this fear is both an imitation of the suffering Christ and a lifting up (rapture) in the Holy Spirit. Müntzer says, "God does this so that we may emulate Christ in his suffering and life through ecstasy in the Holy Spirit, against whom the world rages. . . . Thus faith will be given only to the poor in spirit, who also recognize their unbelief."[102] This awareness allows the believer to be deified, though apparently not to experience union with God, which Müntzer mentions hardly at all. It also gives the true believer a mandate to destroy those who have not attained this status.

Was Müntzer a mystic? Once again, the ambiguity of the designation with regard to Reformation thinkers confronts us. Müntzer certainly incorporated mystical themes into his view of the nature of Christian belief and practice more than many other reformers—and in ways that Luther and his followers rejected. Müntzer might be called a "mystic of the fear of God," since for him the experience of fear is absolutely necessary for destroying self-will and allowing the Holy Spirit to write the message of salvation in the abyss of the soul. Fear makes God truly present to us and begins a process of transformation that has a central christological dimension: being conformed to the "bitter Christ." Attention to the inner voice of the Holy Spirit emphasizes the importance of visions and prophecies. Inner emptying, abandonment, and releasement (*Gelassenheit*) allow the believer to recognize his true self as the temple, house, or throne of God and to become a "friend of God." Müntzer invokes these and other forms of mystical language to describe the life of true faith, such as transformation, deification, and occasionally the birth of the Son in the soul;[103] but he hardly ever talks about uniting with God.[104] The goal of Müntzer's version of the mystical path is not contemplation but action, specifically apocalyptic action. His recombination of the mystical and the apocalyptic dimensions of Christianity was unusual, especially in its conviction that those who had been truly deified had the right, even the obligation, to destroy their opponents in God's name. If Müntzer is a mystic, he is an example of the fact that the mystical element in Christianity (no less than the institutional or intellectual elements), especially when isolated from the others, can become unbalanced and even destructive.

Hans Denck (ca. 1500–1527)

The brief life of Hans Denck, who had some contact with Müntzer and Karlstadt, shows that there were differing models of using medieval mysticism within the world of the Radical Reform.[105] Like many of the radicals, Denck is hard to characterize. He was critical of Luther, as were many other radicals. He was influenced by Müntzer but was not an apocalypticist. Rather, Denck was a pacifist, an irenicist, and something of an early ecumenist in his emphasis that God offers salvation to all, even those who have not heard the gospel. With regard to baptism, Denck preferred adult baptism, but he did not forbid the infant form. Like the Anabaptists, he was against oaths, but, unlike most Anabaptists, he was not a scriptural literalist, nor a community builder. Denck's emphasis on the need for the inner light of the Holy Spirit for turning to God and his spiritual interpretation of baptism and the Lord's Supper, have led many to characterize him as a Spiritual Anabaptist.[106]

Born in Bavaria around 1500, Denck received a humanist education at Ingolstadt (ca. 1517–20). He became a reformer about 1522 at Basel, but by the time he was named head of the St. Sebald School there in September 1523, he had already become critical of Luther. Subsequently, at Nuremberg he ran afoul of the Lutheran reformers of the city, notably Andreas Osiander, and in January of 1525 he was called before the city council to defend his religious views. Denck's *Confession to the City Council of Nuremberg* is our first witness to his thinking.[107] We also possess the *Critical Evaluation of Denck's Confession by the Nuremberg Preachers*, which resulted in his exile. During 1525 and 1526 Denck wandered to several cities (St. Gall, Augsburg, and so on) and was in contact with Anabaptist leaders such as Hans Hut and Balthasar Hubmaier. In these years he wrote some short treatises attacking Luther and setting out his view of Christian faith: *What Scripture Means When It Says God Is the Cause of Good and Evil*; a tract on *The Law of God*; and *The Order of God*. Denck's radical views caused him to be exiled from even tolerant Strassburg in late 1526. He went to Worms and eventually back to Basel, where he died of the plague in November 1527. During his final year Denck wrote several other works, notably a treatise *Concerning Divine Love*, and an irenic *Recantation* (better termed *Reconsideration*), a kind of last will and testament.

Denck's knowledge of late medieval German mysticism was similar to that of Karlstadt and Müntzer–Tauler, the *Theologia Deutsch*, and possibly a few other texts. He does not explicitly cite these sources, however, and his use of mystical terminology is infrequent. Nevertheless, if it is legitimate to speak of a distinctive Spiritualist strand of mysticism in the early sixteenth century, Denck is one of its purest representatives. By Spiritualist mysticism I mean an emphasis on listening to the Spirit of God within the soul as the source for a life dedicated to love of God and neighbor so strong that all the externals of faith (Bible, church, sacraments) become expendable—useful if they help, but not necessary.[108]

From his earliest writing, the *Confession to the Nuremberg Council*, the spiritual tendency in Denck is clear.[109] He begins from the inner turmoil of his "natural obstinate nature," seeking the faith that leads to life. What is the source of this faith? It cannot come from outside, from the parents who raised him, or even (by implication) from the words of scripture or preachers (as Luther insisted). Rather, the source is "something" in the soul, an "inborn poverty of spirit" (a mystical expression), that is, "the truth" he feels in his inward being that enables him to cast out false faith. This interiorization is also true of reading scripture. Again (and contrary to Luther), he insists that scripture is not evident in itself, but only if inner grace-given truth reveals "the testimonies that are in part very strong in attesting Christ to be the power that spurs me on." Denck testifies to his personal anguish in trying to find out what scripture really means, concluding that its significance can be penetrated only by the inner action of the Spirit: "Therefore, Peter (2 Pet. 1:20ff.) states correctly that scripture is not given to one's own interpretation, but that it belongs to the Holy Spirit to expound it correctly, who has also given it in the beginning." This is an example of one of the fundamental issues of the Reformation and the early modern religious project, as Susan Schreiner has shown, namely, where does religious truth reside, and who gets to determine this?[110] Luther broke with papal control over the meaning of scripture to assert that only scripture itself (*sola scriptura*) could be the foundation of true belief. Luther was sure of what the Bible said. The Radical Reformers, as they grew more aware of divergent ways of interpreting the Bible over such issues as Christ's presence in the Lord's Supper, and as they realized that infant baptism was nowhere mentioned in the New Testament, began to insist that it was only the experience of the same Spirit who wrote the original text that could guarantee its real meaning. But if the Spirit gave different interpreters different meanings, what was to be done? More radically, if the Spirit within is the real witness to divine truth, is the outer word necessary at all? Denck was one of the first to pose these questions, especially with regard to baptism and the Lord's Supper, which is why the Lutheran pastors of Nuremberg exiled him under pain of death. Denck's later writings explore aspects of these fundamental issues already outlined in the *Confession*. They are an early witness to a new mystical tendency within Radical Protestantism, one that was to have many later transformations, not only in Spiritualists like Schwenkfeld, Franck, and Weigel, but also in seventeenth-century groups like the Quakers.

Denck's writings do not feature extensive discussions of the divine nature,[111] but they do speak of God as Perfect Love and Absolute Goodness.[112] Denck broke with Luther and his followers by insisting that the good God could not predestine anyone to hell. The treatise *Whether God Is the Cause of Evil*, primarily written against this error, says early on, "For since God is good he can in reality not make anything but the good. Hence, all creatures are made good by God and they are in some respect like God. Any sin beyond this, people do out of their own nature and against God."[113] God's creation of the good universe finds its center in human nature made to the divine image, which image is the "divine something," or "spark," in the depths of the soul. Here Denck introduced an essential element of late medieval German mysticism into his anthropology. Because the divine spark is found within the soul, unmediated contact with God is not only possible but necessary: "Whoever does not learn to know God from God himself has never known him."[114]

Against Luther and most of the later mainline reformers, Denck insisted that humans always retain free will, the ability to sin or refrain from sinning, although the deeply personal aspect of his writings testifies to how difficult he found it to realize choosing the good without the aid of the Spirit acting within. Reaffirming this conviction in chapter 4 of his *Recantation*, on "Free Will," he says that "God does not force anyone to remain in his service who is not found compelled by love.

The devil . . . cannot force anyone to remain in his service who has once known the truth."[115] Hence, justifying faith, for Denck, is not something external and imputed that comes to the fallen creature by preaching and the word of scripture, but it consists in inhering faith given by the Holy Spirit.[116] Although Denck was careful to allow some usefulness to Scripture and outward ceremonies, the logic of his position led him eventually to make it clear that all external practices of religion are secondary, even unnecessary—useful for weak persons but not essential to salvation. "A person who has been elected by God may be saved without preaching or scripture," as he said at the end of his life.[117] This is true of all external practices, such as baptism (whether of infants or adults), as well as the Lord's Supper.[118]

What role does Christ play in the path to salvation for Denck? And what kinds of practices are conducive to helping the believer experience the Spirit within, if the sacramental rituals of the church, and even reading of the Bible, have become peripheral? Denck does not neglect Christ. Jesus Christ is the sole means of salvation, as he teaches in *Whether God Is the Cause of Evil*.[119] For Denck, however, Christ is interiorized and idealized. If the meaning of salvation is the recognition that every human has God dwelling within, then Christ is the exemplar and foremost realization of the inner union of God and human. In *Concerning Genuine Love*, he says, "Therefore, he who desires to know or attain to genuine Love, cannot receive it earlier or more readily than through this Jesus Christ."[120] Christ is not only the best teacher of the return to God but also, and more importantly, the living model of the essential practice of faith: perfect love of God and of neighbor. Possibly echoing Luther, Denck defines love as "a spiritual power by which one is united or through which one desires to be united to another person."[121] The marks of perfect love are complete surrender to the other person, loss of self-concern, willingness to die, and the desire to be united to everyone. Some have described Denck's theology as an essentially ethical system, interested in laying out good and bad practices; but he is more radical than that, in line with the Augustinian axiom (which he does not quote), "Love God and do what you will" (*ama et fac quod vis*).

Denck also talks about the attitudes and practices that assist believers in arriving at awareness of the Spirit in the depths of the soul and thus being able to begin to practice the pure love of God and of neighbor exemplified by Christ. Some of the language he uses to describe these practices is taken over from German mysticism. For example, in some places (e.g., in the treatise *Divine Order*) he adverts to how inner pain, difficulty, and suffering (*Anfechtung*) are necessary in breaking down self-reliance.[122] Inner suffering, however, plays a smaller role in his thought than it does in Luther and Müntzer. Like Karlstadt, Denck at times uses the term "releasement" (*Gelassenheit*), especially in *Whether God Is the Cause of Evil*, to refer to the need for letting go of created self-interest in order to become attentive to the voice of the Spirit within. In order for a sinner to return to God, he needs to become a "truly released person" and recognize God as his true home. "That you, however, seek yourself and not God for his own sake, you show by your un-releasedness (*Ungelassenheyt*), by the fact that you are always looking for a hiding place that you might escape the hand of God."[123] This process involves a losing of the self that Denck describes in mystical terms as God's "breaking-through" of the will. "Yes," he says, "since blood and flesh are so antagonistic that before God all our doing is inactivity, our making before God, a breaking, our something before God, a nothing, we always ought to hear what the Spirit says to us, namely, that what appears to us as God's breaking, is the best making and that God's Nothing (which appears to be nothing to us) is the highest and noblest Something."[124] A later passage in the same work speaks of "surrendering all ownness [*aigenschaft*]" in order "to yield oneself to the freedom which is God,"[125] another set of terms with a long history in German mysticism stretching back to Eckhart.

The necessity for releasement and interiorization forms an essential link between late medieval German mysticism and a number of sixteenth-century reformers. But not all letting-go and interiorization are the same, and it is not likely that Tauler and the author of the *Theologia Deutsch* would have agreed with Denck's conviction that these practices mean that all external religious practices become dispensable, even dangerous. A basic shift in the internalization of religion took place with the sixteenth-century Radical Reformers, one that, for all its similarities to some late medieval mystics, represents something new. This shift is evident in what Denck has to say about the goal of the transformative process of experiencing the Spirit within. In outward practice, as noted above, Denck insists that immediate awareness of God is measured by the authenticity of one's love of God and neighbor. One aspect of this conviction is that Denck was one of the first sixteenth-century authors who took an irenic approach to religious controversy, as we see in his *Recantation*.[126] This attitude was also the source of his pacifism. It also involved a form of universalism. If God acts within all humans, how is it possible to exclude those of other faiths from recognizing God within, as Denck notes several times?[127]

Viewed from within one's own consciousness, what does the experience of the Holy Spirit entail? Here again, Denck employs terminology taken over from medieval mysticism. For example, those who have attained this status can be described as "friends of God," a biblical term, but one that became characteristic of circles of late medieval German mysticism.[128] In *Whether God Is the Cause of Evil*, Denck also speaks of becoming deified in terms as strong as those found in Luther and some other reformers. When a person becomes free in God, he says, "Then a person takes after God, takes on the traits of the divine nature [Rom. 8:17] as one who is a son of God and co-heir with Christ. . . . But it is not he who lives, but Christ within him who does not consider it robbery that he is in some measure equal to God [Phil. 2:20]." To one who objects that this makes us equal to Christ, Denck responds, "In some measure all Christians are equal to Christ. . . . Not, I say, that they are as perfect as Christ was, but that they seek the perfection which Christ never lost. . . . To sum up, all Christians, that is, those who received the Holy Spirit, are in God one with and equal to Christ, so that what pertains to one, pertains to the other. As Christ does, so do they also."[129] At the beginning of his writing career, in the *Confession* at Nuremberg, Denck put this equally strongly. Speaking of the believer who becomes inebriated by drinking the invisible wine out of the invisible cup mixed by the Father through his Son, he says, "He does not know anything about himself any more, but becomes deified [*vergottet*] through the love of God while God becomes incarnate in him [*vermenscht*]. This is what we mean by eating the body of Christ and drinking the blood of Christ."[130]

Along with divinization, Denck speaks of being born from God. In *The Law of God*, for example, he says, "He who is born of God is bound to witness to the truth."[131] He has no detailed discussions, however, of the birth of the Word in the soul, such as we find in Eckhart and other medieval mystics. Given Denck's emphasis on interiority, as well as the passages on deification noted above, it is not surprising that he does speak of "uniting with God" in a number of places. Denck seems to conceive of this union in two fairly traditional ways. The soul is one in God from its creation in that it bears the divine spark within it, but uniting to God can also be conceived of as the deepening realization of our primordial oneness through letting go and learning to love as Christ loved. Chapter 10 of *Divine Order*, for instance, says that the person who seeks the best of all things whether he faces good or ill, has gone beyond the written law (1 Tim. 1:9) and has become a law to himself (Rom. 2:14). In such freedom, Denck continues, echoing John

17:21, one of the most cited scriptural passages about union, "He is one with Christ as Christ is with the Father."[132] In *Concerning Genuine Love* he alludes to another of the oft-cited biblical texts on union, saying, "All those who are saved are one spirit with God" (1 Cor. 6:17). This union is modeled on that of Jesus. "All those," he continues, "who have sought and found the way of God have become one with God, but this very one [i.e., Jesus], who has never faltered in God's ways, has never become separated from God but has from the very beginning been one with God in the Spirit."[133] In sum, union with God is important for Denck, but it would be hard to construct a theology of mystical union from his scattered comments.

These uses of mystical terminology show that Denck, like Karlstadt and Müntzer, was clearly influenced by late medieval Germanic mysticism. They do not necessarily make Denck a "mystical author," at least in the medieval sense of someone laying out a program for attaining contemplative union with God. Furthermore, the interests of the reformers were different from those of late medieval mystics, especially because these sixteenth-century thinkers used their sense of the priority of inner religion to break with the inherited religious structures and to create a new relation between the outer and inner dimensions of belief. Denck's insistence that finding God within is the essential meaning of faith can, nonetheless, be considered a form of mysticism—and one that had influence in later Radical Protestant traditions. Although the young reformer had a deep devotion to Jesus Christ, his rigorously inward mysticism, separated from scripture, institution, and the usual mystical practices, was something new.

Sebastian Franck (1499–1542)

Sebastian Franck was born in Donauwörth in Bavaria in 1499, probably of an artisan family.[134] He studied at Ingolstadt (1515–17), and then at Heidelberg (1518–24). Ordained a Catholic priest, he became a Reformed pastor at Gustenfelden in 1525. Franck, however, was already beginning to distance himself from Luther, perhaps because he was disappointed that Lutheran *sola fide* and *sola scriptura* did not seem to be making a real difference in the moral behavior of the adherents of the Reform. Also important was Franck's translation of and reaction to the *Dialloge* of the humanist reformer Andreas Althamer (ca. 1500–1539), which attempted to reconcile the many contradictions found in the Bible in defense of Luther's view of the clarity of the scriptural text.

The more Franck reflected on these problems, the more he became convinced that only the inner light of the Spirit could resolve such problems, not rational argument.[135] His 1528 *Treatise against Drunkenness* already suggests that true religion depends not on Luther's external criteria for belief but only on the "spark of divine love" within the soul. Franck was thus aligning himself with the "Spiritual" tendency of Hans Denck (recently dead) and Caspar Schwenckfeld, whom he met in 1529.[136]

Franck's abandonment of Lutheranism caused him difficulty for the rest of his life, as he moved from city to city, eventually exiled from each place of refuge due to his radical views. He supported himself as a soapmaker and printer. Franck was a polymath who wrote on history, geography, and language, as well as on theological, biblical, and spiritual topics. His historical works, such as the *Chronicle of the Turks* (1530), *World Chronicle* (1531), and geographical *Worldbook* (1534), had an implied theological agenda, showing how the rise and fall of kingdoms illustrates the futility of history, how ecclesiastical history shows that the decline of the institutional church began right after the time of the apostles, and, finally, how the best hope for true believers rests in a coming spiritual church.[137] After a period at Strassburg (1531–32), where he published his *Letter to Campanus*, a summary of his theology, Franck moved on to Ulm, where he stayed from 1533 to 1539. Here he issued his *Paradoxes(Paradoxa)* in 1534, and in late 1535 gave an important *Declaration* defending his views against those who wished to exile him. His opponents eventually prevailed in 1539, and he then settled in Basel, where he died in late 1542. While at Basel he published his most popular work, a large collection of *Proverbs (Sprichwörterbuch)* drawn from many languages. He also made a Latin paraphrase and expansion of the *Theologia Deutsch*, which he praised as superior even to the Bible in revealing the spiritual essence of religion.[138]

The extent and variety of Franck's writings make him difficult to present in any simple way, especially because he became more and more skeptical of external religion over his lifetime. While Schwenkfeld gathered circles of those devoted to inner religion (Schwenckfeldians, who survive to this day), Franck had no interest in gathering followers. Some of Franck's views are similar to those of Denck, notably his ecumenical universalism, which held that salvation was available to all— Christians, Jews, and Muslims. Franck's positions, however, were very much his own. He seems to have been a disillusioned person, someone at odds with the religious violence of his time and its theological quarrels, follies, and contradictions. His skepticism and universalism explain why some interpreters have found Franck "the most modern figure" of the sixteenth century, despite the anachronism involved in the judgment.

Franck's humanist sympathies, especially for Erasmus, and his reading of late medieval German mysticism were important sources for his spiritualizing program. As with Luther and with a number of the Radical Reformers, Franck was fond of Tauler's sermons and the *Theologia Deutsch*.[139] These German mystics had stressed the necessity for inner contact with God as the essence of faith, although they also spoke about the institutional aspects of the practice of Christian faith. Mystics like Eckhart, Tauler, and the author of the *Theologia Deutsch* affirmed that, *without* interior religion, external practice counts for little or nothing. Denck and Franck said that interior religion was *all* that mattered and external religion should be rejected, not only as secondary but as harmful. The difference is real.[140]

R. Emmet McLaughlin notes, "Franck's letter to Johannes Campanus can claim the status of a classic. Nowhere else was the Radical Spiritualist vision of the church presented so clearly and so unsparingly."[141] Campanus (ca. 1500–1575), born in Belgium, at first was a follower of Luther but broke with him and evolved a religious position close to Unitarianism.[142] Franck wrote to Campanus to urge him to stand fast against attacks of "doctors of the Roman or . . . Christian church," who are denounced as wolves and servants of Antichrist. "I believe," he says, "that the outward church of Christ, including all its gifts and sacraments, because of the breaking in and laying waste by Antichrist right after the death of the Apostles, went up into heaven and lies concealed in the Spirit and in truth. . . . But at the same time nothing has departed from the inner truth of baptism, the Supper, the ban, and gathering for worship. Instead, the Spirit has imparted all this in truth to the faithful in whatever lands they be."[143] The originally useful outward rituals have been taken over by Antichrist for fourteen centuries, but the "Unitary Spirit" continues to give inward baptism "to all the faithful and all who are obedient to the inner Word in whatever part of the world they be." Franck rejects not only the Roman church and its revered teachers from the time of the Fathers but also the Evangelicals who have merely substituted one form of external oppression of faith for the Roman yoke. He also finds the Anabaptists lacking, because they think that the ruin of the church began with Constantine, whereas, for Franck, it goes back virtually to the beginning. What use is there, then, for restoring "outworn sacraments," as the Anabaptists are trying to do? The outward sacraments are like toys given to children by an indulgent Father, things to be left behind when the child grows up.

The second half of the letter features a personal appeal to Campanus. Franck advises him to give up his attempts to reform the "outworn church," and to "let the church of God remain in the Spirit among all peoples and pagans, . . . wherever they be, those who fear God and work righteousness, instructed by God and inwardly drawn by him, even though they have never heard of baptism, indeed, of Christ himself."[144] Franck says that he has more in his heart that he would like to say to Campanus, but any person and even scripture itself can only give a little testimony to the inner truth. "Faith is not learned out of books nor from a person, but rather it is learned and poured in by God in the School of the Lord, that is, under the cross." Franck praises Campanus's theology, especially his questioning of the doctrine of the Trinity, but he cautions that all past understandings of Christian teaching are radically deficient. Truth is coming in the future: "But in the end learned men will arise from among the people and they will impart understanding (Dan., ch. 12)." Finally, he chides Campanus for being too subservient to the letter of scripture and also for withdrawing his heart from the inner teaching of the Holy Spirit. One should not start from the outer scripture; "You should much rather interpret the scripture as a confirmation of your conscience, so that it testifies to the heart and not against it."[145]

The *Letter to Campanus* puts Franck's radical view of universal Christianity forcefully. It does not, however, make use of mystical themes or contain references to mystical writers. In what sense was the mystical tradition helpful for Franck in constructing his spiritual view of Christianity? To find an answer to this question, we can consider two documents from his Ulm period, the *Paradoxes*, probably the closest Franck ever came to summarizing his theology, and the shorter *Defense* of his views he offered to the city's Inquisitorial Board in late 1535.

Sebastian Franck's *Paradoxa* is a kind of *summa* of Radical Spiritualist theology, or better the theology of *a* Radical Spiritualist.[146] With 280 paradoxes, or "wondrous sayings," the work features a very different form of organizing and arguing from the medieval *summae*.[147] In his preface, Franck announces, "I entitled this my philosophy *Paradoxa* and translated 'paradox' by 'wondrous saying' or 'wondrous word,' since theology, the right meaning of Scripture (which alone is God's word), is nothing other than an eternal paradox, certain and true over against every illusion, appearance and the faith and esteem of the entire world."[148] A paradox is a statement contrary to common sense but still true when investigated from the perspective of inner truth. Scripture, of course, is full of such statements (e.g., "the last shall be first," "those who lose their life will keep it") and many of Franck's paradoxes are taken from the Bible. Scripture, indeed, reveals the fundamental logic of Franck's hermeneutic of paradoxical reversal: whatever is true of the literal reading of the Bible is false from the viewpoint of its inner spiritual meaning, and vice versa.

One of the themes of the book is the contrast between Christ and Antichrist: from the literal perspective Christ seems like Antichrist because of the demands he makes on the faithful, while Antichrist is always masquerading as a kind and welcoming savior (think of Müntzer's contrast between the "bitter Christ" and the "sweet Christ").[149] While Franck's book is fundamentally drawn from the Bible, he also scours ancient authors and ecclesiastical writers[150] and makes use of folk wisdom and proverbs to illustrate his fundamental perspective: truth is not what it seems; namely, what the world takes for the truth hides the spiritual truth within, which is diametrically opposed to the world's judgment. In Paradox 57 he summarizes, "I say, therefore, that everything has two appearances, one divine, the other human. These judge and determine the very opposite in everything."[151] Franck's method of argumentation is not unlike Luther's view of God's acting toward us *sub contrario*, but Franck pushes this in ways not found in Luther.

It has been said that there is no order to Franck's *Paradoxes*, but this is only half true. While there is no apparent surface order, Franck often treats successive paradoxes in groups, or follows individual paradoxes with others on similar topics, thus forming treatises that cover the major headings of his theology. The treatment of a topic in one place does not preclude returning to the same issue later in the collection. Among the theological topics given multiple treatments are (1) Evil and Sin (##29–31, 271–78); (2) The Word of God and Christ (##47–50, 98–118, 128–40); (3) The Proper Way to Read Scripture (five unnumbered paradoxes in the preface, and ##83–89, 119–25); (4) Prayer (##166–70, 204–8); and (5) Faith (##181–83, 215–26, plus many individual paradoxes). Single treatises include those on (1) God (##1–10); (2) Predestination and Foreknowledge (##19–22); (3) The World as the Kingdom of Satan (##70–74); (4) The Nature of the Just Person (##75–78); (5) Charity (##227–29); (6) Justification and Works (##243–47); and (7) Freedom and Grace (##266–70). While Franck's treatise is sometimes confusing and often repetitious, there is an inner logic to his approach. A brief exploration of some of the major aspects of the *Paradoxes* will help locate the function of mystical themes in his thought.[152]

Franck's theology is deeply biblical, but from a resolutely spiritual perspective. The literal interpretation of the Bible, he insists, is the original sin of exegesis, making the Bible into "Antichrist's sword." Thus, without a spiritual (or "allegorical" as he often calls it) reading of the Bible, we would necessarily be led astray, even damned. Spiritual reading comes from within, from the Word written in the heart by the Holy Spirit. "The New Testament, because it is not letter, but the Holy Spirit itself, must be learned from God without any mediators. Thus, properly speaking, no book or external word and worship is of the New Testament."[153] According to the concluding paradoxes (## 279–80), "God's word is wind and spirit, whose breath can be readily heard in the ground of a released, quiet soul [*im Grunde der gelassen stillen Seelen*], but whose 'whither and wherefrom' no one knows. It cannot be mastered, advanced, refused or enticed into someone, nor can it be spoken or written." Later he says, "Therefore, the Word became flesh that it may, though hidden in itself, be revealed in us. The Word cannot be shouted into us from outside, but must be found, taught, and perceived within us, stimulated, driven and taught by the Holy Spirit. It cannot be spoken or written, for it is God's Word itself."[154] This insistence on interiority grounds Franck's teaching that because the action of the Holy Spirit is not tied to the Bible itself (#249), salvation is open to all humans, even those who have never heard of Christ, faith, or scripture (e.g., ##92–93, 253, etc.). Paradox 83 states, "God is a God of the gentiles too." An important corollary of this interiorization of salvation is that all the history recounted in the Bible, both of the Old Testament and the life of Christ, while not being denied, finds its true meaning in the depths of the soul. "Therefore, the entire Bible has to be repeated again and again and must follow the same pattern. . . . All this takes place in us internally."[155]

Franck begins the *Paradoxes* with a brief treatment of the nature of God (##1–10) stressing negative theology—the little we can ever really know of the divine mystery. Paradox 1 ("No one knows what God is") cites Cicero, Thomas Aquinas, Plato, Dionysius the Areopagite, and other authorities, such as Tauler and Proclus. God is "the essential ground and the IS of all that is" (#2), and God's supreme goodness is both the source of our being and the goal of our return to deifying union with the Godhead (#4). Franck insists on a reciprocity between God and the creature: "God ought not to be without the creature, for then he would be unknown to himself and not praised. Similarly, the creature should not be without God. Therefore, he has created us for community and partnership with him, so that we might enjoy him and he be praised by us."[156] God is also the perfect goodness and love to which nothing can be added and from which nothing can be subtracted; all that he desires us to do is for our sake and not for his (#9). An important corollary of this teaching on God as love is Franck's insistence throughout the work that there can be no wrath or anger in God—as with Julian of Norwich, anger and wrath are only in us (see ##90, 119–23).

In the *Letter to Campanus,* Franck had already indicated his sympathy for those who questioned traditional teaching about the Trinity. In the *Paradoxes,* he often speaks of Father, Son, and Holy Spirit, but his language seems to suggest a kind of binitarianism in which the Father acts as Holy Spirit in the soul giving witness to the Eternal Word, who is certainly co-eternal but may not be fully equal to the Father. A full exploration of Franck's view of the Trinity, however, would demand an investigation of all his works. Franck's concern in the *Paradoxes* is primarily soteriological and ethical: How we are to be saved and how we are to live? In order to explain this goal he has to deal at length with theological anthropology (the nature of the human), Christology (who is Christ and how does he save us?), and the implications of these for Christian belief and practice.

Franck's anthropology is different from that of the Magisterial Reformers and is, in some aspects at least, close to that of the German mystics, whom he often cites.[157] The central theme is that humans have been created in the image and likeness of God (Gen. 1:26). Eckhart and his followers had distinguished two levels of the reality of human nature—a virtual preexistence of the human in the mind of God (*esse virtuale*) and the actual, or formal, existence of individual human beings (*esse formale*). In Paradox 79 ("There are two persons in everyone") Franck presents his version of this: "Every person is divided in himself and made up of two beings—an outward and figurative and an inward essential being." "The truly essential being is internal and invisible," he goes on to say. "Each of us is created at once out of nothing or out of the dust of the earth [i.e., the outward man] and also from God to the image of God."[158] Franck insists that both of these creations are timeless, because God does not work in time: "He created us all in eternity, both in the inner and the external nature. With those of us who are temporal, however, it begins when we become this." What he seems to mean here is that God's eternal intention is that a human being exists on these two levels, but the actual external nature begins in time. He confuses the point, however, by also applying it to being "born of God in time and to become a new creation and a Christ," asserting that this too "exists in eternity and always."[159] Franck explains this point in terms of the traditional Pauline tripartite distinction of body–soul–spirit (1 Thess. 5:21). Soul and body pertain to the outward person, while the spirit is the inner person, which is "the image of God, born of God."

The image is christological in nature, as explained in the "Treatise on Christ" found in Paradoxes 98–118. After introducing Christ as the eternal God-man who is Lord of all (##98–100), Franck discusses how Christ as the "express image of the splendor of God" is the image in which humankind has been formed (##101–2). The eternal God became visible in Christ in order to spiritualize and deify our flesh. Franck's divided view of inner and outer, however, affects his Christology, because he insists that Christ according to the flesh is only "an image and expression of God," while according to the inner spirit and divinity, "he is the word and Word of God himself."[160] The purpose of the incarnation, according to Franck, is best expressed in the ancient theological axiom that God became man that man might become God. Once again, however, Franck takes this adage in a daring direction similar to what is found in Eckhart. He says:

> All his [Christ's] members in him are of the same kind, too, so that as a result absolutely everything that is said of God can be said of Christ and through Christ of all his anointed. This spreads so far and incomprehensibly everywhere that it remains largely unwritten and is experienced by a released person more than it can be expressed [*und ein Gelassener es mehr zu empfinden als auszusprechen vermag*].

This is why humans are said to be created in the image of God and in Christ. Franck goes on to note the whole range of metaphors for the image placed in "the ground of the soul": model, spark, trace, light, word, will, son, seed, hand, life, and truth. He buttresses his teaching by citing a number of authorities.[161]

Franck speaks about humans as made in the image of God in many other places in the *Paradoxa*,[162] but these two sections provide the essence of his teaching. From time to time he refers to "the ground of the soul,"[163] but this theme does not have a large role in his thought. His understanding of the inner divine image, however, shows that his anthropology differs from that of Luther and Calvin in its insistence that even fallen humans retain the divine spark. Hence, it is not surprising that he teaches that humans maintain the freedom to choose either sin or righteousness, even after the Fall. As he says in Paradoxes 271–74: "Faith is a good, free will of the heart which seeks to undertake for God everything that is good. On the other hand, unbelief is a free turning away from him." "Therefore," he later concludes, "sin and righteousness are primarily free and willing, since they are only in the mind and disposition, will, mind, thought, and passion."[164]

Christ is present throughout the *Paradoxes*, but, as the passages already noted make clear, it is the inner, not the outer Christ who is the focus of Franck's attention. In that sense, Otto Langer has spoken of Franck's "Mysticism of the Logos" (*Logosmystik*).[165] The treatise beginning with Paradox 47 ("The Word of God Lasts Forever") shows this emphasis. Franck says, "The body is never the soul, though it is human; likewise, the flesh of the Word is never the Word, though it is Christ." There can be only one Word by which all things are made. Like Eckhart and his notion of continuous creation (*creatio continua*), Franck insists that "God still speaks this word daily and yet it is never properly spoken; otherwise it would be finite and accomplished. And if God were not still speaking this word today, . . . everything would instantly fall back into nothing."[166] The Word did become incarnate in the historical figure of Jesus Christ, but he did so in order to direct us back to the Word within, that is, the Word both within Christ and in our inner being. Christ outside us (*Christus extra nos*) does not save: "The indwelling Christ is all in all. Outside of you he would be of no use to you" (##135–37). This is not to say that the external Christ does not have a purpose. "Now contemplate the poor life of Christ," says Franck, noting his "poverty, patience, meekness, releasement [*Gelassenheit*], and refusal of all honors." Christ alone is our salvation, but as the "form and expression," we might say the model, for the interior mystical practice of total surrender to God. "Virtues hang together like a chain and there is but one virtue and one good work, John 6. For to believe in God or Christ is to be surrendered to God in total releasement and to offer oneself freely as his possession."[167] Outward and historical events find their meaning only in how they reveal the inner and eternal: "The external Adam and Christ are merely expressions of the inward, indwelling Adam, or of the eternal Christ who was murdered in Abel."[168]

As might be expected, this strongly inward view of Christ and salvation creates problems for any traditional view of the church and its sacraments, whether of the Roman or of the Reformed variety.[169] There is a "church" for Franck, but it has little, or nothing, to do with any of the competing churches he experienced during his lifetime. Starting as a Catholic priest, he became a Lutheran pastor, then abandoned Lutheranism as just another exterior control of true religion. He also found other Radicals, such as the Anabaptists, still caught in external rituals, such as adult baptism. In the discussion of Christ found in Paradoxes 135–37, he says, "The rebirth of baptism does not save. Therefore, Christ must be the baptism which takes place with fire and spirit, Titus 1, John 3."[170] Franck's church is an invisible reality (##232–35), one that has existed through history, but whose reality is timeless. In some writings, such as the *Letter to Campanus*, Franck seems to hold out hope for a coming apocalyptic manifestation of the real heavenly church on earth, but not in the *Paradoxa*, where history has become peripheral. What difference would it make to true believers if the inner church was to be realized on earth?

Granted that history is meaningless, how does Franck counsel the saved to live in the world? Like Denck and other Radicals (as well as some medieval mystics), Franck is not interested in a detailed moral theology involving commands and prohibitions. He concentrates on the fundamental Christian practices of faith and love, although he treats these virtues rather differently from contemporary Catholics and Magisterial Reformers. Faith, for Franck, in accordance with a major theme of Reformed theology, is a general category comprising our whole relation to God. But, as the "Treatise on Faith" in Paradoxes 220–26 makes clear, faith is an inner, noncognitive experience that is independent of scripture and preaching. He says:

> Now this free, living faith is poured out in the school of Christ under the holy cross in greatest releasement, self-emptying and poverty of spirit from sheer grace. And it is experienced and taught in experience more than it is derived from the reading of scripture and the hearing of sermons. It is derived exclusively from being addressed by the living word of God and from the hearing of the same that goes forth unmediated from the mouth of God through the agency of the spirit and of the letter.[171]

Faith is intimately tied to love, the other essential saving practice. In Paradoxes 181–83, he says that love gives way to faith alone, by which he means that the commands of love of neighbor found in the second tablet of Moses yield only to the commands of faith, our relation to God, found in the first tablet. This is because from God's point of view neither love nor necessity can ever be contrary to God.[172] Franck says a good deal about the practice of love of neighbor, [173] and he is especially concerned to unmask the religious hypocrisy that excuses evil actions by appealing to scripture. Paradox 200 even says, paradoxically, "God's word is the spice and adornment of all evil."[174] Like a number of the other radicals, his emphasis on love in practice meant that he was opposed not only to violence and repression in the name of religion (e.g., ##232–35) but also to war in general (#199). Franck's fundamental moral teaching might be reduced to the following formula: External moral commands are either suspect or evil; the internal commands of faith and love alone are salvific.

This brief review of Franck's theology indicates a number of the mystical themes found in the *280 Paradoxes*. It also suggests some analogies between Eckhartian mysticism and Franck's thought, though Franck's contact with Eckhart would have been limited to some sermons collected under Tauler's name in the early printed editions. Franck was clearly influenced by late medieval German mysticism; but it cannot be said that mystical texts, such as Tauler and the *Theologia Deutsch*, were the foundation for his theology. Rather, these sources seem to have been welcomed as aids in the expression of his new understanding of the relation of spirit and word.

Meeting God in *Anfechtung*, the experience of difficulty, temptation, even dereliction and despair, a major theme in late medieval mystics like Tauler, was important to Luther and Müntzer. It also appears in the *Paradoxes* but does not have a central role. Citing the examples of the prophets and apostles, and especially Christ on the cross, Franck says that God is "never closer than when he comes along, storming unceasingly, at enmity with the world and your flesh; consequently appearing to be most remote."[175] A more frequent theme in the *Paradoxes*, as we have seen, is *Gelassenheit*, the necessity for total letting go and emptying of self that was so important to Karlstadt. In speaking of releasement, Franck often joins it to language of uniting to God, or being transformed into God, sometimes explicitly citing Tauler, as in Paradoxes 43–44:

> A person . . . must consider himself as nothing at all if the Teacher is to come who will teach us more in one moment than all external words, sermons and writings could, from now to eternity. For a released person shall be transformed instantly into God and translated into the Kingdom of God which is pure light in which everything is taught and seen in an instant, so that whoever remains in it will have a lifetime to speak about it. See several places in Tauler, notably the first two sermons in which he speaks of the power of the true and living word of God.[176]

Altogether, Franck uses "releasement" and the "released person" about twenty-seven times in the *Paradoxes*, and he sometimes refers to Christ as the truest model of releasement (e.g., ##135–37, 187–89). Although Franck did not make *Gelassenheit* the focal topic of any of the paradoxes, the importance of being released occurs throughout the work and represents an important link with German mysticism.

Franck also speaks of union with God and deification, although here too, he does not provide any extended analysis. His approximately twenty references to union sometimes make use of the traditional language, based on 1 Corinthians 6:17, of becoming "one spirit with God." Thus, in Paradoxes 33–35, we read: "Whoever then leans on God's grace, is given still more, so that his riches increase daily in God until he is deified with him, becomes one spirit with him and in all things God and like God." Or, in Paradox 83, where he says that the Christian who has utterly abandoned books, sacraments, and all external things "has become one spirit in God" and "hears the Lamb alone within himself."[177] Sometimes union is described as becoming one with God or the Godhead, and even with the Holy Spirit (##179–80), and there are a number of passages specifically speaking about becoming one with Christ. A long account of the union of all believers with Christ (the *totus Christus*) occurs in the christological treatise of Paradoxes 109–14. Franck says, "Note here, Christ is in us, not outside us; he is our righteousness, salvation and faith so that we, having been ingrafted into him from Adam, might become in all things like his image and might be guided by the model he has set before us, yes, which he himself lives out within us."[178] Union language is used in conjunction with deification, sometimes in a radical way. "Whoever then leans on God's grace, is given still more, so that his riches increase daily in God until he is deified with him, becomes one spirit with him and in all things God and like God."[179] Deifying union is christological. Christ must be born in us, so that the Word becomes flesh in us as it was in Christ. "The Word must get in," he says, "that we may be one and one Christ with him who has become our flesh that he may spiritualize it [*das ers vergaistet*] and draw it into himself so that we might become his flesh and blood, bone of his bone and flesh of his flesh."[180]

Sebastian Franck's *280 Paradoxes* is not properly a mystical treatise, but an interiorized mystical teaching is important to this summary of his theology. Its teachings were, not unexpectedly, controversial. In 1535, Franck's enemy, the Lutheran minister Martin Frecht, together with the other Lutheran preachers in Ulm, drew up a memorandum listing six errors from the *Paradoxes* and the city council commanded Franck to respond to the document, which he did in September.[181] The paradoxes that were singled out as dangerous were ##124–25

("Scripture as God's Word"), #163 ("To the godless all languages and sciences are impure"); #44 ("All God's works are perfect"), and #171 ("No one can preach without a calling"). Paradoxes 163 and 44 seem to have been suspect because of their teaching about how God reveals truth instantaneously to the "released person." A later attack by the Lutheran pastors on Franck took him to task for his statement in Paradox 280 that God's written word was "not for instruction but for testimony," that is, that the scriptures "serve as witnesses of that which we were first taught by God and heard inwardly."[182] In the wake of the disaster at Münster, both the city council and the school board were concerned that Franck's emphasis on inner religion posed a threat to the powers of church and state that had been ordained by God's *potentia dei ordinata*. Franck's response to his opponents was in the so-called *Declaration*, which Steven Ozment characterizes as "as precise an illustration of mystical theology in the service of dissent as one will find in the sixteenth century."[183] The themes that we have seen in the *Paradoxes* are evident in the *Declaration*: the primacy of the internal word planted in the depths of the soul; God's inward direct teaching of the saved; scripture's marginal relation to conversion and justification; faith and theology as experience rather than science; and the unimportance of all institutions for saving faith. In defending this last point, Franck appeals to both Tauler and "Dr. Eckhart."[184] Franck did not yield an iota in his insistence that it is the inner, spiritual order that is essential, while the literal and external counts for little or nothing. Franck was given a conditional tenure in the city in November of 1535, but his enemies never gave up and he was finally exiled in January of 1539.

Sebastian Franck was an outsider who did not fit into any of the warring camps of Reformed theology in the second quarter of the sixteenth century. Because he was relentlessly nonpartisan (*unparteiisch*), he brought the wrath of all parties down on his head. While Franck was not an original thinker, his rigorously internalized view of Christian faith made him one of the first spokesmen for freedom of conscience and universal toleration in the West. He can also be called a mystical author, at least in the broad sense of the term, as one who taught that direct inner contact with God was the essence of religion.

Valentin Weigel (1533–1588)

Valentin Weigel was a generation younger than the other figures treated here. Müntzer and Denck died before he was born; Karlstadt and Franck when he was still a boy.[185] Unlike these Radicals, Weigel lived out his years as a Lutheran pastor, hiding his true ideas behind the veil of Lutheran orthodoxy and leaving his writings to be published after his death.[186] Weigel's Nicodemism can be explained partly by his historical context and partly by the fact that he had a more positive attitude to the Bible and to religious practices than some of the other Radicals, although he too insisted that it was interior appropriation, not external practice, that was essential to true Christianity.

Weigel was born in the Albertine Saxon town of Grossenhayn in 1533. Since the end of the fifteenth century, Saxony had been split into Ernestine, or princely Saxony, ruled by an elector prince, and Albertine Saxony ruled by a duke. Frederick the Wise, the prince of Ernestine Saxony, was a strong supporter of Luther, while Duke Georg remained faithful to Catholicism. The rivalry between the two Saxonies, as well as the theological disputes within contemporary Lutheranism, colored Weigel's life and help to explain his religious position. Weigel was born a Catholic, but in 1539 Duke Georg died and was succeeded by his Lutheran brother, Heinrich. Albertine Saxony rapidly was made into a Lutheran state. The now-Lutheran Valentin received ducal support to attend the Prince's School at Meissen and then the University of Leipzig, where he matriculated in 1554. He studied there for nine years before going on to the University of Wittenberg from 1563 to 1567. In November of 1567 Weigel was made pastor of the Saxon city of Zschopau, where he remained until his death in 1588.

Weigel grew up in the midst of a confused and violent time in which the struggles between the Protestant princes and the emperor Charles V convulsed Germany before the Peace of Augsburg in 1555, when the principle "The ruler decides the religion" (*cujus regio, eius religio*) brought an uneasy peace. Even more important for his development were the theological disputes that fractured Lutheranism into contending factions during the three decades after Luther's death in 1546.[187] These quarrels led to political backlash and governmental intervention as witnessed in the Formula of Concord of 1577, in which the elector August forced the theologians to come up with a common statement of belief that eventually led to the publication of the *Book of Concord* in 1580, the collection of the fundamental documents of Lutheranism. This exemplified the Lutheran chapter of the process of confessionalization that was central to both Protestantism and Catholicism in the second half of the sixteenth century.

Weigel was much troubled by these disputes and not happy with the mandated "confessional" solution. These factors are central for understanding his version of Radical Reform. An autobiographical passage in chapter 24 of his *The Golden Grasp (Der güldene Griff)* is revelatory. He recounts, "Before I came to the beginning of the true faith, and also when I believed along with others so as to please the crowd, I was often very worried about this or that article [of faith] and I would have liked to know on what I should have built [my belief]. I took up the books of many authors and read through them. But no satisfaction came to me. My heart was more and more uncertain." Weigel proceeds with a summary of the theological disputes that marked these years and recalls his appeal to the Lord to rescue him from darkness and conflict. The answer God gave him was to turn from the outward books of religious controversy to the interior book of life. He says:

> As I thus called and prayed to the Lord, grace was visited upon me from above. For a book was shown to me that delighted me and illuminated my heart, so that I could judge and know all things [and I] could see more clearly than if all the teachers in the entire world had instructed me with their books. For from it all books had been written since the beginning of the world, and this book is in me and in all human beings. . . . But few indeed could read it. Indeed worse still, many of the worldly wise rejected and denied it [and instead] adhered to the dead letter which is outside them and neglect the book of life which is within them.[188]

Experience and grace brought Weigel to the Radical Spiritualist perspective from which he was able to rise above the confessional divisions of his age. It was to be his life's work to explore the truth of this inner religion.

Weigel's anti-dogmatic and anti-confessional writings grew more radical from his first preserved dissenting works of 1570 until his death. His critical stance toward contemporary quarrels among Christians and his insistence on the indispensability of interior religion led him, like other Spiritualists, to a universalist stance, due to his recognition that true religion is an inner not an outer reality. God offers salvation to all. Weigel, however, did not publish his challenging writings in his lifetime, leaving it to his disciples to see his works into print in the seventeenth century and also to mislead readers by publishing pseudonymous works under his name. Weigel continued to function as the pastor of Zschopau in the belief that his preaching and pastoral activity might help his flock turn to true inner religion, but his pastoral tenure was not free of controversy and trials of conscience. In 1572, a neighboring pastor accused him of doctrinal error and he sent a brief reply to the local superintendent defending his Lutheranism. This, and the support of his parishioners, saved the day. A more ticklish moment arrived when he, along with all other Lutheran pastors, had to sign the Formula of Concord. Weigel did sign, although he did not subscribe to its tenets. This was something that continued to bother his conscience. In his 1584 *Dialogue on Christianity* he tries to provide an explanation, or at least an excuse:

> I did not subscribe to their teaching or human books, but rather since their intention was aimed at the apostolic scripture and the same is to be preferred to all human books, as it should be, I could suffer it. . . . Besides, it all [happened in] a rush or an overhastening, so that one was not permitted to think it over for several days or weeks. . . . Third, I poor Auditor [his figure in the *Dialogue*] didn't see fit to prepare and serve a feast for the devil, knowing that the whole lot would have cried out: "There, there, we knew it all along: he is not in conformity with our doctrine."[189]

Weigel's works are too extensive to be fully surveyed here, but an investigation of his early writings on mysticism and a consideration of the role of mysticism in a few of his later works will provide a perspective on how significant mysticism was to his overall intellectual-spiritual project, a form of universal knowledge.[190] As Alexandre Koyré observed, mysticism is important but is just one of the components in Weigel's thinking.[191] His long theological education gave him considerable knowledge of Western theology back to Augustine at least. He never abandoned Lutheranism, and his thinking was formed in relation to intra-Lutheran disputes. (Weigel kept a high regard for the early writings of Luther and for the Reformer's translation of the Bible.) Weigel was also familiar with some of the Radical Spiritualists, especially Franck. Above all, he was deeply influenced by the magico-alchemical thinking of Paracelsus, or Theophrastus Bombastus of Hochheim (1493–1541).[192] Weigel's Paracelsianism, as well as his broad knowledge of mystical literature, gives his form of Spiritual Radicalism a different flavor from the other figures we have examined.[193]

Weigel's writing career falls into three phases: early writings (1570–71); didactic and sermonic writings (1572–76); and mature writings (1576–84). With regard to the mystical element, Weigel began his writing with three short works largely drawn from late medieval mystical literature, especially the *Theologia Deutsch* and Tauler's sermons.[194] These works also make use of a number of Eckhart sermons that Weigel knew through his reading of the 1522 Basel Tauler edition.[195] The early Tauler editions (1498, 1508) had eighty-four sermons, including about six by Eckhart, who remained unnamed.[196] The Basel edition, put together by the humanist Adam Petri and published in 1521 and in a slightly expanded form in 1522, added much more, especially in a final section of sixty sermons, explicitly introduced as depending on Meister Eckhart. This section begins:

> Here follow some very subtle and very precious sermons of some quite learned and pious fathers and teachers from which you can see that Doctor Tauler has taken some of his foundation; namely and especially Meister Eckhart . . . , who was an especially highly learned man and was so highly informed in the subtleties of natural and divine skills that many learned people of his time did not understand him. Therefore, a part of his teaching in some sections and articles was rejected and still is dangerous reading for simple people.[197]

This edition had a role in the history of Eckhartian mysticism in the early modern period, if only because Weigel was the first of the Radical Reformers to have such detailed knowledge of the Dominican mystic. He also employed other mystics (some cited by Franck), notably Pseudo-Dionysius and Nicholas of Cusa. Weigel thus had extensive acquaintance both with German mystical literature and its foundation in Dionysius.

Weigel's three early mystical works were the *Two Useful Treatises (Zwene Nützliche Traktat)*, that is, *On Conversion (Von der Bekehrung des Menschen)*, and *On Poverty of Spirit or True Released Releasement (Von Armut des Geistes, oder waarer gelassener Gelassenheit)*, and what he called the *Report on "The German Theology" (Bericht zur 'Deutschen Theologie')*.[198] The *Two Useful Treatises* feature so many long citations from Eckhart, Tauler, and the *Theologia Deutsch* that they might seem to be merely anthologies, but this would be incorrect. Weigel set the agenda for each treatise, determining what resources he would use from the mystics to contribute to the proper understanding of that key issue of Reformation theology: justification. "Good readers," he says in his introduction to the two treatises, "in this little book about repentance and poverty of spirit that I have drawn together from the sermons of Tauler, and of which I have also written a good part, will be held up a true essential teaching about how a person should resign himself and must keep himself in his conversion or justification."[199] The list of subjects for the chapters in *On Conversion* (original sin, free will, conversion, the new birth, baptism in water, the nature and character of children of both Christians and heathen, the old and new man, Adam's fall and recovery, and the forgiveness of sins) show how Weigel used mystical themes such as the birth of the Word in the soul to explain Reformation issues such as repentance and the nature of baptism. As the ten brief chapters unfold, Weigel cites the *Theologia Deutsch* (nineteen times) more often than he does Tauler (seven times). He uses Eckhart, though sparingly, in chapters 4 and 10.[200] In chapters 2 and 3, key aspects of what Weigel found in German mysticism emerge: the themes of new birth and deification.[201] Weigel insists that Christ's incarnation makes possible our rebirth and deification, and, like the medieval mystics, he says that the process of deification is passive, not active. God does not want our "cooperation" (*mitwercken*), but "A person must bring in a bare empty suffering [*leiden*] with releasement and giving up of the will, in dying to himself, in being still, for as often as a person goes out of himself with his own will, so often God goes in with his own will."[202] The middle chapters 4–8 are a treatise on the disputes over baptism and original sin that had disturbed the Protestant world for a half-century. Although Weigel cites Luther often, he argues for the supremacy of inner spiritual baptism. In chapter 6 he says, "In short, outer baptism does not make holy, but the indwelling new birth [does] through the Holy Spirit, or through faith." Such inner baptism is universal: "One who has this new birth in him, be it man or woman, young or old, Jew or pagan, Christian or Turk, and the like, will be holy, even if he has not already been baptized with water."[203]

The second of the *Two Useful Treatises* is one of the most profound of the mystical works of the Spiritual Reformers. The fact that Weigel focuses on "poverty of spirit" and "released releasement" (the intensive term was also known to Franck) shows his engagement with German mysticism.[204] He makes use of Eckhart's famous "Poverty Sermon" (Pr. 52), which is quoted extensively in chapter 3.[205] In company with the mid-sixteenth-century anonymous Dutch mystics who wrote the *Evangelical Pearl* and the *Arnhem Mystical Sermons*, Weigel made this challenging text central to his teaching. The first two chapters of *True Poverty of Spirit* employ a still-unidentified Tauler sermon with many Eckhartian overtones. Chapter 3 is essentially a long series of quotations from Eckhart's Pr. 52 with its triple theme that poverty of spirit consists in wanting nothing, knowing nothing, and having nothing. Chapters 4–7 further demonstrate the Lutheran pastor's knowledge of late medieval mysticism. Chapter 4 uses German mystics, along with Franck and Boethius, to show how poverty of spirit is identical with total self-forgetfulness and annihilation of self.[206] Chapter 5 employs Eckhart (Pr. 12), Tauler, and the *Theologia Deutsch* to show how releasement and detachment lead to union with God.[207] Weigel ends this chapter with several quotations from a "Sermon for the Feast of the Birth of John the Baptist" that appeared in the 1522 Basel Tauler: "Releasement is the most noble virtue and goes beyond love and knowledge and vision. For from knowledge and through knowledge many have fallen and been deceived."[208] The same limitations exist with regard to love and vision. "But through releasement or poverty of spirit nobody has fallen, either in heaven or on earth." The sermon citations say that love and knowledge discern that God is "ungraspable" (*vnbegrifflich*) and "without ground" (*vnergrundtlich*). Therefore, a person must turn to "purity of heart" and "detachment from self" (*abgescheydenheit seiner selbst*) to discover that God is perfectly proportioned to him (*Gott Jme Ebenmessig Jst*). To rest quietly in God allows us to hear God speaking within. The chapter closes by putting the sermon's last lines in verse form:

> Love makes me dear to God.
> Knowledge makes me to gaze on God,
> But purity makes me like God.
> Grace makes me worthy of God,
> But purity unites me with God.[209]

The final two chapters of Weigel's poverty treatise take up some major themes of late medieval German mysticism, with occasional appeals to the thought of Paracelsus. Chapter 6, for example, condemns "self-will" (*eigenwille*) as the forbidden fruit that grounds all sin, and counsels that it is only through releasement that the "new birth" into God can be achieved, a birth that leads to living "without a why," as Weigel shows, quoting another Eckhart sermon: "A person who has released all things and himself for all things, and does not seek what is his own and all things, and does all his work without a why, and from love, this person is dead to the whole world, and lives in God and God in him."[210] Finally, chapter 7 discusses how releasement allows the believer to become indifferent to all things, even to being consigned to hell were that God's will (*resignatio ad infernum*). Like Eckhart, Weigel holds that such total surrender to God paradoxically puts the annihilated soul in charge of God, "compelling" God to act through it. While there is little that is new in Weigel's treatise, he has impressively pulled together some of the most challenging teachings of German mysticism in a synthetic presentation.

The third of Weigel's early mystical works, *The Short Report and Introduction to the "German Theology,"* purports to be a commentary but is really an independent treatise that sets out a preliminary version of Weigel's view of God, world, and humanity. The preface praises the *Theologia Deutsch*, once again using it along with Eckhart and Tauler.[211] Weigel then summarizes the message of the text in what he calls "The Short and Essential Report" and gives a brief explanation of the first chapter of the *Theologia*.

Weigel treats the *Theologia Deutsch* as almost the equivalent of scripture, saying that the book, along with the first three chapters of Genesis when read spiritually, contain the whole truth about death in Adam and life in Christ, the good and evil principles in each person.[212] Such antitheses were important to the *Theologia Deutsch* and were to be a feature of Weigel's thinking throughout his life.[213] Based on the scriptural notion of the "key of David" that unlocks the mysteries of the seven seals of the book of Revelation (Isa. 22:22; Rev. 3:7), Weigel says that the *Theologia* has enabled him to identify "the kind of Rule found in the light of nature through which a person can make his reason right-ordered to see what was hitherto dark and hidden," namely, "Every being in a natural way has a desire towards that from which it comes; it loves, seeks and finds the same thing."[214]

There are two essential realities, God and creature, which the Rule helps us to understand in the proper way. God is "the eternal, unchanging, and uncreated Good or Being, of which the mutable, temporal, created being is an image or like a shadow" (1:87). God is directed to himself, because he is from nothing else and above all things. The intellectual creature, on the other hand, both humans and angels, must follow the Rule; that is, because they do not come from themselves, they must direct their desire and intention to God who is their source. Intellectual creatures are endowed with freedom, so it is possible for them to close their desire in on themselves and to fall away from God in sin. In the course of a rather meandering exposition of the fall of Lucifer and Adam's fall (1:87–100), Weigel touches on themes that were to remain constant in his writings. God is characterized as the Supreme Light, who creates the universe in such a way that he is the being of all things (*esse omnium*), a Dionysian theme (1:99, 105).[215] Weigel later explains this in terms taken from Nicholas of Cusa. Using the example of a nut in which is found the roots, trunk, branches, and leaves of the tree, although the nut is not any of these, he says, "So God is the being of all beings, and the life of all living things *complicative* [i.e., as enfolding them all], and yet God is not the creature, *scilicet explicative* [i.e., as unfolded in creaturely existence]."[216] Following Eckhart, Adam is described as "a perfect image of God" (*eine vollkommene Bildnuss Gottes*), set "in the middle of time and eternity," and destined to enjoy face-to-face vision of God in heaven. "As little as the Kingdom of God, which is God himself, can be bound to any one place, so each believer bears all things with himself in this world."[217] The notion of humanity as created to God's image, long central to Christian theological anthropology, also finds a prominent place in Weigel's thought.[218] Employing language dear to the German mystics, Weigel says that God is present in the ground of the soul: "the perfect Good will be found, felt, and tasted in the inner ground of the soul; just where the creature ends, God begins."[219]

God's inner presence can be attained only through the "inner light of faith or grace," not the outer "light of nature." This inner light leads us to the self-annihilation and releasement that Weigel had already discussed in the two earlier short treatises. "When I completely die to myself and become nothing, God will become alive in me, he will be everything in me, and God [will be] the person, and the person will remain under God as nothing else but a tool."[220] Thus, the emphasis on God's action and human passive reception, already seen in the early treatises, resurfaces here. "Now as much as the creature lets itself go, so much will God enter in and will himself [become] the person. God wishes to take the person totally to himself and to be all in all, and yet not without the person. The person can accomplish nothing without God and God will do nothing without the person, and therefore God expresses himself actively and the person passively."[221] Releasement (*Gelassenheit*), passivity, and annihilation form the path to the new birth realized through Christ, which was to become a dominant theme in the later Weigel. He says, "It is not beyond our understanding that we can advance to the new birth, because to believers all things are possible, and the spiritual person searches out all things, even the depths of the Godhead [1 Cor. 2:10]); even more can the believer know of what is under God through Christ."[222] The new birth makes us into children of God with Christ: "The knowledge through faith makes us children of God and we are heirs and co-heirs with Christ" (*seinen Erben vnd Miterben mit Christo*; 1:108). Where there is belief, we find not only the new birth but also justification, forgiveness of sins, and life and eternal happiness (1:109). Toward the end of *The Short Report,* Weigel gives five rules for reading the *Theologia Deutsch,* as well as a brief synopsis of Eckhart's Sermon 52 under the title, "A person shall be without knowing, without willing, without loving, and without worrying, or, as Eckhart [says], 'A person shall know nothing, have nothing, will nothing." He closes the treatise with eight rhyming couplets summarizing his mystical teaching. These couplets provide a good sense of what Weigel gleaned from the *Theologia Deutsch* and its forebears: "As long as you seek 'I,' 'mine,' 'me,' 'what is,' / You will not find true Knowledge. / If you want to live in Christ as God, / You have to give him up totally. . . . / If you want to be united to God, / live for his will alone. / Let your own will die / in order to gain the highest Good."[223]

Weigel's important Latin work, the *Blessed Life (De vita beata)*, belongs to this early period (1570–71). It is more philosophical in nature, a consideration of human destiny and happiness based mostly on Boethius's *Consolation of Philosophy* as interpreted through a commentary ascribed to Thomas Aquinas but actually written by the fourteenth-century author William Wheatley. Again, the treatise is more than an anthology, because it shows Weigel mining mystical and philosophical resources to defend his view that inner religion, not external practices, and devotion to God, not doctrinal squabbles, are the foundation of the blessed life, both here and in heaven. In the preface dedicated to "Johann Bufler, student of mystical truth, friend, and his very dear compatriot," Weigel says that the aim of the book is "that he may recognize that the true homeland or Highest Good rests within us, and is not to be sought outside in particular things." The goal is union with God, namely, "that you give yourself to the contemplative life, and finally, when all created things are exceeded, you may cast yourself from divine love into the fountain of the abyss, so that you may become one with the One Itself, in whom all things are one, and this is eternal life."[224] This language has a Dionysian ring, and, indeed, several of the twenty-seven chapters of the work quote the *Divine Names*.[225] In the short Latin tract titled *On Divine Light and Darkness (De luce et caligine divina)*, which appeared in the first printing of the *Blessed Life* in 1609, the Dionysian *Mystical Theology* is also used.[226] Other mystical sources cited in the *Blessed Life* include Cusanus (chaps. 23 and 24), Tauler, the *Theologia Deutsch*, and the *Imitation of Christ* (chaps. 25 and 26).[227]

Weigel's early works form a distinct mystical group. The Lutheran pastor never lost his interest in mystical literature and continued to cite Eckhart, Tauler, the *Theologia Deutsch*, and other mystical texts throughout his later writings. The later works, however, advance Weigel's own thinking using philosophical and theosophical conceptions often dependent on Paracelsus. As Andrew Weeks put it, "Weigel's original thinking is informed by Eckhart and yet, at the same time, it is distinct and original."[228] A detailed analysis of Weigel's later works cannot be pursued here,[229] but a brief glance at several of his speculative writings can show how he continued to use German mysticism as a component in his mature theological/pansophical syntheses.

Self-knowledge as the path to true knowledge of God had been a part of Christian reflection almost from its origins. Christian authors loved to cite the axiom ascribed to the Delphic oracle, "Know yourself" (*Gnothi seauton*). It is not surprising that Weigel's earliest independent work, dating to about 1571, takes as its title *Gnothi seauton, Nosce teipsum.*[230] Anthropology and epistemology were important for Weigel throughout his writings. True knowing as inner appropriation of truth, in contrast to an objective sense of knowing as finding the truth that is "out there in things," was one of Weigel's essential teachings. It was his response to the warring doctrinal parties of his age, which insisted that they alone had the truth. When parties disagreed over objective truth, only inner truth could be relied upon. The principle "Knowing is in the knower, not in the thing known" was foundational for Weigel's subsequent writings.[231]

The printed form of the *Gnothi seauton* consists of two books, the first of twenty-one chapters (only fourteen chapters in the manuscript) dealing with natural knowing, and a second book about the supernatural knowing of faith also in twenty-one chapters (thirteen in the manuscript). The notion of the human as the microcosm, or small world, conforming to the macrocosm of the universe, is the starting point of the treatise (part 1, chap. 2). Thus, to know the human being is to know the whole universe. The microcosm/macrocosm motif was as old as Plato, but Weigel's appropriation of the theme came from Paracelsus.[232] Weigel goes on to examine tripartite parallels between the two worlds,[233] especially the theme of the three eyes of the human being—the eye of flesh, the eye of reason, and the mental eye—a constant theme in his writings taken over from Hugh of St. Victor.[234] Chapters 12–14 in the printed form (not found in the manuscript) emphasize other dimensions of Weigel's thought: that knowledge of scripture comes only from the inner eye, not from the outer letter (chap. 12); that both natural knowing and supernatural knowing are perfected in humanity (chap. 13); and that all external books only serve as reminders for the truth hidden within the mind (chap. 14).

The second book of *Gnothi seauton*, on supernatural knowledge, features the contrast between Adam and Christ, the natural "Old Man" and the "New Man" of supernatural life. Both men are found in all humans, as the title to chapter 4 explains, "The two persons, Adam and Christ, are not outside us (as the world thinks), but must be recognized within us, so that we can philosophize essentially in Christ." Hence, we have to recognize, as Sebastian Franck did, that each person is his own worst enemy (chaps. 5–6). In chapter 7 (= chap. 13 in the printed version), Weigel pursues the mystical theme of the kingdom of God as being within the soul. To explain this he gives a long quotation from a sermon on the Samaritan woman ascribed to Tauler in the 1522 Basel edition, but which is now recognized as being by Eckhart.[235] The remaining chapters (chaps. 14–21 in the printed text) draw on Franck, the *Theologia Deutsch*, and Tauler's sermons to show how the new birth becomes available to us through Christ.[236] The conclusion, or appendix, in both the manuscript and printed versions, contains a treatment of the mutuality of seeing between God and the intellectual creature that comes close to the Eckhartian theme, "The eye with which I see God is the same eye with which God sees me."[237] Weigel says, "When the Father sees his child, he sees himself, for whoever sees his image, sees himself, and as you walk before a mirror and find your image in it, and you see your image (that is, you see yourself), you also see the inconceivable and unchangeable God himself through his image, through his Firstborn Son, who is his will, his hand, his eye, and his Word, Christ is the perfect Image." All created things are made through this perfect Image, through whom they can come to knowledge of the Father. "Therefore, he [the Father] has born for himself an Image from himself, in which he sees himself, and through this Son he grants all creatures to recognize him, and no one can come to the inconceivable and invisible Father save in, with, and through the Son." Weigel finds a scriptural foundation for this inner seeing in John 14:7–9.[238]

The only two treatises of Weigel currently available in English, *On the Place of the World (Vom Ort der Welt)* of 1576 and *The Golden Grasp (Der güldene Griff)* of 1578, form a nice contrast, as pointed out by Andrew Weeks.[239] *The Place of the World* proceeds from the outside world into the inner world, both of the human spirit and the Divine Spirit. *The Golden Grasp*, on the other hand, moves from the inner presence of God out into the created universe.

The Place of the World is divided into two sections: the first ten chapters are a geographical and cosmographical treatment of the nature of place, while chapters 11–29 provide a speculative consideration of the relation of place and spirit. In the first part, Weigel shows how every bodily thing in the universe has its place, but that the world itself cannot be said to have a place, because "[t]he visible world stands in itself, and in accordance with its external aspect it stands in the depths, within the abyss of infinity" (chap. 10; trans., 89). This observation provides the starting point of the longer, second part, as chapter 11 explains why the world has no place and goes on to show how this is also true of God and of spiritual creatures, such as angels. Near and far are the same for the spirit, as Weigel explains citing an Eckhart sermon and other sources.[240] Chapters 13 and 14 discuss the ideal or virtual existence of the visible world in the depths of God, using Nicholas of Cusa and the *Theologia Deutsch.* The essential point is that this form of presence continues to remain true of spiritual beings, even after the creation of the physical universe—they are in God and God is in them. "He is our paradise, our heaven and bliss," says Weigel, "not outside of us but rather within us, therefore bound to no locale, place, ceremonies, gestures, or persons, as some teach against God [that the kingdom of heaven] is linked to ceremonies; it is instead in us, in the inner ground of the soul."[241]

The implications of the true meaning of place are discussed in the remainder of the text (chaps. 18–29), particularly with regard to the proper understanding of heaven and hell, which must be seen as realities internal to souls, not "places." The proper place of rational creatures is in Christ as the Word and Image of God, who is identified with the Will of God (chap. 17). Hence, spiritual practice consists of giving up and abandoning our own will and putting ourselves (or better, allowing ourselves to be put) back into the will of God or Christ. This is rebirth, and Weigel expresses the hope, "Let everyone experience it within himself" (chap. 18; trans., 113). In chapter 22, Weigel introduces what was to become a major motif of his later writings, that is, the claim that in the world to come we will need to be born again, taking on "a supernatural celestial body incarnated from the Holy Spirit," just as the body of Jesus was not coarse material flesh drawn from Adam but rather "a supernatural, celestial, clarified body."[242] The notion of the "heavenly flesh of Christ," originally found in some early Christian Gnostics, was revived by some Radical Reformers of the sixteenth century, such as Melchior Hoffmann and Caspar Schwenckfeld.[243] The last chapters of *The Place of the World* expand upon the role of Christ and rebirth in him. God becomes human in Christ, so Christ or the Will of God is "the single center, and the Unitary [*das einig*] is [identical] with this center" (chap. 26; trans., 134). Chapter 27 continues this reflection, noting that "God is not only a center but a circle of all creatures, that is, God and his will or Word is not only in all creatures but also outside of them, conceiving and encompassing them. . . . Everything has to be in God in accordance with its being, but not according to will" (trans., 135). Therefore, the task of the believer is to remove his or her contrary will through self-abandonment and poverty of spirit in order to achieve rebirth and union of wills with God, "so that God is in me and I am in God, and I and God are one in will" (chap. 28; trans., 138). Weigel says, "There must be a dying, there must be an abandoning of self within and without, in spirit and in nature, if God is to become human in you, that is, should you be born of God for heaven" (chap. 28; trans., 140). Thus the believer becomes another God incarnate.

The Golden Grasp has a similar message but is both more religious in expression (each chapter ends with a prayer) and more polemical, as Weigel strongly criticizes the "pseudo-theologians" of the universities who have perverted true faith with their emphasis on externals.[244] Only the true faithful, like Weigel, who have attained "the golden grasp" of inner faith, can speak about it. Like the *Gnothi seauton*, a number of whose chapters appear here in a recast form, the treatise centers on the nature of the true supernatural knowing that comes from within the heart. "More than any other work," according to Andrew Weeks, "*The Golden Grasp* synthesizes Weigel's themes, interpreting them both as a whole and in what appears to be a personal light."[245] Many of these themes have now become familiar: the human as microcosm (chap. 15); insistence that truth comes from within, not from outside (chaps. 2, 9, 10, 21, 22); the reciprocity of knowledge of self and knowledge of the universe (preface); the three eyes of the soul (chaps. 4, 7, 8); reading books, even the Bible, only in order to confirm the inner message of God written in the soul (chaps. 16, 20); and the distinction between two kinds of knowledge and wisdom—active natural knowing and supernatural knowing in which we are passive to God's infusion of grace (chaps. 5, 6, 12, 15).[246] Both natural and supernatural knowing flow from within, not from external objects, but as chapter 12 points out, "The supernatural knowledge is not based on the capability from nature; instead, grace acts at the point where the human being with all his reason and wisdom comes into a quiet silence when God pours himself into the passive eye, when the human being only waits and receives, and God gives and effects."[247] Supernatural knowledge does, indeed, come from the *objectum*, that is, God as the source; nevertheless, it does not come *from the outside*, because God is always present within the soul and hence knowledge flows from the inside out. Weigel cites the *Theologia Deutsch* in this connection, but this was the constant teaching of the German mystics.

The later chapters of *The Golden Grasp* demonstrate Weigel's growing ability to synthesize his message about spiritual religion. Chapter 13, for example, pushes what we have seen at the end of the *Gnothi seauton* about the identity of the divine and human eye into a succinct formula close to the original Eckhartian version. Emphasizing the necessity for total passivity on the part of the human eye of knowing, Weigel says:

> From this *objectum*, or thing vis-à-vis, knowledge flows into the eye as soon as it comports itself passively, so that God knows himself through himself. . . . Thus, he is the eye and the knowledge itself, in, with, and through the human being, as through his obedient tool. . . . But it is even more amazing still that God or the *objectum* should be the very eye in the human being. Yet whoever knows Christ dare not be amazed at anything. . . . Our eyes are God's eyes; they see what God wants and not what we want.[248]

This is a reaffirmation of an insight found in Eckhart's mysticism, but it is interesting to see what Weigel does with it, because the chapter ends with the affirmation that understanding this truth leads to membership "in the unity of the holy church, which is an assembly of all the faithful in the peace of Christ and indissoluble unity." Eckhart would not have disagreed with this language; but Weigel, living in the midst of the fractured Christianity of the sixteenth century, held that "the unity of the holy church" embraces not only all real Christians but also the truly religious people of other faiths.

From the viewpoint of the mystical dimensions of Weigel's Spiritualism as found in *The Golden Grasp*, there are a number of themes that echo what we have seen in the earlier works. Prominent among these is the contrast, taken over at least in part from the *Theologia Deutsch*, of Adam versus Christ, the bad seed and the good seed in all humans. Salvation means being reborn within the "spirit of God, the Word of God, or Christ in us, indwelling through faith" (chap. 15; trans., 187). Like Eckhart and Tauler, Weigel counsels that the only way to the kingdom of heaven is by turning within with total *Gelassenheit*: a person must "turn inward into the innermost ground of the soul, awaiting God within himself in silent releasement, and coming into a forgetfulness of self and of all things" in order to be divinely illuminated.[249] Later in the same chapter 8, Weigel returns to his favorite Eckhart Sermon 52. Talking about how the highest eye of the soul, the mental eye, can arrive at illumination, he says, "If the uppermost eye, that is the reason, is to know and see an invisible thing, reason must remain silent. If the uppermost eye is to be illuminated, it must do nothing, see nothing, know nothing [*so muss es nichts wirchen, nichts sehen, nichts wissen*]; it must rest in a Sabbath awaiting God."[250] This kind of seeing is a divine seeing, as set forth in chapter 13. At the very end of the treatise, Weigel strikes another note reminiscent of Eckhart: "It must be necessarily concluded that there is a supernatural passive knowledge of truth, in which the human being is passive and remains still. For this, one must obtain understanding through prayer. . . . To ask, however, means to wait for God in spirit and truth, to hear the Father, to learn from the Holy Spirit, as supernatural knowledge requires."[251]

Weigel went on to write more treatises, exegetical and theological, between 1578 and 1584. His *Dialogue on Christianity*, sometimes said to be his most mature work, is even more critical of the religious world in which he lived than *The Golden Grasp*. Adopting the ancient dialogue form allowed Weigel to dramatize his religious views in a more indirect and perhaps safer way than his treatises, although this work also was not published until after his death. Three conversation partners (the Preacher, the Hearer, and Death) converse about the meaning of faith. The Preacher (*Conciniator*) represents dogmatic Lutheranism, while the lay Hearer (*Auditor*) is Weigel and all those who question the rigid dogmatism of the learned religious. Weigel's antiestablishment and universalist view of true Christianity, espoused by the Auditor, is, not surprisingly, vindicated by Death, who is an egalitarian Christ who teaches the readers how to die and arise to new life. As he approached his own death, Valentin Weigel became more and more profoundly disappointed in the state of Christianity.

Weigel meditated deeply on the texts of German mysticism. In the context of late-sixteenth- and early-seventeenth-century German thought, his turn to Paracelsian speculation was significant. More than Karlstadt, Müntzer, Denck, and even Franck,[252] Weigel sought to find a systematic viewpoint, theological and cosmological, as well as anthropological and epistemological, for his spiritual view of true religion. In this effort, he was a predecessor of a better-known figure, Jacob Boehme, who will be treated in the next chapter. Weigel, however, was more than just a forerunner. The seventeenth-century publication of his own works, along with some pseudonymous writings, made him a *bête noire* to the orthodox Lutheran tradition. In his own right, however, Weigel was an independent speculative thinker with strong mystical tendencies, perhaps the most impressive of the Radical Reformers.

Conclusion

Is there, then, a mysticism of the Radical Reformation? The answer lies very much in the eye of the beholder and in the conception of mysticism being used. The historiography of the question is revealing. In 1928, the Quaker scholar Rufus M. Jones treated all the figures considered here, as well as others, under the rubric of "Spiritual Reformers," considering them predecessors of the Quakers and not hesitating to describe them as "mystics." In 1973, Steven E. Ozment argued that Müntzer, Denck, Franck, Weigel, and a few other figures could be seen as mystical dissenters to the Magisterial Reformers. More recent students of the Radicals (e.g., Timothy George, R. Emmet McLaughlin, Andrew Weeks) have not hesitated to use the term "mystical" in relation to the spirituality of the Radical Reformers. The case that I have tried to present in this chapter is that there is a mysticism of the Radical Reformation that was realized, as mysticism always is, in diverse ways in different figures.

We should not conceive of the figures treated here as representing a single approach to the mystical dimension of Christianity, even in the way we speak broadly of a Cistercian mysticism, or a Franciscan mysticism. A more complete theological treatment of the Radicals and the mystical elements in their teaching would show significant differences in their doctrine of God (e.g., with regard to the Trinity), their understanding of Christ (e.g., was his flesh celestial or not?), and their conception of humanity as made to God's image, and in other issues. In their reaction against the Catholicism of their day, as well as the developing orthodoxy of Lutheranism, the Radicals, despite differences among themselves, stressed the primacy of interior religion on issues such as the authority of scripture, the nature of the church, and the role of the sacraments. This shared emphasis on interior religion was much influenced by late medieval German mysticism. As Timothy George put it, "[M]ystical and ascetical impulses from the Middle Ages were blended by the Radicals into their own unique patterns of spiritual life."[253] Mystics such as Tauler, the author of the *Theologia Deutsch*, and Eckhart had insisted that it was only by going within to find God in the ground of the soul that salvation can be realized. The Radical Reformers agreed. The quest for experiencing the immediacy of God in the depths of the soul marked all these figures. The practices that the German mystics taught for facilitating the search for the immediate presence of God, such as recollection, silence, poverty of spirit, releasing the self and all created things (*Gelassenheit*), and even annihilating the created self, were used by many of the Radicals. These practices fostered realizing union with God, which was an important category for some Radicals, although they did not engage in speculative analysis of the meaning of union, or in descriptions of the stages leading to it. The Radicals often used language taken over from late medieval German mysticism that suggests an essential oneness of God and the human, one in which God *is* the soul, at least on some level. What was central to the Radicals in such union was its character as a divine birth, a new creation, a deification of the human person. These were all themes found in late medieval German mystics.

Nonetheless, there were real differences between late medieval German mysticism and the mysticism of the Radicals. The late medieval emphasis on the interior search for God coexisted with acceptance of the external church order of medieval Catholicism with its hierarchy, prayers, practices, and sacraments. The mystics who rejected these things, the so-called Free Spirits, were themselves rejected, not least by figures like Eckhart, Tauler, and their followers. Some have held that it is a logical contradiction to accept the primacy of interior religion and deep union with God and still adhere to the external church; I have argued elsewhere that this need not be the case.[254] The Radical Reformers, however, did feel that it was something of an either/or. The terrible religious quarrels of the sixteenth century, the fact that attempts at Evangelical Reform produced further divisions and more violence, and the observation that rejecting the dogmatism of the pope only led to new forms of dogmatic rigidity pushed many sincere religious people toward positions where all external forms of religion, even the Bible, were secondary and even harmful in the search for salvation. In an era of increasing religious conformity, often mandated by governments for purposes of social control, such views could only be viewed as dangerous. The fact that some of the Radical adherents of inner religion (Müntzer is the example discussed here) eventually argued that radical inwardness should be externally imposed to usher in the millennial kingdom proved that the dangers of social upheaval were real.

There were also other significant differences between the medieval mystics and the Radical Reformers, some mentioned above, that cannot be pursued here. In the long run, however, it is difficult to deny the existence of a mysticism of the Radical Reform, however much we admit the variety among its spokesmen and the complexity of their relation to their forebears in late medieval Germany.

Notes

1. Williams's large book continued to grow in later editions. The third and final edition is *The Radical Reformation*, 3rd ed., Sixteenth Century Essays and Studies 15 (Ann Arbor, MI: Edwards Brothers, 1992), 1,513 pages. See also George H. Williams and Angel M. Mergal, eds., *Spiritual and Anabaptist Writers*, Library of Christian Classics 25 (Philadelphia: Westminster, 1957). This was the first useful English compendium of sources from the Radical Reformation. Since then, many other writings of the radicals have been made available in English.

2. For reflections on the problems of the use of the term "radical," see Adolf Laube, "Radicalism as a Research Problem in the History of the Early Reformation," in *Radical Tendencies in the Reformation: Divergent Perspectives*, ed. Hans J. Hillerbrand, Sixteenth Century Essays and Studies 9 (Ann Arbor, MI: Edwards Brothers, 1988), 9–23; and James M. Stayer, "Introduction: Radicalism and Dissent—A Provisional Assessment," in *Radikalität und Dissent im 16. Jahrhundert / Radicalism and Dissent in the Sixteenth Century*, ed. Hans-Jürgen Goertz and James M. Stayer, Zeitschrift für historische Forschung, Beiheft 27 (Berlin: Duncker & Humblot, 2002), 9–25.

3. A helpful survey is John D. Roth and James M. Stayer, eds, *A Companion to Anabaptism and Spiritualism, 1521–1700*, Brill's Companions to the Christian Tradition 6 (Leiden: Brill, 2007). Shorter introductions include James M. Stayer, "The Radical Reformation," in Brady et al., *Handbook of European History 1400–1600*, 2:249–82; and R. Emmet McLaughlin, "The Radical Reformation," in Hsia, *The Cambridge History of Christianity*, vol. 6, *Christianity: Reform and Expansion 1500–1660*, 37–55.

4. For overviews of the spirituality of the Radical Reformers, see Peter C. Erb, "Anabaptist Spirituality," in Senn, *Protestant Spiritual Traditions*, 80–124; Timothy George, "The Spirituality of the Radical Reformation," in Raitt et al., *Christian Spirituality II: High Middle Ages and Reformation*, 334–71. A number of older works retain value, such as Rufus M. Jones, *Spiritual Reformers in the 16ᵗʰ and 17ᵗʰ Centuries* (London: Macmillan, 1928); Ozment, *Mysticism and Dissent*; and the collection edited by Hans-Jürgen Goertz, ed., *Profiles of Radical Reformers: Biographical Sketches from Thomas Müntzer to Paracelsus* (Kitchener, ON: Herald Press, 1982).

5. For this claim, see Stayer, "Radical Reformation," 249–51.

6. For an introductuion to apocalypticism among the Radicals, see Walter Klassen, *Living at the End of the Ages: Apocalyptic Expectation in the Radical Reformation* (Lanham, MD: University Press of America, 1992).

7. Werner O. Packull, *Mysticism and the Early South German-Austrian Anabaptist Movement, 1525–1531* (Scottdale, PA: Herald Press, 1977).

8. Martyrdom, an important aspect of the mythos of Anabaptism, has been perhaps overstressed in the past. Recent research calculates that there were perhaps five thousand martyrs (those who voluntarily died for their beliefs) during

the Reformation era. About half of these were Anabaptists, which, given their disparity in numbers compared to Catholic and Protestants, is significant. See Brad S. Gregory, *Salvation at Stake: Christian Martyrdom in the Early Modern Period* (Cambridge, MA: Harvard University Press, 1999).

9. On Hans Hut and the relation between his mysticism and that of the late Middle Ages, see Packull, *Mysticism and the Early South German-Austrian Anabaptist Movement*, chapters 3–5.

10. The Anabaptist movement (or movements) had greater structure than the Spiritualists. This means that not only do their descendants continue to exist today as Mennonites, Hutterites, and the like, but that more historical investigation has been devoted to them. For introductions, see James M. Stayer, "The Significance of Anabaptism and Anabaptist Research," in Goertz and Stayer, *Radikalität und Dissent*, 77–78; and Werner O. Packull, "An Introduction to Anabaptist Theology," in Bagchi and Steinmentz, *Cambridge Companion to Reformation Theology*, 194–214, as well as the many essays in Roth and Stayer, *Companion to Anabaptism and Spiritualism, 1521–1700*.

11. On the importance of Strassburg as a center for Reformation currents, see MacCulloch, *Reformation*, 179–89.

12. Much has been written about the tragedy of Münster; for an introduction, see H. C. Erik Midelfort, "Madness and the Millennium at Münster, 1534–1535," in *Fearful Hope: Approaching the New Millennium*, ed. Christopher Kleinhenz and Fannie J. LeMoine (Madison: University of Wisconsin Press, 1999), 115–34.

13. McLaughlin, "Radical Reformation," 17.

14. Karlstadt and Müntzer are treated together by Hans-Jürgen Goertz, "Karlstadt, Müntzer and the Reformation of the Commoners," in Roth and Stayer, *Companion to Anabaptism and Spiritualism, 1521–1700*, 1–44.

15. For a general account, see Ronald J. Sider, *Andreas Bodenstein von Karlstadt: The Development of His Thought, 1517–1525*, Studies in Medieval and Reformation Thought 11 (Leiden: Brill, 1974). For brief summaries, see Ronald J. Sider, "Andreas Bodenstein von Karlstadt: Between Liberal and Radical," in Goertz, *Profiles of Radical Reformers*, 45–53; David Steinmetz, "Andreas Bodenstein von Carlstadt," in idem, *Reformers in the Wings: From Geiler von Kaysersberg to Theodore Beza*, 2nd ed. (Oxford: Oxford University Press, 2001), 123–30; and Ulrich Bubenheimer, "Bodenstein von Karlstadt, Andreas," in *Oxford Encyclopedia*, 1:178–80. Because many of Karlstadt's writings are difficult to find in the original German, I will make use of the anthology by E. J. Furcha, *The Essential Carlstadt: Fifteen Tracts by Andreas Bodenstein (Carlstadt) from Karlstadt*, Classics of the Radical Reformation 8 (Scottdale, PA: Herald Press, 1995).

16. For an engaging account, see Gordon Rupp, "Andrew Karlstadt: The Reformer as Puritan," in idem, *Patterns of Reformation* (London: Epworth, 1969), 49–153.

17. Sigrid Looss ("Radical Views of the Early Andreas Karlstadt [1520–1525]," in Hillerbrand, *Radical Tendencies in the Reformation*, 43–53, puts Karlstadt's increasing radicalization down to his appropriation of the mystical category of *Gelassenheit* as "the motif for his position, in the sense of breaking away and separating from traditional conditions" (47).

18. The famous meeting between Luther and Karlstadt at the Black Bear Inn at Jena, where Luther challenged his former colleague to attack his views in print

by offering him a golden guilder, is recounted in a number of sources. See chapter 3, "Consultation at the Black Bear," in *Karlstadt's Battle with Luther: Documents in a Liberal-Radical Debate*, ed. Ronald J. Sider (Philadelphia: Fortress, 1978), 36–48.

19. *Against the Heavenly Prophets* can be found in WA 18:62–125, and 134–214. On the quarrel between Luther and Karlstadt, see Mark U. Edwards Jr., *Luther and the False Brethren* (Stanford: Stanford University Press, 1975), chapter 2; and Alois M. Haas, *Der Kampf um den Heiligen Geist: Luther und die Schwärmer* (Freiburg, Schweiz: Universitätsverlag, 1997).

20. Rupp, "Andrew Karlstadt," 139: "Karlstadt's program is not only a premonition of the Radical Reformation, but an ingredient in the emergence of the Reformed, as distinct from the Lutheran tradition."

21. On Karlstadt's influence, see Ulrich Bubenheimer, "Karlstadtrezeption von der Reformation bis zum Pietismus im Spiegel der Schriften Karlstadts zur Gelassenheit," in *Andreas Bodenstein von Karlstadt (1486–1541): Ein Theologe der frühen Reformation; Beiträge eines Arbeitsgesprächs vom 24.–25. November 1995 in Wittenberg*, ed. Sigrid Looss and Markus Matthias, Themata Leucoreana (Wittenberg: Hans Lufft, 1998), 25–71.

22. On Karlstadt's relation to the Anabaptist and later Baptist movements, see Calvin Augustine Pater, *Karlstadt as the Father of the Baptist Movements: The Emergence of Lay Protestantism* (Toronto: University of Toronto Press, 1984).

23. Rupp, "Andrew Karlstadt," 152.

24. A general account of Karlstadt's theology can be found in Sider, *Andreas Bodenstein*, chapter 8, "Karlstadt's Orlamünde Theology (1523–early 1525)," 202–303. There are, however, two problems with Sider: (1) a consistent attempt to minimize the differences between Luther and Karlstadt; and (2) a narrow view of the nature of mysticism, especially German mysticism, which leads him to underestimate its role in Karlstadt.

25. Henrik Otto, "Grundlinien der Taulerrezeption Andreas Karlstadts," in *Vor- und frühreformatorische Tauler-Rezeption*, 241–54. Otto shows that Karlstadt studied Tauler intensively, making no fewer that 2,223 marginal notations, though most of these were minor.

26. The *Theologia Deutsch* makes use of the verb *gelassen*, but not the noun *Gelassenheit*, which is found fourteen times in Tauler's sermons.

27. The treatise is translated by Furcha in *Essential Carlstadt*, 27–39.

28. The title in German: *Was gesagt ist / Sich gelassen / und was das wort gelassenheit bedeüt / und wa es in hailiger geschift begriffen.* This was printed twice in 1523 and reprinted three times in the seventeenth century (1618, 1693, and 1698). It is translated by Furcha (*Essential Carlstadt*, 133–68) under the title *The Meaning of the Term Gelassenheit and Where in Holy Scripture It Is Found*.

29. Translated by Furcha, *Essential Carlstadt*, 185–228. Another treatise of Karlstadt that is useful for seeing the mystical dimensions of his theology is the 1524 tract *Regarding the Two Greatest Commandments*, translated by Furcha, 229–46, and in a revised form by Scott Hendrix in *Early Protestant Spirituality*, 151–68.

30. For a survey, see Ludwig Völker, "'Gelassenheit': Zur Enstehung des Wortes in der Sprache Meister Eckharts und seiner Überlieferung in der nacheckhartischen Mystik bis Jacob Böhme," in *'Getempert und Gemischet': Für Wolfgang Mohr zum 65. Geburtstag von seiner Tübinger Schülern*, ed. Franz Hundsnurcher and Ulrich Müller, Göppinger Arbeiten zur Germanistik 65 (Göppingen: Alfred

Kümmerle, 1972), 281–312, which treats Karlstadt on 293–96. On the various understandings of *Gelassenheit* in the German mystics, see the references under "*Gelassenheit* (Releasement)" in the "Index of Subjects," in McGinn, *Harvest*, 718.

31. *Meaning of the Term Gelassenheit*, 135.

32. Ibid., 149.

33. Ibid., 136.

34. Ibid., 138, but my translation is from the German original available in the notes in Sider, *Andreas Bodenstein*, 213 and 229–30.

35. *Meaning of the Term Gelassenheit*, 156. Once again, I translate these texts from the German as given in the notes in Sider, *Andreas Bodenstein*, 226–28. Ecclesiasticus 1:7 was cited by Eckhart and other German mystics as a scriptural warrant for the flowing out and return of all things to their divine source. For another passage on the soul's return to "as it was in the first creation," see *Meaning of the Term Gelassenheit*, 144.

36. Sider denies any return to the pre-creational state, but he has to interpret the texts he cites contrary to what they actually say (e.g., *Andreas Bodenstein*, 218–19, 229–30, 301).

37. On Karlstadt's doctrine of sin, see Sider, *Andreas Bodenstein*, 213–16, who admits considerable dependence on the German mystics.

38. There are a number of passages where Karlstadt asserts that all acts tainted with "mineness" are mortally sinful. For example, "We commit a mortal sin whenever we are afraid, worried, or preoccupied on account of food, or when we trust in, desire, and hope for money and possessions" (*Meaning of the Term Gelassenheit*, 151; see also 160, 167). The puritanical aspect of Karlstadt is evident when he says that "all pleasure is sin" (*Meaning of the Term Gelassenheit*, 139).

39. *Meaning of the Term Gelassenheit*, 140.

40. Ibid., 145–48 and 151. The theme of inner circumcision is also found in Karlstadt's other treatises, such as *Manifold, Singular Will*, 216.

41. *Meaning of the Term Gelassenheit*, 141–42 and 147.

42. The progressive character of *Gelassenheit* appears, for example, in *Meaning of the Term Gelassenheit*, 167; see also *Manifold, Singular Will*, 201.

43. *Meaning of the Term Gelassenheit*, 143–44; see also 154, 155, 157, and 163.

44. Ibid., 143.

45. Ibid., 145–46 and 164.

46. *The Two Greatest Commandments* (Hendrix, *Early Protestant Spirituality*, 154).

47. *Meaning of the Term Gelassenheit*, 144.

48. See ibid., 156–59.

49. Sider (*Andreas Bodenstein*, 254–59) gives a fuller account of "Christ's soteriological role" in Karlstadt's thought.

50. On the importance of the proper relation between the inner and the outer dimensions of faith for Luther, see Hamm, *Early Luther*, 249–52.

51. WA 18:137.5–9 (*Luther's Works* 40:146–47). Luther also criticizes Karlstadt's use of mystical terminology in part 1 (*Luther's Works* 40:88, and 117).

52. WA 18:66.17–20 (*Luther's Works* 40:83).

53. *Meaning of the Term Gelassenheit*, 153–54.

54. For example, *Manifold, Singular Will*, 217: "For this reason a spiritual person is not bound to externals"; and 218: "God's gracious will can be done without any externals." There is a discussion in Sider, *Andreas Karlstadt*, 259–77, "The Problem

of Authority in Theology." Sider minimizes the differences between Luther and Karlstadt but still allows for "a significant spiritualist tendency," which he claims "was still less radically spiritualist than has often been suggested" (276–77).

55. On regeneration as the core of Karlstadt's theology, see Sider, *Andreas Karlstadt*, 212–13, 258–59, and 302–3.

56. *Meaning of the Term Gelassenheit*, 155–56. The original German is available in Sider, *Andreas Bodenstein*, 226–27n121. Deification is mentioned also on 167.

57. I translate here from the German text as given in Sider, *Andreas Bodenstein*, 275–76n288.

58. For passages on union and deification in *Manifold, Singular Will of God*, see Furcha, *Essential Carlstadt*, 186–87, 212, 216–17, and 218–20.

59. "Friend of God" appears eight times in the treatise but is strangely absent from the contemporary *Gelassenheit* treatise.

60. Völker ("'Gelassenheit,'" 296) notes that Carlstadt's view of *Gelassenheit*, for all its differences from the late medieval mystics, did not lose its connection with union.

61. Karlstadt does speak of the *seles grund* from time to time, e.g., at the beginning of *Regarding the Two Greatest Commandments* (Hendrix, *Early Protestant Spirituality*, 153).

62. Accounts that I have found helpful include Rupp, "Thomas Müntzer: The Reformer as Rebel," in idem, *Patterns of Reformation*, 155–353; and Hans-Jürgen Goertz, *Thomas Müntzer: Apocalyptic, Mystic, and Revolutionary* (Edinburgh: T&T Clark, 1993), and more briefly in "Thomas Müntzer: Revolutionary in a Mystical Spirit," in idem, *Profiles of Radical Reformers*, 29–44. For a brief account of Müntzer, see Schreiner, *Are You Alone Wise?*, 92–96. In citing Müntzer, I will generally use the translations of Michael G. Baylor, *Revelation and Revolution: Basic Writings of Thomas Müntzer* (Bethlehem, PA: Lehigh University Press, 1993).

63. An older Marxist account is M. M. Smirin, *Die Volksreformation des Thomas Müntzers und der Grosse Bauernkrieg* (Berlin: Dietz, 1956). More recently, see Günter Vogler, *Thomas Müntzer* (Berlin: Dietz, 1989).

64. A helpful survey of literature on Müntzer and his relation to Luther is Eric W. Gritsch, "Thomas Müntzer and Luther: A Tragedy of Errors," in Hillerbrand, *Radical Tendencies in the Reformation*, 55–83. There is a useful bibliography in Marion Dammaschke and Günter Vogler, *Thomas Müntzer Bibliographie (1519–2012)*, Bibliotheca bibliographica Aureliana 233, Bibliotheca Dissidentium 28 (Baden-Baden: Valentin Koerner, 2013).

65. In my essay "Apocalypticism and Mysticism: Aspects of the History of Their Interaction," *Zeitsprünge: Forschungen zur Frühen Neuzeit* 3 (1999): 292–315, I sketch out the main lines of the relationship of these two elements from the New Testament down to the sixteenth century.

66. For discussions of Müntzer's role in this history, see McGinn, "Apocalypticism and Mysticism," 310–13; and Goertz, *Thomas Müntzer*, 193–207.

67. *On Contrived Faith* (trans. Baylor, 80–81).

68. Müntzer, unlike Luther and Karlstadt, does not talk about his mystical sources, which has given free rein to much speculation. He must have read Tauler and most probably the *Theologia Deutsch*, and he also knew a collection of visionary texts published under the title *Liber trium virorum et trium visibilium virginum*, as well as some other medieval visionary accounts that supported his belief in visions

and revelations. But did he really know other mystical texts, such as the *Book of the Poor in Spirit*, as some have suggested? Two articles investigating Müntzer's mystical sources do not, alas, shed much light on the topic: Max Steinmetz, "Thomas Müntzer und die Mystik: Quellenkritische Bemerkungen," in *Bauer, Reich, und Reformation: Festschrift für Günther Franz zum 80. Geburtstag am 23 Mai 1982*, ed. Peter Blickle (Stuttgart: Ulmer, 1982), 148–59; and Reinhard Schwarz, "Thomas Müntzer und die Mystik," in *Die Theologie Thomas Müntzer: Untersuchungen zu seiner Entwicklung und Lehre*, ed. Siegfried Bräuer and Helmar Junghans (Göttingen: Vandenhoeck & Ruprecht, 1989), 283–301, esp. 283–85. Schwartz does, however, provide a useful sketch of the main themes of Müntzer's mysticism.

69. At the end of *On Contrived Faith*, Müntzer rebuffed accusations that he was dependent on Joachim of Fiore, but admitted that he had read the abbot's *Commentary on Jeremiah* (Baylor trans., 84). On the pseudonymous *Commentary on Jeremiah* (*Super Hieremiam*), the most popular of the works ascribed to Joachim, see Robert Moynihan, "The Development of the 'Pseudo-Joachim' Commentary 'Super Hieremiam': New Manuscript Evidence," *Mélanges de l'école française de Rome: Moyen Age–Temps Modernes* 98 (1986): 109–42.

70. The critical text for the German and Latin is *Thomas Müntzer, Schriften und Briefe: Kritische Gesamtausgabe*, ed. Günther Franz, Quellen und Forschungen zur Reformationsgeschichte 33 (Gütersloh: Gerd Mohn, 1968), 491–511. Although a new critical edition of Müntzer's writings is under way, it is not complete, so I will reference the Franz edition. Franz edits the shorter and longer German versions of the Prague Manifesto (491–511). I will use Baylor's translation of the long version in *Revelation and Revolution*, 53–60.

71. *Prague Manifesto* (Franz ed., 496.1–9; Baylor trans., 53).

72. Müntzer rarely speaks of Christ as the Bridegroom. Along with this text (Franz ed., 498.6–18; Baylor trans., 55), see the longer passage in a letter of May 30, 1524, to Christoph Meinhard, containing an exposition of Psalm 19 (Franz ed., 402–3; trans. Baylor, 166).

73. By the time Müntzer delivered his "Sermon to the Princes" in July of 1524 he had come to recognize the need for some kind of unspecified discernment of spirits (see Baylor, 112–13).

74. *Prague Manifesto* (Franz ed., 498.23–30; Baylor trans., 55).

75. *Prague Manifesto* (Franz ed., 500–501; Baylor trans., 56–57).

76. *Prague Manifesto* (Franz ed., 504.19–22; Baylor trans., 59).

77. The letter is translated in Baylor, 179.

78. The Letter to the League was written April 26 or 27, 1525 (Baylor trans., 191–92).

79. There is an edition of the "Fürstenpredigt" in *Thomas Müntzer: Politische Schriften*, ed. Carl Hinrichs (Halle: Niemeyer, 1950), 1–28. For a translation, see Baylor, 98–114. In this work Müntzer rejects the pacifist view of apocalypticism, that is, that the role of the elect is to faithfully suffer while awaiting divine vindication (Baylor trans., 112–13). There are many discussions of this text; see, e.g., Goertz, *Thomas Müntzer*, 119–29.

80. *Sermon to the Princes* (Baylor trans., 113).

81. The text is in *Schriften und Briefe*, 387–88. The passage that follows here is Franz, 387.19–23; Baylor trans., 157–58.

82. For background, see Bernard McGinn, "The Abyss of Love," in *The Joy of*

Learning and the Love of God: Studies in Honor of Jean Leclercq, ed. E. Rozanne Elder, Cistercian Studies 160 (Kalamazoo, MI: Cistercian Publications, 1995), 95–120; and "Lost in the Abyss: The Function of Abyss Language in Medieval Mysticism," *Franciscan Studies* 73 (2014): 373–89.

83. As far as I can determine, Müntzer rarely uses *grund*, preferring *abgrund*.

84. This text, the *Ausgedrückte Entblössung des Falschen Glaubens* is found in *Schriften und Briefe*, 265–319 (Baylor trans., 115–38). I give the German of this important passage (274.5–17): ". . . do die krafft der allerhoechsten (wie Luce am ersten und letsten beschriben) allen getichten, heymlichen unglauben verwirfft auffs allergestrackste, den er wirt entdeckt durch das anthuon oder durchgang im abgrund der seelen. Paulus sagt: 'Ir solt Christen anthuon', do kan der falsche glaub ueberal keyn stat haben. Wer aber disen durchgang nicht gehabt, der weyss vom glauben gantz und gar nichts."

85. The text is in Franz ed., 21–24 (Baylor trans., 61–63, but without the preface).

86. Franz ed., 21 (my trans.): "Nach der swacheyth, dye dye auserwelten menschen yn der gelassenheit haben, gibt er yhn unde zeuth sye an mit der stercke, dye von ym apgehet."

87. References to poverty of spirit occur eight times in the texts translated by Baylor.

88. Franz ed., 23.5–10 (Baylor trans., 61).

89. On the importance of experienced faith for Müntzer, see Ozment, *Mysticism and Dissent*, 94–96.

90. Found in Franz ed., 424–27 (Baylor trans., 182–84).

91. Franz ed., 425.6–13 (Baylor trans., 183).

92. Again, I provide the German for this important passage (425.19–24): "Dusse erdulden nicht den swynden screyber, der do screybet nicht mit tynten adder ander materien, sundern myt den griffel seyns geysts yn apgrundt der seln, do der mensche erkent, das her sey eyn son Gottis, und Christus sey der uberste yn den sonen Gottis. Wan das alle auserwelten seynt von gnaden, das ist her durch gotlich nature."

93. Franz ed., 426.28–29.

94. The two forms of the *Ausgedrückte Entblössung* are available in *Schriften und Briefe*, 265–319; the main form is translated in Baylor, 115–38. Helpful for situating these mystical themes within the full context of Müntzer's theology is Rupp, "The Gospel according to Thomas Müntzer," chapter 19 in idem, *Patterns of Reformation*, 251–304. See also the analysis by Ozment, *Mysticism and Dissent*, 79–97.

95. Franz ed., 272.30–33 (Baylor trans., 117).

96. Franz ed., 277.23–25 (Baylor trans., 119).

97. Franz ed., 281.16–32 (Baylor trans., 121).

98. Franz ed., 292.1–8 (Baylor trans., 126).

99. Franz ed., 300.34–301.11 (Baylor trans., 130 modified): "Ja, drumb ist in also spoetlich, das sie die langweyl nit gekost haben, durch welche Gottes werck allein erfunden wirt, psalm 40, zum ersten durch die besprengung, nume. 19, da die wasser goetlicher weyssheyt sich erregen, eccle. 15. Da wirt der traurig gewar, das Got gantz ueberschweckliche ding an im anhebet. Drumb entsetzt er sich zum ersten vor Gottes namen, der im eroeffnet wirt aus der ersten bewegung goettlichs wercks." The term *langweil*, found a few other times in Müntzer, seems to

be something like *Gelassenheit*. Some authors (e.g., Rupp, *Patterns of Reformation*, 338–39) have claimed that it is typical of German mysticism, but it seems rare among these mystics. For a selection of texts, see Rupp, *Patterns*, 283–84.

100. Franz ed., 308.31–309.7 (Baylor trans., 133).

101. Franz ed., 309.39–310.27 (trans. Baylor, 134).

102. Franz ed., 318.29–37 (trans. Baylor, 138).

103. A text from Müntzer's German liturgy explaining the "Sanctus" invokes the Father giving birth to the Son in the soul: "Nemlich: er sol und muss wissen, das God in ym sey, das er yn nicht austichte odder ausssinne, wie er tausent meilen von ym sey, sonder wie himel und erden vol, vol Gottes seint, und wie der vatter den son in uns on unterlass gebiret, und der heilige geist nit an ders dan den gecreutzigten in uns durch hertzliche betrubniss ercleret" (Franz ed., 210.33–211.2; see Baylor trans., 88).

104. On of the few mentions of union I have found is in the treatise *On Contrived Faith* 12, which says of the patriarchs of the Old Testament, "None of them was united [*mit yme eins geworden ist*] with God until he had triumphed over his suffering" (Franz ed., 223.12–14; Baylor trans., 81).

105. For introductions to Hans Denck, see Rufus Jones, "Hans Denck and the Inward Word," in idem, *Spiritual Reformers in the 16th and 17th Centuries*, 17–30; Steven Ozment, "Hans Denck," in *Mysticism and Dissent*, 116–33; Werner Packull, "Hans Denck: Fugitive from Dogmatism," in Goertz, *Profiles of Radical Reformers*, 62–71; and Geoffrey Dipple, "The Spiritualist Anabaptists," in Roth and Stayer, *Companion to Anabaptism and Spiritualism, 1521–1700*, 257–71.

106. On the ambiguities of the term "Spiritual Anabaptist," see Dipple, "Spiritual Anabaptists," 257–60.

107. Denck's writings are edited by Georg Baring and Walter Fellmann, *Hans Denck Schriften*, 3 vols. (Gütersloh: Bertelsmann, 1955-60). I will use the English translation of Edward J. Furcha, *Selected Writings of Hans Denck* (Pittsburgh: Pickwick, 1975), reissued in an expanded form as *Selected Writings of Hans Denck 1500–1527* (Lewiston, NY: Edwin Mellen, 1989). There are also translations of *Concerning True Love* and *Divine Order* in *Early Anabaptist Spirituality*, ed. and trans. Daniel Liechty, Classics of Western Spirituality (New York: Paulist Press, 1994), 111–34. Selections from Denck's writings with the German original can be found in Clarence Bauman, *The Spiritual Legacy of Hans Denck: Interpretation and Translation of Key Texts*, Studies in Medieval and Reformation Thought 47 (Leiden: Brill, 1991).

108. For a discussion of the evolution and ambiguities of the term, see R. Emmet McLaughlin, "Spiritualism," in *Oxford Encyclopedia*, 4:105–7.

109. I use the translation in Furcha (1975), 13–23, in what follows.

110. See Schreiner, *Are You Alone Wise?*, 247–50.

111. It is revealing that, although the title of chapter 10 of the treatise *Divine Order* (Furcha 1975, 93–94) says it is about the Trinity, it never actually mentions the three persons.

112. On God as Perfect Love, see *Concerning Genuine Love* (Furcha 1975, 102–3), while chapter 1 of *Divine Order* (Furcha 1975, 78–79) emphasizes God's goodness. *Whether God Is the Cause of Evil* mentions Exodus 3:14 on God as "He who is" (Furcha 1989, 210).

113. *Whether God Is the Cause of Evil* (Furcha 1989, 183); and *Divine Order*, chapter 1 (Furcha 1975, 78–80).

114. Denck, *The Law of God* (Furcha 1975, 64).

115. *Recantation* IV (Furcha 1975, 126).

116. On inherent faith, see *Law of God* (Furcha 1975, 49–53); *Recantation* III (Furcha 1975, 125).

117. *Recantation* I (Furcha 1975, 124).

118. On Denck's final views on baptism and the Lord's Supper, see *Recantation* VIII and IX (Furcha 1975, 128–30).

119. *Whether God Is the Cause of Evil* (Furcha 1989, 198–99, 209).

120. *Concerning Genuine Love* (Furcha 1975, 104; see 103–6, and 118–19).

121. *Concerning Genuine Love* (Furcha 1975, 101). A note on this passage (Furcha, 154) suggests that this is close to the definition of love that Luther gives in his *Lectures on Romans* (WA 56:241.5ff.).

122. *Divine Order*, chapters 6–7 (Furcha 1975, 86–88).

123. *Whether God Is the Cause of Evil* (Furcha 1989, 187–90; quotation from 190). For other appearances of *Gelassenheit* translated as "yieldedness," see Furcha 1989, 194 and 201.

124. *Whether God Is the Cause of Evil* (Furcha 1989, 191).

125. *Whether God Is the Cause of Evil* (Furcha 1989, 194–95).

126. *Recantation*, Prologue (Furcha 1975, 122–23). See also *Law of God* (Furcha 1975, 45–46).

127. *Whether God Is the Cause of Evil* (Furcha 1989, 191–92, 201, and 211).

128. "Friends of God" is found in *Divine Order* and *Concerning Genuine Love* (Furcha 1975, 80, 84, 112, and 117).

129. *Whether God Is the Cause of Evil* (Furcha 1989, 197). See also Furcha, 200, which uses the term *vergottet*.

130. *Confession* (Furcha 1975, 21).

131. *Law of God* (Furcha 1975, 72).

132. *Divine Order*, chapter 8 (Furcha 1975, 90). See also chapters 4 and 5 (Furcha 83, 85).

133. *Concerning Genuine Love* (Furcha 1975, 104–5).

134. Among the English treatments of Franck, see Rufus Jones, "Sebastian Franck: An Apostle of Inward Religion," in *Spiritual Reformers in the 16th and 17th Centuries*, 46–63; Hans J. Hillerbrand, "The Lonely Individualist: *Sebastian Franck*," in idem, *A Fellowship of Discontent* (New York: Harper & Row, 1967), 31–64; Steven Ozment, "Sebastian Franck," in idem, *Mysticism and Dissent*, 137–67; George Huntston Williams, "Sebastian Franck, 1531, to his Death in 1542," in idem, *Radical Reformation* (3rd ed.), 694–703; and Patrick Hayden-Roy, "Franck, Sebastian," in *Oxford Encyclopedia*, 2:134–35. There is more literature in German, especially Siegfried Wollgast, *Der deutsche Pantheismus der 16. Jahrhundert: Sebastian Franck und seine Wirkungen auf die Entwicklung der pantheistischen Philosophie in Deutschland* (Berlin: Deutscher Verlag der Wissenschaften, 1972); and the essays in Jan-Dirk Müller, ed., *Sebastian Franck (1499–1542)*, Wolfenbütteler Forschungen 56 (Wiesbaden: Harrassowitz, 1993). Still useful despite its age is Alfred Hegler, *Geist und Schrift bei Sebastian Franck* (Freiburg-im-Breisgau: J. C. B. Mohr, 1892). For a bibliography, see Christoph Dejung, "Sebastian Franck," in *Bibliotheca Dissidentium*, vol. 7 (Baden-Baden: Valentin Koerner, 1986), 39–119.

135. This is the thesis of Hegler, *Geist und Schrift*, esp. 30–48. I thank Andrew Weeks for his comments on this. For Althamer, see the brief summary of Irmgard Höss, "Althamer, Andreas," in *Oxford Encyclopedia*, 1:21.

136. On the relations between Franck and Schwenkfeld, see R. Emmet McLaughlin, "Sebastian Franck and Caspar Schwenkfeld: Two Spiritualist *Viae*," in Müller, *Sebastian Franck (1499–1542)*, 71–86.

137. A critical edition of Franck's works in under way, but only three volumes have appeared, mostly of the historical writings. See *Sebastian Franck, Sämtlicher Werke: Kritische Ausgabe mit Kommentar*, ed. Peter Klaus Knauer (Bern: Peter Lang, 1992–). Many of Franck's works are only available in rare sixteenth-century editions, or in modern photographic reprints.

138. For a partial edition and study, see Alfred Hegler, ed., *Sebastian Francks lateinischen Paraphrase der Deutschen Theologie und seine holländisch erhaltenen Traktate* (Tübingen: G. Schnürlen, 1901).

139. The most helpful analyses of the role of German mysticism in Franck are Ozment, "Sebastian Franck"; and Otto Langer, "Inneres Wort und inwohnender Christus: Zum mystischen Spiritualismus Sebastian Francks und seiner Implikation," in Müller, *Sebastian Franck (1499–1524)*, 55–69. Both authors, in my opinion, tend to overstress the similarities between Franck and the German mystics.

140. The essential difference between Franck and the mystics on *Heilsgeschichte* and the institutional church have been noted by Hillerbrand, "Lonely Individualist," 53–54.

141. McLaughlin, "Spiritualism: Schwenkfeld and Franck and Their Early Modern Resonances," in Roth and Stayer, *Companion to Anabaptism and Spiritualism, 1521–1700*, 119–61 (quotation at 135). The Latin original of the letter is lost, but Dutch and German versions survive. I use the translation of Williams in Williams and Mergal, *Spiritual and Anabaptist Writers*, 147–60, who provides bibliographic information about the work and editions.

142. Horst Weigelt, "Campanus, Johannes," in *Oxford Encyclopedia*, 1:249–50.

143. *Letter to Campanus* (Williams, 149).

144. *Letter to Campanus* (Williams, 155–56).

145. These passages are taken from the *Letter to Campanus* (Williams, 158–59).

146. Franck's *Paradoxa ducenta octoginta* was first published in 1534 and reprinted in 1542. There is an abridged modern German version by Heinrich Ziegler, *Sebastian Franck, Paradoxa* (Jena: Eugen Dietrichs, 1909). I will use the English version of E. J. Furcha, *Sebastian Franck, 280 Paradoxes or Wondrous Sayings* (Lewiston, NY: Edwin Mellen, 1986), occasionally adjusting the translations.

147. As Furcha notes, there are actually 292 paradoxes in the surviving work, because some numbers are left out and others are repeated in the surviving copies. He keeps the original numbering (e.g., #17) and adds numbers when needed (e.g., #17a, 17b). Not all of Franck's "paradoxes" are technically a paradox, or contradiction, but all represent difficult or opposing statements.

148. *280 Paradoxes*, preface (Furcha, 2).

149. The paradox of the Christ who appears as Antichrist and vice versa appears in ##15–16, 177–177a, and 187.

150. Despite his dismissal of all the early church writers in the *Letter to Campanus*, Franck makes extensive use of many patristic authors in the *280 Paradoxes* (for example, Cyril, Chrysostom, Jerome, and Augustine). He at times cites medi-

eval authors, such as Bernard of Clairvaux, Thomas Aquinas (three times), and Nicholas of Cusa, and also uses both Petrarch and Erasmus.

151. *280 Paradoxes* #57, entitled "Bifrons Janus Omnia. All things have two appearances" (Furcha, 106). For more expressions of the law of opposites, see, e.g., ##60, 177–177a, 185, 187–193, and 252.

152. A good summary of Franck's thought is "Sébastian Franck (1499–1542)," in Alexandre Koyré, *Mystiques, Spirituels, Alchimistes du XVI siècle allemande* (Paris: Librarie Armand Colin, 1955), 21–43.

153. *280 Paradoxes*, ##83–85 (Furcha, 138).

154. *280 Paradoxes* ##279–80 (Furcha, 486–87).

155. *280 Paradoxes* ##106–8 (Furcha, 190–91).

156. *280 Paradoxes* #8 (Furcha, 26).

157. Franck cites Tauler and the *Theologia Deutsch* about twenty times each, sometimes summarizing or quoting passages.

158. *280 Paradoxes* #79 (Furcha, 124). I use my own translation of the second passage to better reflect the German: "Wir sind jeder einmal aus Nichte oder Staub von der erden gemacht, nachmals aus Gott zu dem Bilde Gottes" (Ziegler, 97).

159. *280 Paradoxes* #79 (Furcha, 125–26).

160. *280 Paradoxes* #99 (Furcha, 182–83).

161. *280 Paradoxes* ##101–2 (Furcha, 186–87, trans. adapted). Besides a range of biblical passages, Franck cites Fulgentius, the *Imitatio Christi*, the *Theologia Deutsch*, Jerome, Augustine, Origen, Cyril, Tauler, and Thomas Aquinas.

162. For other treatments of humans as *imago dei*, see *280 Paradoxa* ##19, 27b, 67, 115–18, 138–40, 266–70 (Furcha, 53, 69, 116, 209, 262, 447, and 470).

163. Along with the mention in ##101–2, *grunt der seelen* also appears in ##271–74 and 279–80 (Furcha, 477, 486).

164. *280 Paradoxes* ##271–74 (Furcha, 475–76). For more on the freedom of the will, see #28 (Furcha, 71–73).

165. Langer, "Inneres Wort und inwohnender Christus," 62–68.

166. *280 Paradoxes* ##47–50 (Furcha, 99–101).

167. *280 Paradoxes* ##135–37 (Furcha, 230, 235). See also #133 (*Christus extra nos non prodest quicquam*), where Franck begins by citing the *Theologia Deutsch*. For more on Christ as ethical example, see ##130–31 (Furcha, 224–26)

168. *280 Paradoxes* #231 (Furcha, 392). This view is summarized by Koyré, "Sébastien Franck," 32: "le fait historique et métaphysique deviant un processus pyschologique dans chaque individu."

169. See the attack on all forms of external religion in #89 (Furcha, 158–65).

170. *280 Paradoxes* ##135–37 (Furcha, 245).

171. *280 Paradoxes* ##220–26 (Furcha, 376).

172. *280 Paradoxa* ##181–83 (Furcha, 328–29).

173. For Franck's teaching on love of neighbor, see ##151a, 155–57, 179–80, and 227–29.

174. *280 Paradoxes* ##200–203 (Furcha, 357–61).

175. *280 Paradoxes* ##40–41 (Furcha, 90–91). See also ##37–39, and 195–96.

176. *280 Paradoxes* ##43–44 (Furcha, 93). Although it would depend on which edition of Tauler's sermons Franck was using, it is likely that the sermons he is referring to were actually by Eckhart.

177. *280 Paradoxes* ##33–35, 83–85 (Furcha, 85, 140). See also ##135–37.

178. *280 Paradoxes* ##109–14 (Furcha, 199). For other appearances of union with Christ, see ##23, 138–40, 151b (Furcha, 62–63, 263, 279).

179. *280 Paradoxes* ##33–35 (Furcha, 85). Deification language is found about ten times in the book.

180. *280 Paradoxes* ##138-40 (Furcha, 263).

181. A good account of the affair and an analysis of Franck's *Declaration* are in Ozment, *Mysticism and Dissent*, 151–67.

182. *280 Paradoxes* #280 (Furcha, 488–89).

183. Ozment, *Mysticism and Dissent*, 159. The *Declaration* was edited by Alfred Hegler and W. Köhler, *Beiträge zur Geschichte der Mystik in der Reformationszeit*, Archiv für Reformationsgeschichte, Ergänzungsband 1 (Berlin: C. A. Schwetschke, 1906), 137–77.

184. See the texts cited in Ozment, *Mysticism and Dissent*, 163.

185. There is considerable literature about Weigel in German. In English, see especially Andrew Weeks, *Valentin Weigel (1533–1588): German Religious Dissenter, Speculative Theorist, and Advocate of Tolerance* (Albany: State University of New York Press, 2000), as well as the anthology produced by Weeks, *Valentin Weigel, Selected Spiritual Writings*, Classics of Western Spirituality (New York: Paulist Press, 2003). See also Jones, *Spiritual Reformers of the 16th and 17th Centuries*, 133–50; and Ozment, *Mysticism and Dissent*, 203–45. Other literature will be cited below.

186. The new critical edition of Weigel's works is now complete: *Valentin Weigel–Sämtliche Schriften*, ed. Horst Pfefferl, 15 vols. (Stuttgart-Bad Canstatt: frommann-holzboog, 1996–2016). I will cite from this edition, using the abbreviation *SS*.

187. These intra-Lutheran disputes, the "Gnesio-Lutheran controversies," are too complicated to be explored here, but there is a summary in Weeks, *Valentin Weigel*, chapter 2. On the debates over Lutheran orthodoxy, see the general sketch by Robert Kolb, "Lutheranism: Theology," in *Oxford Encyclopedia*, 2:470–73; and the more detailed essay of James Arne Nestingen, "Gnesio-Lutherans," ibid., 2:177–80.

188. *SS* 8:89–91, using the translation of Weeks, *Selected Spiritual Writings*, 205–6.

189. I use the translation in Weeks, *Selected Spiritual Writings*, 18.

190. For general accounts, see Alexandre Koyré, "Un mystique protestant: Valentin Weigel (1533–1588)," in *Mystiques, Spirituels, Alchimistes*, 80–116 (helpful despite its use of some pseudonymous works); Bernard Gorceix, *La mystique de Valentin Weigel* (Paris: Université de Paris, 1972); and Winfried Zeller, "Der ferne Weg des Geistes: Zur Würdigung Valentin Weigels," in idem, *Theologie und Frömmigkeit: Gesammelte Aufsätze*, ed. Bernd Jaspert, 2 vols. (Marburg: Elwert, 1978), 2:89–102.

191. Koyré, "Un mystique protestant," 82–83.

192. Paracelsus himself, a complex and fascinating figure, can be said to have both theological and mystical elements in his thought, but he is often seen as a medical and alchemical thinker. For an introduction to his thought that pays attention to the theological aspects, see Andrew Weeks, *Paracelsus: Speculative Theory and the Crisis of the Early Reformation* (Albany: State University of New York

Press, 1997), as well as Charles Webster, *Paracelsus: Medicine, Magic, and Mission at the End of Time* (New Haven: Yale University Press, 2009).

193. This is not the place to try to explore what Weigel took from Paracelsus. The Paracelsian elements are evident in both his cosmology and his anthropology (e.g., the notion of the human as the microcosm of the macrocosmic world).

194. On Weigel and the *Theologia Deutsch*, see G. Baring, "Valentin Weigel und die 'Deutsche Theologie,'" *Archiv für Reformationsgeschichte* 55 (1964): 5–16.

195. On Weigel's knowledge of Eckhart, see Winfried Zeller, "Meister Eckhart bei Valentin Weigel," in idem, *Theologie und Frömmigkeit*, 2:56–88 (first published in 1938 but still valuable); and Andrew Weeks, "Meister Eckhart and Valentin Weigel," in *A Companion to Meister Eckhart*, ed. Jeremiah M. Hackett, Brill's Companions to the Christian Tradition 36 (Leiden: Brill, 2013), 607–27.

196. For the story of the early Tauler editions, see Louise Gnädinger, *Joannes Tauler: Lebenswelt und mystische Lehre* (Munich: C. H. Beck, 1993), 411–21.

197. This note is at the beginning of the fourth section of the 1522 edition (f. 242v). The section (ff. 242v–318r) contains sixty sermons and mentions Eckhart also on ff. 300v and 316v. By my count, about thirty of the sermons can be found in the critical edition of Eckhart's works (DW 1–4), while some others are in Pfeiffer's 1857 Eckhart edition.

198. The three works are edited in *SS* 1:3–76 for the two treatises, and 79–114 for the *Bericht zur 'Deutschen Theologie'* (translations are my own).

199. *Von der Bekehrung*, Foreword (1:5): "Günstiger Lesser, Jnn diesen Büchlein, von der Busse, vnd Armut des Geistes, welches Jst aus dem Predigten Tauleri, von mir zusammen gezogen vnd auch ein gutt Theil, von mir selber geschrieben, wirdt furgehaltten, ein waarer grundlicher Vnterricht, wie sich ein Mensch Schicken, und haltten soll, vnd muss Jnn seiner bekehrung, oder Rechtfertigung." Zeller ("Meister Eckhart bei Valentin Weigel," 63–64) emphasizes Weigel's turn to mysticism as his way of approaching contemporary problems in Lutheranism.

200. Chapter 4 (1:23) quotes Eckhart's Pr. 27 (DW 2:51), while chapter 10 cites Pr. 42 (DW 2:306).

201. Koyré ("Valentin Weigel," 85) sees the inner religion of the "new birth" as the core of Weigel's thought.

202. *Von der Bekehrung*, chap. 3 (1:17): "Ein bloses lautter leiden, muss der Mensch bringen, mit gelassenheit, vnd Ergebenen *Willen*, Jnn absterben sein selbst, Jn still haltten, denn so baldt der Mensch sein selbst ausgehet mit seinen Willen, So baldt gehet Gott ein mit seinen Willen,...."

203. *Von der Bekehrung*, Chap. 6 (1:27–28): "Kurtz, das auswendige Zeugnus macht nicht selig, Sondern die Jnnwendige Newe geburt, durch den H[eiligen] Geist, oder glauben. Wer diese Newe geburt Jnn Jme hat, er sey Weib oder Man, Jung oder Altt, Jude oder Heyde, Christ oder Turcke etc. der wirdt Seelig, vnd ob er schon am leibe mit Wasser nicht getaufft ist."

204. The term "released releasement" (*gelassenen Gelassenheit*) comes from Tauler (e.g., Sermon 13, in Vetter, *Die Predigten Taulers*, 62.6–9). *Gelassenheit* is used about forty-five times in the treatise; its kin *Abgeschiedenheit* only two or three times. Zeller ("Meister Eckhart bei Valentin Weigel," 66–68) has a discussion of the difference between Karlstadt's and Weigel's views of *Gelassenheit*, in which he argues that Karlstadt's view is more "ethical" and Weigel's more "religious," though I find the distinction problematic.

205. Eckhart's "Poverty Sermon," preached on the text of Matthew 5:8, "Beati pauperes spiritu," is in DW 2:478–524. It appears in the 1522 Basel Tauler edition on ff. 306v–308r.

206. *Von waarer Armut des Geistes*, chap. 6 (1:62–63).

207. Weigel often talks about becoming one with God, but he never gives the topic a detailed analysis. Ozment (*Mysticism and Dissent*, 233–34 and 239–40) characterizes Weigel's view of union as "essential union," because he at times used the adjective *wesentlich* in relation to becoming one with God.

208. This sermon, entitled "Vff Johannis Baptiste geburt Die ander predig," is in the 1522 Basel Tauler on ff. 277r–78r. It is not by Eckhart but by John of Steerngassen, one of Eckhart's contemporaries and a noted mystical preacher (see Gnädinger, *Johannes Tauler*, 419).

209. *Von waarer Armut des Geistes*, chap. 5 (1:67): "Liebe machet mich Gott lieb sein. / Erkendtnus, Thut mich Gott Schawen, / Aber Lauterkeit mich Gott gleich wesen. / Gnade machet mich Gott würdig, / Aber Lauterkeit, vereiniget mich mit Gott."

210. *Von waarer Armut des Geistes*, chap. 6 (1:72): "Ein mensch der da alle Ding gelassen hat, vnd sich selber fur allen Dingen, vnd der da des seinen nichts suchet, ann keinen Dingen, vnd wircket alle seine Werck, ohne warumb, vnd von liebe etc., Dieser Mensch Jst Todt alle der Weldt, vnd lebet Jnn Gott, vnnd Gott Jnn Jme." This section is a quotation from a sermon of Eckhart on the Ascension, Pr. 29 (DW 2:70–89) found in the 1522 Tauler edition on ff. 262v–264r.

211. Eckhart is used in several places in the treatise, notably Pr. 47 (1:95), Pr. 16b (1:97), and Pr. 4 (1:106).

212. *Kurtzer Bericht* (1:81–83).

213. On Weigel's thinking by way of binaries, see Weeks, "Introduction," in *Valentin Weigel: Selected Spiritual Writings*, 30–31.

214. *Kurtzer Bericht* (1:84): "Ein jedes Wesen begehret natuerliche Weiss zu dem dauon es kommen ist / libet / suchet vnd findet dasselbige."

215. On the role of light in Weigel's thought, see Kurt Goldhammer, "Lichtsymbolik in philosophischer Weltanschauung, Mystik und Theosophie vom 15. bis zum 17. Jahrhundert," *Studium Generale* 13 (1960): 678–79.

216. *Kurtzer Bericht* (1:106): "Also Gott is aller Wesen Wesen / vnnd aller lebendigen Leben *complicative*, vnd doch ist Gott nivht Creatur / *sc[ilicet] explicative*." In his *De visione dei*, chap. 7, Cusa uses the example of the nut tree to explain how God contains all things. Weigel refers to the Cusan paradigm of *complicatio-explicatio* in other works, e.g., *De vita beata* 23 (SS 2:90).

217. *Kurtzer Bericht* (1:95): "Dann so wenig als das Reich Gottes / welches Gott selber ist / an einen Ohrt gebunden ist / sondern ein jeder Glaubiger tregt alles bey sich selber in dieser Welt." The account of Adam's nature as the image of God given here cites both Eckhart (Pr. 47) and the *Theologia Deutsch*, chapters 51 and 9. Weigel also cites Eckhart on humans as the image of God in 1:97 (Pr. 16b) and 1:98, with a formula taken from the 1522 Basel Tauler: "Es sagt der Taulerus aus dem Eccardo."

218. Weigel's anthropology, based on humanity as *imago dei* understood according to the Pauline trichotomy of body–soul–spirit (1 Thess. 5:21), is a variant of the most general form of mystical anthropology in medieval and early modern times. For more detail, see Ozment, *Mysticism and Dissent*, 210–19. For the

importance of the *imago dei* motif in Weigel, see Weeks, *Valentin Weigel,* 70–71, 111–12, 140–41, and 170–72.

219. *Kurtzer Bericht* (1:107): "da wirdt das vollkommene Gut im inwendigen Grundt der Seelen gefunden / gefuelet / geschmecket / so bald Creatur auffhoeret / so fehet Gott an." In his later works Weigel speaks of both "the ground of the soul" and "the ground of the heart." See *The Golden Grasp,* trans. Weeks, *Valentin Weigel: Selected Spiritual Writings,* 154, 165, 172, 182, 186, 187, 189.

220. *Kurtzer Bericht* (1:107): "Wenn ich mir gar sterbe vnd zu nicht werde / so wirdt Gott in mir lebendig / wirdt alle Ding in mir / also wirdt Gott der Mensche / vnd der Mensch bleibet vnter Gott nichts dann ein Werckzeug."

221. *Kurtzer Bericht* (1:101): "So viel nun Creatur von jhr selbst lasset / so viel gehet Gott ein / vnd wird selber der Mensch. Dann Gott will den Menschen gar an sich nehmen vnd alles in allem sein / doch nicht ohne den Menschen / der Mensch vermag nichts ihne Gott / vnd Gott wil nicht ohne den Menschen / drumb helt sich Gott wircklich vnd der Mensch leidlich."

222. *Kurtzer Bericht* (1:103): "Es were nicht vber vnsern Verstand / so wir nur in die newe Geburt tretten / dann dem Glaubigen seind alle Ding mueglich / vnnd der Geistliche erforschet alle Ding / auch die tieffe der Gottheit / vielmehr noch was vnter Gott ist / wirdt ein Glaubiger durch Christum erkennen."

223. *Kurtzer Bericht* (1:114): "So lange du suchest ich / mir / mich /icht / So bekommestu ware Erkantnuss nicht. Wenn du in Christo Gotte wilt leben / So mustu dich jhme gantz ergeben. . . . Wiltu mit gott vereinigt seyn / So lebe seines willens allein. Lass deinen eignen Willen sterben / So wirstu das hoechste Gut erweben."

224. *De vita beata,* Praefatio (*SS* 2:5): ". . . ut animadvertas veram patriam seu Summum Bonum intra nos ipsos latere, nec ab extra in particularibus quaerendum esse, . . . conferas te ad vitam contemplativam, et tandem omnia creata supergressus, praecipites te ex amore divino in fontem abyssi, ut Vnum fias in ipso Vno, in quo omnia sunt Vnum, et haec est Vita Aeterna." The language of uniting with God and plunging into the divine abyss recurs in the final chapter 27 (2:107): "O Infinitum, absorbe me abysso infinitudinis tuae. O Unum, unito me tibi intime, ut relicta omni multiplicitate mea, te unum cogitare, tibi uni adhaerere discam."

225. *De vita beata* 13 (*SS* 2:55–56) is dependent in part on DN 1, while chapter 14 cites DN 13 (2:57–58). Later, chapter 26 (2:102–4) makes considerable use of Dionysius's discussion of evil in DN 4.

226. The *De luce et caligine divina* is edited in *SS* 2:110–17, with the quotation from the MT on 116–17.

227. Chapter 15 (*SS* 2:60–62) treats the mystical theme of becoming sons of God and deiform.

228. Weeks, "Meister Eckhart and Valentin Weigel," 625.

229. A study of Weigel's sermons, especially the important *Kirchen- oder Hauspostille* edited in the two volumes of *SS* 12, would reveal some other uses of mystical themes.

230. The *Gnothi seauton,* which survives in somewhat different manuscript and printed versions, is edited in *SS* 3:49–197. There is overlap between some of the chapters in this work and sections of the later treatises, *About the Law or Will of God* and the *Golden Grasp.* For accounts, see Weeks, *Valentin Weigel,* 74–83; and Koyré, "Valentin Weigel," 114–15.

231. This principle appears in the *Gnothi seauton* I.10 (3:77): ". . . dass dass sehen vnnd erkhennen nicht von gegenwurff sondern auge selbe herkomme. . . ." This is repeated often in later works, such as *Der güldene Griff* and *Vom Ort der Welt.*

232. For an introduction, see Rudolph Allers, "Microcosmos from Anaximandros to Paracelsus," *Traditio* 2 (1944): 319–409. For Paracelsus, see John D. North, "Microcosm and Macrocosm in Paracelsus," in *Neue Beiträge zur Paracelsus-Forschung,* ed. Peter Dilg and Hartmut Rudolph, Hohenheimer Protokolle 47 (Stuttgart: Akademie der Diözese Rottenburg-Stuttgart, 1995), 41–58.

233. See, e.g., *Gnothi seauton* I.12 (3:83–85) on the parallels between the three heavens of 2 Corinthians 12:2 and human knowing.

234. The theme of the three eyes is introduced in *Gnothi seauton* I.8 (3:71–72) and expanded on in the subsequent chapters. The source is probably Hugh of St. Victor; see his *De sacramentis* I.10 (*PL* 176:329).

235. *Gnothi seauton* II.7 (3:115–19), quoting Eckhart, Pr. 66 (DW 3:113–19), which is found in the 1522 edition on ff. 309v–311r.

236. Eckhart appears one more time, a quotation on the nothingness of creatures from Pr. 4 (DW 1:69) found in chap. 9 (= chap. 15 in printed version; see 3:125).

237. "The eye with which I see God is the same eye with which God sees me," one of the most powerful of Eckhart's images for union of identity with God, is found several places in the Dominican's sermons, e.g., Pr. 12 (DW 1:201).

238. *Gnothi seauton,* appendix (3:144): "Wann der Vatter sein Khindt ansiehet so siehet Er sich selbst, dann wer sein bildnuss siehet, der siehet sich selbst, vnnd wie du für einen Spiegel trittest, vnndt dein bild feldt hinein vnd du siehest dein buldnus, das ist du siehest dich selbst, also siehet der vnbegreiflihe, vnwandelbare Gott sich selbst, durch sein bildnus, durch seinen erstgebornen, der ist sin Wille, Handt, Auge, vnd Wordt, Christus Jst ebenbildt. . . . Darumb gebüeret Er Jme ein Bildnus auss im selber, darin Ersiehet er such selber, vnd durch disen Sohn gibet Er sich allen Creturn zuerkennen, vnd keinner mag zum Vnbegreiflihen, Vnsichtbaren Vatter alss in, mit, vnd durch den Sohn."

239. Weeks, "Introduction," in *Valentin Weigel: Selected Spiritual Writings,* 42. *Vom Ort der Welt* can be found in *SS* 10:1–83; *Der güldene Griff* is edited in *SS* 8:3–102. I will cite these treatises from the translation of Weeks and provide references to the German original only when needed.

240. *Vom Ort der Welt,* chap. 12 (ed., 35; trans., 95). The Eckhart sermon is Pr. 38 (DW 2:233).

241. *Vom Ort der Welt,* chap. 14 (trans., 101). This chapter (ed., 39–42) cited both the *Theologia Deutsch* and Boethius.

242. *Vom Ort der Welt,* chap. 22 (trans., 121–25). The heavenly flesh of Christ is discussed also in *Der güldene Griff,* chap. 17 (trans., 194), and at length in *Von Betrachtung des Lebens Christi* in *SS* 7.

243. On the heavenly flesh of Christ, see Hans Joachim Schoeps, *Vom himmlischen Fleisch Christi: Eine dogmengeschichtliche Untersuchung* (Tübingen: J. C. B. Mohr, 1951), who discusses Weigel on 56–62; and Ozment, *Mysticism and Dissent,* 228–34.

244. Attacks on the "pseudo-theologians" can be found in *Der güldene Griff,* chaps. 8, 14, 27, and in the conclusion (trans., 159, 184, 211, 213–14).

245. Weeks, *Valentin Weigel*, 114. Weeks gives a summary of the treatise on 114–22.

246. There are, to be sure, a number of new themes taken up in *Der güldene Griff*, such as the treatment of the nature of faith, discernment of spirits, and the book of the heart in chaps. 23–26.

247. *Der güldene Griff*, chap. 12 (trans., 178–79).

248. *Der güldene Griff*, chap. 13 (trans., 183).

249. *Der güldene Griff*, chap. 8 (*SS* 8:30; my trans.): ". . . vnnd sich hinein keren in den Jnwendigsten grundt der seelen, in stiller gelassenheit auf gott warten in ihm selber, vnnd in ein Vergessen kommen seiner selbest vnnd aller dingen." A similar passage on self-abandonment in the ground of the soul can be found in chap. 14 (trans., 186).

250. *Der güldene Griff*, chap. 8 (*SS* 8:33; I have slightly adapted Weeks's version found on 167).

251. *Der güldene Griff*, chap. 28 (trans., 213).

252. Weigel did make use of Franck's work, including his method of arguing by paradox; see *Der güldene Griff*, chap. 17 (trans., 192–95).

253. George, "Spirituality of the Radical Reformation," 366.

254. See McGinn, *Foundations*, 334–36, in agreement with Gershom Scholem.

CHAPTER 3

Two Lutheran Mystics

JOHANN ARNDT (1555–1621) AND JACOB BOEHME (1575–1624) were contemporaries in the world of Northern German Lutheranism of the late sixteenth and early seventeenth centuries.[1] Their writing careers (1597–1620 and 1612–24) overlapped. Arndt was an important figure in the Lutheran clerical world; Boehme was a layman, a cobbler by trade. Both writers were criticized by the Lutheran establishment and have remained controversial. This did not prevent them from being widely read. Arndt's *True Christianity*, first published in four volumes between 1606 and 1610, and later expanded into six books after his death, was immensely popular, going through close to two hundred editions prior to the twentieth century and being translated into at least a dozen languages. With the exception of the *Imitation of Christ* no other spiritual treatise seems to have found so many readers. Arndt was read within Protestant, especially Lutheran, circles, but also by Catholics and Orthodox. Boehme's challenging views also had a readership in many contexts. His influence was large, both among the "Boehmists," the circles of those who identified themselves as his followers, and through the impact of his thinking on philosophers (e.g., G. W. F. Hegel), theologians (e.g., William Law), and writers (e.g., William Blake). The differences between the two thinkers were substantial, especially because Arndt fits

---

I would like to thank Prof. Cyril O'Regan of the Department of Theology of the University of Notre Dame for reading this chapter and making important suggestions for its improvement, especially with regard to Boehme.

within the broad tradition of Christian mysticism, while it is legitimate to ask to what extent Boehme can be considered a Christian mystic. Both writers were shaped by the intellectual and religious culture of their time.[2] Both questioned the Protestant Scholasticism that had developed in the latter part of the sixteenth century, but they remained Lutherans. While they are different in many ways, Arndt and Boehme represent polarities important for understanding the Protestant mysticism of the time.

Johann Arndt: Integrating Mysticism into the Lutheran Tradition[3]

I argued in chapter 1 that aspects of medieval mysticism were vital to understanding Luther's new evangelical theology, whether or not one wants to call the Wittenberger himself a mystic.[4] The brunt of chapter 2 was to show how important strands of medieval German mysticism used by Luther were developed by some of the Radical Reformers who broke with him and his followers to help create a vision of an inward universal and mystical Christian faith. Johann Arndt represents a third option—what can be called an Evangelical (i.e., Lutheran) mysticism, or mystical theology, one created as a challenge to the regnant Protestant Scholasticism of Lutheranism of ca. 1575–1625. This mysticism can be described as *evangelical* in the sense that it remains true to the basic insights of Luther and his followers about the message of saving faith, but it is also explicitly *mystical* in the sense that Arndt showed less interest in the objective aspects of faith, but rather emphasized inner appropriation of the kingdom of God within the soul and the new birth that leads to deepening union with God.

Life, Writings, Sources, Historiography

Johann Arndt was born at the end of 1555, the son of the Lutheran pastor of Edderitz bei Köthen in the province of Anhalt in central Germany. Arndt's birth year corresponded to the Peace of Augsburg, which gave formal recognition to Lutheranism, and he was a young man when the imposition of the Formula of Concord of 1577 and the publication of the *Book of Concord* in 1580 established Lutheran orthodoxy.[5] This confessionalization encouraged the formation of Protestant Scholasticism, a formal and analytic mode of theology that flourished between ca. 1560 and 1650 and lived on well beyond that time.[6] While

Lutheran orthodoxy included diverse currents, this "School Theology" was something that Arndt reacted against with vigor, because he felt it neglected inner renewal as the goal of true theology. Arndt studied at Halberstadt and Magdeburg before going to the University of Helmstedt to pursue medicine. He soon turned to theology and studied at Wittenberg, Strassburg, and Basel. In 1584, Arndt became the pastor of Badeborn, a village near Quedlinburg. During the 1590s, first in Badeborn and then in Mansfeld and Quedlinburg, he became involved in controversy with the Calvinistically leaning authorities of the area. Eventually, in 1599 he moved to Braunschweig. During his decade there, Arndt published the first editions of his most famous work, *Vier Bücher vom Wahren Christentum (Four Books on True Christianity)*. Controversy over the orthodoxy of this work continued to dog him in life and after. In 1609, he was named pastor of Eisleben (Luther's birthplace), and in 1611 he was appointed the General Superintendent in Celle, where he remained until his death on May 11, 1621.

Johann Arndt wrote extensively in many genres, though a number of his works survive in title only. A variety of scriptural commentaries, sermons, letters, introductions, and treatises appeared between 1597 and his death; other works were published posthumously. Like Luther, he was interested in German mysticism. In 1597 he published an edition of the *Theologia Deutsch* with an introduction. This was reworked and reprinted in 1605 with the addition of the always popular *Imitation of Christ*.[7] Arndt's appreciation for this key work in the history of German mysticism was emphasized at the end of his life in the third part of book VI of *True Christianity*, consisting of two essays defending and explaining the *Theologia Deutsch*. Here he says:

> Joseph was released from prison by a dream (Gen. 41). . . . As Joseph when he was released from his imprisonment still had on his old servant's cloak, so this old *Theologia Deutsch* steps forward in its rude German farmer's cloak, that is, in its old, rude speech in which it still teaches very high spiritual and lovely things, namely, to take on Christ's life, to practice the teaching of Christ in life, how Christ is to live in us and Adam is to die in us.[8]

Arndt also edited some spiritual works of Johann von Staupitz, Luther's friend and mentor. Closely related to *True Christianity* was a collection of prayers called *Paradiesgärtlein (Little Garden of Paradise)* that first appeared in 1612. A collection of *Sermons on the Catechism* was published in 1616. Arndt's popular sermons on the Gospels and the Psalms (1616–17) made considerable use of medieval mystics like Bernard. In

the year of his death, Arndt wrote an "Introduction" to *Tauler's Postille*
(i.e., sermons). The core works of Arndt's subsequent influence, however, were *True Christianity* and the *Little Garden of Paradise*. In later
years, the two works were often printed together to form a massive
collection on mystical teaching and prayer.[9]
Arndt's use of sources in his great work and in other writings has
been the subject of considerable study.[10] First of all, it must be stressed
that Arndt was a deeply biblical theologian—there is hardly a page of
True Christianity that does not feature many biblical quotations.[11] It
is clear that he developed his theology with the help of many mystical sources, some favored by Luther, such as the *Theologia Deutsch* and
Tauler.[12] Like Luther, he was also influenced by Augustine,[13] Bernard
of Clairvaux,[14] and Johann von Staupitz. Arndt used medieval mystical
materials not found in Luther, such as the *Imitation of Christ* and the
writings of the Franciscan mystic Angela of Foligno (d. 1309).[15] Arndt
was aware that his use of these medieval sources was questionable in
the world of rigid Lutheran orthodoxy. In the foreword to book I, he
defends his employing the mystics as follows: "It is true that I have
quoted, especially in the Frankfort edition, some earlier writers, such
as Tauler, à Kempis, and others, who may seem to ascribe more than is
due to human ability and works, but my whole book strives against such
an error." Arndt goes on to insist on his adherence to the fundamental
Lutheran doctrines of "the abomination of original sin" and ascribing
all salvation to Christ alone. "All this has been written and abundantly
explained in many passages of this book," he continues, and therefore, "the doctrines of the Papists, Synergists, and Majorists have been
expressly refuted and rejected. The doctrine of faith by justification,
moreover, has been set forth in this book, and especially in Book II."[16]
Given Arndt's career as a Lutheran pastor, we should not think of this
statement as some kind of ploy or excuse. Arndt was convinced that
he needed to rescue Lutheranism from its present, merely external
piety and that medieval mystical texts were an important resource for
achieving this goal. As Johannes Wallmann put it, "Arndt found in
pre-Reformation mysticism the necessary inspiration and power for
religious renewal for his time. The incorporation and treatment of
mystical ideas is what constitutes the uniqueness of Arndt's main work,
True Christianity."[17]
Arndt's disaffection with the Lutheranism of his day is evident also
in his willingness to use the works of the Spiritual Reformers, especially
Valentin Weigel,[18] and probably also Caspar Schwenckfeld. Although
he later sought to distance himself from the suspect Weigel, Arndt

did not criticize the Radical Reformers, as many other Lutherans did. Finally, as book IV of *True Christianity* demonstrates, Arndt was deeply imbued with the thought of Paracelsus.[19] Reformation theology in the decades before and after 1600 obviously included diverse theological tendencies, despite the predominance of Lutheran Scholasticism. Arndt's Lutheranism, deeply impregnated with medieval mysticism and other sources, was one option among others. It was to prove an influential and long-lived option, though that part of the story cannot be taken up here. It is important to insist, however, that Arndt's *True Christianity* was not just an eclectic compilation of materials; it was an original contribution to Western mysticism.

What is most surprising about *True Christianity* is that it uses little of Luther, at least directly, and hardly anything of classic or contemporary Lutheran theology.[20] Luther is praised, of course,[21] and Arndt avers that his teaching is in conformity with the confessional documents of the Lutheran church.[22] Nevertheless, it is hard to agree with Christian Braw's claim that Arndt saw *True Christianity* as a supplement to the dogmatic volumes of Lutheran beliefs.[23] Rather, Hermann Geyer seems more correct in his argument that Arndt was deliberately setting up his model of true inner theology *against* the outer, fleshly, dead theology of Lutheran orthodoxy.[24] This interpretive difference raises the issue of exactly what kind of Lutheran Johann Arndt was.

From the beginning, Arndt was a divisive figure. Contemporary Orthodox Lutherans, such as Lucas Osiander the Younger (1571–1638),[25] attacked him as an "Enthusiast" and crypto-papist who was advancing not "Christianity" (*Christentum*) but "Tauleranity" (*Taulerdom*). Other orthodox theologians, such as Arndt's friend Johann Gerhard, defended his intentions, if not always his manner of expression. These attacks, however, did nothing to hinder the popularity of *True Christianity*. Arndt was later favored by the Pietists. The founder of Pietism, Jacob Philipp Spener (1635–1705), hailed him as the third Elijah. Arndt's divided reputation continued into the modern era. Albrecht Ritschl (1822–89) in his *Geschichte des Pietismus* (3 vols., 1880–86) singled out Arndt as a suspect figure, the forebear of Pietism, which Ritschl felt had too many mystical tendencies to be theologically orthodox.[26] The major early twentieth-century monograph on Arndt, Wilhelm Koepp's *Johann Arndt* of 1912, came out of the Ritschlian school and sought to separate the Lutheran basis of Arndt's theology from the dangerous mysticism he had added to it.[27] From the 1960s on, new work on the so-called *Frömmigkeitskrise* (crisis of piety) around 1600, as well as investigations of the origins of Pietism, led to more appreciative analyses of the role of mysticism in Arndt and his place in the history of spirituality.[28] Two major studies on Arndt of the past quarter century took divergent views on his mysticism. In 1986, the Danish theologian Christian Braw published *Bücher im Staube (Books in the Dust)*, employing a phrase Arndt used in referring to the forgotten medieval mystical literature he incorporated into his teaching. Braw attempted to vindicate Arndt's Lutheran orthodoxy, while also showing that his basic concern was to reform Lutheran Christianity by bringing attention back to the mystical goal of inner renewal originally taught by Luther. Hermann Geyer's *Verborgene Weisheit (Hidden Wisdom)*, the largest work devoted to Arndt, took a different stance. For Geyer, Arndt is a major "non-Orthodox" figure in the history of Lutheranism, the representative of an alternative view of evangelical faith, one based on experience and a distinctive Reformation form of "mystical theology." Geyer finds Arndt closer to the Spiritual Reformers (a term he finds problematic), as well as to the Hermetic and Theosophical trends evident in Germany at the time, rather than to mainline Lutheranism. Even so brief a survey of the "Arndt Question" shows that he remains a contested figure in the history of Lutheranism, not least because he raised the question of the role of mysticism among Protestants in what has been called "The Era of Confessionalization." In order to evaluate the significance of Arndt's mysticism, we need to explore how he set out his case for "true Christianity" in his famous book.

What Is True Christianity?

Arndt's book grew in stages. He may have been considering it in 1597, when the foreword to his first edition of the *Theologia Deutsch* already featured a sharp attack on "School Theology." "It is a great mistake," he says, "for a person to strive to attain pure teaching only with writing and disputing in schools and in churches and to forget Christian living." Christian living itself is the true theology: "To turn Christ's teaching into living, or how Christ should live in us and Adam die, or how a person should be united to God, this is the perfection of humanity and the goal of all theology."[29] Arndt worked on the four books intensively in the early years of the seventeenth century, publishing the first version of book I in 1605, and in either 1609 or 1610 the first edition of all four of the original books. A number of other editions followed. What became book V was originally a freestanding text published in 1620. In the same year, he also put out a *Repetitio Apologetica, or Repetition and Defense of the Teaching of True Christianity.*

Posthumously this became the first part of book VI. The last two books were not added to the first four until 1679, and both the short and long forms of *True Christianity* continued to circulate widely. Despite their varied publication history, all six books are authentic works of Arndt.

The foreword to book I declares that the subject of the book is to show "simple readers [*Einfaltigen*] wherein true Christianity consists, namely, in the exhibition of a true, living faith, active in genuine godliness and in the fruits of righteousness." The contrast of Adam and Christ, Pauline in origin but also emphasized in the *Theologia Deutsch*, is mentioned, setting up the main theme of *True Christianity*: "It is not enough to know God's word; one must also practice it in a living, active manner."[30] The foreword warns the reader not to confuse the righteousness of faith with the righteousness of a Christian life—for *true* Christianity both are needed. As he says later in the first book: "True Christianity consists only in pure faith, in love and a holy life" (I.20.1). True Christianity and true theology are one and the same: "If we live in Christ alone and walk in love and humility and direct our total energy and theology to this, we are to mortify the flesh and live in Christ."[31] Arndt repeated and expanded on this message of the meaning of true Christianity in the later books, lest the reader forget. The defense of *True Christianity* in the *Repetitio Apologetica* of book VI gives the phrase a christological and Trinitarian emphasis:

> The foundation and ground of true Christianity is the true knowledge of Our Lord Jesus Christ according to his holy person and Mediatorship in which he "is made by God to be for us Wisdom, and Righteousness, and Sanctification, and Redemption" (1 Cor. 1:30). . . . Therefore, Christ is clearly revealed for us in God's holy word, so that we see and hear him in a clear mirror and bright light and through God's grace and spirit we can grasp him through faith and fasten him in our heart.

A person who holds Christ in his heart and in all his good deeds has the whole Trinity living within him and has restored the Trinitarian image in which we were made (Gen. 1:26).[32] Arndt's theology is, above all, a theology of the heart. While there can be no question about his adherence to the doctrine of justification by faith, Johannes Wallmann is correct in saying that "Arndt shifted the accent from justification to the beginning of a new life or to sanctification."[33]

Among the reasons for which Luther and Arndt loved the *Theologia Deutsch* was the way in which this medieval text set out the fundamental contrasts of Christian faith and life: Adam versus Christ; the flesh-letter versus the spirit; the outer man versus the inner; darkness versus light. Arndt saw this dualism also realized in the contrast between two kinds of theology. In the foreword to book I, he says, "Many think that theology is a mere science or rhetoric, whereas it is a living experience and practice" (I.Vorrede.2). One can be as wise as Solomon and have all the wisdom of the scriptures, but if true love of God and neighbor is not present, one's damnation will be even greater (I.35.9). In chapter 39 he summarizes his view of real theology, attacking the heretics of the early church and "the false practices of the Papists," but also all those who rely on "heavy disputations, polemical sermons, writings and tracts," and forget about holy living. Polemical books may be necessary to detect error, but, says Arndt, "[a] person who confesses Christ's teaching and not his life confesses only half of Christ." He queries, "How can the truth of pure doctrine be upheld without a holy life?"[34] The foreword to book III sharpens the distinction between two ways of gaining wisdom and understanding:

> The first comes through much reading and disputation. Those who take this way one calls *doctos*, learned ones. The other way is through prayer and love, and those who take this way one calls *sanctos*, saints. Between the two is a great distinction. The first, because they are learned and not lovers, are blown up with pride. The others are lowly and humble. By the first way you will not find your inner treasure; by the second way, however, you will find it in yourself.[35]

Given this contrast, it is not surprising that Arndt presented the theology set forth in *True Christianity* as a "practical theology" (*theologia practica/praxis theologiae*), that is, a theology centered on ethical action.[36] Deeply troubled by the triumph of Aristotelian analytic thinking and the polemical disputations among contemporary Lutherans, he proclaimed that theology must be above all practical: a mode of life involving penance, prayer, and love of God and neighbor. In his early Latin *Dissertatio*, which was not published until 1616, he laid out three principles for the proper study of theology: first, that "use and praxis" must be especially employed in theology; second, "The praxis of theology is the exercise of faith and of the Christian life, or true piety"; and, third, "Therefore, theological study that is concerned only with theology [in the narrow sense] and the art of disputation should be totally forsaken as reprehensible."[37] Although *True Christianity* tends to favor biblical terms like "wisdom," a theology that is lived and not just thought about is the core of its message.

Given Arndt's rejection of the dogmatic categories of Lutheran orthodoxy (not the truth of the Lutheran Confessions), his theology needs to be investigated on its own terms, so I will proceed by a succinct analysis of the structure and content of the books of *True Christianity*.[38] In the foreword to book III, Arndt says that the first three books were constructed according to the traditional three stages of progress in the Christian life:

> Just as our natural life has its steps, . . . so also does our spiritual or Christian life. [It] has its beginning in repentance [i.e., *via purgativa*], by which man daily betters himself. Thereafter follows middle age, more illumination [*via illuminativa*], through the contemplation of divine things, through prayer, and through suffering. . . . Finally, the perfection of old age comes. It consists in full union through love [*via unitiva*], which Saint Paul called the perfect age of Christ and a perfect man in Christ (Eph. 4:13).[39]

Nevertheless, Arndt also gave the individual books their own titles that do not necessarily reflect this threefold pattern of spiritual progress. Book I is called the "Book of Scripture" with forty-two chapters. Deeply influenced by the *Theologia Deutsch*, it serves as a foundation for what comes afterward, both in terms of setting out dogmatic truths and ascetical practices. Book II, the "Book of Life" (i.e., Christ) consists of fifty-eight chapters dealing with the central role of Christ and various practices of the Christian life, such as prayer (chaps. 34–43) and patience under tribulation (chaps. 44–58). It is mostly in this book that Angela of Foligno appears. Book III, with twenty-three chapters, is the "Book of Conscience" describing inner union with God and making much use of the Basel Tauler edition of 1522, citing long passages from Tauler and at times even Meister Eckhart.[40] Book III is not a mere compilation, however, but shows how Arndt, like Valentin Weigel, absorbed and recast medieval German mysticism in the service of his own vision of the mystical life. Book IV shifts gear. Arndt begins by appealing to the ancient motif of the two witnesses, or books, by which God reveals his truth—the greater world of the cosmos and the smaller world of humanity. If the first three books investigated anthropology, that is, the human *microcosmos*, then book IV will show how "the great book of the world of nature," the macrocosm, reveals the same truths, because creatures are designed to lead us to God. Book IV is divided into two parts: Part 1 consists of six long chapters interpreting the Hexaemeron account of creation; part 2 of forty chapters is devoted to humanity, the special creation of the sixth day.[41]

The four books of *True Christianity* have a coherent general structure, though the internal development of books I and II are often digressive. The collection gives the heart of Arndt's teaching about true Christianity. The later addition of books V–VI, while enshrining authentic Arndtian writing, was not part of his original plan. Book V, called the *Liber Confessionis*, consists of three parts. The first has eleven chapters "On True Belief and Holy Life." The second part has fifteen chapters and was published separately in 1620 under the title *Concerning the Very Wonderful and Grace-filled Union of the Believer with the Almighty, Immortal, and Unassailable Head of the Church, Jesus Christ.* Arndt had made sparing use of the mystical theme of the marriage between Christ and the faithful soul in the first four books of *True Christianity*, several times referring to Bernard of Clairvaux. In these chapters, however, mystical marriage emerges as a major theme, especially in chapter 7, which seems to have been written with Bernard's *Sermons on the Song of Songs* on his desk. Still, Arndt puts this Bernardine mysticism in the context of a treatise on mystical union of a distinctly evangelical flavor. Three brief chapters on the Trinity, Christ's person and work, and the gifts of the Holy Spirit close off book V. Finally, book VI, the *Liber Demonstrationis*, also has three parts: the *Repetitio Apologetica*, defending some chapters of books I–III; a selection of nine letters Arndt wrote to friends explaining and defending his views; and two reflections on the meaning of that central source for Protestant mysticism, the *Theologia Deutsch.*

Mystical Themes in True Christianity

A full review of Arndt's large work is not possible here, but in order to understand his contribution it is important to consider some of the major themes of *True Christianity* in the context of Arndt's full theology. Five themes will be treated: (1) humans as created in God's image and likeness; (2) the loss of the image in Adam's sin and its restoration in Christ's saving action; (3) the necessity of experiencing the new birth given by Christ's saving action; (4) the practices that further restore the *imago dei*, especially love of God and neighbor; and (5) union with God in Christ. Other themes will be touched on in passing.

Book I provides the underpinning of Arndt's evangelical mystical theology, which he insists is the basic message of the Bible (*Liber Scripturae* being the title of the book). Arndt begins not with a consideration of God's nature as one and three,[42] as might be expected in the case in Protestant Scholasticism, but with five chapters that set out the fundamental contours of his theology: humanity as created in the image of God (chap. 1); Adam's Fall (chap. 2); the new birth in Christ (chap. 3); true repentance as the beginning of the new birth (chap. 4); and justifying faith (chap. 5).

The doctrine of humanity as created in God's image and likeness is fundamental to Arndt's message.[43] This connects him with one of the central themes of patristic and medieval mysticism. Arndt begins with humanity's participation in the Trinity: "The image of God in man is the conformity of the human soul, understanding, spirit, mind, will, and all internal and external bodily and spiritual powers with God and the Holy Trinity." Immediately after he adds, "From this it is clear that the Holy Trinity has placed its image in man," and then notes, "There are three chief powers created in the human soul by God: understanding, will, and memory." It might seem, therefore, that Arndt's view of the image of the Trinity in humans is essentially Augustinian, identifying the three higher powers of the soul (memory/intellect/will) with the Father, Son, and Holy Spirit. But this is not quite the case. The first and most decisive difference is that, for Arndt, like Calvin, the image of God is holistic, found in the entire human person ("all internal and external bodily and spiritual powers"), not just in the faculties of the soul.[44] Second, Arndt, unlike Augustine and many of his medieval followers, has little interest in faculty psychology or speculative analysis of how the faculties relate to the persons of the Trinity.[45] He is mainly concerned with two other aspects of the *imago dei*. The first is the christological character of the image. Following Paul (Rom. 8:29; 1 Cor. 15:49; 2 Cor. 3:18; Eph. 4:23; Col. 1:15-20) and the main tradition in Western theology, he teaches that the Word alone is the true image of God, so that humans are images formed *according* to the Word made flesh in Jesus.[46] The christological core of Arndt's image theology is summarized at the end of book II.33, where he says, "Just as God created man to his perfect image through his Wisdom, so too, through his Beloved Son, who is Eternal Wisdom, has he created him anew and given him birth into the new image of God, in which his wisdom, glory, and justice shall forever shine. For it is in this especially that the image of God consists."[47]

The second main theme in Arndt's theology is the contrast between the true image which God created in Adam and the image of Satan into which humans were plunged after the Fall. This is already introduced in chapter 2, where Arndt tells the reader, "Learn to know yourself, what you have become through the fall of Adam. Out of God's image came forth Satan's image in which all false qualities, characteristics, and evils of Satan are contained. In God's image all true qualities, characteristics, and virtues are contained."[48] The teaching is often repeated in subsequent chapters of book I and throughout *True Christianity*.[49] Arndt's teaching about the *imago dei* is practical, not speculative. He wants the reader to understand that humans were created in excellence, made in the image of God; but, because of the loss of the image in Adam's Fall, the only way to restore human excellence as God's image and therefore to attain happiness is through justifying faith in Christ and the living out of this faith in Christian life. Discussions of the image of God as created, lost, and regained appear throughout book I,[50] as well as in the later books. An important treatment is found in book IV, part 2, chapters 23–25, where Arndt discusses the order among creatures in the Genesis account, demonstrating that man, as made in God's image, is the goal of all creation, made to show love to God and to his fellow humans, who were also made in the image of God.[51] As Braw notes, mystics like Eckhart and Tauler investigated the *imago dei* as the place where God always resides in the ground of the soul, whereas Arndt, in the tradition of Luther and evangelical theology in general, concentrates on how the radically injured, almost effaced, image can be restored by justification in Christ to become the ground for sanctification.[52]

Arndt's distance from the anthropology of the medieval German mystics can be seen in how he uses the metaphor of the *grunt/grund* with regard to both God and humans. Ground is only very rarely used of God, and seemingly only in quotations from mystical sources.[53] The language of ground does, however, have an important place in Arndt's theological anthropology in the form of the "inner ground of the heart" (*innerlich Grund des Herzens*), a phrase that occurs often, being first used in I.4.2: "Repentence does not only occur when one ceases to give freedom to gross external sins and leave them, but when one enters oneself, changes and makes better the internal ground of one's heart." Chapter 23 of book I shows that the phrase also has a christological dimension: "A tree does not grow better than in its own ground and earth. Thus, the inner man does not grow better than in the inner ground of the heart, which is Christ."[54] Like the notion of the image of God, Arndt's conception of the inner ground of the heart is holistic. In book I.41.8, he states, "You must understand the use of the word 'heart' in the Scriptures as meaning all the powers of the soul: understanding, will, affections, and desires." References to the inner ground of the heart are especially frequent in book III, which is not surprising given its emphasis on union with God.[55]

Like many Protestant mystics, with the exception of Valentin Weigel, Arndt does not have the kind of speculative mystical anthropology found in many of the medieval mystics. His contact with these mystics, however, did lead him to include some texts where he echoes aspects of their teaching about the soul's origin in God and its return to the divine source. For example, in a passage in book I.23, speaking of fleeing the worldly community, he says that "there is nothing better for the soul than to be in its own house, that is, to rest in God from which it has flown forth and to which it must flow back again if it is to be whole."[56] A text from book III.2.3 speaks of returning to the Principle from which we flowed out, as well as of God breaking through his divine nature "to offer us the abyss of his Godhead and the fullness of his being and his nature." This is a quotation from a sermon of Eckhart's found in the 1522 Tauler edition.[57]

Arndt, like other Protestant theologians, had a deeply pessimistic view of human nature's condition after Adam's Fall. Because *True Christianity* was written for earnest believers, however, he did not engage in long discussions of the nature of original sin and its effects.[58] Nevertheless, chapters 2 and 41 of book I lay out an evangelical understanding of the "destruction of the holy image of God" in humanity. Adam's sin was what "changed God's image into Satan's image," and led humanity to become the instrument of the Evil One (I.2.3). Chapter 41 explains in more detail that original sin leaves all humans in a situation of true enmity toward God in which they sin against all the commandments, especially those of the first tablet (i.e., relating to God himself). With regard to the commandments that rule our relations to others, "a spark of free will remains in the soul," but it rules only external works and cannot be perfected, that is, perform saving works. God allows "the natural flame of love to remain so that we might know and sense what a high good and beautiful image of God the perfect love of God is, and how great a good we have lost."[59] Natural man does not have anything of the spiritual light (see 1 Cor. 2:14) that leads to the kingdom of God within.

Arndt's attention is concentrated on the renewal of the image, that is, the new birth in Christ, which he begins to discuss in book I, chapter 3. The new creation achieved by Christ's indwelling forms the beginning and the progression of the true Christian life, which centers on our deepening union with God. The new birth is the work of the Holy Spirit alone, and it has two chief aspects: justification and sanctification or renewal (I.3.1). Arndt will focus on sanctification, something he felt had largely been forgotten in contemporary Lutheranism. This new birth, conceived of in biblical terms, is not the atemporal Eckhartian birth of the Word in the soul but the historical event of fallen humanity's new birth in Christ. Hence, Christ is the proper rule and model for the sanctification process. "The suffering of Christ," says Arndt, "is two things; namely, a payment for all our sins and a renewal of man through faith and true repentance" (I.3.12). In the long chapter 11 of book I, Arndt returns to the discussion of the new birth, emphasizing that it means that we must now live in Christ and Christ in us. The greatest proof of this is found in love. Citing 1 John 4:7–8, he says, "it is clear that the new birth is from God and that its fruits and the new life do not consist in words alone or in external appearance, but in the highest virtue, which is God himself, namely, in love."[60] As with the other themes introduced in these beginning chapters of *True Christianity*, the new birth in Christ frequently reappears in the remainder of the work.[61]

With the fundamentals established, Arndt proceeds in a leisurely manner, discussing both the ascetical aspects of the sanctification process, and sometimes touching on the mystical dimensions, which will be treated in greater detail in book III and in the appended book V. Repentance, for example, is treated in chapters 4 and 8, while true faith is discussed in chapters 5 and 6. A mini-treatise on the Christian life is found in chapters 12–16, one of the places in book I where Arndt makes use of the *Imitation of Christ*. Chapter 14 contains the earliest mention of a theme that will grow stronger in the later books, the marriage between the faithful soul and Christ, the Divine Bridegroom (I.14.9). Other chapters deal with the use of temporal goods, the nature of Christian sorrow, and true worship. One of the constant themes running through book I, as well as the subsequent books, is the need for experience, not book learning. Book I.21.9 says, "This is the true knowledge of God, which arises out of experience and consists in living faith"; and chapter 26.6 insists, "The knowledge of God and Christ must proceed from the experience and reception of Christ." Another constant theme is the necessary relation between faith and love. What makes the true Christian is not miracles, or other great deeds, but faith active in love (see Gal. 5:6).[62] Chapters 22–30 form a treatise on love of God and love of neighbor, the first of a number of such treatments in *True Christianity*. The mystical dimensions of the work are given more explicit consideration in chapter 36, which speaks of the experience of union with God, using the well-known passage from 1 Corinthians 6:17 about attaining unity of spirit with God.[63] Finally, the long chapter 41 consists of a summary of the whole of book I, thus serving as a kind of introduction to the following books.[64]

The foreword to book II provides an outline of the sections into which Arndt divided this treatment of the *Liber Vitae*, that is, Christ conceived of as the book and/or mirror in which we find the model and meaning of the life of "the new spiritual man." Christ is also our ladder to God. Picking up on a theme that goes back at least as far as Augustine, Arndt says, "In Christ's humanity we must begin and arise into his divinity."[65] Chapters 1–3 treat of Christ as the remedy for original sin, while chapters 4–6 deal with faith. Chapters 7–10 concern the distinction between flesh and spirit and the necessity for daily repentance. Four long sections follow. Chapters 11–25 consider Christ's life as our mirror, followed by a treatment of "the chief aspects of the contemplative life" (chaps. 26–33). Then chapters 34–43 turn to prayer, while finally chapters 44–58 treat "patience under tribulation, the chief spiritual trials, and how to overcome them." Arndt had already expressed in book I his double sense of Christ's mission as both Redeemer and Exemplar (e.g., I.11.1–4; 14.7; 24.16). In book II he pursues both themes but concentrates on the Savior's exemplary role.[66] We cannot consider this long book in detail, but a glance at a few chapters dealing with mystical motifs is important.

In the section on faith, Arndt not only insists on justification by faith but also emphasizes that faith finds its true expression in a sanctified life. The outcome of such a life is perfection and union with God, as we are told in chapter 6. Just as the union between the divine and human natures in Christ cannot be destroyed, "so too must Christ our Head be united with his members, so that we cannot be separated from Christ in life or in death. Thus, the prophet Hosea speaking in the person of Christ says, 'I will betroth myself to you in eternity' (Hos. 2:19)."[67] In tones that echo those of the German mystics, Arndt says that we contribute nothing to this new birth; all is God's work, to which we must surrender our will, honor, and wisdom (II.6.4–5). Quoting a range of authorities (Augustine, Bonaventure, even Seneca), he says, "Your self-will [*Eigenwille*] is nothing else but a falling away from God. . . . The will is imprisoned; the works are dead. Christ must give all the help in the beginning, middle, and end" (II.6.7).

In chapters 11–25 Arndt spells out how Christ's life is the mirror for our imitation. The essential mode of imitation is the practice of the three theological virtues of faith, hope, and charity (II.12). Arndt presents other aspects of Christ's life that his followers are called to imitate, such as poverty (II.13), humility (II.15), patience and meek-ness (II.17). Because Christ suffered tribulation, we also ought to suffer willingly out of love for him. (II.18). In emphasizing Christ crucified as the book of life, written internally and externally, in chapter 19 Arndt utilized the Latin version of the writings of Angela of Foligno. The important chapter 20, devoted to "The Power and Necessity of Prayer in Spiritual Considerations," also employs the Franciscan tertiary, as well as John Tauler. Prayer has three steps, says Arndt: (1) oral prayer; followed by (2) inner prayer "without cease in belief, spirit, and inner mind [*Gemuethe*], as mentioned in John 4:23." This is meant to lead on to (3) "supernatural prayer, which takes place, as Tauler says, through true union with God through faith, in which our created spirit melts into and sinks into the Uncreated Spirit of God, that happens altogether in a blink of the eye."[68] What is interesting here is Arndt's willingness to use language about deep union with God that would have been sus-pect to the early Luther and especially to later Protestants. Once again, prayer is seen from a christological perspective: "This threefold exam-ple, teaching, skill, and mode we have found in Our Lord Jesus Christ, when we rightly consider his way of praying" (II.20.10). The treatise on imitating Christ does not propose these practices in any external way; rather, Arndt insists, following Christ is an expression of the inner love that unites us to him (e.g., II.24.12–14).

Arndt's treatment of the contemplative life (chaps. 26–33) does not deal with contemplation in the medieval sense of forms of special con-centration on, and possible "seeing," of God, but rather continues the christological emphasis characteristic of book II, despite occasional references to such things as contemplating God's beauty in creation and in a higher way in Christ (II.30). The treatise on prayer that fol-lows in chapters 34–43 provides further insight into Arndt's use of sus-pect mystical sources. The outline of prayer given in the long chapter 34 (ed., 388–411) contains twelve headings based on Valentin Weigel's *Little Book of Prayer (Gebetbüchlein)*, although the details of Arndt's treat-ment feature materials from his own prayers. Book II closes with a treatment of the patience required for the true Christian amid the trials and tribulations of life.

Book III of *True Christianity* has been described as the key to the whole work, as the reference to it representing the final stage of the spiritual life found in the foreword and cited above suggests.[69] A vital theme of Arndt's mysticism also appears in the foreword. "So that you may properly understand this third book," says Arndt, "know that it is intended to point out how you are to seek and find the kingdom of God in yourself" (Luke 17:21).[70] The inner kingdom of God was a major motif of medieval German mysticism, so it is not surprising that it appears here and throughout *True Christianity*. Realizing the kingdom of God within is to attain the perfection of the Christian life, a completion that consists not in great deeds but in self-denial, fulfilling God's will, and love of God and neighbor (III.Foreword.7).

The first chapter of book III invokes a number of other themes of Arndt's teaching, such as the necessity of experiencing God the Trinity in the inner Sabbath (III.1.1–2), and the movement from the outward man into the "inner ground of the heart," which Arndt says he will expound on the basis of Tauler's [*sic*] *Theologia Deutsch* (III.1.3). The first mention of union occurs toward the end of this initial chapter: "You must have this treasure [the kingdom of God] in yourself. You must be united with Christ through faith" (III.1.5). Union with God is always faith-based and therefore christological for Arndt, as is evident in chapters 2–3, where he refers to Luther's notion of the "happy exchange" between God and human in the incarnation and life of the God-man (III.3.3). The mystical practices that Arndt invokes, such as turning within (III.2.1) and letting go (III.9.2, III.16.2), are always described as works of faith. Arndt has no hesitation, however, in using the language of medieval mystics to express the believer's union with Christ established in baptism and lived in faith. This is evident in his reference to God offering us the "abyss of his Godhead" and the call for total emptying of inner forms in order to see God (III.2.3). Spousal language appears in chapter 3: "Faith unites our soul with Christ as a bride with her bridegroom [Hos. 2:19–20]. . . . For whatever Christ has will belong to the believing soul, and what the soul has belongs to Christ."[71] Chapter 4 picks up on an important motif of Tauler and other German mystics, the need for seeking God both in a working way (*wuerkender Weise*) and in a receiving or suffering way (*leidender Weise*). Even closer to Tauler is the use of the language of the ground and releasement:

> If the soul is emptied of all intellectual and sensible created things that are not God himself, then a person will come into the ground, where he will find nothing but God with his light and his being. In summary, one must let all things go [*es muss alles gelassen seyn*] if you wish to find the ground. . . . Then they no longer cling to creatures, as natural persons do, but they are united in and with God, and God with them.[72]

Those who are united with God in this manner are "godly [*goettlich*], not by nature, but by grace," an appeal to one of the standard expressions of deification.[73]

The language of empting and releasing as the way to union in the ground is complemented by other motifs drawn from German mysticism, such as the appeal to poverty of spirit (III.5.1)[74] and the need for the soul to sink into stillness, rest, and darkness to find God.[75] "That is the darkness," he says, "in which the Lord dwells, and the night in which the will sleeps and is united with God." The one who seeks God must go beyond memory, intellect, and will, so that "he does not remain in the powers of the soul, but is hidden in the innermost ground and being of the soul [*ist verborgen im innersten Grund und Wesen der Seelen*]."[76] Chapter 8 heightens this kind of language. God's whole being calls to us to return to him, so we must sink into our own nothingness in total humility and self-surrender. In language that echoes Eckhart, he says, "If in yourself you were free of the images of creatures, you would have and possess God without ceasing, because he cannot keep himself back, either in heaven or on earth; he must turn to you, he must fill your soul, when he finds you empty."[77] Arndt sometimes cites whole passages from Eckhart as found in the last part of the 1522 Basel Tauler edition. For example, chapter 13 says, "Whoever seeks God and seeks anything with God, does not find him. But whoever seeks God alone in the truth, he finds God and everything that God is and what God can give and do."[78] After a number of quotations from Eckhart and Tauler (e.g., chap. 15), Arndt closes off book III by discussing the role of the Holy Spirit in uniting us with God (chaps. 16–18), as well as explaining the need for humility (chap. 20). The final chapter of book III, "On the Mystery of the Cross, how we are drawn through it to God," summarizes something dear to Tauler and Luther, that is, how willingness to suffer and to undergo *Anfechtung* is a necessary stage in the path to God and more salutary than experiencing the sweetness of God's gifts.[79]

Book III may be said to illustrate a tension in Arndt's notion of the path to union with God. The Lutheran pastor insisted on the distinction between Creator and creature, and most of the passages on union in books I–II of *True Christianity* would seem to fit into the tradition of conceiving union as a loving union of wills between God and the human person as illustrated in 1 Corinthians 6:17 (i.e., becoming one spirit with God). Nevertheless, Arndt's reliance on Tauler and Eckhart in book III allows him to use language that at times suggests a deeper understanding of becoming one with God. He was scarcely alone in this, because a number of late medieval mystics had also employed varied language to describe mystical union, which, after all, is something that cannot really be captured in words.

Book IV turns from the microcosm to the macrocosm, that is, the Book of Nature, although the second part treats of humanity as a particular part of God's creation. Along with heavy use of Paracelsus, as well as other alchemical and Hermetic materials, Arndt includes some chapters that are important for the theological foundation of his mysticism. As mentioned above, the first six chapters deal with the six days of creation, while the shorter forty chapters of part 2 concern humanity. The first ten chapters of this second part treat God as the creator, especially the pleasure God takes in his image, the human creature (IV.4; see also IV.23), and the relation of the image to the Creator (IV.5–10). Chapters 11–18 concern our obligation to love God above all things. Chapters 19–22 treat of the double command of love of God and love of neighbor (a frequent theme, as we have seen). The major concern of this second part is a long and somewhat disorganized treatment of the relation of love of God, love of self, and love of neighbor (chaps. 24–40). Arndt insists that it is not possible to be united to God in love without also being one with our neighbor: "The more a person loves God, the more he also loves those whom God loves. The more a person loves another person, the more will he be united with him" (IV.26.1). This appeal to the union of believers in Christ's Body (see 1 Cor. 12) is a frequent theme in *True Christianity*.[80] After a series of chapters contrasting good love of God and evil self-love, Arndt concludes by repeating that the whole work on the true living of the Christian life was written for justified believers, not unbelievers, "so that you let Christ live in you, rule in you, and the Holy Spirit direct you, so that your Christianity is not a sham" (IV.Conclusion.1).

We are not sure of the motivation of the editors who added books V and VI to Arndt's original four. The Lutheran pastor composed these brief works more than fifteen years after the first books. Book VI is a defense of the message of the original *True Christianity* against its critics, while the three parts of book V, especially part 2, "On the Highly Wonderful and Grace-Rich Union of Believers with . . . Christ Their Head," are a reprisal, but also a deepening, of Arndt's mystical teaching. The first part of this *Liber Confessionis*, the eleven chapters on "True Belief and the Holy Life," are a summary of Arndt's teaching on humanity as God's image, the role of the Incarnate Christ, justification by faith, and the role of conversion and the "new godly life" in deepening of the union with God given in baptism. It includes a chapter on the nature of prayer (V.Pt.1.10, ed., 827–31). Part 3 of book V has three brief dogmatic chapters. Our concern here is with the fifteen chapters of part 2, a central text for Arndt's mysticism.

The topics treated in part 2 are not new, but the heightened ways in which Arndt treats spousal union with Christ, especially in chapters 7 and 8, are. Chapter 1 begins, as in book I, with humanity's creation in the image of God, the Fall, which broke and dissolved the image, and the incarnation, which restores the image so that the Holy Spirit can once again dwell in humans.[81] In chapter 5, Arndt situates his teaching in the context of the history of salvation, saying that union with God "is established and witnessed by the three chief works of grace: first, the creation of man to God's image . . . ; second, the Incarnation of the Son of God; third, the sending of the Holy Spirit."[82] Chapter 2 explains the relation of our union to that of the Trinity. Only the Son is the "essential Image" of the Father and therefore enjoys "essential union" (*wesentliche Vereinigung*) with him; what humans possess is "likeness of this union" given us by God's infinite goodness.[83] The new birth and indwelling of the Holy Spirit (chap. 5) given in Christ's incarnation (chaps. 3–4) and treated in chapters 4, 5, 11, 14, etc., are the foundation for our present union with God, which is the foretaste of the perfect union of heaven (chap. 2.3–4). Arndt has much to say about the rooting of union in the full Christian life, such as its dependence on justifying faith (chaps. 6, 12), the themes of conversion and repentance (chaps. 6, 15), the role of word and sacrament (chaps. 3, 11, 12), and the importance of prayer (chap. 13). The focus of the treatise, however, rests squarely on "spiritual marriage and union" (*die geistliche Verehligung und Vereinigung*: 6.1). Chapters 7 and 8 explore these in detail.

Chapter 7 is entitled "The Union of the Lord Christ with the Believing Soul Takes Place through the Spiritual Marriage and Wedding." Far more lyrical and passionate than the passages on spiritual marriage in the first four books, it is a long prose poem on the nuptial bond between Christ and the believer making heavy use of the Song of Songs.[84] While Arndt does not directly reference Bernard of Clairvaux, his fervent rhetoric is reminiscent of the Cistercian abbot. Arndt begins in the voice of the lover, if not in the first person:

> If the Bridegroom comes, the holy soul rejoices and looks closely and eagerly toward his presence [*seine Gegenwart*]. By his joyous, enlivening, and holy arrival he drives out darkness and night and the heart has sweet joy, the waters of meditation flow in upon it, the soul melts for love, the spirit rejoices, the affections and desires become fervid,

love is ignited, the mind rejoices, the mouth gives praise and honor, man takes vows, and all the powers of the soul rejoice in and because of the Bridegroom.

These reflections move Arndt to break into a hymn of praise and joy: "Oh what a love! Of what a fiery desire! Of what a loving conversation! Oh how chaste a kiss!"[85] I cite these opening lines at length, because they are typical of the whole chapter with its heightened language, a style that is more easily read than summarized.

Arndt continues with a meditation on the soul as the temple of God, the "deeply beloved bride who is sick with love" (Song 2:5). He insists that "[n]o one can know this [joy and love] except the person who has experienced it," an appeal to personal experience found often in the treatise.[86] Later he says, "This spiritual marriage is far beyond all human understanding, all self-will, all [human] marital life, for it is a heavenly gift." Only humble, pure, prayerful souls are worthy of the coming of the Bridegroom, "this spiritual and mysterious wedding and marriage with the Son of God" (7.6). In order to describe it further, Arndt gives a long series of quotations from the Song of Songs (Song 2:10; 1:13–14; 4:11–13; 5:10). He even makes the surprising statement that the person who has been made "a partaker of the Lord's loveliness . . . at all times enjoys [*geneusset allezeit*] the presence of him whom he loves" (7.7). Toward the end of the chapter, Arndt turns to another of the motifs of erotic mysticism in describing the experience as *sacra ebri-etas*: "O holy drunkenness, which is full of sobriety, which according to its overflowing and taste, as it is enjoyed, lifts one to God and unites him with God so that they become one!"[87] The short chapter 8 contin-ues the same love-rhetoric, making use of another of the metaphors found so often in mystical traditions: "O sweet Lord Jesus, penetrate our hearts with the fiery arrows of your love!"[88]

The remaining chapters of this treatise on the love union with the Divine Bridegroom are less fervent, turning to the effects of our unit-ing with Christ as members of his body. Christ wishes to "clothe him-self and transform himself in each person so that through the bond of love each person might be renewed and reformed in him" (chap. 9.2). Becoming one with Christ means not only sharing in the delights of his presence but also willingness to suffer innocently, as he suffered. As members of his body, we can unite the inner word of his testimony and the outer word of the preacher (9.3).[89] In line with Luther and the broad evangelical tradition, chapter 11 insists that this union begins in the waters of baptism, where "the Bridegroom takes the soul and marries himself to the soul with an eternal binding" (chap. 11.4). Those who are living in and from this union, however, must "also be united to him through the use and enjoyment of his essential body and blood" (chap. 12.1), that is, through the reception of the Lord's Supper. Just as the highest blessedness of this life is to be so united with God (chap. 14), so too "the greatest and highest misery of man is to be eternally cut off from God" through sin (chap. 15). Thus, Arndt closes off his most extensive treatment of what some (but not he) called mystical union.[90]

Conclusion

There have been many attempts to characterize Johann Arndt's teaching. At the beginning of the eighteenth century, the Pietist Gottfried Arnold included Arndt as a major figure in his *History and Description of Mystical Theology or Godly Teaching* (1702). Early in the twentieth century (1912), Wilhelm Koepp, despite using the word mysticism in the title of his book on Arndt, saw him not as a theologian or a mystical theologian but as a writer concerned with piety and ethical instruction. That Arndt is indeed a theologian and a mystic has emerged more clearly in recent decades, though these claims are still contested, depending on one's view of mysticism. Winfried Zeller (1978) included Arndt in his study of the relation of Lutheranism and mysticism, and Berndt Hamm (1982) spoke of Arndt's "theology of piety" (*Frömmigkeitstheologie*). Johannes Wallmann hesitated, claiming, "[Arndt] was no mystic, but a lover of mysticism. He did not build his own type of Protestant mysticism. . . . Johann Arndt is not a representative of Protestant mysticism, but the mediator of mystical piety to Protestantism."[91] The two major recent studies of Arndt have not hesitated to see him as a theologian and in some way a mystic, though they evaluate his mysticism in different ways. Christian Braw (1986) speaks of Arndt's "new mysticism" as a form of confessional evangelical mysticism, stressing the deep Lutheran roots of his teaching and presenting it according to the categories of orthodox Lutheran theology.[92] Hermann Geyer (2001) speaks of Arndt's "mystical theology" and sees *True Christianity* as a "theological-theosophical program," one that, while not departing from the fundamentals of the Lutheran confessional documents, represents an explicit challenge to Lutheran orthodox theology in its mode of presentation, rich range of sources, and in the fundamentals of its message.[93]

True Christianity fits within the parameters of late medieval and early modern mysticism, not least because of its sources and its treatment of key aspects of the mystical tradition. This is what Martin Schmidt meant by speaking of *True Christianity* as "a catholic book" (with emphasis on the small c).[94] But there are also new, and specifically evangelical, elements in Arndt, ones that helped ensure the popularity and later influence of the book in Protestant circles. From the Protestant perspective, Arndt represents a shift from concentrating on justification by faith to emphasis on the process of sanctification realized by the indwelling of the Word and the Spirit in the restored *imago dei*. As with Luther, the union of Christ and the believer is rooted in baptism, but Arndt is more concerned than Luther was with the deepening of union through the life of prayer and sanctification, a process he describes in erotic language beyond that used by Luther. Like Weigel, Arndt was also willing to take over some of the late medieval language of deep union of identity not found in Luther. Without ever questioning the importance of the external and objective features of the Bible, the church, preaching the word, and sacramental observance, Arndt's message that external faith does not save without internal appropriation of sanctification was a gauntlet thrown down to the Confessional Lutheranism of his day. In this sense, Hermann Geyer is correct to say that Arndt "spiritualizes" Lutheranism, but from within, not from without, as the Radical Spiritualists attempted.[95] Berndt Hamm claims that, in the long run, Arndt does not convey "a Lutheran theology," summarizing his position: "Arndt goes his own way between Luther, Orthodoxy, and radical Protestant Spiritualism and by so doing shows a singular path to Pietist spirituality insofar as it moves within the ecclesiastical realm and seeks connections to the Lutheran teaching tradition."[96] However he is judged, I would argue that Johann Arndt was an original voice in the story of early modern mysticism.

Jacob Boehme: "The Philosopher of the Simple"

Jacob Boehme was born in 1575 into a peasant family in a village near Görlitz in Lusatia, one of the northern crown lands of the Kingdom of Bohemia (today the city is on the German–Polish border).[97] He was sent to school to learn his ABCs but never received higher education and hence was ignorant of Latin and wrote only in German.[98] Apprenticed as a shoemaker, Boehme wandered for several years as a journeyman before settling in Görlitz in 1592 and setting up shop. Lusatia was an area of religious diversity where different groups mingled: various Lutheran parties, Schwenkfeldians, Paracelsians, Humanists, and even students of Kabbalah (the Kabbalist R. Jehudah Löw visited the city in 1600). Boehme's pastor, Martin Moller (d. 1606), was mystically inclined and appears to have had some influence on the shoemaker. The religious picture had begun to shift in 1592 in favor of orthodox Lutheranism when neighboring Saxony introduced a series of Articles of Visitation, which insisted on strict adherence to the Formula of Concord. Boehme continued to attend the Lutheran church in Görlitz, but it became increasingly clear that his Lutheranism was latitudinarian and some thought unorthodox.[99] Still, Lutheranism was the major element in Boehme's background, and Luther's Bible was his essential book.[100] Boehme's reaction against the narrowness of contemporary Lutheran theology allied him with Johann Arndt, but his reaction led him in a different path.

Young Jacob, who married in 1599, had an inquiring mind. His first work, the *Aurora* of 1612, tells of his fascination with the deepest puzzles of theology and cosmology and the intense melancholy he experienced in not being able to find satisfactory answers to his questions. He says, "I have read the writings of many exalted masters" (*Aurora* 10.27), but detecting precise sources for Boehme's elaborate speculations is a difficult task.[101] One day in 1600, as he wrestled with trying to understand God's love and mercy, he says, "at that point he blessed me, that is, illuminated me with his Holy Spirit, so that I might understand his will and be rid of my sadness; at that point, the spirit broke through [*So Brach der Geist durch*]." Several lines later, he continues:

> . . . at last, after several firm assaults, my spirit broke through the gates of hell and into the innermost birth of the divinity [*Biss in die Inreste geburtt der Gottheit*], there to be embraced by love as a bridegroom embraces his beloved bride. As for my exultation of spirit, I cannot convey it in writing or in speech. . . . In this light my spirit soon saw everything, recognizing God in all creatures, in vegetation and grass; I recognized who he is, and how he is, and what is his intention [*wer der sey / vnd wie der Sey / vnd was sein willen sey*].[102]

Boehme says that he immediately determined "to describe the being of God," but the illumination was so deep and comprehensive that he admits he could not immediately apprehend all that he had seen, so twelve years passed before he plumbed its meaning sufficiently to sit down to write his account of what had been revealed to him in the *Aurora*.[103] It is important not to dwell too much or too little on this event. Boehme was not a visionary in the medieval sense of someone who enjoyed a series of imaginative showings of God and the other world; he was a "see-er," that is, a person whose life was devoted to deepening mental penetration into the reality of God and the world. What Boehme "saw" was a new construction of the universe, one with ties to other philosophical, religious, and mystical traditions, but still quite original. Boehme was constructing a new *mythos*, a likely story about the deepest nature of all things—something revealed to him and therefore personally indisputable,[104] but which he also knew would be hard to make convincing to his contemporaries.

Boehme gave up shoe making in 1612 and became a small trades-man. The *Aurora* was not published but circulated in manuscript form and came to the attention of the pastor of Görlitz, Gregor Richter, in 1613. He confiscated the copies and forbade Boehme from further writing. The unassuming Boehme, who had begun to gather a circle of like-minded seekers around him, obeyed this injunction until 1619. Prompted by another illumination and the encouragement of his friends, he began writing and circulating more works. An avalanche of treatises, long and short, poured from his pen in the last five years of his life, the same years that saw the beginnings of the disastrous Thirty Years' War that ravaged Germany.[105] In 1619, he finished the *De tribus principiis (Three Principles of Divine Being)*, and 1620 saw the appearance of five works: *The Threefold Life of Man*; *Forty Questions on the Soul*; *The Human Genesis of Christ*; *Six Theosophical Points*; and *Six Mystical Points*. During the early 1620s he was also penning a series of *Theosophical Letters* to friends and disciples. The *De signatura rerum (The Birth and Designation of All Things)*, his most important cosmo-logical work, dates from 1622. *Election to Grace* and *The Heavenly and Earthly Mysteries* also come from this time. Boehme's longest work, an exposition of Genesis called *Mysterium Magnum*, was written between 1622 and 1624; and the short *Clavis (Key)*, a guide to his fundamental themes and terms, was written in spring of 1624. Other minor writ-ings, some polemical, were also being produced. At the beginning of 1624, a small collection of treatises was printed under the title *The Way to Christ*. This brought him once again to the attention of Pas-tor Richter, who denounced him from the pulpit as the "Shoemaker Antichrist."[106] The town council advised Boehme to leave Görlitz. By late 1624 Richter had died, and Boehme, in ill health, returned to the city where he succumbed to illness on November 17. His circle of disciples, however, had already begun to disseminate his writings. The first of these was an expanded version of the *Christosophia, or The Way to Christ*. (Later editions added more treatises until there were nine in all.) Stories about the quiet cobbler which pictured him as a prophet, visionary, and unrivaled savant began to spread. The legend of Jacob Boehme had begun.

It is not easy to write about legends, especially those who left so many thousands of pages. Boehme's "impulse to describe the being of God" resulted in a speculative theosophy that has always been difficult to analyze, especially because of his intention to describe the whole divine mystery.[107] Boehme remains a bone of contention for interpreters, old and new.[108] Hegel lauded him as the "first German philosopher," and a more recent student, David Walsh, claims that "Boehme created the new symbolic form that has dominated the self-understanding of modern Western civilization: the historical myth of innerworldly perfection."[109] Is Boehme really the beginning of the modern world? Others might rather be inclined to agree with John Wesley, writing on June 4, 1742, who said of Boehme's *Mysterium Magnum*, "it is most sublime nonsense; inimitable bombast; fustian not to be paralleled!"[110] Even a sympathetic reader, such as Cyril O'Regan, says that Boehme presents a "coagulated cyclone of language, a form or nonform of linguistic implosion that repels and excludes," admitting that "Boehme is simply one of the most difficult reads in the history of Christian thought."[111] In what follows I make no pretense to survey all of Boehme's works, let alone to give a full account of his theosophy;[112] but the fact that the Lutheran shoemaker has been seen by many as an important mystic, however untraditional, means that we need to investigate why this claim has been made and what it might mean.[113]

Given the extent of Boehme's writings (about twenty-five works, some quite large), a closer look at just a few of his treatises will have to suffice for providing a sense of his thinking and its peculiar form of mysticism.[114] I begin with the *Aurora*, which, despite its early date and the preliminary form of his views found in it, remains Boehme's most read work. What kind of book is the *Aurora*, or *Morning Redness in Rising (Morgen-Röte im auffgang)*? The long subtitle and the author's preface indicate the scope of the volume: "*I have given this book the title, the mother or root of Philosophia, Astrologia, and Theologia*" (Preface 84; Weeks, 104–5). *Philosophia*, Boehme explains, treats of the divine nature and power and how all things are constituted in God, while *Astrologia* concerns all the forces of nature. *Theologia* considers the realm of Christ and how it is opposed to the realm of hell (Preface 84–88; Weeks, 104–7). Boehme concludes, "*The uppermost title*, Morning Glow in ascent, is a secret and *mysterium*" (Preface 89; Weeks, 106–7). Therefore, the book, embracing as it does the root of philosophy, astrology, and theology, is a speculative explanation of everything (i.e., pansophy).

At the outset and throughout the book (first printed in 1634), Boehme alerts the reader to the fact that the work needs to be supplemented by his later writings, especially *The Three Principles* and *The Threefold Life of Man*. There is, then, an unfinished quality to the book, though it features an optimistic rhetoric and passionate intensity often missing in the shoemaker's later, more pessimistic writings. The passion is reflected in the title: the "Morning Glow" indicates the beginning of a new era, the end of the old world of ignorance and evil, and the dawn of an age of enlightenment. With vatic confidence at the end of the book, Boehme gives one of several personal *apologiae*:

> This is the true gate of the mystery of God. The reader will take note that it does not lie within the capacity of a human being to understand such things or to know about them, if the morning glow in the center were not breaking forth in the soul. For these are divine mysteries that no human being can research by the power of human reason. . . . I will have enough scoffers, for the ruined nature is terribly ashamed before the light. But I cannot for this reason desist. [115]

Like many sixteenth-century mystics, both Protestant and Catholic, Boehme insists on the necessity of inner experience. In a series of *apologiae* scattered throughout the *Aurora*, he asserts that he has no personal expertise as a philosopher, alchemist, or astrologer, but it was God who gave him insight into the inner mysteries and it is God (or sometimes Nature) who compels him to write, no matter what others might say against him.[116] Those skilled in these disciplines are correct in their descriptions of the outer phenomena, Boehme says, but he has been given the vision of the inner relationships of the divine nature and the fabric of the universe. Although Boehme admits that there are aspects of the mysteries he does not fully understand,[117] he says he is compelled to set the message forth. At times he invites his readers to pray to be given illumination that will allow them to see what he has seen.[118] Despite his lack of higher education, Boehme writes with self-confidence: "For I have not taken my writing and book from other masters, even if I use many examples and much testimony of the Holy Spirit in it. Rather all of this comes from God, written in my own way of thinking."[119] Late in the *Aurora*, when considering the role of the seven planets, he says, "Nor can any human being instruct me in these matters. For I do not owe my knowledge to studies. . . . I was not there when God created them. But since in my spirit the gates of the depths and the gates of anger and the chamber of death have all been opened wide by the love of God, the spirit sees through." He concludes, "But since I see the gates of God in my spirit, and have an urge to do so, I intend to write according to what I see and to pay no heed to any human authority."[120] Jacob Boehme, lay worker and autodidact, is part of a broad late medieval and early modern movement in which divinely inspired laity challenge the authority of the university-trained clerics, which is why he aptly characterized himself as "a philosopher of the simple" (*ein Philosophus der einfeltigen* [*Aurora* 18.80]).

Boehme also has his opponents in mind in the *Aurora*. The philosophers, astrologers, and theologians who deal with outward things are not condemned as long as they keep to their limited fields, but he rejects those who might question the truth of his more penetrating universal view of God and the world. Boehme reserves special scorn for those he calls the "Grace-Choosers" (*Gnaden-Waler*), or "Electionists," that is, the Calvinist predestinarians, who insist that God only gives grace to some and rejects others from all eternity.[121] He attacks them often, even naming Calvin in one place.[122] Boehme, like the Radical Spiritualists examined in the previous chapter, insisted on the continued existence of human freedom after Adam's Fall and on the possible salvation of all, even Turks, Jews, and heathen.[123] Like the Radical Spiritualists, he came to doubt the saving efficacy of the institutional church(es)—the dead *Steinkirchen* (churches of stone)—in favor of the invisible church of true inner believers.

The *Aurora* is long and at times confusing to those not familiar with Boehme's symbolism and repetitious style.[124] Much is said about God, angels and humans, the Fall of Lucifer and that of Adam, the creation of the physical universe, the elements and humors, and even the heliocentric view of the cosmos. A central motif repeated over hundreds of pages concerns what Boehme calls "the seven spirits of God" (*Die sieben geister Gottes*), or the "Source-Spirits" (*quel geister* [*Aurora* 9.41–46]), which are also characterized as "qualities" (*Aurora* 8.19–24). At the outset of the treatise Boehme defines "quality" as "the motility or activity, the surging or urging of a thing, as for example the heat that burns, consumes, and acts upon everything that enters into it that is not its property."[125] The seven qualities reveal a fundamental characteristic of Boehme's thought: the necessity for contrariety and opposition, both in the created universe and in the divine realm on which our world is based. The dynamic movement of the seven essential qualities is at the heart of all things, even the divine activity; it is what allows Boehme to find an inner pattern, an interlocking series of universal concordances achieved by the interaction of contraries in all things. Toward the end of the book, he tries to bring his thoughts on the universality of seven spirits together into a kind of summary: "When you reflect and consider what exists both in this world and outside of it, you speculate and reflect about the entire body of God who is the being of all beings [*das wesen aller wesen*], a being without beginning. But in his own seat he possesses no mobility, rationality, or palpability, but is rather a dark depth without beginning or end." Nonetheless, "In this dark vale, there are the seven spirits of God. They have no beginning or end. . . . The seven spirits generate each the other from eternity to eternity."[126] The seven spirits, or qualities (probably based on the action of the seven planets), are a tool for explaining the relation of the realms of reality, as well as the evil introduced by the Fall of Lucifer and compounded in Adam's Fall, a tragedy now being overcome by the work of Christ.

A survey of the *Aurora* reveals some of the dimensions of this holistic picture of the relation of the divine and created realms. Chapters 1–7 deal with God and the angels. Chapter 1, as noted above, introduces the notion of spirit-quality, which can be of a good or bad nature. The six qualities listed here are heat (containing both light and wrath), cold (which lessens heat and also causes destruction), and the four elements—bitter, sweet, sour, and stringent or salty.[127] The account becomes more complex in chapter 2, which claims that all creatures are created from these qualities, and goes on to introduce another key aspect of Boehme's thought: the parallel between man the microcosm created in God's image and likeness and the macrocosm of the universe. Chapter 3 contains the first of several discussions of the Trinity, none of which conforms to traditional Trinitarian speculation.[128] Chapter 4 takes up the creation of the angels and introduces the notion of *salnitter/salitter* (4.10, 28), an alchemical term whose meaning seems to shift. In the *Aurora* it signifies something like the explosive life force found in pure form in the divine realm and impurely in the natural realm.[129] Chapter 6 shows how both angels and humans are made to God's image.

Chapter 8 contains an account of how the seven spirit-qualities in God form the basis for the cosmos, not only the Angelic Kingdom but also the heliocentric physical universe. Here the seven qualities, which conform to the seven planets, are (1) dry (Saturn); (2) sweet (Jupiter); (3) bitter (Mars); (4) water/fire (Moon/Sun); (5) love (Venus); (6) sound (Mercury); and finally (7) corpus or body (Earth).[130] The remainder of the long *Aurora* features treatments of the interaction of the seven spirit-qualities in all the realms of divine and created being.[131] One way to understand this repetition is to see it as Boehme's vehicle for showing how God is the essence of all things (e.g., *Aurora* 26.53–62). God is ubiquitous and immanent in all things; therefore, from one perspective, all things are consubstantial with God.[132] For the Görlitz seer, everything that lives and moves is *in* God and all that is formed or made is *out of* God. As he puts it in a rhetorical challenge in chapter 23, "Look, you uncomprehending fellow! I intend to show you the true ground of the divinity. If this entire being is not God, then you are not God's image."[133] Like a number of earlier thinkers (e.g., John Scottus Eriugena), Boehme understands creation from nothing (*creatio ex nihilo*) as *creatio ex Deo*. The insistence that all things are in God and out of God but not identical with God's totally good and simple nature (*Aurora* 23.77–81) shows that, despite statements about the world being the body of God (e.g., *Aurora* 2.16–18), Boehme is concerned to point out how God both *is* the world and yet is *beyond* the world. He is not a pantheist, though some might describe him as a kind of spiritual materialist.

Boehme returns to the creation of the angels in chapter 12 of the *Aurora* and then begins a discussion of the creation and fall of Lucifer that stretches through chapters 13–16, followed by a shorter reflection on the Fall of humanity (chap. 17). In order to understand the role of the spirit-qualities in the making of the angels, it is necessary to analyze their action in "the birth or geniture of God in his innermost being" (*Aurora* 13.68). The activity of the seven qualities in the divine birth (13.69–89) uses the analogy of the turning of the wheels within wheels that Boehme adopted from the chariot vision of Ezekiel 1:15–21 and to which he often returned.[134] These chapters feature the shoemaker's initial attempt at theodicy, or an explanation of how evil entered the world. Boehme insists that God is totally good (e.g., *Aurora* 2.35), but the seven spirit-qualities found in God and in creation form the root of evil when they are no longer kept in balance in creatures, beginning with King Lucifer, "the brightest among the three kings of angels" (*Aurora* 12.133). Lucifer's pride led to his free decision to pervert this balance, a situation in which the wrathful side of the spirits in God is enkindled and the cosmos is thrown into disarray (e.g., *Aurora* 4.7, 9; 16.57–78). It is not easy to follow Boehme's thought here, or in his subsequent considerations of evil. He does not appear to be a consistent dualist. In the *Aurora*, evil does not seem to originate directly in God, though it sets constraints on God subsequent to Lucifer's Fall.[135] Boehme's treatment of evil serves as a basis for those, like Cyril O'Regan, who see him representing "the proximate emergence of Gnosticism in modern discourse."[136] The problem of evil, however, will be overcome in the expected "Dawn," the approaching millennium when the unfortunate consequences of the disharmony of the seven spirits will be expunged by the action of Christ, who is the Father's answer to the crisis created by Lucifer's Fall. Thus, there is a distinct apocalyptic dimension to Boehme's thought, albeit intermingled with many other speculative tendencies. Be this as it may, the apocalyptic side is not further developed, because the later chapters of the *Aurora* do not focus on soteriology, here or in the future, but rather on cosmology, as Boehme pursues a meandering account of the seven days of creation (chaps. 18–26).

In the course of his lengthy first work, Boehme touches on a variety of topics. He does so with a sense of prophetic conviction and a desire to inspire his readers to see *into* the mysteries he has been shown and even into the loving union with God he has experienced. This impetus toward union helps explain the popularity of this long and difficult work, which might be described as speculative theosophy of a mystical cast. The divine marriage between God and the soul appears in a number of places. For example, chapter 8 on "The Mystery of the Angelic Kingdom" contains a passage on how the fifth spirit-quality of "blessed, friendly, and joyous *love*" affects the person who is seeking God (*Aurora* 8.91–109). Boehme composes a hymn to the sweet power of love. When love arrives, God's lovers taste it and come to life. "*What comes then is an amiable heralding and triumphing,*" he says, "a friendly greeting and great love. Oh yes, an amiable and blessed kissing and good tasting! The bridegroom kisses the bride. Oh, bliss and profound love! How sweet you are! How amicable! Yet how lovely your taste, how mellow your smell."[137] Later, he has an impassioned address to the blind human beings whom the devil is deceiving:

> Oh, wretched human creature, turn around! The heavenly father has stretched out both arms and is calling to you: *Come!* He wants to embrace you in his love. You are his child. If he were set against you, he would have to be divided in himself. . . . Oh, you guardians of Israel, why do you sleep! Awake from the slumber of whorishness and adorn your lamps. The bridegroom nears!

As the passage goes on, Boehme again becomes more ecstatic: "*Awaken! Awaken!* Give birth, you sad woman! Behold! The bridegroom draws near and asks of you the fruit. Why do you sleep! See how he knocks. Oh blessed love and radiant light! Abide by us. For evening draws near."[138] Boehme's language evokes both the Song of Songs and New

Testament texts on the approach of the Divine Bridegroom, such as Matthew 9:15, John 3:29, Revelation 21:9, and especially the Parable of the Wise and Foolish Virgins (Matt. 25:1–13). Such texts also contain a strong apocalyptic dimension.

Important themes of Boehme's developing theosophy do not yet appear in the *Aurora*. The extent to which any summary of these themes may be said to constitute a "Boehmist system" is a subject of disagreement. Boehme himself seems to have tried to give some system to his teaching in his late work, the *Clavis*, where he says, "Because the lovers [of truth] desire a *Clavis*, or key of my writings, so I am happy to please them in this and will sketch a short summary of the ground of these strange words."[139] Some modern students of Boehme, such as Hans Grunsky, have followed this line, speaking of Boehme's "closed system" and providing a systematic lexicon of his terminology.[140] Given the kaleidoscopic variety of Boehme's writings, however, and the fact that even key terms and themes seem to shift meaning, other interpreters have found any systematic approach misleading. Andrew Weeks, for example, decries attempts to find "a full-blown philosophical system in his writing," speaking of Boehme's works as "more like great series of thematic cycles and epicycles," circles of symbolic images.[141] Given his stress on the role of imagination (*Einbildung/Imaginatio*),[142] attempts to reduce Boehme's thought to a logically coherent system seem to miss the mark. Hence, I will not try to evaluate the whole of Boehme's thought, but only consider some key themes and images from several of his later works as an opening for considering what Boehme may be said to have contributed to the history of Christian mysticism.

The Three Principles of the Divine Being appeared in 1619, but probably took several years to write.[143] Although Boehme says he is now writing in a "better style" than the *Aurora*, later readers have not found this to be the case. The book is fearfully dense, and Weeks characterizes it as "a many-layered complex of relationships and references, a kind of symbolist-esoteric palimpsest."[144] The three principles announced on the title page are: (1) the eternal birth of the Holy Trinity; (2) the creation of man and his Fall from Paradise; and (3) the meaning of God's wrath (sin, death, the devil, and hell). Several significant shifts in Boehme's thinking are evident as the book unfolds. Scripturally, Boehme uses both Genesis 1 and the Gospel of John, but he says that John's Prologue provides a deeper account of the divine and human worlds. Second, emphasis is now placed on *principium* more than on spirit-qualities. "A principle," Boehme says, "is nothing else but a new birth, a new life,"[145] in other words, a place, origin, or force in which the spirit is reborn.

Wesen, being or substance, is the reality within which principles give rise to new life. The central role of the principles seems to reflect the importance of the alchemical triad of sulphur, mercury, and salt. In the *Aurora*, Boehme had already wrestled with the problem of theodicy in relation to Lucifer's Fall; in the *Three Principles* he presents an account of evil that roots it more directly in the divine nature itself, not unlike what can be found in esoteric Kabbalah. Chapter 4 advances a case for God before creation as Nothing: "He is a spirit, and before our eyes he is like a nothing; hence, if we did not know him from creation, we would know nothing of him; if he had not become from all eternity, he would be nothing at all."[146] Because the devil was created out of God, not out of nothing, it seems that evil extends back into the divine nature (e.g., 4.33–37), that is, when God begins to express himself in creation, evil is already present in some way. David Walsh puts it as follows: "He [Boehme] focused attention on the necessity for a negative self-assertive force in the unfolding process of reality, and he inevitably blurred the distinction between moral evil and the consuming powers of the physical world. . . . The logic of his speculation . . . maintained the necessity for a negative and even evil reality so that the divine light and love may be manifested."[147] Correlative to this shift in understanding God is the emergence of the transcendental divine will as a fundamental category. There had not been much discussion of will in *Aurora*, but beginning in chapter 7 of the *Three Principles* will as the force that impels the unknown darkness of the Nothing-God to come to expression and self-knowledge becomes important. In chapter 7.14, Boehme makes God's will the source of creation, and even the birthing in the Trinity. "One should understand," he says, "how the divine power shines in all things, yet is not the thing itself, but the Spirit of God is in the other as principle. The thing is its mirror, which comes to be in this way from its yearning will." He continues, "Now the heart of God in the Father is the first will, and the Father is the first desire for the Son, and the Son is the Father's power and light."[148] Will in this sense is prior to being (*Wesen*); it is that which impels the hidden God to come into being—the being of God, of the Trinity, and of the angelic and visible worlds. Boehme's theosophy is thus fundamentally voluntarist. For Boehme, however, will is closely aligned with Imagination, the supernatural power to create images in one's own likeness found in both God and humans.

In the *Aurora*, considerable attention was given to Lucifer's Fall, but the *Three Principles*, without neglecting Lucifer, gives more space to a mythic account of Adam and his Fall, as well as his relation to the archetypal figure of the Virgin Divine Wisdom developed from Old Testament accounts of *Sophia* (e.g., Proverbs 8). Thus, the theosophical emphasis of the *Aurora* is complemented by a developing anthropology, or better "anthroposophy,"[149] intimately tied to a "sophiology," or teaching on the Virgin Sophia. This begins to be laid out in chapters 12–13 of the *Three Principles*. Here Adam is seen as a celestial androgynous figure, combining male and female principles but going beyond them. In his paradisiacal perfection, Adam did not need to eat and could self-propagate. However, God allowed Adam to be tempted for forty days, during which time he began to lust after Divine Wisdom, conceived of as the serene and reflective aspect of the Deity, "the mirror of God." Wisdom was meant to assist Adam but could not be his mate because she was of the divine realm. As a result of his lust, Adam was cast into sleep (the First Fall), the Virgin Sophia left him, and he received the earthly Eve, his female side, as wife. They both then sinned by desiring unlawful knowledge symbolized in the eating of the apple (the Second Fall) and were cast out of the Garden of Paradise. From here on Divine Wisdom would play a major role in Boehme's thought, something that did not endear him to orthodox Lutheran critics, who accused him of heresy by introducing a fourth figure into the divine realm. Wisdom as the feminine aspect of God is described in a myriad of ways in Boehme's later writings. Many of these are summarized in the *Clavis*, where he says, "Wisdom is the outflown Word of the divine power, knowledge, and holiness, a *Subjectum* or 'counterstroke' in which the Holy Spirit works, forms, and models." Wisdom is also "the great mystery of the divine art." She is "the divine understanding, that is, the divine contemplation wherein Unity is manifest." Finally, "She is the true divine chaos in which all things lie as a divine imagination in which the ideas of angels and souls have been seen from all eternity in a divine resemblance."[150]

Boehme was now entering into a period of amazing productivity, as treatises long and short flew from his pen. The years 1619–1620 saw the writing of three substantial works: *The Threefold Life of Man; Forty Questions on the Soul;* and *The Human Genesis of Christ (De incarnatione Verbi, oder Von der Menschwerdung Jesu Christi)*. These middle works deal with anthropology and Christology, particularly the issue of human freedom. Two short works also come from this time, the *Six Theosophical Points*, and the *Six Mystical Points*. *The Threefold Life of Man* considers the alienated life that is the fate of fallen humanity, making considerable use of the Bible, especially Genesis and the Apocalypse. *The Forty Questions on the Soul* is of importance because it is the first place in Boehme's writings where he talks about the primal "God beyond God," what he called the *Ungrund*.

Boehme seems to have been meditating on the ultimate source of all differentiation, divine and created, from the time of his illumination in 1600. In the *Aurora* he had made use of the terms *Grund* ("ground") and *Abgrund* ("abyss"), favored by medieval mystics. In *The Three Principles* he experimented with *Urkund* (perhaps "primal manifestation"). He now created the neologism *Ungrund* (literally "no-ground," or "without-ground"), which Virginie Pektas identifies as "the non-revealed Deity, included in itself, outside the movement of creation, without any determination, pure silence without essence."[151] *Ungrund* was central to Boehme's subsequent thought.

Given its biblical foundations, *abyssus* (German *Abgrund*) had played a role in Christian discourse from early days, though most often in the negative sense of the abyss of chaos at the beginning of creation, or the depths of hell. In some medieval mystics *Abgrund* gradually emerged as a term to indicate the boundless and unknowable divine depths, and also the deepest reaches of the human spirit created in God's image.[152] Mystical use of the language of "ground" (Middle High German *grunt* and its equivalents) was initiated by Eckhart and richly developed in the Germanic languages of the late medieval and early modern periods as a key "master metaphor" of mystical discourse.[153] The interaction of *abgrunt* and *grunt* language in various mystics was complicated. While related to both these inherited mystical categories, Boehme's *Ungrund* was a new creation that underscores his role in the history of apophatic mysticism.

The *Forty Questions on the Soul* is unusual among Boehme's works in being a response to issues posed by his learned friend Balthasar Walther,[154] who was supposedly acquainted with Kabbalah.[155] Although the questions are forty in number, the essence of the treatise is presented in the first question, which occupies about a third of the work. Question 1 concerns the issue, "Where does the Soul originally come from at the Beginning of the World?"[156] Boehme's account of the origin of the soul proceeds according to ten forms of fire, which some have seen as reflecting the ten *sephirot*, or manifestations of the hidden God, found in the Kabbalists. Once again, the divine will functions as the central agent (e.g., 1.6–9). The first form is characterized as "the eternal liberty which has the will and is itself the will; now every will has a seeking to do or desire something; and herein it beholds itself and sees in eternity what it is. It makes for itself a glass of its own likeness, for it sees what it is, and so, finding nothing but itself, it desires itself."[157]

This comment sets the stage for the second form of fire, where *Ungrund* receives its initial treatment.[158] Will is again the motivating force, but since this pre-cosmic desire exists by itself, it can only want itself. Thus, seeking a model of itself, Will makes itself pregnant so that a kind of darkness comes over it. Boehme tries to explain how this free-willing "nothingness in itself" constitutes itself by employing the analogy of an eye gazing into a mirror (i.e., the mirror of itself). "It is all things," he says, "and yet as a nothing; it beholds itself, and yet finds nothing but an A, which is its eye. AV [German *Auge*], that is, the eternal original that something is, for it is an eternal beginning and the eternal end. Thus, the *Ungrund* sees in itself and finds itself [*Also siehet der Ungrund in sich, und findet sich selber*]." He continues with a dense analysis of how this mystery is to be interpreted. The eye signifies both A and O, as in the Apocalypse text about Christ being the Alpha and Omega (Rev. 22:13). The eye of God gazes into the A and V as into a mirror and yet sees something more than itself, namely, "the globe of eternity, wherein lies the foundation of heaven and earth, of the elements, and also the starry spheres." In this globe all things are seen from eternity, yet before they have essence, so only as reflections in "the eye of the *Ungrund*, concerning which we have neither pen, tongue, nor utterance, either to write or to speak; only the spirit of eternity [which] leads the eye of the soul into it; and so we see it; otherwise, it would remain silent, and this hand could not describe anything of it."

While Boehme also continued to use the term "abyss" of the hidden God,[159] his neologism *Ungrund* was a major development. The metaphor, which might be paraphrased as "the ungraspable non-ground," has been written about by many Boehme scholars, such as the Russian philosopher Nicholas Berdyaev, who spoke of *Ungrund* as, "an absolutely original freedom, something that is not even the meonotic freedom determined by God."[160] But the *Ungrund* appears to be more like the "whence" (though not the place) where freedom arises, rather than freedom itself. All human words are insufficient to describe its primordiality. Although *Ungrund* has affinities with Eckhart's master metaphor *grunt* (e.g., the way in which it is spoken of metaphorically as "hunting" or "desiring" all things), it also has significant differences, especially in its lack of an anthropological reciprocity. There is no human *Ungrund*, while for Eckhart the *grunt* is found both in the deepest recesses of God and of the soul. For Boehme the *Ungrund* is not really so much a ground of all that comes after it, as it is a presupposition for the grounding activity of transcendental will/desire, or imagination. *Ungrund* is limitless neediness—an indeterminate aspiration to come to knowledge of itself and of what follows from this, that is, knowledge of the universe.[161] Although it can be described in terms reminiscent of those found in mystics like Eriugena and Eckhart, such as "Nothing," "the One beyond being," and "perfect silence and stillness," in its pre-intellective and deep neediness *Ungrund* contrasts with silent and hidden pleroma of the divine "No-thing" of these earlier mystics, which is a hiddenness that overflows from itself in sharing the good, rather than from the desperate need to find itself.[162]

Given the significance of the *Ungrund*, a look at some other appearances of the term will be helpful. The first of the *Six Theosophical Points*, written about the same time as the *Forty Questions*, features another attempt to clarify the *Ungrund*.[163] "So the first will is an *Ungrund* . . . ," Boehme begins, "an eternal nothing; we know it to be like a mirror, wherein one sees his own image." What is significant here is that once again will and desire are the fundamental categories for speaking about the *Ungrund*. Although *Ungrund* is a Nothingness beyond all concepts, words, and categories, when Boehme tries to express its hyper-transcendentalism, volitional language comes to the fore. This passage from the beginning of the *Six Theosophical Points* goes on to discuss how the *Ungrund* emerges into the "triad of the Deity," that is, Father, Son, and Holy Spirit, and also how the *Ungrund* is related to *Magia*, another major theme in Boehme's later thought, one closely related to the creative power of Imagination. "All is together an eternal *Magia*," he assets, "and dwells with the center of the heart in itself, and by the spirit goes forth from the center out of itself." In the fifth of his *Six Mystical Points*, another short treatise from this period, he speaks of *Magia* as "the desiring spirit of being," "the formative power in the Eternal Wisdom," "the Mother from which nature comes," "the activity in the Will-Spirit," and "the best theology."[164] *Magia*, therefore, is necessary for *Ungrund* to come to expression.

In the brief collection of nine texts known as *Pansophical Mystery (Mysterium Pansophicum)*, the first text is devoted to the *Ungrund*. Boehme says, "The *Ungrund* is an eternal nothing, but it makes an eternal beginning as a craving [*Sucht*], for the Nothing is a craving after something. And because there is nothing that can give anything, the craving itself is the giving of it, and yet it is a Nothing as purely a desiring craving. And that is the eternal origin of *Magia*, which makes in itself where there is nothing. It makes something out of nothing, and that only in itself."[165] *Ungrund* appears in many of Boehme's later works.[166] A passage from the *De signatura rerum* tries to express the relation between *Ungrund* and the other terms that Boehme uses in relation to it, such as Nothing, Eye, and Will.[167] There is also a passage in *On Divine Contemplation (Theoscopia)*, where, rather than employing the usual metaphor of the self-reflecting eye, Boehme says, "Since the *Ungrund*, as God, is an eternal speaking as a breathing forth of himself, so also the *Ungrund* is spoken into the resigned life, for the breathing of the *Ungrund* speaks through the stationary ground of life."[168] This turn to a metaphor of breathing rather than seeing reminds us of the limitations of all descriptions of the *Ungrund* as hidden source.[169]

There are many other aspects of Boehme's theosophy that cannot be pursued here,[170] but it is important to consider his view of Christ, if only briefly. Boehme's Christology (perhaps better Christosophy) forms the final stage of his fourfold anthroposophy, consisting of humanity's integral state before the Fall; the nature of the Fall itself; life in the fallen world; and the ongoing restoration initiated by the incarnation. This picture looks traditional, but what Boehme does with it is original. His most important christological work, *On the Human Genesis of Christ (De incarnatione verbi, oder Von der Menschwerdung Jesu Christi)*, was completed in 1620 and helps elucidate this dimension of his thought.[171] The work is divided into three parts and thirty-two chapters. The fundamental theme is rebirth in Christ. The historical events of the human genesis of Christ are not neglected, but Boehme's focus is not on the exterior events remembered in historical faith but on the inner mystery of being born again in and through the Heavenly Christ, who completes what Adam failed to do. Reason, which cannot grasp this truth, is the enemy. "The Spirit of God reveals the incarnation of Christ to each person in one's self, and without the Spirit there is no finding it. . . . The incarnation of Christ is such a mystery that external reason knows nothing of it."[172] Boehme expresses his opposition to all external forensic notions of justification, such as that taught by Lutheran orthodoxy: "Therefore reflect, dear children, and enter in at the right door. It is necessary not merely to be forgiven, but to be born. Then we are to be regarded as forgiven, that is, sin is then but a husk. The new man grows out of this husk and throws the husk away: that constitutes God's forgiveness."[173] In his emphasis on the necessity of the new birth Boehme was at one with Arndt. What differentiates him from the Lutheran pastor and others is the theosophical and partly docetic speculation in which he framed the new birth in Christ.

Adam, as we have seen, was born an androgynous virgin following the pattern of the Virgin Divine Wisdom. But Adam fell, Eve was created (a good creation, be it noted), and their Fall meant that supernal virginity was lost to the world, even to Mary. The name of Jesus, however, placed its image in the Virgin Wisdom from all eternity, and from thence, according to the divine plan, when Mary gave her consent to the Incarnation (Lk. 1:38), she was filled with the virginity of Divine Wisdom and gave birth to the Virgin Christ, who, like Adam, is androgynous (1.9.17), and the offspring of two mothers. Although Boehme uses the formulae of the Chalcedonian hypostatic union (e.g., "God and humankind have become one person, one Christ, one God, one Lord . . .": 1.9.23), he also employs docetic expressions, for example, statements that Christ was only seemingly a real human: "He thus became human in the heavenly virgin, and the earthly quality merely hung on him" (1.9.20). This docetic cast is heightened in the ten essential christological points Boehme says he was given by divine illumination and which he sets out at the end of chapter 14 of the first part of this treatise. These axioms are mostly alchemical and show little overlap with traditional christological formulations.[174]

Boehme agrees with tradition in asserting that God became man so that man might become God (e.g., 1.10–11), but what is essential to him is that believers come to rebirth by their participation in the inner meaning of the outward events of Christ's life, not by any external *imitatio Christi*. Merely historical faith, like reason, is the enemy. The new birth is the function of true faith and creative imagination:

> For the word "faith" is not historical; rather it is a taking from God's being, eating from God's being, introducing God's being with one's imagination into God's soul-fire, and quieting its hunger therewith, and therefore putting on God's being, not as a garment, but rather as the body of the soul. The soul must have God's being in its fire; it must eat God's bread, if it wants to be a child.[175]

In the final chapter, he puts the point more strongly:

> The son of history is a stranger. You must be born of God in Christ so that you may become a true son, then you will be God's son and an heir of the suffering and death of Christ. Christ's death is your death, his resurrection from the grave is your resurrection, his ascension is your ascension, and his eternal kingdom is your kingdom. In that you are born his true son of his Flesh and Blood you are an heir of all his goods.[176]

Boehme labored at his longest work, the *Great Mystery (Mysterium Magnum)*, during 1622–23.[177] The shoemaker's prolixity reaches its climax here. Commentary on Genesis had long formed a central strand in Christian thought, not least for Luther.[178] Although Boehme had

devoted a part of his *Aurora* to exegesis of the Hexaemeron, here he
goes back over this, correcting and expanding on his earlier views,
before embarking on a lengthy reading of Genesis 3–51. His conclusion strikes an odd note to anyone who has waded through these pages:
"This is a brief summary [*summarische Erklärung*] of the first book of
Moses from a right true ground and divine gift. . . . We admonish the
reader of this that when he finds something that in any place of our
deep sense seems to be obscure that he does not condemn it according to the manner of the evil world, but diligently read and pray to
God, who will surely open the door of his heart."[179] One of the fundamental features of the commentary is its christological focus. Boehme
reads Genesis as a vast christological typology, seeing the Old Testament events and persons as prophetic of the aspects of Christ's life in
their historical and cosmological significance. In this context I will
look at only three areas that may help clarify some of what has been
presented above.

The first area involves the emanation of all things from the unknown
Nothing into the Trinity of persons and then into the created world.
Chapters 1–16 offer another version of the Boehmian view of emanative origin.[180] Nothing seems to be added to what was set forth in
previous works, although new details appear. A second major area of
interest in the *Mysterium Magnum* concerns the creation of Adam in
God's image and likeness (primarily chaps. 15–16). Here Boehme provides a summary of Adam's original creation as both a heavenly and
an earthly man, as well as an account of the three souls in man that
are still yet one (the eternal soul, the spiritual soul, and the rational
soul in the vegetative bestial life; chap. 15.14–31). The third area concerns the Fall. While the *Aurora* concentrated on Lucifer's Fall, in this
work the attention shifts to the Fall of Adam and Eve, both Adam's
first Fall before his sleep and the Fall of the first couple, the now sexu-
ally divided halves of the originally androgynous Adam, as recounted
in the story of the eating of the forbidden fruit (chaps. 17–25). The
general picture is much like what was set forth in the *Three Principles*,
though more richly developed.

In the preface to the *Mysterium Magnum*, Boehme lists ten points
summarizing "the Great Mystery of the eternal spiritual nature."[181]
Texts like this and the earlier *Six Theosophical Points* indicate that the
Görlitz seer was trying to bring his complex thinking into some kind
of order. The most noted of these attempts was the brief *Clavis* or *Key*,
written in the spring of 1624 but not published until 1647.[182] Boehme
divides the treatise into seventeen short headings. The first deals with

"How God is to be considered without Nature and Creature," that is, the hidden source of Deity. What is interesting in this section is that Boehme begins with a series of biblical passages on God's unity and goodness and does not use his neologism *Ungrund*. The second section turns to the Trinity. Boehme once again uses the analogy of the Father as will, the Son as pleasure and delight, and the Holy Spirit as the life of will and virtue. More typical of his distinctive Trinitarianism is the statement at the end: "If there were not such a desiring receptivity [*begierliche Empfindlichkeit*] and outgoing operation of the Trinity in the eternal Unity, the Unity would be an eternal silence and like a Nothing, and there would be neither nature nor creature."[183] The next three sections also concern the divine nature, dealing with the Eternal Word of God (III), the Holy Name Jehova (IV), and Divine Wisdom (V).

Boehme then turns his attention to the emanative process by which God flows out into the world. Section VI deals with the *Mysterium Magnum*, that is, God as eternal nature, the source of other natures and essences. Boehme says the outflow contains two substances: "the Unity of God, i.e., the divine power and virtue, the outflowing wisdom," and "the separable will," which seems to be the desire to create properties and distinctions, such as the difference between the loving and merciful God and the angry jealous God (VI.20–21). According to Boehme, the Great Mystery is "chaos" (VI.23), that is, the source of good and evil and all contraries, as well as "the ground and principle" of all creation. It is also, as we are told in chapter VII, the "Center of the Eternal Nature," "the innermost ground where its will that rises up leads it to 'I-ness' [*Ichheit*] through a receptivity, as in a natural working."[184] The stage is now set for a treatment (VIII–IX) of Boehme's seven essential properties, what were earlier called the spirit-qualities. These are the created manifestations of the divine ideas: "What the Eternal Mind [*ewige Gemüth*] models in God's Wisdom through the divine power and brings into an Idea, that Nature forms into a property" (VIII.27). First, the seven properties are named (desire, attraction, perception, fire, light/love, sound, and finally the subject, or body [VIII.29–35]). All of these have both a divine and a natural substance (VIII.36–37). Then, section IX.38–80 takes up an analysis of their characteristics and interaction. Section X considers the visible world and its inward ground in the spiritual world, featuring yet another exegesis of the Genesis Hexaemeron (X.83–95). Section XI turns to the *Spiritus Mundi*, that is, the hidden spiritual world in which the corporeal world subsists, considering the four elements that flow out from this world (XI.98–117). The sections that close the *Clavis* are merely lists of terms and definitions. The first (XII) summarizes the *Clavis* itself, while XIII is an exposition of words found in Boehme's other works.[185] Sections XIV–XVII are lists partly compiled by Boehme and partly by his friends and followers.

The *Clavis* has the advantage of brevity, but it is no less obscure than Boehme's other writings, nor does it take up all aspects of his pansophy. Without attempting to confine Boehme's thought into a rigid system, some recent investigators have tried to give a synoptic view of the major narrative moments in his overall schema. Cyril O'Regan, for example, proposes a six-stage narrative of divine self-appropriation in what he calls Boehme's "erotic-agonistic speculative narrative discourse."[186] The first stage is that of the hidden divine source prior to any determination, what the later Boehme often called the *Ungrund*. In some way, Will/Imagination arises in the *Ungrund*, and, in its desire to see itself, although it has nothing to see because it is nothing, begins a process of bringing itself forth so that it can come to know and love itself and be known and loved (e.g., *Clavis* VIII.37; MM 5.10). This bringing forth has two dimensions: first, the immanent Trinity of Father, Son, and Spirit; and then, the emergence of Eternal Wisdom as the *Mysterium Magnum* containing the forms of all things as archetypes. The second stage of the emanative process, according to O'Regan, is that of Eternal Nature (e.g., MM 3), which is a kind of antitype to Wisdom. Constituted by "desire" (*Sucht*), it is the principle responsible for the production of essence (*Wesen*) and the source of the contradictory forces (good and evil, light and dark, etc.) found within God and therefore also in all nondivine reality. Eternal Nature as forceful anger is the First of the Principles responsible for the world; the Second is its contrary, the "counter-will" of love (e.g., MM 40.7–8). The conflict of these two principles produces the seven properties, or spirit-qualities, so often featured in Boehme's works.

The third stage is the creation of the material world and human nature, the result of what Boehme often calls the *turba*, the dramatic displacement of the harmonious original state into the conflict of the two Primary Principles. This first occurs in Lucifer's Fall. As a result, the created world is not evil in itself, although it necessarily contains evil. "The essence of the world consists in good and evil, and the one cannot be without the other" (MM 11.15; also 10.15). The world is an expression of God's desire for self-manifestation, but such an expression, by its very nature, given the contrariety of the properties in the spiritual world and in God as emanative, must contain both good and evil, although evil will eventually be overcome. Thus, the created world is the Third Principle, the "signature" of the invisible world. The preface to the *Mysterium Magnum* begins: "When we consider the visible world with its essence and consider the life of creatures, then we find therein the likeness of the invisible spiritual world, which is hidden in the visible world as the soul in the body." The creation of Adam is the goal of this third stage, since he exists both on the spiritual side of the divide, as made in God's image and likeness, but also on the material side, as made from the clay of the earth—man as the microcosm. Adam's paradisiacal condition, as noted above, was one of androgyny and perfect knowledge and power, but it only lasted for forty days. Thus, the fourth stage in the story is Adam's Fall, touched on above.

The final two chapters in Boehme's theosophical narrative, according to O'Regan, constitute the restitution process. These stages center on Christ. Like everything else in his theosophy, Boehme's view of Christ is idiosyncratic, because, to use David Walsh's terms, Boehme has both a Christology and a Christosophy.[187] In the *Aurora,* he says that after Lucifer's Fall "[God] made within our time another king out of the same divinity out of which Lucifer was created . . . , out of the salitter that was external to the body of King Lucifer, and then placed him on the royal throne of Lucifer, and gave him the power and authority Lucifer had before his fall. *This king is called Jesus Christ and is the Son of God and Man.*"[188] Christ's central position is evident from the fact that he alone experiences the three births ("genitures") that constitute the world: the innermost birth of the soul, the supernal birth of heaven, and the outermost birth in this world (*Aurora* 19.28–37). Christ restores the image of God damaged in Adam's Fall.

Boehme tries to avoid a docetic view of Christ but only partly succeeds, due to Christ's relation to two mothers, Mary and Divine Wisdom. Mary is the mother of the human aspect of Jesus, but the eternal Christ is born from Divine Wisdom, which, however, is said to dwell in Mary's soul. In the *Human Genesis of Christ* the relation of Christ to Wisdom dominates, and, although the *Mysterium Magnum* elaborates many typologies between the events of Genesis and aspects of the life of Jesus on earth, it is hard to escape the suspicion that Boehme's Christology is fundamentally cosmic and universal.[189] This does not lessen his devotion to Christ. In his *Theosophical Letters,* for example, Boehme speaks of himself as a true follower of Christ,[190] and the *Six Theosophical Points* show that he thought of Christ both as the cosmic Redeemer, the Head of the body of the redeemed, and the model for the imitation of his followers.[191] Nonetheless, the distance between the

Görlitz shoemaker's view of Christ and what was presented in contemporary Lutheran or Catholic traditions was large.

The sixth stage of O'Regan's depiction of Boehme's narrative is described as "Eschatology and Narrative Circularity," comprising the shoemaker's view of the ongoing struggle between good and evil typologized in the conflict between Cain/Lucifer and Abel/Christ (see MM 26–28). This conflict is set to end in the eventual reintegration of all things in Christ and the return of his kingdom to the Father—the eschatological fulfillment. Thus, there is a grand circular pattern to Boehme's theosophy in which the *Endzeit* repeats the *Urzeit*, although it may well be that he views the end as a higher spiral of the supernal story of divine emanation. Helpful as O'Regan's six narrative moments are for a general picture of Boehme's theosophy, any attempt at systematization is bound to distort to some degree the Görlitz shoemaker's dense symbolic presentations of his obscure vision of reality.

Boehme's thinking features a program for rebirth and inner transformation that has often been described as mystical. Some have wondered, however, how far it is legitimate to consider him a *Christian* mystic. The shoemaker himself never broke with the Lutheran church of his day, though he experienced rejection and even persecution. It is easy to identify aspects of his thought that are at odds with Lutheranism and, indeed, with almost any established form of Christianity. Boehme's true loyalties are not always easy to discern. Although he disagreed with Luther and contemporary Lutherans on such issues as forensic justification, and sided with the Radicals on the universal offer of salvation to non-Christians, in other particulars, such as the doctrine of the sacraments, he seems to have defended Lutheran positions. Like the Spirituals and Arndt, although very much in his own way, he wrote to enlighten his fellow Christians about the need for the inner appropriation of belief, not mere outward conformity. This is evident in his most directly mystical work, the *Christosophia, or The Way to Christ.*

This collection of nine treatises (not completely published until after his death) gives us an insight into the more specifically Christian dimensions of Boehme's thinking in his last years.[192] The treatises concern a variety of topics. Some can be described as practical-ascetical, such as the second work *The First Treatise on True Repentance* (1623), and the third tract *On Holy Prayer*, following the liturgical order of the week (1624). The remaining treatises take up issues central to mysticism, such as *The Treatise on True Repentance* (1622); *On True Resignation* (1622); *On the New Birth* (1622); *On the Supersensual Life* (1622); *On Divine Contemplation* (1620); and *The Conversation between the Enlightened and*

Unenlightened Soul (1624). The final short work, *Consolation Treatise on the Four Humors* (1624), has been described as a treatise on spiritual guidance.

The First Treatise on True Repentance deals with a theme basic to Reformation faith and piety, but what Boehme does with it is unusual. The relation of Adam and Adam's descendants to the Virgin Divine Wisdom had been important in Boehme's thought for some time, but here he describes it in terms of a fervent love mysticism. In good Lutheran fashion, Boehme says that our covenant with God and marriage to Sophia begins at baptism (1.30), but he is at pains to make this marriage real for each believer through descriptions of courting the Virgin, addressing love prayers to her, and retelling the amorous conversation between the soul and the Celestial Virgin. Boehme starts out with general considerations about the three chains that bind us to sin and the eight motivations for conversion; he then provides a confessional prayer for the start of the life of repentance (1.19–25). True repentance, however, is not in outward words: "If the soul wishes to obtain Christ Conquerer's crown from the noble Virgin Sophia, [it] must court her with great love-desire."[193] This summons introduces the first long section (1.27–39) on the soul's marriage to Sophia. Christ said we must forsake all things to gain the love of Sophia, who is described as "the flower of Sharon, the rose of the valley" (Song 2:1). Throughout this section, Boehme interweaves language of devotion to the sweetest name of Jesus with praise of Sophia, who gives the devout soul a kiss in the name of Jesus. The kiss is the betrothal, but the marriage will not happen until the soul has faithfully followed Jesus for some time. This is how the reward is described:

> Then the Virgin will come to the soul. She has revealed herself in the precious Name JESUS as Christ the serpent-treader, as the anointed of God. She kisses [the soul] completely inwardly with her sweet love and presses love into its desire as a sign of victory. Here Adam according to his heavenly part is resurrected from the dead in Christ. Of this I cannot write; there is no pen in the world with which to do it for this is the marriage of the Lamb when the noble pearl is sown with great triumph, although it is first but small, like mustard seed, as Christ says [Matt. 17:20].[194]

The final reward, bestowal of the pearl, will not be given the soul until heaven.

Similar language, mingling prayer to Jesus and instructions about gaining Sophia, is found throughout the remainder of the treatise.

It reaches a climax in the conversation between the soul and Sophia found at the end. Christ moves into the corrupted image of God in the soul when conversion and repentance take place. He brings with him the treasure of Sophia. "We who have tasted this heavenly treasure," says Boehme, "understand this but no one else does." (A prominent feature of the *Treatise on True Repentance* is the appeal to the need for experience to understand its message.) Boehme continues, "But the noble Sophia draws herself near to the soul's being and kisses it in a friendly manner and tinctures [i.e., changes] the dark fire of the soul with her love beams and penetrates the soul with her loving kiss. Then the soul leaps in its body for great joy in the virginal power of this love."[195] The love-colloquy of Virgin Sophia and the male Soul extends over several pages (1.46–51).[196]

Four of the other treatises in *The Way to Christ* also deserve notice for what they tell us about Boehme's mystical teaching. The 1622 *On True Resignation (Von wahrer Gelassenheit)* sheds light on how Boehme understood this term that many Protestant mystics had treated at length. The first part of chapter 1 (1.1–18) is a dense summary of major themes of Boehme's theosophy that tells us little about the announced topic, but the remainder of the chapter (1.19–48), based on the contrast between human reason and resignation/releasement, is more helpful. Reason blocks the way to God, says Boehme. What is needed is for the will to let go of reason and desire and sink into itself and then into Christ: "[The will] is only to sink itself unaffected and simply into the love and grace of God in Christ Jesus, and being dead to its desires, give itself completely to the life of God in love."[197] Boehme describes this as sinking into nothing, the nothing of deep humility before God (1.30).[198] The second chapter returns to issues both theosophical and practical about the nature of *Gelassenheit*.

Boehme, like Johann Arndt, insisted on the necessity of the new birth from God for salvation, and not merely external justification. He describes the *Treatise on the New Birth* as "a short summary on this new birth" taken from his "other very deep writings" (Preface 1). The eight chapters of the treatise provide a good account of much of Boehme's more practical teaching. Man's existence in the three worlds is featured in chapter 1 (1.19). Chapter 2 revisits Boehme's view of the Adamic myth, while chapter 3 talks about the effects of the Fall. Chapter 4 returns to an essential theme of the whole collection—the marriage to Sophia (4.13–16). The later chapters focus on Boehme's insistence that true religion is not found in external churches of stone (though these are not evil in themselves), but only in hearing and obeying God within

(6.2–18). Like the Radical Spirituals, Boehme lays stress on the ecumenical and universalistic aspects of the new birth. "A Christian has no sect," he says. "He can dwell among the sects, even appear in their services, and yet hang on to none. He has only a single knowledge and that is Christ in him" (7.5). Hence, "[i]t is the greatest folly in Babel that the devil has made the world argue about religion so that they argue about self-made ideas, about the letter" (7.8).

Two of the last treatises in *The Way to Christ* reveal Boehme's debt to late medieval German mysticism, especially themes initiated by Meister Eckhart. Nonetheless, the mysticism in these two works is transmuted through the shoemaker's distinctive theosophy. Treatise VI on *The Supersensual Life: The Conversation of a Teacher and a Student* (1622) is a brief didactic work, daring in how it employs the language of the ground as divine nothingness and stresses the need for total releasement (*Gelassenheit*) into the ground. It also emphasizes love and will as the motivating forces that bring us into the deepest source of reality. The Master advises the Student that absolute silence from all thinking and willing is necessary for true releasement, although he must not forget awareness of the cross of Christ (6.3–6). Later the Master insists that it is only through love "in its power and virtue and in its height and greatness" (6.26) that one can find God in everything and in nothing, providing an analysis of each of these four characteristics of love. The Master also gives a detailed explanation of how "He who finds love finds nothing and everything, . . . for he finds a supernatural, supersensual abyss that has no place as its dwelling and finds nothing that can be compared to it" (6.27). Thus, the resigned soul loses itself in the divine ground (e.g., 6.38).

In the final mystical tract in *The Way to Christ*, entitled *The Precious Gate on Divine Contemplation*, or *Theoscopia* (1620), Boehme sets out a similar message, but one more consonant with his own terminology. Reason cannot attain the hidden God who has brought himself forth into nature (1.2–3), but Reason can ask why God could not have created a better world in which there would be no suffering. The answer is given in terms of one of the fundamental tenets of Boehme's thought: "No thing may be revealed to itself without contrariety. If it has no thing that resists it, it always goes out from itself and does not go into itself again."[199] Hence, if there were no contrariety, natural life would never ask about its source and the hidden God would remain unknown. Therefore, it was necessary for the unitary hidden God (i.e., the *Ungrund*) "to lead himself by his will out of himself" into divisibility of wills and into strife, implied or explicit, so that the created world could exist and have the possibility of returning to its source (1.10–11). The opposition of evil moves the good to press back toward its cause, that is, to desire God (1.13). Boehme summarizes, "We can . . . say concerning the single good that he in himself can desire nothing, for he has nothing in or before himself that can give him anything, and therefore he brings himself out of himself into divisibility . . . so that the contrariety arises in the over-flow . . . so that the good might become perceptive, working and willing in the evil, that is, desiring to divide itself from evil and desiring to go back again into the simple will of God."[200]

The later chapters of the treatise fill in some details of this basic picture of voluntaristic emanation and return. Chapter 2, for example, deals with humanity as the *imago dei*. "The life of man is a form of the divine will that was breathed into the created image of man by the breath of the divine," but it has become poisoned by the devil and the imbalance of the forces in the temporal world (2.2). Boehme goes on to explain this in terms of the damage done to the three principles of human life, before turning to how the return process is being effected by "the new source-spring of divine love and unity through its out-flow in Christ" (2.12). The primary practices that Boehme advocates to realize the return were well known to the medieval mystics, especially *Gelassenheit*, that is, sinking one's innermost ground into the embodied grace of God, and inner silence (2.16). He says, "For if life stands quiet in its own willing, when it stands in the abyss of nature and creature, in the eternal speaking out of God, then God speaks in it."[201] Chapter 3 features discussions of several other topics: the Word as the revelation of God's will; the *Mysterium Magnum*, or the likeness of all things in the eternal will; God as the creator of all; the three kinds of life; and even the Trinity. The fourth chapter, on the "in" and "out" of the Eternal Will, remained unfinished.

This look at *The Way to Christ* indicates that Boehme thought of himself as teaching within the boundaries of the Christian tradition, however much some of his contemporaries and successors were criti-cal of his orthodoxy. But in what sense can Boehme be thought of as providing Christian mystical teaching? Certainly, key themes charac-teristic of late medieval and Protestant mysticism appear across his works, such as *Gelassenheit*, contemplation, divine indwelling, and rebirth in God. The Görlitz seer also makes use of erotic language known in Christian tradition for describing the soul's relationship with God, specifically the marriage with the Virgin Sophia. Boehme does not have a developed teaching on forms of union with God, although he cites 1 Corinthians 6:17 about "becoming one spirit with God" from time-to-time.[202] Uniting with God, however, can be said to be built into the structure of his thinking, as his language about sinking into nothingness with God in the *Mysterium Magnum* shows.[203] Above all, Boehme concentrates on the inner transformation in God that takes place through the perception of divine truth, conversion to a higher life, and the practice of love of God and love of neighbor, although for him this often takes on the accents of an alchemical conversion back into our true substance. Boehme's thinking is scarcely traditional, but it is certainly "mystical," or hidden, in both the etymological and trans-formational senses of the word.

The Görlitz shoemaker pushes the envelope of what constitutes Christian mysticism. There is no denying that his heritage has been for the most part in philosophical, alchemical, and theosophical circles, rather than in theological and ecclesiastical contexts. Boehme's dense theosophy comes into conflict with traditional Christian doctrine in a number of places. Although the language of the medieval mystics on the hidden God (*nihil/grund/abgrund*) never formed part of official church teaching, Boehme's view of the *Ungrund* differs from theirs. The divine *nihil* of Eriugena, or the *grund/abgrund* of Eckhart, Tauler, Ruusbroec, and others, is a transcendent Nothing, a plenipotent self-awareness that overflows to form the world of created reality.[204] Boehme's *Ungrund*, on the other hand, is a kind of "Hyper-Defectivity," an ignorance that stirs itself to will in an emanative process in order to reveal its conflicted self in a world of dialectical opposites. This is a form of emanation, or manifestation, but one can doubt if it should be called self-manifestation, because *Ungrund* does not appear to be any kind of "self," even in a transcendent sense.

In many of his writings Boehme speculates on the Trinity of Father, Son, and Holy Spirit, and the relation of the three to the divine unity. What we have seen of his understanding of the Trinitarian life reveals itself as different from most previous mystical views of the Trinity, sug-gesting a quasi-Sabellian Trinitariansim in which the "three" are mani-festations of the one God, rather than subsistent persons identical with the one God. In this, as in so much else, Boehme's views are outliers to the main Christian tradition. Similarly, while Christianity had a role for Divine Wisdom, usually understood as an appropriated term for speaking of the Word, Boehme's Heavenly Virgin Sophia threatens to become a fourth "something" in God, one whose status in relation to the Word and the Trinity is not always clear.

With regard to the origin of evil, Boehme also distances himself from customary Christian teaching. He was no dualist, at least in the sense of seeing evil as equipotent with God. Nonetheless, Boehme thought that divine manifestation is not possible without contrariety and opposition, so that the root of evil is present from the beginning in the conflicting creative potentialities of the emanative spirit-qualities in God. The actual introduction of evil into the world, however, was the result of choice, specifically the primeval decision of Lucifer to choose pride and thus disrupt the balance of the spirit-qualities. The power of evil in the created universe was further enhanced by the Fall of Adam, the primordial androgynous human. Boehme's mythic narrative of the presexual Adam and his double Fall has affinities with the speculations of some early Christian Gnostics, which are also distant from the standard teaching of Catholic and Protestant theology. Boehme's view of Christ, however evident his devotion to the God-man as redeemer and model, also has features that conflict with traditional Christology, such as Christ's dual mothers (Sophia and Mary), as well as the reality of his earthly flesh. Finally, we can ask about the place of the visible church. Unlike some of the Radical Spiritualists, Boehme did not totally reject the need for "stone churches" and the sacraments and preaching found within them. He lived as a Lutheran, despite his run-ins with Pastor Richter. It is clear, however, that Boehme thought the visible church had at best a secondary role in salvation. Without the internal rebirth realized in true believers, the actions of the visible church count for nothing. Thus, Cyril O'Regan can summarize Boehme's relation to Christianity: "For Boehme, Christianity is not a doctrinal religion, but a religion of internal transformation and, finally, a religion of speculative vision."[205]

It is not easy to give a sketch of a thinker as original, as difficult, and as elusive as Jacob Boehme. Nor is it simple to characterize his contribution to mysticism. Andrew Weeks speaks of Boehme's "mysticism of divine ubiquity,"[206] and David Walsh of his "mysticism of fire."[207] These descriptions may be helpful for capturing aspects of his thinking but are not fully adequate for discerning the breadth of Boehme's contribution and influence. If labels are needed, it may be best to stick to terms that the Görlitz seer himself employed—theosophy and pansophy—and thus characterize him as a theosophical or pansophical mystic.

Arndt and Boehme as Lutheran Mystics

I have treated these two contemporaries together, because, despite their differences, they testify to the power of the mystical element in

Lutheranism, both in the seventeenth century and after. This is not the place to attempt to give even a sketch of their influence in subsequent centuries. Both Arndt and Boehme were significant for the Pietist movement that originated at the end of the seventeenth century and that had so many ramifications in the eighteenth and nineteenth centuries. Arndt was much read by devotional Pietists like Philip Jacob Spener (d. 1705); Boehme had a role in the development of the more speculative currents in Pietism, such as we see in Friedrich Christoph Oetinger (d. 1782). Both Arndt and Boehme, however, had a broad readership, not only in Lutheranism but in other Christian denominations and in a variety of intellectual circles. From the perspective of the history of mysticism, Arndt represents a major connection between the Catholic mysticism of the Middle Ages and those elements of mysticism that remained alive and well in Evangelical Christianity. Boehme, as pointed out above, is more difficult to evaluate. The Görlitz cobbler was an outsider, brilliant and obscure, attractive and mystifying. He absorbed many traditional mystical motifs into his original thought, along with other intellectual currents too numerous to mention. Boehme created his own reenvisioning of Christianity, one in which the mystical and the theosophical-speculative aspects are deeply entwined. Both in his time and in ours, he remains a bone of contention.

Notes

1. For an introduction to Lutheranism in this period, see Hartmut Lehmann, "Lutheranism in the Seventeenth Century," in *The Cambridge History of Christianity*, vol. 6, *Christianity: Reform and Expansion, 1500–1600*, ed. R. Po-chia Hsia (Cambridge: Cambridge University Press, 2007), 56–72.

2. On the theology and piety of Lutheran Germany in the seventeenth century, see Winfried Zeller, "Protestantische Frömmigkeit im 17. Jahrhundert," originally published as the introduction to the collection of texts, *Der Protestantismus des 17. Jahrhunderts*, Klassiker des Protestantismus 5 (Bremen: C. Schünemann, 1962), and reprinted in revised form in Zeller, *Theologie und Frömmigkeit*, 1:85–116.

3. There is a partial English translation of Arndt's major book by Peter Erb, *Johann Arndt. True Christianity*, Classics of Western Spirituality (New York: Paulist Press, 1979). With the exception of a few unpublished dissertations, however, there is little on him in English. See Johannes Wallmann, "Johann Arndt (1555–1621)," in *The Pietist Theologians: An Introduction to Theology in the Seventeenth and Eighteenth Centuries*, ed. Carter Lindberg, The Great Theologians (Oxford: Blackwell, 2005), 21–37. There is a significant literature in German. On his mysticism, see esp. Christian Braw, *Bücher im Staube: Die Theologie Johann Arndts in ihrem Verhältnis zur Mystik*, Studies in Medieval and Reformation Thought 39 (Leiden: Brill, 1986); and

Hermann Geyer, *Verborgene Weisheit: Johann Arndts "Vier Bücher vom Wahren Chris-tentum" als Programm einer spiritualistisch-hermetischen Theologie*, 3 vols., Arbeiten zur Kirchengeschichte 80 (Berlin: Walter de Gruyter, 2001). For a short introduc-tion, see Martin Schmidt, "Arndt, Johann (1555–1621)," *TRE* 4:121–29.

4. On the relation between Lutheranism and mysticism in general, see Winfried Zeller, "Luthertum und Mystik," in idem, *Theologie und Frömmigkeit*, 2:35–54.

5. On the formation of Lutheran confessionalism, see Robert Kolb, "Confes-sional Lutheran theology," in Bagchi and Steinmentz, *Cambridge Companion to Reformation Theology*, 68–79.

6. On Protestant Scholasticism, see Robert D. Preus, *The Theology of Post-Reformation Lutheranism*, 2 vols. (St. Louis: Concordia, 1970–72). The foremost figure of Lutheran Scholasticism was Johann Gerhard (1582–1637), who had Arndt as his pastor as a young man and remained close to him throughout his life. Gerhard's major work was the nine-volume *Loci Theologici* (1610–22), and he also wrote a series of popular *Meditationes* (1606). A translation of some of these and of the Lutheran devotional hymns of the era can be found in Eric Lund, ed., *Seventeenth-Century Lutheran Meditations and Hymns*, Classics of Western Spiritual-ity (New York: Paulist Press, 2011).

7. For a description of these editions and their place among the 190 editions of the *Theologia Deutsch* until 1960, see Georg Baring, *Bibliographie der Ausgaben der "Theologia Deutsch" (1516–1961): Ein Beitrag zur Lutherbibliographie* (Baden-Baden: Heitz, 1963). Like many others, Arndt seems to have thought that the work was written by John Tauler.

8. *Vom Wahren Christenthum*, book VI, part 3.2.13 (trans. Erb, 280).

9. I will make use of the edition published by Johann Christoph Leidenfrost at Hof in 1753 (*Herrn Johann Arndts Sechs Bücher vom Wahren Christenthum . . . Nebst dem Paradies-Gärtlein*, 7th ed. [Hof: Johann Christoph Leidenfrost, 1753]). Leidenfrost's edition includes all six books of *Vom Wahren Christenthum* in 1,035 pages, not including forty-four pages of prefatory materials and four unpaginated indices. (I will cite with the abbreviation WC by book, chapter, and section; e.g., WC III.1.3.) With this edition is also bound Leidenfrost's 1752 edition of the *Para-diesgärtlein* of 239 pages with three unpaginated indices. I will use Peter Erb's translation where available; other translations are my own. I will generally not cite the German text, save in the case of a few passages important for their mystical terminology.

10. The most detailed treatment of Arndt's sources is Edmund Weber, *Johann Arndts Vier Bücher vom Wahren Christentum als Beitrag zur protestantischen Irenik des 17. Jahrhundert: Eine quellenkritische Untersuchung* (Marburg/Lahn: Elwert, 1969). Weber does not consider the Bible but takes up the mystical, Paracelsian, and other sources. Rich materials on Arndt's sources are also found in Geyer, *Verbor-gene Weisheit*. See also Johannes Wallmann, "Johann Arndt und die protestan-tische Frömmigkeit: Zur Rezeption der mittelalterlichen Mystik im Luthertum," in *Frömmigkeit in der frühen Neuzeit: Studien zur religiösen Literatur des 17. Jahrhunderts in Deutschland*, ed. Dieter Breuer, Chloe 2 (Amsterdam: Rodopi, 1984), 50–74.

11. In treating the Bible in the WC, Arndt insisted above all that the biblical text and its stories must be experienced from within, so that "they might become living in us in spirit and faith and that a completely new inner man might arise"

(I.6.2; ed., 27). This chapter is the fullest discussion of Arndt's experiential herme-neutics, but see also I.12, I.21, I.36, II.37, and II.39.

12. Tauler is referred to by name eight times in the WC: I.Vorrede.8 (ed., 43); I.13.14 (ed., 59); I.37.17 (ed., 181); I.39.6 (ed., 193); II.20.4 (ed., 330); III.Vorrede.3 (ed., 559); III.15.1 (ed., 606); and VI.Pt.1.3.5 (ed., 931). Arndt also quotes often from Tauler's sermons without naming him.

13. Augustine's influence on Arndt is obvious in many aspects of his theology, such as his doctrine on God as Supreme Good, the nature of man as *imago Trinitatis*, and on sin and grace. Augustine is explicitly named and cited seven times: WC I.18.2; II.6.6; II.28.5; III.5.2; III.6.2; III.17.2; and V.Pt. 2.13.2.

14. Bernard is named and cited in WC I.37.13; III.Vorrede.6; and VI.Pt 3.2.11. In addition, Bonaventure is cited in II.6.6.

15. Arndt came to know Angela's writings through a Latin translation published at Cologne in 1601: *Angela de Fulginio, ostendens nobis veram viam qua possumus sequi vestigia nostri Redemptoris.* On his use of Angela, see Weber, *Johann Arndts Vier Bücher*, 63–71; and Braw, *Bücher im Staube*, passim.

16. WC I.Vorrede.8 (ed., 43-44; trans. Erb, 25).

17. Wallmann, "Johann Arndt (1555-1621)," 30.

18. On the influence of Weigel and the Pseudo-Weigeliana on Arndt, see Geyer, *Verborgene Weisheit*, 1:230–57; see also Weeks, *Valentin Weigel (1533–1588)*, 99-100. The long chapter on prayer in WC II.34 is mostly taken from Weigel's *Gebetbüchlein*.

19. On the role of Paracelsus, see Weber, *Johann Arndts Vier Bücher*, 108–67; and Geyer, *Verborgene Weisheit*, 3:1–104.

20. This point is emphasized by Geyer, *Verborgene Weisheit*, 1:196–97.

21. For praise of Luther, see, e.g., WC I.39.2 (ed., 191; trans. Erb, 173). Luther is also quoted in WC VI.Pt.1.II.2.2 (ed., 920). WC III.3 seems to use Luther's *Freedom of the Christian* without naming him.

22. Expressions of agreement with the Lutheran confessions can be found, e.g., in WC IV.Vorrede.9 (ed., 639); and WC VI.Vorrede.1 (ed., 892).

23. Braw, *Bücher im Staube*, 21, 220.

24. Fundamental to Geyer's book is his insistence that Arndt set out to create a different model of theology from that of Lutheran Scholastic orthodoxy; see, e.g., *Verborgene Weisheit*, 1:96–97, 107, 113–14, 167–68, 201–2, 214–15, 227, 309, etc.

25. Bodo Nischan, "Osiander, Lucas II," in *Oxford Encyclopedia*, 3:185.

26. Albrecht Ritschl treats Arndt in *Geschichte des Pietismus*, 3 vols. (Bonn: A. Marcus, 1880–86), 2:34–62.

27. Wilhelm Koepp, *Johann Arndt: Eine Untersuchung über die Mystik im Luthertum* (Berlin: Protestantische Schriftenvertrieb, 1912). Koepp expressed a more positive view in a later work: *Johann Arndt und sein "Wahres Christentum": Lutherisches Bekenntnis und Oekumene*, Aufsätze und Vorträge zur Theologie und Religionswissenschaft 7 (Berlin: Evangelische Verlaganstalt, 1959).

28. Representatives of this chapter of scholarship include Winfried Zeller, some of whose essays have been already cited, as well as Berndt Hamm, "Johann Arndts Wortverständnis: Ein Beitrag zu dem Anfängen des Pietismus," in *Pietismus und Neuzeit*, vol. 8, *Der radikale Pietismus* (Göttingen: Vandenhoeck & Ruprecht, 1982), 43–73; and Johannes Wallmann, "Johann Arndt und die protestantische Frömmigkeit."

29. I translate these passages from the *Vorrede Theologia Deutsch* 1 and 12, as quoted by Geyer, *Verborgene Weisheit*, 1:96-97. Geyer discusses the importance of this foreword on 91-99.

30. WC I.Vorrede.1 (ed., 40; trans. Erb, 21).

31. WC I.38.12 (ed., 188; trans. Erb, 171).

32. WC VI.Pt.1.1 (ed., 894-95).

33. Wallmann, "Johann Arndt (1555-1621)," 28.

34. WC I. 39.2-6 (ed., 191-93; trans. Erb, 173-75).

35. WC III.Vorrede.3 (ed., 555; trans. Erb, 222).

36. Braw (*Bücher im Staube*) emphasizes the ethical dimension of Arndt's teaching; e.g., 31-32, 182-83, 195ff., and 223ff.

37. *Dissertatio* 1-3, as cited in Geyer, *Verborgene Weisheit*, 1:160, who treats the practical character of Arndt's notion of theology on 160-69, and 205.

38. The second volume of Geyer's *Verborgene Weisheit* contains a detailed analysis of the first four books under the title "*libri dei*. Die metaphorische Programmatik der 'Vier Bücher vom Wahren Christentum.'" There is also a treatment of books III-IV in Birgit Gruebner, *Gott und die Lebendigkeit in der Natur: Eine Interpretation des Dritten und Vierten Buches von Johann Arndts "Wahrem Christentum,"* Arbeiten zur Theologiegeschichte 4 (Rheinbach: CMZ, 1998).

39. WC III.Vorrede.1 (ed., 554; trans. Erb, 221).

40. Weber (*Johann Arndts Vier Bücher*, 77-107) lists and discusses Arndt's use of the 1522 Tauler edition in book III, calculating that Arndt cites forty-four sermons (thirty-four from Tauler, five from Eckhart, and five from unknown preachers). Weber's tallies, however, are not complete. For example, he misses the quotation from Eckhart's Pr. 26 (DW 2:26; BT ff. 251v-252v) in WC III.13.4 (ed., 630).

41. The six chapters of part 1, the most Paracelsian section of Arndt's work, take up pp, 640-723 of the 1753 edition, while the forty chapters of part 2 are found on pp. 723-81.

42. Arndt does have a doctrine of God, which often appears in *True Christianity*. For a summary, see Braw, *Bücher im Staube*, 55-71. Braw points out that a major difference between Arndt and the medieval German mystics is Arndt's lack of an apophatic theology (68).

43. As noted by Schmidt, "Arndt, Johannes," *TRE* 4:125.

44. On the holistic nature of Arndt's notion of the *imago dei*, see esp. WC I.41.7-8 (ed., 207-8; trans., Erb, 185-86). See the discussion in Braw, *Bücher im Staube*, 78-79.

45. This is evident, for example, in WC I.27.7 (ed., 131; trans. Erb, 139-40).

46. On Christ as the Image of God to whom we are conformed, see WC I.22.2-3 (ed., 107, trans. Erb, 117-18).

47. WC II.33.14 (ed., 387; my trans.).

48. WC I.2.8 (ed., 11; trans. Erb, 35). For more on the image of God as contrasted with the image of Satan, see I.11.4-9 (ed., 46-47; trans. Erb, 64-65); I.13.12-17 (ed., 59-60; trans. Erb, 76-77); and I.41.8-11, 16 (ed., 208-9, 211; trans. Erb, 187-89).

49. The contrast "image of God/image of Satan" is not found explicitly in the *Theologia Deutsch*, but it is suggested in places (e.g., chap. 50 in the text known to Luther and Arndt). The formula was explicitly used by mystics whom Arndt could not have read, such as Walter Hilton.

50. For some later treatments of *imago dei* in WC I, see chapters 13.14–16 (ed., 59–60; trans. Erb, 76–77), 18.12 (ed., 83–84; trans. Erb, 97–98), 23.4 (ed., 110; trans. Erb, 121), and esp. 41 (ed., 205–7, 209, 211, 213–14, 216; trans. Erb, 184–94 passim).

51. WC IV.Pt.2.23–25 (ed., 753–58). For some other passages on the *imago dei*, see WC II.15; III.Vorrede; III.10; IV.Vorrede; IV.Pt.2.4; V.Pt.1.2; V.Pt.2.1, 2, and 5.

52. On the contrast between the understanding of *imago dei* in Tauler and Arndt, see Braw, *Bücher im Staube*, 81–88, 91–92.

53. For example, the reference to sinking into *den Grund des goettlichen Wesens* in WC III.23.4 (ed., 633) comes in the midst of a quotation from a sermon in the 1522 Basel Tauler edition (see Weber, *Johann Arndts Vier Bücher*, 97).

54. WC I.23.8 (ed., 112; trans. Erb, 122). Other appearances of the ground of the heart in WC I can be found in chapters 22.4 (ed., 107) and 26.3 (ed., 124). See also WC II.4.1 (ed., 245).

55. For appearance of the *Grund des Herzens* in book III, see Vorrede.4 (ed., 555: *ein gelassen Gottergeben Herz*); III.1 (559, 561), III.3 (574); III.5 (576); III.12 (599); III.16 (610); III.18 (615); III.20 (four times on 618); and III.21 (622).

56. WC I.23 (ed., 109; trans. Erb, 120).

57. WC III.2.3 (ed., 565), a long quotation from Eckhart's Pr. 12 (DW 1:194), which Arndt had access to in the 1522 Basel Tauler edition (ff. 312v–314v).

58. On original sin in Arndt, see Braw, *Bücher im Staube*, 97–101.

59. WC I.41.24–25 (ed., 215; trans. Erb, 192–93). See the long discussion of original sin and its effects in 41.9–17 (ed., 208–11; trans. Erb, 187–90).

60. WC I.16–17 (ed., 50; trans. Erb, 68–69).

61. For more on the new birth, see such texts as I.22.1 (ed., 107; trans. Erb, 117); I.31.10 (ed., 150; trans. Erb, 150); I.38.2 (ed., 185; trans. Erb, 169); and I.41 passim. In the later books there are discussions in II.6; II.11; III.19; and esp. V.Pt.2 (ed., 789–92).

62. WC I.26.8 (ed., 126; trans. Erb, 134). See also I.30.1 (ed., 142; trans. Erb, 145); the whole of I.32 and I.33 (ed., 151–57) and I.39.10 (ed., 195; trans. Erb, 177).

63. WC I.36.6 (ed., 169; trans. Erb, 170–71); see also I.39.

64. I.41 (ed., 204–17; trans. Erb, 184–94). This chapter also includes mystical material, such as the reference to the kiss of the mouth from Song of Songs 1:1 (41.8 in ed., 208).

65. WC II.Vorrede.3 (ed., 225; trans. Erb, 202). This theme is found in many mystics; for Augustine, see, e.g., *Sermo* 81.6 (*PL* 38:503): "Agnosce Christum, et per hominem ascende ad Deum."

66. For a summary of Arndt's Christology, see Braw, *Bücher im Staube*, 104–43.

67. WC II.6.2 (ed., 259; my trans.).

68. WC II.20.4 (ed., 330; my trans.). Weber's restriction of his investigation of the Tauler sources in Arndt to book III leaves this passage still open to identification.

69. Geyer discusses why book III is central (*Verborgene Weisheit*, 1:214–16).

70. WC III.Vorrede.3 (ed., 554; trans. Erb, 221). Other references to the kingdom of God within can be found in III.1, III.4, III.6, and III.21.

71. WC III.3.3 (ed., 569; my trans.). Spousal language about union is also found in III 6.2, 7.1-2, and 12.3.

72. WC III.4.1 (ed., 574; my trans.), making use of a Tauler sermon found

in the 1522 Basel edition, f. 79r. References to *gelassen* can also be found in III. Vorrede.4; III.20.3; and III.22.2 (ed., 555, 620, 624). *Gelassenheit* (rare in the noun form) seems to play a more restricted role in Arndt than in Karlstadt, Weigel, and other figures. For a brief treatment, see Gruebner, *Gott und die Lebendigkeit in der Natur*, 48–49.

73. WC III.4.2 (ed., 574). Arndt does not use the term "deification," but he does say that union makes the soul like God; see, e.g., IV.Pt.2.28.2 (ed., 762); IV.Pt.2.29.2 (ed., 763); and V.Pt.2.5.3 (ed., 847). On deification in Arndt, see Braw, *Bücher im Staube*, 189–91.

74. In book VI.Pt.1.3 (ed., 931), Arndt defends chap. 5 by saying that it refers to "Christian releasement" (*christliche Gelassenheit*) and gives references to Tauler.

75. There is a discussion of the silent inner Sabbath of the soul also in WC III.10.4 (ed., 594). The notion of rest (*Ruhe*) plays a significant role in Arndt's teaching; see Braw, *Bücher im Staube*, 176–79.

76. WC III.6.1 (ed., 579; my trans.).

77. WC III.8.3 (ed., 587; my trans.): "Warest du allein ledig der Bilde der Creaturen, du würdest Gott ohn Underlass haben und besitzen, denn er möchte sich nicht enthalten, weder im Himmel und Erden, er müste in dich kehren, er müste deine Seele erfüllen, so er sie ledig fande." Expressions regarding God being "compelled" to come into the empty soul in Eckhart are especially strong in the doubtful treatise *Vom abegescheidenheit* (e.g., DW 5:402-11), but are found throughout his sermons as well.

78. WC III.13.4 (ed., 603; my trans.), using Eckhart's Pr. 26 (DW 2:26), found in BT 1522, ff. 251v–252v.

79. WC III.23 (ed., 628–34). Sharing in Christ's cross by suffering and *Anfechtung*, and even the willingness to be consigned to hell if that be God's will (*resignatio ad infernum*) is treated often in book III (e.g., 9.3, 14.1–2, 15.2, 17.2, and 18.2). These motifs are also present in other books.

80. See the remarks on the union of believers in Christ's body in WC III.9.2 (ed., 589–90); IV.34.2 (ed., 769); and especially V.Pt.2.9 (ed., 858–60).

81. In characterizing our union with God in chapter 1 (WC V.Pt. 2.1.5; ed., 838–39; trans. Erb, 247), Arndt uses a whole series of standard New Testament proof-texts: 1 Cor. 6:17; John 17:22; 15:2ff.; Gal. 2:20; and 2 Cor. 13:5.

82. WC V.Pt.2.5.1 (ed., 846; trans. Erb, 252).

83. WC V.Pt.2.2.1 (ed., 840; trans. Erb, 248).

84. WC V.Pt.2.7 (ed., 851–56; trans. Erb, 255–60). In its poetic nature and use of the Song of Songs, this chapter can be compared to the Third Prayer of the Sixth Commandment, "Prayer of Thanks for the Spiritual Marriage of Christ and the Soul," found in part 1 of the *Paradiesgärtlein* (1753 ed., 60–62).

85. WC V.Pt.2.7.1 (ed., 851–52; trans. Erb, 255–56). Although there are no direct parallels, such a passage can be compared with Bernard's *Sermo super Cantica* 74, where he describes the Word's visit to the soul (*Sancti Bernardi Opera* 2:239–44).

86. Chapter 7.5 (ed., 854; trans. Erb, 257). Appeals to the necessity for personal experience are also found in chap. 8.2 (ed., 857; trans. Erb, 260) and chap. 10.3 (ed., 862; trans. Erb, 264).

87. WC V.7.8 (ed., 856; trans. Erb, 259).

88. WC V.Pt.2.8.1 (ed., 857; trans. Erb, 260).

89. On the relation between inner and outer word in Arndt and an argument for his difference from Luther, see Hamm, "Johann Arndts Wortverständnis." This is a contested issue in Arndt studies; for a survey of positions, see Gruebner, *Gott und die Lebendigkeit in der Natur*, 22–24.

90. The teaching on union found in part 2 of book V, and scattered throughout books I–IV, is illuminated by the claim made at the end of book VI, speaking of the *Theologia Deutsch*, that "union with Christ through living faith, a renewal in Christ through the death of the old man, is the purpose and goal of this writing" (WC VI.Pt.3.2.12; ed., 983). The same could be said for *True Christianity*.

91. Wallmann, "Johann Arndt und die protestantische Frömmigkeit," 74.

92. Braw, *Bücher im Staube*, e.g., 21, 36, 50, 198–99, 220, 227–29.

93. Geyer, *Verborgene Weisheit*, esp. 3:337–72, "Die Konzeption der 'Vier Bücher als theologisch-theosophisches Programm."

94. Schmidt, "Arndt, Johann (1555–1621)," *TRE* 4:126.

95. Geyer, *Verborgene Weisheit*, 1:217–18.

96. Hamm, "Johann Arndts Wortverständnis," 73.

97. For the historical context and Boehme's life, see Andrew Weeks, *Boehme: An Intellectual Biography of the Seventeenth-Century Philosopher and Mystic* (Albany: State University of New York Press, 1991).

98. Boehme's writings are most conveniently found in the 1730 edition, photographically reprinted as *Jacob Böhme, Sämtliche Schriften*, ed. August Faust and Will-Erich Peuckert, 11 vols. (Stuttgart: Frommann, 1955–60). Citations from the SS will be by chapter and section of the individual works with the volume and page of the edition in parentheses. English translations will be cited below. I will not generally cite the German original, except when it is important for mystical vocabulary. A new critical edition has begun, though thus far only vol. 1 containing the *Aurora (Morgen-Röte im Aufganck)* and the *De signatura rerum* has appeared in *Jacob Böhme Werke*, ed. Ferdinand van Ingen (Frankfurt-am-Main: Deutsche Klassiker Verlag, 1997). For the English reader of the *Aurora* we now have an excellent edition, translation, and commentary, *Jacob Boehme, Aurora (Morgen Röte im auffgang, 1612)* and *Fundamental Report (Gründlicher Bericht, Mysterium Pansophicum, 1620)*, ed. and trans. Andrew Weeks (Leiden: Brill, 2013), which edition and translation will be used here. I will cite the German text by chapter and paragraph and Weeks's translation by page; e.g., *Aurora* 3.18 (Weeks, 166–67).

99. In his works Boehme distinguished between historical faith concerned with the surface events of Christianity and nonhistorical, or imaginative, faith dealing with the deeper meaning (e.g., *Aurora* 20.14–16; Weeks, 586–87).

100. On the Lutheran background of Boehme, see especially Weeks, "Introduction," *Aurora (Morgen Röte im auffgang, 1612)*, 8 and 13–25.

101. A great deal has been written about Boehme's sources and the influence of other religious, philosophical, and mystical systems on his thinking. He was, of course, quite familiar with Lutheran theology and Luther's Bible; but other currents were important—Paracelsian, alchemical, astrological, Hermetic, Neoplatonic, and Kabbalist. With regard to mystical authors, he had knowledge of the Radical Spirituals, especially Caspar Schwenckfeld and Valentin Weigel, and also would have had some familiarity with late medieval German mysticism, such as Tauler, the *Theologia Deutsch*, and some Eckhart sermons through the 1522 Basel Tauler edition. For a sketch of some of these sources, see Weeks, "Introduction,"

Aurora, 13–44. Cyril O'Regan (*Gnostic Apocalypse: Jacob Boehme's Haunted Narrative* [Albany: State University of New York Press, 2002]) discusses many of these possible connections and comparisons, arguing, along with F. C. Baur in his *Die christliche Gnosis* (1835), that Boehme represents the reemergence of Gnosticism in modern discourse, even though he did not have direct access to Gnostic sources.

102. *Aurora* 19.10–13 (Weeks, 550–51 adapted). On the importance of this "break-through," see Donata Schoeller Reisch, *Enthöhter Gott–vertiefter Mensch: Zur Bedeutung der Demut, ausgehend von Meister Eckhart und Jakob Böhme*, Alber-Reihe Philosophie (Munich: Karl Alber, 2009), 142–44.

103. *Aurora* 19.13–14 (Weeks, 552–53). This incident is also recounted in an expanded form in Boehme's later *Letter* XII.7–20 (SS IX:44–47), which mentions later illuminations (possibly 1610 and 1618). The letter, in which Boehme surveys his writings to about 1620, acknowledges his debt to Caspar Schwenckfeldt (XII.54; SS IX:54–55) and Valentin Weigel (XII.59–60; SS IX:55–56). Later accounts of the vision add details, such as meditating on water gleaming in a pewter dish and a duration of a quarter hour, that are not in the original account in the *Aurora*.

104. In the *Aurora* Boehme frequently claims that his message comes directly from God; e.g., *Aurora* 3.48–49, 11.76–83, 18.4–9, and 23.77.

105. For an introduction to this decisive event in German history, see the essays in Geoffrey Parker, ed., *The Thirty Years' War*, 2nd ed. (London and New York: Routledge, 1987).

106. On the conflict between Boehme and Richter, see Bo Andersson, "Jacob Böhme's polemischer Konflikt mit Gregorius Richter," in *Offenbarung und Episteme: Zur europäischen Wirkung Jacob Böhmes im 17. und 18. Jahrhundert*, ed. Willhelm Kühlmann and Friedrich Vollhardt, 33–46, Frühe Neuzeit 173 (Berlin: Walter de Gruyter, 2012).

107. In *Aurora* 22.107, he says, "My opinion is directed only toward giving an account of entire divinity, to the extent that such things are comprehensible to me in my weakness" (Weeks, 674–75).

108. There is a large literature on Boehme's reception. For recent surveys, see the essays in Ariel Hessayon and Sarah Apetrei, eds., *An Introduction to Jacob Boehme: Four Centuries of Thought and Reception*, Routledge Studies in Religion 31 (New York and London: Routledge, 2014); and Kühlmann and Vollhardt, *Offenbarung und Episteme*. For Boehme's place in modern esoteric traditions, see Arthur Versluis, *Wisdom's Children: A Christian Esoteric Tradition* (Albany: State University of New York Press, 1999).

109. David Walsh, *Mysticism of Innerworldly Fulfullment: A Study of Jacob Boehme* (Gainesville: University Presses of Florida, 1983), 22; see also 108.

110. W. Reginald Ward and Richard P. Heitzenrater, eds., *The Works of John Wesley*, vol. 19, *Journals and Diaries II (1738–43)* (Nashville: Abingdon, 1990), 272.

111. O'Regan, *Gnostic Apocalypse*, 3.

112. Boehme used both the terms "theosophy" (divine wisdom) and the related "pansophy" (universal wisdom). His followers often identified him as a theosophist. *Theo-sophia* first appeared in ancient magical papyri and was used by the fourth-century Neoplatonist Porphyry to characterize the teaching of Indian Brahmans (e.g., *De abstinentia* 4.17). Dionysius used *theosophi* to describe theologians (e.g., *De hierarchia caelesti* 2.5), and from him it passed into the West through

Eriugena's *Commentary on the Celestial Hierarchy* (e.g., *PL* 122:169c). *Theosophia* and *theosophus* were sparingly used in the Middle Ages as synonyms for theology and theologians, but in the late sixteenth and seventeenth centuries the words began to be more widely employed to characterize teaching about God and the world that went beyond the confessional doctrines of the churches. Theosophy received institutional embodiment in the foundation of the Theosophical Society in 1875 by Madame Blavatsky and Col. H. S. Olcott. For a brief history, see Antoine Faivre, "Théosophie," *DS* 15:548–62.

113. Many of those who have written on Boehme take up the question of his mysticism, and more than a few works concentrate on the issue; see, e.g., *Colloque Boehme, Jacob Boehme ou l'obscure lumière de la connaissance mystique: Homage à Jacob Boehme dans le cadre du Centre d'études et de recherches interdisciplinaires de Chantilly*, Bibliothèque d'histoire de la philosophie (Paris: J. Vrin, 1979); and Andreas Gauger, *Jacob Böhme und das Wesen seiner Mystik* (Berlin: Weissensee, 1999).

114. My approach to Boehme has been much aided by Weeks, *Boehme;* O'Regan, *Gnostic Apocalypse*; and Walsh, *Mysticism of Innerworldly Fulfillment*. In addition, I note the following important works: Heinrich Bornkamm, *Luther und Böhme* (Bonn: A. Markus and E. Weber, 1925); Alexandre Koyré, *La philosophie de Jacob Boehme* (Paris: Vrin, 1929; repr., 1968); and Hans Grunsky, *Jacob Böhme* (Stuttgart: Frommann, 1956). Other literature will be cited in what follows.

115. *Aurora* 26.131 (Weeks, 788–89). Boehme also speaks of the rosy dawn of the new era in Pref. 6, and in 26.116–21.

116. Important *apologiae* can be found in *Aurora*, Pref. 91–95; 13.22–28; 16.30–31; 18.4–9; 19.98–102; 20.71–72, 89; 22.8–19; 24.75–77; and 25.3–11.

117. For admissions of partial ignorance, see, e.g., *Aurora* 21.62–64; 22.41–42.

118. Boehme invites the reader to pray for illumination in 13.26–28.

119. *Aurora* 3.48 (Weeks, 166–67).

120. *Aurora* 25.44–50 (Weeks, 738–41).

121. The *gnaden waler* appear in chap. 26.137 (Weeks, 788–89). For other passages rejecting predestination, see, e.g., 13.7–12, 64; and 15.57. Boehme later wrote a treatise on *Von der Gnaden Wahl (On the Election of Grace).*

122. Calvin is attacked in *Aurora* 20.76 (Weeks, 600–601). In contrast, Boehme's only reference to Luther, "a poor despised monk," is favorable (*Aurora* 9.7).

123. See, e.g., *Aurora* 20.22–25; 22.51–65. Similar passages occur in later works.

124. On the relation between experience and speech in the work, see Alois M. Haas, "Erfahrung und Sprache in Böhme's *Aurora*," in *Gott, Natur und Mensch in der Sicht Jacob Böhmes und seiner Rezeption*, ed. Jan Garewicz and Alois M. Haas, Wolfenbütteler Arbeiten zur Barockforschung 24 (Wiesbaden: Harrassowitz, 1994), 1–21.

125. *Aurora* 1.3 (Weeks, 116–17): ". . . qualitet ist die Beweglicheit. quallent / oder treiben Eines dinges / Als da ist die Hitze / die Brennet ver zehret vnd Treiband alles das in siekompt / das nicht ihrer eigendschafft ist."

126. *Aurora* 26.53–57 (Weeks, 770–71). The seven spirits can be said to be the major theme of the *Aurora*; for some representative passages, see 9.4–46; 10.39–47; 11.4; 12.49–51; etc. Consult the index under "source-spirits (seven)" in Weeks, *Aurora*, 834, for a full listing.

127. *Aurora* 1.3–24 (Weeks, 116–25). Later (*Aurora* 4.6 and 26–29) Boehme adds the seventh quality of tone, or resonance (also called *marcurius*).

128. *Aurora* 3 (Weeks, 144–67). God the Father is discussed in 3.2–12; the Son in 3.13–23, while the Holy Spirit appears in 3.24–31. The whole Trinity is treated in 3.32–49. Other discussions of the Trinity are found in *Aurora* 7.25–35; and 23.34–52, 63–83.

129. *Salitter* seems to be derived from the three basic principles of nature investigated by alchemists and other early scientists: sulpher, mercury, and salt. Boehme makes them into universal metaphysical principles. See the note on the passages in *Aurora* 4 in F. van Ingen's edition of the *Aurora*, 930; and Weeks, "Introduction," *Aurora*, 34–35.

130. On the role of the seven spirits in the *Aurora*, see Weeks, *Boehme*, 70–76; and idem, "Introduction," *Aurora*, 27–30.

131. Two brief, but useful, summaries of how the seven spirits are the source of all things can be found in *Aurora* 9.41–46 and 21.73–117.

132. On the importance of consubstantiality in Boehme, see Walsh, *Mysticism of Innerworldly Fulfillment*, 12–13, 22–23, 63–66, 86–87.

133. *Aurora* 23.4 (Weeks, 676–77).

134. Other appearances of the "wheels within wheels" (often seven rather than the four of Ezekiel) can be found in *Aurora* 3.10, 13.71, 21.61, and 23.18 and 55.

135. On evil as limiting God in some way, see Walsh, *Mysticism of Innerworldly Fulfillment*, 92–93.

136. O'Regan, *Gnostic Apocalypse*, 2. The contours and implications of O'Regan's argument concerning Boehme as the first representative of the "Gnostic return," specifically Valentinian Gnosticism, cannot be pursued here.

137. *Aurora* 8.96–97 (Weeks, 260–61). The language of kissing, smelling, and tasting in this passage recalls the Song of Songs.

138. *Aurora* 8.106–9 (Weeks, 262–65). For other texts on the bridegroom drawing near, see 9.9–10, 12.43–44 (also including the birthing motif), and 19.11-12.

139. Jacob Boehme, *Clavis*, Preface 6 (SS IX:77; my translation).

140. Grunsky, *Jacob Böhme*, whose Second Section is entitled *Die Lehre als geschlossenes System* (63–304); see also his "Kleines Lexikon von Böhmes Begriffen" (319–39).

141. Weeks, *Boehme*, 170; see the discussion on 170–75, as well as 219.

142. In considering the importance of imagination in Boehme's writings, I acknowledge my indebtedness to a paper by Hugh B. Urban on this topic for one of my mysticism seminars decades ago—"Mysticism and Imagination in the 16th and 17th Centuries: A Comparison of Ignatius Loyola and Jacob Boehme." My thanks to the author.

143. *De tribus principiis oder Beschreibung der drey Principien Göttliches Wesens* takes up Vol. II of SS and contains 27 chapters and 493 pages.

144. Weeks, *Boehme*, 90. Weeks's account (90–126) is helpful for getting an overview.

145. *Drey Principien* 5.6 (SS II:49).

146. *Drey Principien* 4.31 (SS II:36). Naming God as Nothing was found in a number of former mystics, such as Eriugena and Meister Eckhart.

147. Walsh, *Mysticism of Innerworldly Fulfillment*, 18. See also Weeks, *Boehme*, 105.

148. *Drey Prinzipien* 7.14 (SS II:66; my translation): "Und verstehet man, wie

die Göttliche Kraft in allen Dingen erscheinet, und ist doch nicht das Ding selber, sondern der Geist Gottes ist im andern Principio; das Ding ist aber ein Glast, welches von dem sehenden Willen also worden ist. Nun ist aber das Hertze Gottes in dem Vater der erste Wille, und der Vater ist das erste Begehren nach dem Sohne, und der Sohn ist des Vaters Kraft und Licht." On the relation of the three principles to the will, see 7.26 (SS II:69).

149. I adopt this expression from another seminar paper, that of Ulrike Peinze, "'From Fiery Source to Divine Light': The Theological Anthropology of Jacob Boehme." Again I wish to thank the author for the use of insights from this study.

150. *Clavis* V. Von Göttlicher Weisheit (SS IX:82–83; my trans.). For sketches of Sophia and its function in Boehme's thought, see Walsh, *Mysticism of Inner-worldly Fulfillment*, 74–78; and Weeks, *Boehme*, 121–26.

151. Virginie Pektas, *Mystique et philosophie: Grunt, Abgrunt et Urgrund chez Maître Eckhart et Jacob Böhme*, Bochumer Studien zur Philosophie 45 (Amsterdam: B. R. Grüner, 2006), 103. See also the discussions on 117–19, 183, 207, 217–20, 233–41, 291–98. Pektas's study is a useful account of Boehme's *Ungrund* and its relation to earlier attempts to name a state of absolute origination.

152. See part 1 of Pektas, *Mystique et philosophie*, as well as McGinn, "Abyss of Love," 95–120; and idem, "Lost in the Abyss," 373–89.

153. I have analyzed Eckhart's mysticism as a "mysticism of the ground" in McGinn, *The Mystical Thought of Meister Eckhart: The Man from Whom God Hid Nothing*, Edward Cadbury Lectures 2000–2001 (New York: Crossroad, 2001), chapter 3.

154. See Leigh T. J. Penman, "Böhme's Student and Mentor: The Liegnitz Physician Balthasar Walther (c. 1558–c. 1630)," in Kühlmann and Vollhardt, *Offenbarung und Episteme*, 47–65.

155. Pektas (*Mystique et philosophie*, 206–29) argues that Boehme's conception of the *Ungrund* and also his later views on the relation of the three in the Trinity and the seven qualities reflect Kabbalistic views of the unnameable *En-Sof* ("without end") and the ten divine emanations or *sephirot* that might have been mediated to him by Balthasar Walthar. This is possible, and there are certainly similarities (and not a few substantial differences) between Boehme's views and those features of Kabbalah that would have been known to German-speaking Christians through texts such as Johannes Reuchlin's *De arte cabbalistica*. Along with Pektas, some others claim Kabbalistic sources for Boehme's views, such as John Schulitz, *Jakob Böhme und die Kabbalah: Eine vergleichende Werkanalyse* (Frankfurt am Main: P. Lang, 1993). For a more critical position, see O'Regan, *Gnostic Apocalypse*, 193–209, who admits Kabbalistic influence but cautions against an essentially Kabbalistic reading of these features of Boehme's thought.

156. In the edition found in SS III, the text has 184 pages, of which Question 1 occupies the first 62. I will adapt the old translation of John Sparrow, reprinted as *The Forty Questions of the Soul* (Kila, MT: Kessinger Publishing, n.d.).

157. *Forty Questions* 1.13 (SS III:10; trans. Sparrow, 7). (Here and afterwards I cite the paragraph numbers from the SS III text, which are different from those in Sparrow.)

158. The passages that follow are taken from *Forty Questions* 1.14–22 (SS III:11–12; trans. Sparrow, 7–11).

159. E.g., *Forty Questions* 1.51–54, 108, 127 (SS III:19, 31, 35).

160. Nicholas Berdyaev's "Unground and Freedom," can be found as the Introductory Essay in *Six Theosophical Points and Other Writings by Jacob Boehme*, trans. John Rolleston Earle (Ann Arbor: University of Michigan Press, 1958), v–xxxvii; quotation from xiv. I will use this translation with some adaptations.

161. Andrew Weeks summarizes: "At root, the world is God's struggle for self-understanding and self-expression" (*German Mysticism from Hildegard of Bingen to Ludwig Wittgenstein* [Albany: State University of New York Press, 1993], 183).

162. Pektas (*Mystique et philosophie*) describes insightful contrasts between Eckhart's view of the *grunt* and Boehme's *Ungrund* (see 21, 110, 183, 207, 241, 282, 293–94, and 296–98).

163. *Sex Puncta Theosophica* I.1.7–19 (SS IV:4–7; trans. Earle, 6–10, adapted).

164. The *Sex Puncta Mystica* are found in SS IV:83–96, with Point 5 on 93–96. There is a translation by Earle in *Six Theosophical Points and Other Writings*, 115–37.

165. *Mysterium Pansophicum*, Point 1, chapter 1, in SS IV:97. There is a translation by Earle in *Six Theosophical Points and Other Writings*, 141–62, where this text is at 141.

166. E.g., *Vom Menschenwerdung* 2.2.1–2, 2.3.5, 2.10.6 (SS IV:122–23, 127–28, and 179); Letter XII.71 (SS IX:58); *Clavis*, Point 1.2, and Point 3.15 (SS IX:79 and 81); and the *Mysterium Magnum* 1.2 and 8; 2.1; 3.22–24; and 7.6–8 (SS VII:5–6, 7, 16–17, 37).

167. *De signatura rerum* 3.2 (SS VI:18): "Ausser der Natur ist Gott ein Mysterium, verstehet in dem Nichts, dann ausser der Natur ist das Nichts, das ist ein Auge der Ewigkeit, ein ungründlich Auge, das in nichts stehet oder siehet, dann es ist der Ungrund; und dasselbe Auge ist ein Wille, verstehet ein Sehnen nach der Offenbarung, das Nichts zu finden."

168. *Von göttlichen Beschaulichkeit* 2.21 (SS IV:182; my translation).

169. For other interpretations of Boehme's *Ungrund*, see Koyré, *La philosophie de Jacob Boehme*, 280–82; Walsh, *Mysticism of Innerworldly Fulfillment*, 68–70; Weeks, *Boehme*, 171–73; O'Regan, *Gnostic Apocalypse*, 32–37, 134–35; Arthur Versluis, "The Mystery of Böhme's 'Ungrund,'" *Studies in Spirituality* 11 (2001): 205–11; and especially Pektas, *Mystique et philosophie*, part III, chapter 3.

170. Among these are the first appearances in the middle works of what will become a major theme in his later writings, the doctrine of the three worlds: the dark fire-world, the light world of freedom, and the outer world of bodies. See *Six Theosophical Points* 1.2.33–40; 6.7; *Six Mystical Points* 2.1; and the *Mysterium Magnum* 4.12.

171. *Von der Menschwerdung Jesu Christi* is found in SS IV:1–221. There is an English version by John Rolleston Earle, *Of the Incarnation of Jesus Christ by Jacob Böhme* (London: Constable, 1934), as well as a partial translation in Michael L. Birkel and Jeff Bach, eds., *Genius of the Transcendent, Mystical Writings of Jakob Boehme* (Boston and London: Shambala, 2010), 126–50.

172. *Von der Menschwerdung* 1.10.1–2 (SS IV:78–79; trans. Birkel-Bach, 139). See also 3.8.3–4.

173. *Von der Menschwerdung* 2.10.12 (SS IV:182; trans. Earle, 233).

174. *Von der Menschwerdung* 1.14.10 (SS IV:115–17; trans. Earle, 145–47).

175. *Von der Menschwerdung* 1.11.8 (SS IV:88; trans. Birkel-Bach, 149).

176. *Von der Menschwerdung* 3.8.1 (SS IV:218; trans. Earle, 280).

177. The *Mysterium Magnum, oder Erklärung über Das Erste Buch Mosis*, consist-

ing of seventy-eight chapters, is found in SSVII–VIII and altogether contains 892 pages. I will generally use the old translation of John Sparrow, reprinted in 2 vols. (Kila, MT: Kessinger Publishing, n.d.), containing 935 pages. I abbreviate the text as MM with chapter and section number.

178. For a comparison of Luther and Boehme on Genesis, see Arlene A. Miller, "The Theologies of Luther and Boehme in the Light of their *Genesis* Commentaries," *Harvard Theological Review* 63 (1970): 261–303.

179. MM 78.8–9 (SS VIII:891; trans. Sparrow, 2:935).

180. MM 6–7 offer a summary of how the *Ungrund* manifests itself in the seven qualities. Boehme also provides a brief and more comprehensible view of the emanative process in MM 29.1–15 (trans. Sparrow, 1:255–57).

181. The ten points (SS VII:3) are (1) the center and ground of all essences, (2) what the divine manifestation is, (3) how evil and good and all contraries originate from one ground, (4) how all things have their ground from the Great Mystery, (5) how the Eternal One comes into sensation and perception, (6) how man can attain knowledge of God and nature, (7) how man may attain contemplation of the Being of beings, (8) the creation of the world, (9) the Origin, Fall, and Restoration of man, and (10) the understanding of the Old and New Testaments.

182. The *Clavis* can be found in SS IX:75–120.

183. *Clavis* II.11 (SS IX:80–81; my translation). Boehme's view of the Trinity as three modes of working (*dreyerley Wirckungen*) and one essence has a Sabellian tone, which is enhanced by the fact that in other places he rejects the language of person with regard to the three (e.g., MM 7.5).

184. *Clavis* VII.24 (SS IX:84; my translation): ". . . als den innersten Grund, da sich der eigene enstandene Wille in eine Annehmlichkeit zur Ichheit einführet, als in ein natüliches Wircken."

185. The list includes *turba magna, ternarius sanctus, sul* and *phur, mysterium magnum, scienz,* and so on.

186. O'Regan, *Gnostic Apocalypse,* 207. The six stages are set out in chapter 1, "Narrative Trajectory of the Self-Manifesting Divine," esp. 32–50.

187. Walsh, *Mysticism in Innerworldly Fulfillment,* 44.

188. *Aurora* 14.36 (Weeks, 424–25).

189. On Boehme's Christology, which obviously demands a more detailed treatment than can be given here, see also Weeks, *Boehme,* 176–78.

190. For Boehme's devotion to Christ, see, e.g., Letters XLVI.1ff., LVIII.2, and LXIV.2, in SS IX:165ff., 226, and 244.

191. On imitating Christ, see *Six Theosophical Points* III, 4.24–25 (SS IV:38–39); on Christ as Redeemer, see V, 7.26 (SS IV:54). Many other texts could be cited.

192. *Christophia, oder der Weg zu Christo* is available in SS IV:1–252. There is a translation by Peter Erb, *Jacob Boehme: The Way to Christ,* Classics of Western Spirituality (New York: Paulist Press, 1978). See the "Introduction" by Erb, 1–26; and Weeks, *Boehme,* 205–8.

193. *Von wahrer Busse* 1.26 (SS IV:14; trans. Erb, 39).

194. *Von wahrer Busse* 1.38 (SS IV:20; trans. Erb, 45).

195. *Von wahrer Busse* 1.45 (SS IV:30; trans. Erb, 56–57).

196. There is also a reference to the marriage with Sophia in the second treatise at 2.16–17 (SS IV:41–42; trans. Erb, 69–70).

197. *Von wahrer Gelassenheit* 1.23 (SS IV:91; trans. Erb, 119).

198. Humility (*Demut*), both of God and humans, has been identified as a key theme in Boehme by D. Schoeller Reisch, *Enthöhter Gott–verteiften Mensch*, part 3.

199. *Von göttlicher Beschaulichkeit* 1.8 (SS IV:167; trans. Erb, 196).

200. *Von göttlicher Beschaulichkeit* 1.14 (SS IV:169; trans. Erb, 197 adapted). Boehme goes on to explain this in further, if obscure, detail in 1.15-31 (SS IV:169-73; trans. Erb, 199-201).

201. *Von göttlicher Beschaulichkeit* 2.19 (SS IV:182; trans. Erb, 209).

202. For some uses of 1 Corinthians 6:17, see *Von den Menschwerdung* II.10.7 and III.1.3; *Sex Puncta Theosophica* IV.6.5-6; and *Clavis*, Vorrede 2.

203. On sinking into nothingness, see, e.g., MM 27.5, 39.8, and 52.4-7.

204. For John Scottus Eriugena, the hidden God does not know himself, but that is because he cannot be *conceptually* known. John describes this *ignorantia* as *ineffabilis intelligentia*.

205. O'Regan, *Gnostic Apocalypse*, 48–49. O'Regan also discusses Boehme's relation to Christianity on 91-101 and 138-40. Walsh, *Mysticism of Innerworldly Fulfillment*, highlights Boehme's break with Christianity (*Mysticism of Innerworldly Fulfillment*, e.g., 14-15, 22-23, 51, 53, 71, 89, 92, 97-98).

206. Weeks, *Boehme*, 46, 56-57.

207. Walsh, *Mysticism of Innerworldly Fulfillment*, 17-18.

CHAPTER 4

Mysticism in the English Reformation

Historical Background

THE REFORMATION IN ENGLAND took a different direction than it did on the Continent.[1] The growing power of rulers in the early modern period had an important role in the triumph of the Evangelical reforms on the Continent (e.g., Luther and Frederick of Saxony), but it was not always necessary for success, as shown by the reform movements that were mostly supported by cities. England, however, was a self-contained monarchy, one in which the will of the king proved decisive in religious matters. Another difference between the English reform and movements on the Continent was leadership. Sixteenth-century England had important reformers, such as Thomas Cranmer (1489–1556), archbishop of Canterbury, who played a pivotal role in moving the English church toward the reformed camp, but no one has ever called English Protestants "Cranmerites," the way German Evangelicals were first called "Martinites," and later "Lutherans."

The Church of England, which in the modern era has developed into the Anglican Communion with its many branches around the world, evolved as a "middle way" between Catholi-

My gratitude is due to Prof. Mark McIntosh of the Department of Theology of Loyola University, Chicago, for his comments and suggestions on this chapter.

cism and the strong rejection of medieval religion found in both Lutheranism and Calvinism.[2] As T. S. Eliot put it, the English church under Queen Elizabeth I was persistent "in finding a mean between Papacy and Presbytery."[3] Anglicanism (a nineteenth-century term) has been marked by an effort to tolerate a plurality of theologies and views of the church, though often with much inner squabbling.[4] The emphasis on moderation and compromise that the English Reformation achieved through its internal struggles allowed for a variety of interpretations of Christian faith within an overall consensus about a state church whose system survives in England, if much altered, down to the present.

Henry VIII (ruled 1509–47) was one of the new monarchs who came on the scene early in the sixteenth century. As Luther's ideas percolated through Europe, in 1521 Henry commissioned his advisors to write a rebuttal to the Reformer's theology of the sacraments, a treatise for which Henry was ironically given the title "Defender of the Faith" by Leo X. By 1527, however, Henry had rejected his first wife, the Spanish Catherine of Aragon, who had not provided him with a male heir. He then began a six-year attempt to obtain a papal dispensation so that he could marry his mistress, Anne Boleyn. The pope was unyielding, so in 1534 Henry ordered the Parliament to issue the "Acts of Supremacy," which declared Henry "the only supreme head on earth of the Church of England, called *Ecclesia Anglicana*." Between 1532 and 1540, Henry's chief minister, Thomas Cromwell, oversaw the dissolution of the monasteries and furthered a growing evangelical turn in the English church.

Henry was not enamored of many of the Protestant changes in theology and liturgy, but some of the bishops he appointed, such as Thomas Cranmer, were. Cranmer's role in the evolution of the Anglican Church was decisive in a number of ways, not least in his efforts beginning in 1549 to create an official vernacular prayer book for both clergy and laity, what eventually became the *Book of Common Prayer*.[5] This "integrated view of prayer and the Christian life" has been described as "the heart of Anglican spirituality."[6] After the king's death, Cranmer and other bishops steered the English church in a more strongly Reformed Protestant direction during the brief reign of Henry's sickly son, Edward VI (1547–53). The situation was reversed under the succeeding rule of Mary Tudor (1553–58), daughter of Henry and Catherine, who tried to "Re-catholicize" the country. The death of the unpopular Mary brought her stepsister Elizabeth (daughter of Henry and Anne Boleyn) to the throne, where she was to reign from 1558 to 1603.

Elizabeth presided over what the English have always looked on as the golden "Elizabethan Age." The queen sympathized with the Protestant cause, both religiously and politically, but she adhered to a middle path between those who thought that the reform in England had not gone far enough, especially in retaining bishops and older liturgical forms, and those, Catholics and other conservatives, who wanted the clock turned back. Elizabeth resisted further reforms in the church, especially through the Settlement of 1559 and the "Thirty-Nine Articles" of belief officially approved in 1571.[7] By the end of the sixteenth century England had emerged as the great Protestant nation-state. Within the country, however, there were competing views of what Protestant meant that led to argument and eventually armed conflict.

From the 1560s on, currents among the English clergy and laity had expressed dissatisfaction with the 1559 Settlement. These "precise," or "godly" folk, later called Puritans, believed that the English church needed to draw closer to the theological and organizational view of the Reformed wing of Continental Protestantism as represented in Geneva, dropping bishops and adopting a Presbyterian structure for the church, as well as simplifying the liturgy and giving greater emphasis to preaching.[8] The Conformists to the 1559 Settlement opposed the Puritans and, after considerable struggle, won out politically at the end of the sixteenth century. Their views found expression in the writings of Richard Hooker (1554–1600), whose *Laws of Ecclesiastical Polity* have been seen as the classic expression of the Elizabethan Settlement and the intellectual foundation of Anglican Christianity.

The Puritans were initially defeated, but they bided their time. For some sixty years after 1600 the Church of England was convulsed with the struggles between the establishment "Conformers" (Anglicans) and the Non-Conformist "Puritan" members of the church who sought to purge it of its imperfections. Elizabeth died in 1603 and was succeeded by the King of Scotland, James VI Stuart, who reigned in England as James I down to 1625. Under James, another pillar of the Anglican tradition, the "Authorized Version of the Bible" (AV, or King James Bible), was published in 1611. James advanced bishops like Lancelot Andrewes (1555–1626), whose sermons and prayers represent the essence of Anglican piety. James's son, Charles I (1625–49), favored a theological and ecclesiastical policy (called "Arminianism") that was closer to Catholicism than most English, especially the Puritans, wanted. His Arminian appointee to the see of Canterbury, William Laud (archbishop 1633–45), enraged the Puritan faction. The tensions between Charles I, not a skillful ruler, and the increasingly radical

Puritan Parliament led to a decisive split in 1640 and the outbreak of civil war in 1642. Laud was imprisoned and executed, and by 1648 Charles himself was defeated and taken prisoner. The English religious quarrels went further than anything that had happened on the Continent, when in 1649 Charles, the established head of the Church of England, was executed by the order of the leaders of the Puritan army who controlled Parliament. For the next decade (1649–58) England was a commonwealth under the rule of the Lord Protector, Oliver Cromwell (1599–1658), the most powerful of the Puritan generals. The Puritan government and its attempts to introduce strict Presbyterianism and to regulate the morals and manners of the citizens grew increasingly unpopular with the bulk of the populace. The new regime collapsed after Cromwell's death in 1658, and by 1660 the Parliament had invited Charles I's eldest son back to rule as Charles II (1660–85).

Anglican Spirituality and Mysticism

Late sixteenth- and seventeenth-century English religious writers made significant contributions to the history of mysticism. In this chapter, I will investigate only those who thought of themselves as belonging to the *Ecclesia Anglicana*, including both those who are today identified as "Anglican" and those who are identified as "Puritans." I will not treat the "Separatists," especially the Quakers, who broke with established religion of any kind, nor the Catholics, who refused to conform to the Elizabethan Settlement and who fled to the Continent (often called "Recusants").

Anglicanism is notorious for resisting definition. Although Anglicanism may be hard to define, the *Ecclesia Anglicana* has had a distinct history, and there are some basic traits that characterize the tradition of those loyal to the Elizabethan Settlement. Recent articles and books on Anglican spirituality argue that the essentials of Anglican spirituality and mysticism were established between ca. 1580 and 1640.[9] The group of religious leaders often called the Caroline Divines (many of whom were more active under Elizabeth and James I than under Charles I) are often seen as forming the heart of the early Anglican tradition. While critics see the Anglican "middle way" as an amorphous compromise, its defenders view it as a sensible solution for the divisions among the Christian communions. George Herbert summed up this view in his poem "The British Church," answering attacks from both Rome and Geneva with the lines: "But dearest Mother, (what those [i.e., the critics] miss) / The mean [i.e., *via media*] thy praise and glory is, / And long may be."

The Anglican tradition is, first and foremost, biblical, formed by its devotion to scripture as expressed in the magnificent prose of the King James Version. Anglicanism also had a pronounced corporate and liturgical emphasis based on the *Book of Common Prayer*.[10] Part of the genius of the *Prayer Book* was its inclusion of the whole worshiping community, clerical and lay. Theologically, the Anglican Church was traditional, looking back to the "Fathers of the Undivided Church" of both the East and the West, although many Anglican divines were also familiar with medieval authors, including the Scholastics. Still, the early Fathers and their liturgies and creeds were felt to be closer to the wellsprings of biblical faith and practice, and therefore essential to Anglican identity. There was also a deep aesthetic dimension in Anglicanism, partly expressed in church music, but even more by the intimate bond between literature and religion, and especially poetry and belief.

Mystical literature was not new in England. The fourteenth century had seen a flowering of mysticism.[11] These medieval writings, however, did not have much impact during the English Reformation, as deep quarrels over the nature of true belief, the dismantling of ecclesiastical structures and pious practices, the end of the monasteries, and religious persecution left little space for the reading or production of mystical literature. By the end of the sixteenth century, however, and during the first half of the seventeenth, both camps in the English church produced writings that form a distinctive chapter in the history of mysticism. Among those who adhered to the Elizabethan Settlement—pastors, professors, preachers, and laity—the most important mystical writing was in the form of poetry. I will begin, however, by looking at some of the prose works of the early Anglican tradition that can be said to have mystical aspects.[12]

Mystical Themes of Early Anglican Preachers

Along with Richard Hooker, Lancelot Andrewes (1555–1626), the bishop of Winchester, was central to the creation of mainstream Anglicanism.[13] Andrewes was born when the Catholic Mary reigned, but he grew up under Elizabeth, receiving ecclesiastical preferment from 1590 on. Favored by James I, he served successively as bishop of three dioceses, court preacher, and in numerous ecclesiastical and royal appointments. Andrewes was deeply learned and sincerely pastoral, though he has been accused of undue subservience to James I due to their shared belief in the "Divine Right of Kings." Among his contemporaries, he left a reputation for probity, kindness, and a deep prayer life, but in what sense might he be called a mystic? The evidence for the claim is based in two of the three aspects of his literary production (leaving out the polemical writings against Catholics): first, his sermons; and, second, the *Private Devotions (Preces Privatae)* that he composed for his own use but which were published after his death.

Andrewes was said to have prayed as much as five hours every day, not only in the public liturgies of the Anglican Church, but with his *Preces Privatae.* As he neared death, he gave a copy of the book to his friend Archbishop Laud, thus indicating a hope for a wider audience.[14] The *Preces Privatae* had to be translated for all but the most learned, since they were written mostly in Latin and Greek with some sections in Andrewes's imperfect Hebrew.[15] The prayers should not be read merely as prose; rather, their hymn-like form is meant to be prayed as a quasi-liturgical exercise, or meditated upon to bring out their inner meaning. There is little in the content of the *Preces* that is original with Andrewes, save for the organization and spirit that pervade the collection.[16] Most of the book is citations from scripture, but there are also ample passages from the liturgies of Eastern and Western Christianity, as well as citations from patristic and medieval authors.[17] Most of the *Preces* is taken up with morning and evening prayers, with sections expanding on the particular parts of these devotions.

Andrewes's collection highlights three essential motifs of Christian prayer: praise, penance, and petition. In terms of the last, he is inclusive (today we might say ecumenical) in his intercessions for all Christians (indeed, all humans) and for his sense of the unity of the one "Mystical Body of Christ." Andrewes's prayers are Trinitarian, and, above all, incarnational, in the sense that they focus on the "dispensation," or economy, of the divine plan for salvation effected through God becoming man in Jesus Christ, and especially in his death on the cross.[18] Salvation is realized especially through contact with Christ in the Eucharist ("a memorial of the dispensation," as he calls it). By the sacrament we come to dwell in Christ and he in us. This theme of "mutual indwelling," which includes an element of being made conformable to Christ,[19] along with a few references to deification,[20] is as close as Andrewes comes to the themes of traditional mystical literature. The emphasis of Andrewes's private liturgy is on faith, penance, intercession, and thanksgiving, not on uniting with God.

Andrewes's hundred or so sermons have been variously interpreted, for both style and content.[21] There is no question that their doctrinally solid and ingeniously varied teaching on incarnation, redemption, and the doctrine of the Holy Spirit make them classic statements of the Anglican *via media*; but, despite the praise of T. S. Eliot, who held that Andrewes's sermons "rank with the finest English prose of their time, or any time," G. M. Story notes that "he is among the least read of Elizabethan and Jacobean writers."[22] To the modern reader their witty metaphysical style, constant use of foreign-language quotations, length, and intricate development tend to be off-putting. Our concern, however, is with the theological content, and specifically with mysticism. Nicholas Lossky presents a case for Andrewes as a mystic, claiming, "The ultimate objective of the spiritual life being union with God, it could be said that the theology of Lancelot Andrewes is a mystical theology." He continues, "It is not a matter . . . of any exceptional experience, reserved for a few, in some way outside the traditional ways of theology. It is on the contrary a matter of the interiorization of the revealed Christian mystery. . . . This theology is mystical in the sense that it is not an abstract reflection, but a matter of living the mystery concretely through a deepening of the faith in prayer and by renunciation of one's own will."[23] Whatever Lossky may have in mind by his reference to "mystical theology . . . as abstract reflection" (he names no names), he seems to mean that Andrewes is a mystical theologian *in the sense of the mysticism of the early church*, where sound incarnational theology was, by definition, always mystical. This may well be the case, and Andrewes is surely one of the best representatives of an integral vision of Christian belief and practice in the early seventeenth century. Nevertheless, it remains a question how far Andrewes should be read as a "mystic," rather than as a theological witness to the core values of the Anglican *via media*.

The sermons of Andrewes are deeply biblical, doctrinally rich, and stylistically ingenious. They contain impressive treatments of the mysteries of salvation, but only a few of the sermons seem to touch on specific themes of the mystical tradition, such as contemplation, ascent to God, union, deification, and the like. Andrewes excludes none of these, but they are not where his interest lies. The bishop wished to instruct his learned audience (many of the sermons were preached to the court of James I) about the theological meaning of the readings for the feasts of the liturgical year.

In preaching on the Nativity, for example, Andrewes follows Bernard of Clairvaux in using the meeting of Mercy and Truth and the kiss

of Righteousness and Peace (Ps. 85:10) to present the significance of
Christ's redeeming birth. He thinks that the same four virtues should
meet in his audience: ". . . looke, what in His *birth*, now; in the new *birth*
of every one, that shall be better by it; even the same *meeting* of the very
same virtues, all."[24] This is a hint at the mystical theme of the birth
of the Word in the soul. At the end of his "Sermon 2 of the Passion:
Good-Friday 1604," he asks his listeners to "Regard," that is, carefully
consider, Christ's passion by thinking upon it, thanking him for it, and
then to "stay and see, whether he will regard us, or no." Andrewes continues, "Sure he wil, and we shal feele our hearts pricked with sorrow. .
. . And againe, warme within us, by consideration of the cause in him,
his Love; till by some motion of his Grace he answere us, and shew,
that our Regard is accepted of him."[25] Andrewes wishes to move his
listeners to devotion and the reception of an inner movement of grace,
but the extent to which we might wish to call this mystical will depend
on how broad a notion of mysticism we are ready to entertain. A third
and final example can be found in "Sermon 14 on the Resurrection:
Easter 1620," which considers the story of Mary Magdalene at the
tomb and her meeting with Christ, ever a favorite of mystical preachers (Andrewes cites Pseudo-Origen, Gregory, and Bernard). This sermon emphasizes Mary's love for Jesus (he even refers to her being "in
a kind of extasie all the while"), but for the most part we look at the
Magdalene from the outside, so to speak, as someone to be admired
more than imitated. Only at the conclusion, where Andrewes insists
that the hearing of faith is more important than seeing, does he turn
to the hope that Christ will deal with us as he did with the Magdalene,
so that we *"know Him and the virtue of His Resurrection*; and make us
partakers of both, by both of the meanes before remembered, by His
blessed Word, by His holy mysteries [i.e., sacraments]; the meanes to
raise our soules here, the pledges of the raising up of our bodies hereafter. Of which *He* make us partakers, who is the Author of both, *Jesus
Christ the Righteous, etc."*[26] So, the raising up of the soul in this life is
mentioned by Andrewes, but not featured.

Similar claims for a mystical dimension have been made for the
prose writings of John Donne (1572–1631).[27] Donne was born into a
staunch Catholic family and took a degree at Oxford before going to
London to study law. During the 1590s, he acquired a reputation as
a rake and began distancing himself from Catholicism, but Donne's
progress from Catholicism to Anglicanism was a slow and difficult process, as he describes in his "Satire III." Although he was influenced by
his Catholic background, there can be no question of the sincerity of

Donne's eventual adherence to Anglicanism's "middle way." As Frank Kermode put it, "What made him a poet also made him an Anglican: the revaluation of a tradition."[28] In 1597, Donne became secretary to the influential courtier Sir Thomas Egerton. While in his employ, Donne met Ann More and secretly married her in 1601. As a result, he lost his position, and from 1602 to 1615 the family, with an increasing number of children, lived a life of marginality and poverty. It was apparently during this period that most of his religious poems were written. In 1615, Donne was ordained and his fortunes began to improve as a number of important clerical posts came his way. The death of his beloved wife in 1617 was a severe blow. Donne was installed as dean of St. Paul's Cathedral in London in 1621 and became a noted preacher. The last decade of his life was marked by illness, and he died on March 31, 1631.

Now most famous as a poet, in his own day Donne was best known as a preacher.[29] Most of Donne's poetry was published after his death, and while he was always read, his reputation greatly increased in the twentieth century. This modern fame has helped attract readers and critics to his 160 surviving sermons preached between 1616 and 1631, sermons no less learned, intricate, and difficult than those of Andrewes, if in his own way.[30] Donne's sermons are classical orations, examples of epideictic rhetoric, but they also display the meditative techniques that became popular in the sixteenth century among both Catholics and Protestants.[31] According to Peter McCollough, "his sermons are like vast, dramatic canvasses by Titian or Rubens," which Izaak Walton, one of his hearers, says affected his audience in various ways, including "carrying some, as St. Paul was, to Heaven in holy raptures."[32] The sermons reveal knowledge of some mystical authors and give attention, from time to time, to mystical themes, without ever making these a major aspect of his preaching.[33] Donne's sermons emphasize doctrinal and especially moral themes, rather than the transformation of consciousness due to a sense of God's interior presence.[34]

One example of Donne's use of mystical themes can be found in the "Sermon on Matthew 5:8" ("Blessed are the pure of heart for they shall see God"), one of the premier texts in the history of Christian mysticism.[35] The primary concern of the sermon is with the beatific vision, which Donne analyzes by means of a typical *divisio* of three parts based on the biblical text: the price (cleanness of heart), the purchase (blessedness), and the term or goal (everlasting enjoyment of God). The homily sets forth a teaching found across Donne's preaching, namely, that although the fullness of the vision of God comes only in the next life,

it is begun here—"so the Joy, and the sense of Salvation, which the pure
of heart have here, is not a joy severed from the Joy of Heaven, but a
Joy that begins in us here, and continues, and accompanies us thither,
and there flowes on, and dilates it selfe to an infinite expansion."[36]
The impossibility of a full vision of God's essence in this life is put
in a wider context in a sermon preached at St. Paul's on Easter 1628,
on 1 Corinthians 13:12, "For now we see through a glasse darkly, but
then face to face."[37] Donne distinguishes various ways of seeing God,
beginning with the obscurity of the light of natural reason's vision of
God in the "Booke of Creatures," moving on to the higher knowledge
found in the church through the light of faith, and following Augustine in ascribing some kind of vision of God to Moses. He notes that
"the Schoole" (i.e., the medieval Scholastics) distinguished four ways
of knowing God: faith, contemplation, apparition (i.e., visions),[38] and
"cleare manifestation of himself in heaven." Donne shows his Protestant perspective in claiming that the faith of the Scholastics is mere
intellectual assent, and in giving a reformed twist to contemplation.
"They [the Scholastics] make their second way Contemplation, that is,
An union with God in this life; which is truly the same thing we mean
by Faith; for we do not call an assent to the Gospell, faith, but faith is
the application of the Gospell to our selves; not an assent that Christ
dyed, but an assurance that Christ dyed for all." Donne thinks little
of knowledge by apparition, so for him knowing God is centered in
"Faith [as] a blessed presence, but compared with heavenly vision, [it]
is but an absence."[39] Like Luther, Donne holds that union with God is
fundamentally a union in faith.

Although the full vision of God's essence is not possible in this life,
Donne did hold out the possibility of contemplative ecstasy as a foretaste of heaven, and even seems to aspire to it for himself. In an Easter
sermon preached on Psalm 89:48, Donne meditates on how the blood
of Christ running in his veins and the breath of the Holy Spirit in his
body make all his deaths turn into resurrections, starting with natural
death and death through sin. He continues with a passage on a third
death:

> . . . but I will finde out another death, *mortem raptus*, a death of rap-
> ture, and of extasie, that death which S. *Paul* died more than once,
> The death which S. *Gregory* speaks of, *Divina contemplatio quoddam*
> *sepulchrum animae*, The contemplation of God, and heaven, is a kind
> of buriall, and Sepulchre, and rest of the soule; and in this death of
> rapture, and extasie, in this death of the Contemplation of my inter-

est in my Saviour, I shall finde my self, and all my sins entered; and entombed in his wounds, and like a Lily in Paradise . . . I shall rise out of his blade . . . acceptable in the sight of his Father.[40]

This death of ecstasy does not involve a direct and permanent vision of God's essence. In the sermon on 1 Corinthians 13:12 cited above, Donne agrees with the teaching of Thomas Aquinas on the matter and even cites the brief experience of touching God enjoyed by Augustine and Monica in *Confessions* 9.10. He concludes "That neither *Adam* in his extasie in Paradise, nor *Moses* in his conversation in the Mount, nor the other Apostles in the Transfiguration of Christ, nor S. *Paul* in his rapture to the third heavens, saw the Essence of God."[41]

Donne sometimes uses strong language regarding union with God in this life. The "Sermon on Psalm 32:8" is a discussion of God's instruction of his people and guidance with "his eye."[42] The preacher distinguishes two effects of this guidance by God's eye: (1) conversion to him, and (2) union with him. These effects create a mutuality between God and ourselves. Donne says:

> The other great effect of his guiding us with his eye, is, That it unites us to himselfe; when he fixes his eye upon us, and accepts the returne of ours to him, then he *keepes* us as the *Apple* of his *eye* (Ps. 17:8). . . . And these are the two great effects of his guiding us by his eye, that first, the eye turns us to himselfe, and then he turns us into himself; first, his eye turnes ours to him, and then, that makes us all one with himselfe. . . . [W]ee cannot be safer then by being his; but thus, we are not onely His, but He . . . .[43]

Such union would seem to imply a kind of deification. Donne does not mention deification here, but the theme occurs elsewhere, at least in terms of a participation in the divine nature (2 Pet. 2:4) begun in this life through the ministry of the church and its sacraments but one that will only reach its fullness in the life to come.[44]

Donne speaks of being identified with Christ in the major mysteries of salvation. The notion of the birth of the Word in the soul is also found in Donne. He refers to the inner divine birth several times in his Christmas sermons, for example: "In this fulnesse [of the birth of Christ within], in this comming of our Saviour into us . . . we should find a threefold fullnesse in ourselves"—a fullness of nature, a fullness of grace, that is, "a daily sense of improvement," and finally, "a fulnesse of glory, that is an apprehension and inchoation of heaven in this life."[45] Donne also emphasizes the need to be identified with

Christ in his dying on the cross, a theme found both in the sermons
and in his poetry.[46] Both forms of participation in Christ are rooted
in the sonship we share with the Only-Begotten Son of the Father. In
a sermon preached at St. Paul's Cross on May 6, 1627, Donne says,
"So high, so very high a *filiation*, hath God given man, as that, having
another Sonne, by another filiation, then this, by an *eternall generation*,
yet he was content, that that Sonne should become this Sonne, that the
Sonne of *God* should become the Sonne of *Man*.[47]

Union between Christ and the believer can even be expressed in
terms of the mystical marriage. Regina Schwartz has suggested that
"marriage is the governing trope" of Donne's theology.[48] In a 1627 sermon he makes the marriage of God and human the center of the whole
work of creation, re-creation, and consummation:

> In thy first work, the *Creation*, the last *seale* of thy whole work was
> a *Mariage* [i.e., of Adam and Eve]. In thy Sonnes great work, the
> *Redemption*, the first seale of that whole work, was a miracle at a *Mar-
> iage*. In the work of thy blessed Spirit, our *Sanctification*, he refreshes
> us, that promise in one Prophet, *That thou wilt mary thy selfe to us
> for ever* . . . (Hos. 2:19).[49]

In a sermon preached before the king at Whitehall in 1625, Donne
speaks of the soul's permanent marriage to Christ: "GOD is *Love*, and
the *Holy Ghost* is amorous in his *Metaphors*; everie where his *Scriptures*
abound with the notions of *Love*, of *Spouse*, and *Husband*, and *Marriadge Songs*, and *Marriadge Supper*, and *Marriadge-Bedde*. But for words
of *Separation*, and *Divorce*, and *Spirituall Divorce* for ever . . . *God* dis-
avowes it."[50] Christ, who is the spouse of the Church,[51] also has a "second marriage." "And of this second, the spiritual marriage," continues
Donne, "much needs not to be said; There is another priest that con-
tracts that, another Preacher that celebrates it, the spirit of God to
our spirit . . . there is a marriage and Christ marries me. . . . And he
hath married it in *aeternum*, for ever." He goes on, "but this eternity
is not begun in this world, but from all eternity in the Book of Life in
God's eternal Decree for my election, there Christ was married to my
soul."[52] Donne even speaks of the mystical kiss of the soul and Christ:
"But though this act of love, be so defamed both ways, by treachery,
by licentiousness, yet God chooses this Metaphor, he bids us kiss the
Sonne. . . . [F]or if we be truly in love with him, it will be a holy and
acceptable Metaphore unto us."[53]

Other of Donne's prose works, such as the *Devotions* he composed
in 1623 during a grave illness, witness more to his sense of the power

of sin in his life and the continuing need for repentance and trust in God's loving mercy than to mystical themes.[54] His earliest theological writing, the *Essays in Divinity* composed about 1614–15, is a series of meditative considerations of Genesis and Exodus testifying to his extensive reading and growing engagement with exegesis and theology.[55] The *Essays* contain mystical overtones of desire for a deeper contact with God in the four "Prayers" that close off the work. Here he asks God to "hasten mine Exodus and deliverance, for I desire to be dissolved, and to be with thee," and he goes on to request to be removed "to a more solitary and desert retiredness, where I may more safely feed upon both thy Mannaes, thy self in thy sacrament, and that other, which is Angells food, contemplation of thee."[56] This may be rhetoric, but it still expresses Donne's hope.

Anglican Mystical Poetry[57]

The prose writings, especially the sermons, of Donne and others provide some evidence for an Anglican mysticism, but a stronger witness is found in poetry. Speaking of the Anglican "metaphysical poets," the critic Cleanth Brooks said, "It is because of [their] sense of reality in spiritual experience that we value the metaphysical poets. . . . There is literally nothing else like them in the religious poetry of the past. Though they have a deep and abiding value for all Christians, a universality which takes them past the bounds of any mere nationalism, they are the special glory of the English church."[58] English metaphysical poets like Donne, Herbert, Vaughan, and Traherne have also long been seen as "mystical poets."[59] But what is a mystical poet?

The relation between poetical expression and mystical discourse has often been a topic of discussion.[60] I will not attempt to give any detailed analysis of the issues involved in speaking of the relation between poetry and mysticism, but two questions need to be confronted: First, when does devotional poetry pass over into mystical poetry? And, second, does mystical poetry need to reflect the personal experience of the poet? These questions are not susceptible of easy answers. The line between devotional poetry reflecting the "merely" religious views of the poet and "mystical poetry" seen as in some way reflecting a special consciousness of God's presence depends on one's view of the meaning of mysticism, and also on how one conceives of the poet's desire (and ability) to relate his or her inner life to general truths about human nature. Mystical poems, like mystical prose texts, cannot adequately *denote* the mystical consciousness that lies beyond words, but they may be able to *connote* it by reflection, indirection, metaphor, and other verbal strategies.[61] Images are necessary but never sufficient for the mystic, who must, as Henry Suso once put it, "Use images to drive out images." Second, under the influence of the once-dominant "autobiographical fallacy" regarding mystical discourse (crudely: "It ain't mysticism unless the author is talking directly about his or her own experience"), many previous studies of the relation of poetry and mysticism made autobiographical "witness" the norm for determining what was truly "mystical" and what was only attempting to describe mysticism from the outside. In his book on the mysticism of the seventeenth-century English poets Itrat Husain argued that Donne, Herbert, and Vaughan were true mystical poets because he could identify autobiographical elements of their poems that conformed to the traditional threefold mystical path of purgation–illumination–union, while Husain judged that the poetry of Richard Crashaw "is really the poetic apprehension of mystical experience rather than an account of his own journey on the Mystic Way."[62] Would that it were so easy! Determining what is a mystical poem will remain a highly personal choice.

John Donne

Donne wrote erotic poems early in his career; most of his devotional poems seem to have come later.[63] His erotic verse, whether autobiographical, or exercises in what an Elizabethan poet was expected to write about physical love,[64] exhibits a variety of styles and attitudes. Some poems are Petrarchan exercises in describing how the lover pursues and longs for the unattainable object of his love; others are Ovidian—frank, cynical, misogynist exercises in male sexual dominance. There are also a number of poems in which the mutual fulfillment of both lovers is emphasized. These poems have been seen as revolutionary in Christian attitudes toward sexuality, because, as Achsah Guibbory put it, "Donne's figurative language makes sexual love sacred, suggesting that it offers an experience of transcendence, a taste of the divine."[65] That is to say, orgasm is holy. In contrast to Jewish Kabbalistic mysticism, in which the Sabbath joining of the rabbi and his wife was an important part of the mystical path, Christian mysticism, in large part due to the triumph of the ideal of virginity in the fourth century, made use of forms of erotic language, especially from the Song of Songs, in presenting the love between Christ and the soul, but shied away from thinking that actual sexual practice, even in marriage, could have a place in the path to God.[66] Sex was at best a distraction; more often a danger. Donne was among the first to challenge this view, although his sacral view of sexual love does not show much explicit relation to love of God.[67] Still, in "Holy Sonnet I (later XVII)," written in honor of his recently deceased wife, Donne says that "the admiring her my mind did whett / To seeke thee God."[68]

Donne's notion of sacred sexuality is private, being realized in the mutual ecstasy of man and woman. Sometimes, however, the poems invite the reader to ponder the significance of the lovers. In "The Extasie," two lovers embrace and gaze into each other's eyes so intently that their souls go out from their bodies in rapture and become one in loving union ("Love, these mixt souls, doth mixe againe, / And makes both one, each this and that"). But ecstatic love cannot remain on the level of spirit alone; it must return to physical sexual union: "Soe soule into the soule may flow, / Though it to body first repaire. / As our blood labors to beget / Spirits as like soules as it can. . . ." The souls of pure lovers must honor the body's affections and faculties, "Else a great Prince in prison lies." So, "To'our bodies turn wee then, that so / Weake men on love reveal'd may looke; / Loves mysteries in soules doe grow, / But yet the body is his booke."[69]

Other of Donne's erotic poems celebrate sexual union in religious, even mystical, terms. In "The Canonization," for example, the lover begins by abruptly ordering his beloved, "For Godsake hold your tongue, and let me love" without complaint about his faults, because, "By us, we two being one, are it. / So to one neutral thing [i.e., the hermaphrodite] both sexes fit, / Wee dye and rise the same, and prove / Mysterious by this love." The sacred mystery has a transcendental dimension, because the depth of their love will make the lovers into saints—"Us *Canoniz'd* for Love."[70] "The Good Morrow" says that in love the lovers acquire a certain eternity, while "The Sunne Rising" presents a cosmic dimension to the lovers on their bed.[71] The eternal dimension of sexual love is further emphasized in "The Anniversary."[72] One of the most direct of all Donne's erotic poems, Elegy XIX "To His Mistris Going to Bed," sees the woman's divesting herself of her clothes to "Full nakedness" as a kind of spiritual trope: "As souls unbodied, bodies uncloth'd must be, / To taste whole joys. . . ." Hence, women "Themselves are mystic books, which only wee / (Whom their imputed grace will dignifie) / Must see reveal'd. . . ."[73] (The idea of the woman "imputing grace" to her lover was shocking to some in his age, and perhaps even today.) Donne gave a transcendent dimension to sexual love, both in this life and in the world to come.

Many accounts of Donne's spirituality and mysticism have been nervous about the early verses and have concentrated on his later devotional poems that seem to represent a criticism of the early erotic verse, or at least the more crude and cynical examples.[74] Nevertheless, the use of erotic images in many of the later poems shows that there is a strong, if complicated, relation between the secular love poems and the later divine poems. As Anthony Low put it, "Donne does not succeed in bringing together the love of woman with the love of God without experiencing agonizing inner conflicts and difficulties."[75] Donne's "Divine Poems," which John Booty reads as intended to draw the reader "into a salvific process,"[76] include some of the most noted religious poems in English.[77] Again, we can ask how far these devotional poems may be termed "mystical."[78] Louis Martz prefers the term "meditative poetry," but, given the porous boundary between meditation and contemplation in the seventeenth century, he is willing to admit that "the term 'mystical' may, with some justice, be applied to the English meditative poets," such as Donne, Herbert, Vaughan, Crashaw, and Traherne.[79]

Some of Donne's divine poems are quasi-liturgical hymns; others, especially among "Holy Sonnets," are meditative and personal. Most are devotional in their encouragement of penance and hope for God's mercy; but in some cases they are more than that—not only concerned with the themes of sin and repentance, holy fear and holy love, and not just featuring meditations on the mysteries of Christ's life (important as these are), but also revealing the need to express how God's love transforms the believer. In this sense, Donne is a mystical poet, although he often plays with and reverses traditional mystical motifs.[80]

Donne's "Divine Poems" have four main sections. The sonnets in "La Corona" are meditations on the mysteries of Christ's life. The "Holy Sonnets" were originally twelve in number in the 1633 edition, but seven were later added. "The Litanie" is a quasi-liturgical poem in twenty-eight stanzas, while five "Occasional Poems" and three "Hymns" close off the corpus. I cannot comment on all these poems but will highlight mystical elements in a few. The first six of the original "Holy Sonnets" are primarily concerned with the fear of God, something never far from Donne's mind, while the last six give more space to God's love for sinners. Sonnet 10 (earlier 14), beginning "Batter my heart, three person'd God," portrays the situation of the tortured soul who asks God to attack and destroy it in order to set it free and make it new. The soul loves God but feels trapped in evil ("Yet dearly'I love you, and would be lov'd faine, / But am betroth'd unto your enemie"). Like Augustine, Donne is powerless, unable to free himself from sin. He can only be rescued by grace. Donne begs for the grace that will paradoxically imprison him in order to free him—"Take mee to you, imprison mee, for I / Except you'enthrall mee, never shall be free, / Nor ever chast, except you ravish mee."[81] The violence of the love relationship with God in these lines is reminiscent of some late medieval mystics, especially women. Donne reverses the usual pattern, however, by pleading for a divinely powerful rapture that will draw him out of his sins.

Another mystical theme, the soul as temple of God, is also found in the Holy Sonnets. Sonnet 11 asks the soul to meditate on "How God the Spirit, by Angels waited on / In heaven, doth make a Temple in thy brest, / The Father having begot a Sonne most blest, / And still begetting, (for he ne't begonne) / Hath deign'd to chuse thee by adoption, / Coheire to'his glory, and Sabbaths endlesse rest."[82] These lines not only identify the soul as God's temple, a theme also found in the sermons,[83] but summarize other major mystical motifs, such as the divine birth in the soul,[84] our adoptive sonship in Christ, and the Sabbath rest. Of course, these are doctrinal headings, but their lived experience as expressed in the poem is in the realm of the mystical life, which, Donne reminds the reader, is always christological: "Twas much, that man was made like God before, / But, that God should be made like man, much more."

Two other poems, one from the "Occasional Poems," and one from the "Hymns," can close off this brief treatment. "Good Friday, 1613. Riding Westward" is one of Donne's most striking lyrics. Its witty comparison of the soul to a sphere and play with the reversals of the East–West directions are typical of the metaphysical poets, but the wit is placed in the service of an inner appropriation of the meaning of Christ's death, one that invokes the biblical mystical theme of the vision of "God's face." Thinking on the crucifixion, Donne says, "Yet dare I'almost be glad, I do not see / That spectacle of too much weight for mee. / Who sees Gods face, that is selfe life, must dye; / What a death it were then to see God dye?" Although Donne allows that he can look on neither the dying Christ, nor his mother, he expresses a confidence that the same divine gaze/face that looked on the event of our salvation now also looks at him: "Though these things, as I ride, be from mine eye, / They'are present yet unto my memory, / For that looks towards them; and thou look'st towards mee." Donne concludes by noting the mutual knowing-gazing between God and the soul: "Restore thine Image, so much, by the grace, / That thou may'st know mee, and I'll turn my face."[85]

A final example of a mystical poem is "A Hymne to Christ, at the Authors last going into Germany," composed in 1619 when Donne accompanied Lord Doncaster on a diplomatic journey to Germany. Again, the poet focuses on the divine gaze that is his hope for salvation: "Thou with clouds of anger do disguise / Thy face; yet through that maske I know those eyes, / Which, though they turne away sometimes, they never will despise." His treatment of God's continuing attention leads him to a meditation on love in which he begs God to bring the Divine and human lovers to a deep inner mutuality in which each allows the other the freedom to give totally of the self: "As thou / Art jealous, Lord, so I am jealous now, / Thou lov'st not, till from loving more, thou free / My soul: Who ever gives, takes libertie: / Or, if thou car'st not whom I love, Alas, thou lov'st not mee."[86]

That the older Donne was a sincerely religious man is not in doubt. Throughout this period a deep, almost crippling, sense of his sinfulness continued to struggle with his conviction of the saving love of God manifest in Christ's death and resurrection. This agonistic spirituality, especially given Donne's sensuality (perhaps abandoned but never forgotten), makes him a troubling figure for those who like their mystics to be serene and faultless. Donne is too complex to fit such a straitjacket.

George Herbert

Born in 1593, the seventh child of Richard and Magdalene Herbert, George Herbert was of a higher station than Donne.[87] His life provides insight into the personal connections of the founders of Anglican spirituality.[88] A precocious if sickly child, he was a student of Lancelot Andrewes at the Westminster School in London and was acquainted with John Donne, a close friend of his mother. Herbert had a distinguished early career at Cambridge (1609–19), where he attained the important position of Greek and Latin Orator of the University. Although his piety seemed to destine him for a clerical life, Herbert delayed, trying to balance civil and ecclesiastical careers, even serving as a member of Parliament in 1623–24. It is possible that disillusionment over his time in Parliament moved him to take ordination as deacon in 1624 and priest in 1630. In the same year he was given the small parish of Bemerton, not far from Salisbury, where he served as a conscientious pastor for a brief three years before his death on March 1, 1633.

Herbert left his book of religious poems to Nicholas Ferrar (1592–1637), the founder of the quasi-monastic community at Little Gidding near Cambridge. According to Izaak Walton, on his deathbed Herbert told another friend, Mr. Duncan: "Sir, I pray deliver this little book to my dear brother Ferrar. And tell him he shall find in it a picture of the many spiritual conflicts that have passed betwixt God and my soul, before I could subject mine will to the will of Jesus my Master, in whose service I have now found perfect freedom." Herbert left Ferrar to judge whether the book's publication might be of use to "any poor dejected soul . . . , for I and it are less than the least of God's mercies."[89] Ferrar published the poems under the title *The Temple* in 1633, and the collection rapidly went through many editions.[90] Izaak Walton (1593–1683) put out his *Life of Mr. George Herbert* in 1670, a work that presented Herbert as a kind of Anglican saint.[91] Both with regard to the poems in *The Temple* and on the basis of Walton's *Life* and the handbook that Herbert wrote for clergy entitled *A Priest to the Temple, or The Country Parson* (first published in 1652), Herbert became a model of the Anglican poet-priest-mystic.[92] Given its primarily didactic character, I will not use *The Country Parson* here but will concentrate on the poems.

Herbert's poetry, like that of the other metaphysical poets, has been a source of debate over the past half century.[93] Older scholars, such as Helen White, T. S. Eliot, Rosemund Tuve,[94] and Louis Martz, stressed an Anglican and even Anglo-Catholic view of Herbert. Beginning in the 1970s, a number of writers argued for a Protestant view that brought Herbert closer to Calvin and the Puritans.[95] There are also historicist and postmodern views of Herbert, which emphasize the sociopolitical rooting of the poems and deconstruct their religious content and meaning.[96] What these divergent interpretations make clear is that Herbert is a poet who elicits strong feelings and whose apparent simplicity and straightforwardness are often deceiving.[97] Herbert's transparency invites the reader to an interpretive collaboration that is more difficult than it seems at first glance.

As T. S. Eliot put it, "*The Temple* . . . [is] a coherent sequence of poems setting down the fluctuations of emotion between despair and bliss, between agitation and serenity, and the discipline of suffering which leads to peace of spirit."[98] *The Temple* models not only a church building, like the small Bemerton structure Herbert served, but also images the whole church on earth, the place in which the salvation of sinful humanity is effected by the grace of Jesus Christ through the mediation of sacrament and liturgical prayer. *The Temple* is ecclesial and liturgical, but no less exemplary and paradigmatic, in the sense that Herbert wished to use his own struggles for interior peace to instruct, even to catechize, his readers.[99] Given the importance of joy,

peace, loving union, and even merging with Jesus in *The Temple*, there
is good reason to speak of the work as an example of mystical poetry.

Herbert developed *The Temple* over a number of years, as a surviving earlier version of many of the poems (the "Williams manuscript")
shows. The structure mirrors the poet's message, with "The Dedication" emphasizing his dependence on God: "Lord, let my first fruits
present themselves to thee; / Yet not mine neither: for from thee
they come, / And must return. Accept them of me; / And make us
strive, who shall sing best thy name."[100] The collection has three parts.
The first is a long moralizing poem entitled "The Church Porch" (or
"Perirrhanterium," holy-water sprinkler), addressed to a young person
of high birth and inviting him to approach the sacred precincts.[101] After
this comes a connecting piece that Herbert called "Superliminare," a
brief poem placed above the threshold of the church proper function-
ing as both an invitation to the eucharistic banquet (the culmination
of what happens within) and a warning to dissuade the unworthy from
approaching.[102]

The long body of *The Temple*, entitled "The Church," consists of 165
poems. The verses are liturgical, as shown not only by the overall structure of the collection but by many poems devoted to feast days and
sacramental rituals. *The Temple* is also, as we might expect, biblical,
a kind of re-creation of the Psalms, with many of the pieces having
scriptural resonances central to grasping their theological and mystical content.[103] Herbert's theology is incarnational and eucharistic,
echoing the ancient theme that "God became man so that man might
become God," and focusing the divinization process on the Eucharist
as the apex of the life of prayer and sacrament by which salvation and
divinization become accessible.[104] Incarnational theology is common
to most Christian thinkers, but Herbert gives it a distinctive mystical
twist.

"The Church" begins with a short piece, "The Altar," in which
Herbert constructs an altar-shaped poem offering his hard heart to
God as a sacrifice, and expressing his desire for union with Christ: "O
let thy blessed SACRIFICE be mine, / And sanctifie this ALTAR to be
thine."[105] This is followed by the longest poem in the collection, "The
Sacrifice," unique in that it is the only piece put in Christ's voice. Using
the traditional liturgical text from Lamentations 1:12 for the Good
Friday "Reproaches" (*Improperia*), "See if there be any sorrow like to
my sorrow," Christ recounts all the sufferings of his passion, asking the
reader "Was ever grief like mine?" The poem ends on a note of resignation inviting compassion: "But now I die; now all is finished. / My wo,

mans weal: and now I bow my head. / Onely let others say, when I am dead, / Never was grief like mine."[106] Christ's sacrifice elicits the believer's response in two poems of thanksgiving ("The Thanksgiving," and "The Reprisal"), as well as a group of poems on the major mysteries of Christ's salvific action.[107]

The poems that follow touch on a variety of topics: poems about physical aspects of the church (e.g., "Church-Monuments," "The Windows"); about sacramental rituals and offices (e.g., "Holy Baptism," "The Holy Communion," "Confession," "The Priesthood," "The Banquet"); about the feasts of the church year (e.g., "Whitsunday," "Christmas," "Trinity Sunday," "Lent"); and about virtues and spiritual practices (e.g., "The Thanksgiving," "Praise" [three poems], "Prayer" [two poems], "Obedience," "Hope," "Peace," "Justice," "Discipline"). But there is much more—poems on vices, two poems on sin, three on love, three on "Affliction," and some poems developed from biblical texts (e.g., Col. 3:3; Matt. 13:45; Eph. 4:30; Ps. 23; and 2 Cor. 2). There are poems on the passion, such as "The Agony," "Good Friday," and "The Cross";[108] and a group of four poems on the "Four Last Things" closes the central section of the work. Even this enumeration, however, only suggests the many topics presented in the collection. Herbert placed one of his most moving eucharistic poems, "Love (III)," at the end of the long second part, thus bookending "The Church" with two poems on the Eucharist. *The Temple* concludes with a third part, a long poem, part historical survey and part prophecy, which Herbert called "The Church Militant," ending with the doxology: "Blessed be God alone, / Thrice blessed Three in One."[109]

It is not possible here to try to survey a large number of these poems. Rather, I will look at a few to present the main spiritual and mystical themes of *The Temple*.[110] Literary critics have spoken of "the two Herberts," that is, the coexistence in the poet of accounts of conflict with God, times of fear and trembling, along with descriptions of deep inner peace and joy. Christ's suffering on the cross represents the theological correlative of Herbert's fear, trembling, and suffering. For example, "Affliction (III)" begins with the poet's groaning address to God: "My heart did heave, and there came forth, *O God!*" By the third stanza, however, Herbert has come to terms with his suffering by recognizing that Christ's suffering was not just a past act, but one that continues in our own pain:

> Thy life on earth was grief, and thou art still
> Constant unto it, making it to be

A point of honour, now to grieve in me,
And in thy members suffer ill.
They who lament one crosse,
Thou dying daily, praise thee to thy losse.[111]

Just as Christ's passion provides the key to Herbert's grief and suffering, so too the resurrection serves as the root of his joy, peace, and resting in God. If the passion lasts through all time, Easter both was and is unto eternity.[112]

Sin and the pain and affliction accompanying it are present throughout *The Temple*. Herbert often wrestles with God. He also finds God, though in unexpected ways, through sudden reversals in what seem to be moments of deep affliction—reversals and paradoxes typical of the metaphysical poets, and also of many mystics. In this sense, Herbert's poems frequently hinge on unexpected manifestations of God's grace—the "suddenly" (*exaiphnēs*) character of divine irruptions in human life.[113] Although Herbert apparently did not lead the kind of dissolute youth that haunted John Donne, in good seventeenth-century fashion he provides evidence for an almost obsessive sense of sinfulness and failure.[114] Herbert's conviction of his sinfulness is redeemed, if never totally overcome, by the power of hope in God's saving love, which is central to why Christians of many persuasions have found *The Temple* a meaningful resource for their own spiritual lives. While there is nothing like a mystical itinerary in Herbert, there are many accounts of a process of spiritual struggle, followed by acts of submission to God's merciful love, and the inner peace and union with God that this surrender brings. Submissive obedience is crucial to Herbert's presentation of the relation between God and the soul.

In "Artillerie," for example, Herbert uses a military metaphor with a scriptural basis (see Lam. 3:13) for presenting his conflict with God and ultimate surrender. In stanza 1, God shoots a star into his breast and reminds him not to expel good motions from his heart. In stanza 2, Herbert seems to give in to God, but it is a feigned surrender, as shown in stanza 3, where he says that he too has "starrs and shooters," namely, the tears and prayers by which he assails God night and day. Stanza 4 brings the resolution. Even though God and Herbert are both "shooters" who are in conflict, the combat is totally unequal. Herbert requests a parley, knowing that there is really no contest with God, but only surrender to him who is our very being, our true self: "Shunne not my arrows, and behold my breast. / Yet if thou shunnest, I am thine: /

I must be so, if I am mine. / There is no articling [arguing] with thee: / I am but finite, yet thine infinitely."[115]

Another poem that features surrender is "The Reprisall" (or "The Second Thanksgiving"), where the speaker's desire to die for Christ in imitation of the passion is expressed as a contest in the first three stanzas, until he finally realizes confession is the only way to God: "Yet by confession will I come / Into the conquest. Though I can do nought / Against thee, in thee I will overcome / The man, who once against thee fought."[116] Similarly, in "The Cross," a quasi-autobiographical poem, Herbert complains about his unfulfilled ambitions and illnesses in a tone close to despair ("These contrarities crush me"). But at the end he suddenly sees his difficulties as the way to identify with Christ in his perfect obedience: "And yet since these thy contradictions / Are properly a crosse felt by thy sonne, / With but foure words, my words, *Thy will be done*."[117]

As long as we remain in this life, our peace and joy can never be perfect. From beginning to end *The Temple* is filled with alternating experiences of desolation and consolation, dereliction and delight, unrest and peace, fear and hope, distance and union. Poems of pain and suffering abound, not only in the series entitled "Affliction" but in such other pieces as "Denial," "Sighs and Groans," "Love Unknown," "Complaining," "Grief," "The Cross," and "Discipline."[118] "Affliction (I)" is autobiographical, sketching Herbert's passage from an early time of joy in God's service (stanzas 1–3), when "There was no month but May," to a period of sickness, sorrow, and loss of friends (stanzas 4–5), and then to his unhappy time at the university and in civil service (stanzas 6–8). The final two stanzas address Herbert's current perplexity about what is to come—"Now I am here, what thou will do with me / None of my books will show." Although he is tempted to seek some other master than God, the final two lines return to loving trust: "Ah my deare God! though I am clean forgot, / Let me not love thee, if I love thee not."[119] The other "Affliction" poems speak to the poet's ongoing search for meaning in the midst of his trials. In the short "Affliction (II)," Herbert begs relief from God in the first two stanzas and then comes to the awareness, as Meister Eckhart said in his *Book of Divine Consolation*, "I find God my suffering." In Herbert's words, "Thou art my grief alone, / Thou Lord conceale it not: and as thou art / All my delight, so all my smart: / Thy crosse took up in one, / By way of imprest [advance payment] all my future mone [moan].[120]

"Affliction (III)," noted above, continues the theme of identity with Christ in his suffering. Using a passage from Psalm 31:14, "Affliction (IV)" returns to the message of the first poem with its stress on continuous suffering that can only be borne in the hope that the poet's assailants might eventually come to work together with Christ, "With care and courage building me, / Till I reach heav'n, and much more thee." The final poem in the sequence widens the perspective to the whole of salvation history. Using the plural "we," Herbert expresses a universal conviction that both pleasure and displeasure, joy and grief are used by God at different times in order to "Furnish thy [God's] table to thy mind," that is, prepare a fitting repast for Divine Wisdom (Prov. 9:2). Herbert concludes, "My God, so temper joy and woe, / That thy bright beams may tame thy bow."[121] The mystery of suffering is not solved, but its place in God's plan is affirmed.[122] The ongoing oscillation, even concomitance, of grief and joy is simply and movingly expressed in the brief poem "Bitter-sweet": "Ah my deare angrie Lord, / Since thou dost love, yet strike; / Cast down, yet help afford; / Sure I will do the like." Therefore, Herbert will complain and praise, bewail and approve, "And all my sowre-sweet dayes / I will lament and love."[123] Herbert's genius in movingly reflecting on such dualities is at the heart of his art and spiritual teaching.

Herbert's trust in the grace that rescues him from his sins and failings is anchored in the faith and life of the church—there is no independent access to God. *The Temple* is more than an account of "George Herbert's" path to salvation; it is an invitation to its readers to "write the message in their souls," as Origen once said of the goal of studying the Bible. It is precisely in this sense of presenting the inner appropriation of the essence of salvation that *The Temple* can be termed a mystical book. In contrast to the theologically articulated teaching on contemplation and the stages of union of many sixteenth- and seventeenth-century Catholic mystics, *The Temple* presents an integrated view of God's presence in the lives of believers, something close to the "everyday mysticism" discussed by some recent interpreters. Herbert's teaching about attaining God in this life can be described as fundamentally relational and transformational in the sense that it is in the dialogue between the poet and Christ in the context of the church that the mystery of our transformation and deification comes to be realized, if never in an absolute or perfect way. By subtle evocation, as well as by direct statement, Herbert shows how by benevolent grace, not our own efforts, we come to see that our actions are really God's actions and vice versa.

Herbert's poems touch on many major mystical themes. For instance, at the outset of "The Temper (II)" the poet asks, "Where is that mighty joy, / Which just now took up all my heart?"—an overpowering moment of grace, whether we want to conceive of it as a rapture or not. With regard to prayer, the foundation of mystical consciousness, Herbert does not try to describe mystical prayer as such, but in "Prayer (I)," he suggests the nature and power of prayer by constructing a hymn of praise through piling up a host of metaphors without a main verb to indicate the ineffable nature of the prayer that lies beyond all defining.[124] Thus, prayer is "the Churches banquet," "Christ-side-piercing spear," "Exalted Manna," "Heaven in ordinarie," and "the bird of Paradise," to mention only a few epithets. He concludes, "Church-bels beyond the starres heard, the souls bloud, / The land of spices; something understood." What is understood? It is not clear, but some critics suggest an appeal to 1 Corinthians 13:12, "Then shall I know even as I am known."[125]

A number of poems express a longing to see God or to gain a sense of the divine presence. An example is "Home" with its constant almost-liturgical refrain, "O show thyself to me, / Or take me up to thee!" The same longing is found in the impassioned lyric "Longing," which draws on the language of the Psalms and Job to beg "Lord JESU" to come to the poet amid the grief and trouble of his life: "My love, my sweetness, heare! / By these thy feet, at which my heart / Lies all the yeare, / Pluck out thy dart, / And heal my troubled breast which cryes, / Which dyes."[126] In "The Glance," however, Herbert shows that it is actually God's longing for us, as imaged in his loving gaze (see Ps. 119:132), that is the source of our longing for him. He addresses God, "When first thy sweet and gracious eye / Vouchsaf'd ev'n in the midst of youth and night / To look upon me . . . ; / I felt a sugared strange delight / Surpassing all cordials. . . ." Even in the midst of "many a bitter storm . . . thy sweet originall joy / Sprung from thine eye, did work within my soul." The final stanza expresses hope for the enjoyment of God's "full-ey'd love" in heaven, "When thou shalt look us out of pain."[127]

In Herbert's poems, longing for God is realized through a relational dialogue that gradually shows that we are one with, even in a sense identical to, the Redeemer. Such consciousness of union with God both deifies the person and is the source for a life of loving service to God, the church, and its members. This dynamic is evident in a number of poems, especially those that involve dialogues between Herbert and God.[128] The punning title of "The Collar" introduces a complex piece.[129] The poem is built on an interior dialogue. First the angry "I" (wayward heart, or the body) in lines 1–16 announces his intention to go abroad, that is, to escape the obligations owed to God and to live for himself. A second anonymous voice (probably reason) cautions restraint in lines 17–26, but "I" responds with another angry outburst, "Away, take heed: / I will abroad." The sudden denouement comes with the moving one-word entry of the divine voice: "But as I rav'd and grew more fierce and wild / At every word, / Me thoughts I heard one calling, *Childe*: / And I reply'd, *My Lord.*" The suddenness of the manifestation of the divine (the *exaiphnēs* experience) is masterfully displayed.

A similar burst of grace occurs at the end of "A true Hymne," a poem about the difficulty of composing an adequate hymn. Herbert says that even good words like "My joy, my life, my crown!" are lacking in the face of God. The fundamental quality of a true hymn exists "when the soul unto the lines accord," but this aspect is still missing from his poem. What is lacking can only be supplied by God. If the heart is moved, God will "supplie the want." Then God enters in as a kind of co-author by writing (not speaking): "As when th'heart says (sighing to be approved) / *O, could I love!* And stops: God writeth, *Loved.*"[130] This is a poetic rendering of 1 John 4:19, "We love him because he first loved us." A longer description of a divine intervention leading to submission is found in the "Dialogue." Again the poet's voice begins on a complaining note, asking what hope remains for a "wretch so full of stains" (stanza 1). God responds to his "childe" in stanza 2, noting that the judgment about the balance of good and evil in anyone's life belongs to him alone. The sinner, however, continues his complaints in stanza 3 with his admission of being under the dominion of sin and having no merit in himself (good Reformation theology). In stanza 4, God switches from justice to love and mercy. If only the sinner could resign himself without complaint and attend to God, he might be able to understand the mystery of salvation. God reminds him: "*That as I did freely part / With my glorie and desert, / Left all joyes to feel all smart*"–At last the sinner gets the point and breaks in with, "Ah! No more: thou break'st my heart."[131]

There are a number of poems in which Herbert evokes other traditional mystical themes, such as the soul being wed to Christ ("Frailtie"), or uniting with God (e.g., "Easter-Wings," "Even-song," "The Search"), or divine indwelling ("Man"). Nevertheless, what is distinctive of Herbert's mystical poetry is not the appeal to such inherited mystical topoi, but his explorations of the language of the mutuality and reciprocity between God and human, especially his use of the relation of "mine and thine."[132] At times this language leads to a kind of implosion of the subject, or a deconstruction of the boundaries between the divine "thine" and the human "mine."

We have already seen some examples of the "mine–thine" dialectic. In some poems it functions only at key moments, such as in "The Quip," in which the poet turns back the temptations of senses, riches, glory, and cleverness, by repeating the refrain, "But thou shalt answer, Lord, for me." When the time comes for the final answer at Judgment Day, the speaker asks God, "Speak not at large [i.e., length], say, I am thine: / And then they have their answer home." Similarly, in "Judgement," when the sinner is called upon to open the book of his life and failings, Herbert says that he intends to thrust a "Testament" (i.e., the New Testament) into God's hands to read. "There thou shalt finde my faults are thine."[133] If our sins have been taken over by Christ, then, by the logic of the incarnation, what is Christ's is ours. The full extent of this insight is evident in several of the most powerful identity poems.

"The Holdfast" (i.e., clamp) is an investigation of what role humans can play, if any, on the road to salvation. It begins with the speaker's statement of agency, "I threatned to observe the strict decree / Of my deare God with all my power & might." But he is told that he cannot do this and that he should only trust in God, although he recognizes that "ev'n to trust in him, was also his: / We must confesse, that nothing is our own." But the speaker is still puzzled by the meaning of having nothing, until the voice of a friend (probably Christ) explains: "That all things were more ours by being his. / What Adam had and forfeited for all, / Christ keepeth now, who cannot fail or fall."[134] In other words, the freedom lost by Adam has been restored to us, not as *our* freedom but as the freedom of the members of Christ's body. The truth that things are more ours by being his finds its root not only in redemption but also in creation itself, as proclaimed in "The Flower," a poem that features, once again, both suffering and restoration, though with the emphasis on the latter. Stanza 3 summarizes:

> These are thy wonders, Lord of power,
> Killing and quickening, bringing down to hell
>   And up to heaven in an houre;
> Making a chiming [i.e., celebration] of a passing-bell.
>   We say amisse,
>   That this or that is:
> Thy word is all, if we could spell.[135]

Meister Eckhart insisted that the created "this or that" was nothing in itself. Herbert joins him with these brief and potent lines—if we could only understand or learn to "spell" correctly, we would see that created beings have no reality in themselves; God's powerful work IS all things.

The "mine–thine" paradox attains its fullest expression in "The Clasping of Hands," a poem that has its basis in Song of Songs 2:16, "My beloved is mine, and I am his." The poem reads as almost nonsense verse, with seventeen lines out of twenty featuring the interplay of mine and thine. The opening lines set the stage: "Lord, thou art mine, and I am thine, / If mine I am: and thine much more, / Then I or ought, or can be mine." In other words, in God alone can we possess all things. The mutuality, even identity, of the "mine–thine" is first expressed from the human point of view: "If I without thee would be mine, / I should be neither mine nor thine." The second stanza, however, turns to something like mystical indistinction in exploring how we might ever resolve what is mine and thine in the plan of salvation in which the divine Son becomes human so that humans can become God:

> For thou didst suffer to restore
> Not thee, but me, and to be mine:
> And with advantage mine the more,
> Since thou in death wast none of thine,
> Yet then as mine didst me restore.
> 　　　O be mine still! Still make me thine!
> 　　　Or rather make no Thine and Mine![136]

How to realize this fusion of the created "me" and the infinite loving "Thee" was what Herbert strove to achieve in *The Temple*, not through any prosaic theology but by the suggestiveness of a poetry that reveals while it conceals. Despite the effective use of the personal voice found in so many of these poems, Herbert's genius in combining the personal with the universal (i.e., the ecclesial and sacramental) gives the *Temple* its special quality. This is evident in the poem he chose to end "The Church" section of the collection—"Love (III)," perhaps his most studied dialogue poem, one whose evocation of union with Christ seamlessly weaves together human frailty, divine love, and the gift of the Eucharist. Almost all who have written on Herbert have had something to say about this poem. Here, I offer it without comment:

> Love bade me welcome: yet my soule drew back,
> 　　　Guilty of dust and sinne.

But quick-ey'd Love, observing me grow slack
    From my first entrance in,
Drew nearer to me, sweetly questioning,
    If I lacked anything.
  A guest, I answer'd, worthy to be here:
    Love said, you shall be he.
I the unkind, ungrateful? Ah, my deare,
    I cannot look on thee.
Love took my hand, and smiling did reply,
    Who made the eyes but I?
Truth Lord, but I have marr'd them: let my shame
    Go where it doth deserve.
And know you not, sayes Love, who bore the blame?
    My deare, then I will serve.
You must sit down, sayes Love, and taste my meat:
    So I did sit and eat.[137]

What is the effect of realizing oneness with Christ in the Eucharist, of submitting our sinfulness to God's overwhelming love, of attaining the insight that with regard to God there is really no difference between "mine" and "thine"? Here, too, Herbert does not disappoint the reader, especially in those poems that accord with an insight common to many great mystics—God can be found everywhere and in everything. It is not in some special experience (though these can be granted), or in a privileged location and action (important as prayer, liturgy, and sacrament may be), but in the insight that God is omnipresent and active in all things, that the mystical presence of God can become a motivating force for life. This teaching is set forth especially in "The Elixer," one of Herbert's most quoted verses. He took special care with this poem, as the three surviving versions show. Herbert begins by asking God to be given the gift to see and to work for him in all he does. He goes on to give alchemical examples of transforming ordinary things for higher purposes, as changing base metal into gold. From this perspective everything reveals God. The new outlook is the transformative elixer, or alchemical "tincture," that shows all creation as theophany, a revelation of God. Therefore, "A servant with this clause [understanding] / Makes drudgerie divine: Who sweeps a room, as for thy laws, / Makes this and th'action fine." This is the "everyday mysticism" that a number of students of Herbert have stressed, a view that puts him in the company of mystics, both medieval (e.g., Eckhart, Catherine of Siena, Julian of Norwich) and modern (e.g., Thomas Merton).[138]

We may close by asking what effect this sense of God's presence had on Herbert's life. The parson-poet, humble but not altogether self-effacing, tried to live out his delicate sense of God's present-absence by a life of devotion to his calling as a devoted pastor and by his willingness to reflect on this life for the benefit of other priests in his handbook, *The Country Parson*. Herbert did not often treat of the relation between his consciousness of God and his pastoral duties, but a few poems in *The Temple*, such as "The Priesthood" and "Aaron," provide some sense of how his contact with God empowered his ministry. In the latter poem, Herbert contrasts his sacerdotal weakness with Aaron anointed and clothed by God in head and breast, before once again realizing it is not *him*, but Christ *in him* who matters: "So holy in my head, / Perfect and light in my deare breast, / My doctrine tun'd by Christ, (who is not dead, / But lives in me while I do rest). /Come people; Aaron's drest.[139] It is easy for the modern reader who finds Herbert's view of the intimate relation of God and the soul attractive to forget that, like the other mystics, this Anglican priest thought that contact with God was not just for himself but also for the people he served.

Henry Vaughan

The later seventeenth-century Anglican poets represent an inward turn in which the poet's relationship to God has less connection with the ecclesial and liturgical context found in Herbert.[140] Henry Vaughan (1621–1695) was born in Breconshire near the river Usk in Wales (hence his sobriquet, the "Silurist," from an ancient Welsh tribe). He studied at Oxford (1638–40), and then pursued law in London. Vaughan also took up medicine at some stage. A committed Royalist, Vaughan was involved in the Civil War. Retiring to Wales, sometime between 1647 and 1654 he underwent a conversion, not in the sense of changing his religious affiliation but in coming to a deeper level of his Anglican faith, then under attack in Puritan England. In 1646, he published a book of translations and mildly amative poems (*Olor Iscanus*, or *The Swan of Usk*), but his fame rests on the two volumes of his *Silex Scintillans (The Flashing Flint)*, the first edition of which appeared in 1650, the second expanded version in 1655. Vaughan also put out a series of prose meditations, *The Mount of Olives* and other works, in 1652, as well as a later collection of sacred verses, *Thalia Rediviva*, in 1678.[141] He led a long life as a doctor in his beloved valley of the Usk, but his productive period was relatively brief.

Vaughan is generally not considered the equal of Donne and Herbert, but he has had his champions, who admit that, while he may not challenge these earlier metaphysical poets in consistency and genius, his ability to present images that break through ordinary consciousness to open up new worlds of meaning is at times unrivaled. The *Silex Scintillans* is a collection of 134 devotional verses. Vaughan says that he undertook the work after his conversion, which he claims took place partly under the influence of reading Herbert, and partly due to crises in his life, such as the defeat of the Royalist and High Church cause in the Civil War,[142] his own illness, and the death of his younger brother.[143] Herbert's influence is undeniable (Vaughan took twenty-eight of his titles from him); nonetheless, Vaughan is more than just an imitator.[144]

A few distinguished critics, such as T. S. Eliot and Frank Kermode, have denied that Vaughan is a "mystical poet," but a number of scholars have been willing to speak of him as a mystic, though often by way of tortuous arguments trying to show how far he agrees with John of the Cross (and Evelyn Underhill!) on such issues as the dark night, mystical union, and other categories of early modern Catholic mysticism.[145] This approach, perhaps understandable in its day, is scarcely sufficient today. If he is in some way a mystical poet, Vaughan must be judged on the basis of his own writings, not according to the yardstick of mystics whom he never cites. Whether or not he "experienced" John of the Cross's "Dark Night," and, even more, if he ever achieved some Sanjuanist form of union with God, is unknown and not really relevant to the question of his mysticism.

On the basis of his poems, a good case can be made that Henry Vaughan is a mystical poet, at least in the sense that many of his poems witness to seeking and in some way finding a transformative presence of God. Anthony Low goes so far as to say that "He is England's chief poet of traditional contemplative experience."[146] Like the works of his hero Herbert, almost all of Vaughan's poems in the *Silex Scintillans* are devotional, but Vaughan often goes beyond standard forms of prayer and meditation and at times at least testifies to the gift of a direct consciousness of God's presence. As Edmund Blunden says, "His verse is chiefly the intimate record of his spiritual life."[147] R. A. Durr goes further, arguing that, while Vaughan may not actually have enjoyed union with God (who knows?), "the poet has shown us, even though in a glass darkly, something *of*, as well as something *like*, that [mystical] region itself."[148]

Vaughan has been called a nature poet, an ancestor of Wordsworth and the Romantics, but his attention to nature is not couched in

terms of detailed descriptions of natural phenomena, or as expressing an attunement to immanent divine power in the universe; it rather
reflects a Christian (one might almost say Franciscan) sense that everything in the universe reveals its Creator. According to Helen White, for
Vaughan, "Almost always nature comes suffused with feeling, with the
light of its implications upon its calm surface."[149] Vaughan makes his
view of nature as God's messenger clear in many poems. For example,
in "The Tempest," he says: "O that man could do so! That he would
hear / The world read to him! . . . / All things here show him heaven;
Waters that fall / Chide, and fly up; *Mists* of corruptest fome / Quit
their first beds & mount; trees, herbs, flowers, all / Strive upwards
stil, and point him the way home."[150] Although tinged with the Her-
meticism that Vaughan learned from his twin brother, Thomas, who
made translations of Hermetic treatises, Henry Vaughan's view of
nature was essentially Christian.[151] In a similar vein, Vaughan's poems
in praise of childhood have nothing to do with Romantic adulation of
the child, but are rather based on the Gospel adage about becoming
like little children in order to enter the kingdom of God (Matt. 18:3;
Luke 18:17).[152]

Like other Anglican poets, Vaughan was strongly biblical, not only
through frequent citation of scriptural texts at the beginning and end
of his poems but also in the themes of many verses, which often make
use of the typology in which Old Testament figures and events foretell
the events of the New Covenant and Christ's continuing salvific activity.[153] Figures like Jacob and Job have special status in the Silurist's biblical hermeneutics. Like Herbert, Vaughan devotes poems to praising
scripture ("H. Scriptures," and "To the Holy Bible"). He also has a number of verses on specific theological doctrines.[154] The *Silex Scintillans*
contains poems on the liturgy and feasts of the liturgical year, including three on the Eucharist ("Dressing," "Holy Communion," and "The
Feast"), as well as ten elegies. The Welsh poet often paid tribute to the
economy of salvation, especially how the incarnation of the Word is
the sole means of rescuing fallen humanity from its sinful state. Again
like Herbert, he is christological and strongly eucharistic in orientation. Even in his doctrinal and liturgical poems, however, Vaughan
concentrates on his own inner states. Although perhaps less negative
in tone than Donne and Herbert, Vaughan's verses feature the sense of
personal sinfulness that hung over seventeenth-century England. The
Silurist, however, is more convincing in his expressions of hope and joy
than in his moments of doubt and despair.

A number of Vaughan's poems are meditative in structure in the manner of other metaphysical poets, such as "Day of Judgement," "I Walkt the other day (to spend my hour)," "The Shepheards," and "Man." In other poems Vaughan seems to be striving to express the limits of rational meditation in reaching God. "The Search" is a meditation on the places and events of salvation history of both the Old and the New Testaments, one that leads to remarks critical of all merely external knowledge. At the conclusion, the poet hears a mysterious singing voice in a different rhyme scheme, advising that "gadding thoughts" must be left behind and that "The skinne and shell of things / Though faire, / are not / Thy wish, nor pray'r." No, the deepest truth must be sought not in meditating on this world but in another realm, as expressed in the concluding lines: "Search well another world; who studies this [world], / Travels in Clouds, seeks *Manna*, where none is."[155] In other poems, Vaughan tries to present aspects of a mystical contemplation of the other world, difficult as the task may be.

The poem "Regeneration" that begins the *Silex Scintillans* expresses a personal mystical itinerary enshrining what Vaughan was aiming for in the collection.[156] The first three of ten stanzas begin with the picture of the difficult journey of the pilgrim through frost, winds, and the clouds of sin. The ascent to the pinnacle of a mountain reveals "a paire of scales" in which the smoke and pleasures of the world outweigh the "late paines" of his ascetic efforts. The poem shifts locale in stanza 4 as a divinely sent voice cries "Away," and the pilgrim is led to the East, where "a faire, fresh field could [I] spy / Some call'd it, *Jacob's Bed*; / A Virgin-soile, which no / Rude feet ere trod, / Where (since he stept there) only go / Prophets, and friends of God." This is Jacob's bed in Bethel, where the patriarch received the vision of angels descending and ascending and where God is present and speaks to him (Gen. 28:10–22). The pilgrim has been led into one of the "thin places" where heaven and earth interact. The remainder of the poem gives a series of vignettes of beautiful locations signifying different experiences of grace.

In stanza 5, he sees "A grove . . . / Of stately height, whose branches met / And mixt on every side." The pilgrim enters the grove, and stanza 6 describes its visual beauties in lush detail. The only sound is that of a little fountain, which he approaches to find "The Cisterne full / Of divers stones, some bright, some round / Other's ill-shaped, and dull" (stanza 7). Stanza 8 suggests that the dancing bright stones are souls attuned to God, while the heavy dull stones that remain stuck in the bottom of the fountain are sinners. The same message is conveyed in the next vision, that of a "banke of flowers" in which some are fast asleep, "others broad-eyed / And taking in the Ray [of the sun]," that is, absorbing grace (stanza 9). At this point, the pilgrim hears "A rushing wind," but cannot tell where it is coming from. The final stanza reveals that it is the wind of the spirit of God:

> But while I listning sought
> My mind to ease
> By knowing, where t'was, or where not,
> It whisper'd; *Where I please* [John 3:8].
> Lord, then said I, *On me one breath,*
> *And let me dye before my death!*

Invoking both Jesus's night conversation with Nicodemus (on which we will see more later), as well as the Bride of the Song of Songs (Vaughan closes by citing Song 5:17), "Regeneration" reveals that the pilgrim's true destination is *mors mystica*, the mystical death of ecstasy, the death that comes before physical death.

The *mors mystica* appears elsewhere in the *Silex Scintillans*.[157] Other images, themes, and metaphors well known in mystical traditions also occur. For example, "Christ's Nativity" speaks of the birth of God in the soul:

> Sweet *Jesu*! Will then; Let no more
> This Leper haunt, and soyl thy door,
> Cure him, Ease him
> O release him!
> And let once more by mystick birth
> The Lord of life be borne on earth.[158]

Reference to the "divine seed" planted by God in the soul is found in several poems (e.g., "Disorder *and* frailty," "Cock-crowing").[159] "The Search" speaks of ecstasy, and the motif of the face of God occurs in poems like "Childhood" and "The Book." In "The dwelling-place," a descant on John 1:38–39, where Jesus invites the disciples to see where he lives, Vaughan describes how Christ has often visited his heart:

> My dear, dear God! I do not know
> What lodged thee then, nor where, nor how;
> But I am sure, thou dost now come

> Oft to a narrow, homely room,
> Where thou too hast but the least part,
> My God, I mean *my sinful heart.*[160]

"Quickness" contrasts the false life of everyday existence with the "Life" that is a "fix'd, discerning light, A knowing Joy." This vivifying, never-cloying, blissful thing is an inexpressible gift from God: "But life is, what none can express, / *A quickness, which my God hath kist.*"[161] Given this use of the metaphor of the divine kiss, we should not be surprised by Vaughan's appeal to the language of marriage between Christ and the human person, especially as realized in the Eucharist.[162]

It might be objected that Vaughan does not talk about *his* inner union with Christ, and it is true that union is mentioned only rarely in the *Silex Scintillans.*[163] Nonetheless, union is only one of the ways to speak about a direct and transforming presence of God, and Vaughan, like many mystics, presents his ineffable experience mostly by poetic indirection and suggestion. The two poems on Christ's Ascension, "Ascension-day" and "Ascension-Hymn," are powerful evocations, often in the first person, of how we can share in the Lord's ascent to heaven, if only briefly, while in this life. In the first poem, Vaughan says, "I soar and rise / Up to the skies, / Leaving the world their day, / And in my flight, / For the true light / Go seeking all the way." "Ascension-Hymn" begins on an equivalent note: "Dust and clay / Mans antient wear! / Here you must stay, / But I elsewhere; / Souls sojourn here, but may not rest; / Who will ascend, must be undrest."

Along with the stripping off of the old self, once again there is a reference to mystical death: "And yet some / That know to die / Before death come, / Walk to the skie / Even in this life. . . ." The poem ends with two verses praising the light of the risen and ascended Christ, who not only makes us white by his blood, but in his Second Coming will rebuild man "bone to bone": "And by his all subduing might / Make clay ascend more quick than light."[164]

The invocations of light in the Ascension poems remind us how often Vaughan emphasizes a desire for experiencing the light of God in this life as a foretaste of the eternal brightness of heaven. As a number of critics have noted, Vaughan is a poet of movement, vision, and especially of light—the divine illumination of which the lights of this world are only a pale shadow.[165] It is no accident that Vaughan's perhaps most famous poem—with some of the most memorable opening lines in all English literature—is an evocation of supernal light with distinct Boethian overtones:

> I saw Eternity the other night
> Like a great *Ring* of pure and endless light.
>   All calm, as it was bright,
> And round beneath it, Time in hours, days, years
>   Driv'n by the spheres
> Like a vast shadow moves, In which the world
> And all her train were hurl'd; . . .[166]

This vision of eternity is without equal in English literature. Critics have noted that the rest of the four-stanza poem falls off from the beginning (as if anything would not!). For Vaughan's mysticism, however, it is worth noting that the cosmic vision with which he starts is not just a beautiful evocation of time and eternity but is intended to show the moral failure of those who do not focus their lives on Eternity (e.g., "the doting Lover," "the darksome States-man," "the fearfull miser," "the down-right Epicure"). The vision can never be gained by human effort, but only by repentance and the joy given by grace: "Yet some, who all this while did weep and sing, / and sing and weep, soar'd up into the *Ring*." The poem concludes with a warning to those who "prefer dark night" and hate the day because it shows the way to God:

> A way where you might tread the Sun, and be
>   More bright than he.
> But as I did their madness so discusss
>   One whisper'd thus,
> *This Ring the Bride-groome did for none provide*
> *But for his bride.*

Vaughan closes by citing John 2:16–17, about the world and its lusts passing away, but the reference to the union of the lovers of the Song of Songs shows that it is only through the ring of mystical marriage to Christ that we can have access to the ring of eternity.

Many other poems in the *Silex Scintillans* focus on the light of nature as a sign of the breakthrough of divine light into the earthly realm. In the course of the collection, Vaughan included eight elegies without title, one of which begins with another of his magnificent openings, this time concerning the deceased: "They are all gone into the world of light! / And I alone sit lingring here; / Their very memory is fair and bright, / And my sad thoughts doth clear." Later in the poem Vaughan says, "I see them walking in an Air of glory, / whose light doth trample on my days." The desire for experiencing the full light of heaven gains in intensity as the poem proceeds, closing with the metaphor of a star (i.e., the human soul) being confined in a tomb where it is dimmed but always ready to shine out again. Then comes a prayer:

> O Father of eternal life, and all
>   Created glories under thee!
> Resume thy spirit from this world of thrall
>   Into true liberty.
> Either disperse these mists, which blot and fill
>   My perspective [i.e., telescope] still as they pass,
> Or else remove me hence unto that hill,
>   Where I shall need no glass.[167]

Other poems witness to Vaughan's abiding sense of the divine illuminations that begin in this life but that will only be fully achieved in heaven.[168] Paradoxically, however, another of Vaughan's most noted poems, one often called his masterpiece, takes a different approach, that of darkness and the apophatic way. "The Night" is among the most studied of Vaughan's poems, but how its reversal of the usual values of light and darkness fits into his oeuvre is not immediately clear.[169] If we recognize that mystical language is always an intricate combination of positive and negative, light and darkness, we can begin to appreciate how tellingly Vaughan uses the apophatic register in this poem in order to veil what light elsewhere attempts to unveil, suggesting that both procedures are necessary to approach the mystery of Christ's presence. Although Vaughan does not cite the text here, he may well have had Psalm 138:11–12 (AV) in mind: "If I say, Surely the darkness shall cover me; even the night shall be light about me. Yea, the darkness hideth not from thee; but the night shineth as the day: the darkness and the light are both alike to thee."

The poem begins with Nicodemus's night visit to Jesus recounted in John 3, but calls upon many biblical typologies, including the description of the tabernacle and its furniture in Exodus 25, Jacob's experience at Bethel (Gen. 28), and the sleep of the Bride in Song of Songs 5:2. Witty wordplay on light and darkness throughout the poem add to its complexity. "The Night" has often been analyzed as a poem of meditation, with stanzas 1–2 providing a composition of place (the night meeting of Christ and Nicodemus), stanzas 3–6 a meditation on night, and stanzas 7–9 constituting a "colloquy," or prayer. "The Night," however, goes beyond discursive meditation, breaking through into dark contemplation in many places.

The first three stanzas praise Nicodemus as the model for seeing the incarnate Redeemer, the person who "Did at mid-night speak with the Sun!", through "that pure *Virgin-shrine*," that is, the veil of flesh derived from Mary in which God was hidden (but also partly revealed). "Wise Nicodemus," says Vaughan, "saw such light / As made him know his God by night." Stanza 4 switches to a salvation-historical dimension, saying that God is no longer accessible in the external "mercy seat of gold, no dead and dusty *Cherub*, nor carv'd stone" of the Old Testament, but only in "his own living works." Stanzas 5–7 are the center of the poem, an evocation of how the Christian can experience the presence of the Savior in this life, which Vaughan places not in light and illumination but in night (in French, *la mystique nocturne*), in stillness, and in hints of the divine presence. The poet praises: "Dear night! This worlds defeat; / . . . The day of spirits; my souls calm retreat / Which none disturb!" Night has become heaven, the time of prayer, the time when spirits are met, and even Christ himself.[170] The following stanza seems to me to be among Vaughan's most moving attempts to convey his experience of God as the Divine Lover, when the soul has become passive, "asleep," and "dumb" in the face of divine action:

> Gods silent, searching flight:
> When my Lords head is fill'd with dew, and all
> His locks are wet with the clear drops of night [Song 5:2];
>   His still, soft call [1 Sam. 3:4–9]
> His knocking time [Apoc. 3:20]; The souls dumb watch,
> When Spirits their fair kindred catch.

The next stanza underlines the personal significance of this evocation by stating that if "all my loud evil days" were like the "dark Tent" [Num. 10:15], then the poet would feel he was already in heaven. But, as Vaughan insists in stanza 8, he still lives under the light of the created sun where he continually runs into the mire of sin, erring more than he can do by night. The poem concludes with a bow toward the Dionysian apophatic tradition, which some have seen as Vaughan's admission that he has never "experienced" divine darkness. This seems to me a misreading. Vaughan is rather expressing the hope that his own consciousness of God's hiddenness accords with a long mystical tradition[171] and, more importantly, is destined to achieve fulfillment:

> There is in God (some say)
> A deep, but dazzling darkness [see MT 1]; As men here

> Say it is late and dusky, because they
>   See not all clear;
> O for that night! Where I in him
> Might live invisible and dim.

For the mystic Henry Vaughan, as for Dionysius, the resplendence of God's light can only render humans "invisible and dim."

Thomas Traherne (1637–1674)

Traherne is a modern discovery, since only a few of his prose works were published in his life and shortly afterwards. In 1896, manuscripts of some of his poems and the prose *Centuries of Meditations* were purchased for a few pennies. The poems were published by Bertram Dobell in 1903 and the *Centuries* in 1908.[172] A few years later, a series of poems heavily reworked by Thomas's brother Philip was discovered and also published. These two collections, the thirty-seven poems of the "Dobell Collection" and the thirty-four new "Felicity Poems" edited by Philip, are the best known of his poetry. New manuscripts of Traherne's poems and prose works, such as the *Select Meditations*, *The Kingdom of God*, and *Commentaries of Heaven*, have been discovered in the second half of the twentieth century. These are substantially revising our view of his theology, so that Traherne is emerging as one of the most important voices of the Anglican tradition.[173]

Thomas Traherne was born in Hereford probably in 1637 and studied at Brasenose College in Oxford (ca. 1653–57).[174] At this stage he was probably a moderate Puritan, but he was ordained in 1660 after the Restoration of Charles II and became an adherent of the Established Church. Traherne had a pastoral appointment at Credenhill near Hereford, and in later years served as chaplain to Sir Orlando Bridgeman, Lord Keeper of the Great Seal, before his early death. Traherne is unusual among the seventeenth-century Anglicans in leaving us both mystical poetry and extensive prose writings. This treatment will concentrate on his poetry, since the relation between his prose and poetry is still a topic of ongoing research. Traherne's poetry is ecstatic and sometimes excessive; his prose works have been praised for their more measured style, especially the prose-poetry of the *Centuries*.[175] Many older investigators have seen Traherne as a mystical poet,[176] an identification generally not challenged by most recent students, who, however, tend to concentrate on his doctrinal theology. Despite flashes of brilliance, the repetitiveness, abstract language, didacticism, and excess of the poems, even those judged fully his (as contrasted with those edited by his brother), make the reservations of some critics about the quality of his verse understandable.[177] Traherne seems to be playing an organ with only a few registers, often at full blast. A. L. Clements, however, praises Traherne's "appositional" style, in which catalogues of recurrent biblical and mystical symbols are piled up, as an apt vehicle for expressing mystical experience.[178] In that sense, Traherne is reminiscent of an earlier English mystic, Richard Rolle, who invented his own extravagant style in his Latin works, especially the *Melos Amoris*.[179]

No seventeenth-century poet concentrates more on the inner relation of God and the "I/eye" of the mystic than Traherne, and none offers greater evidence of the use of mystical symbols, themes, and tropes.[180] Traherne gives the reader the impression that he is writing "out of" his inner mystical consciousness, using various verbal strategies to suggest the imperfect memory of what cannot really be put into words.[181] A passage from the *Select Meditations* IV.3 testifies to the personal experience at the basis of his poems:

> This Endless Comprehension of my Immortal Soul when I first saw it, so Wholly Ravished and Transported my spirit, that for a fortnight after I could scarsly Think or speak or write any other Thing. But like a man Doteing with Delight and Extasie, Talk of it Night and Day as if all the Joy of Heaven and Earth were shut up in it. For in the very Deed there I saw the Divine Image Relucent and Shining, There I saw the foundation of mans Excellency, and that which made Him a Son of God. Nor shall I be able to forget its Glory.[182]

The passionate conviction of Traherne's poems becomes obvious on this basis.

Traherne's poetry attempts to portray the prelapsarian innocent vision of God and reality enjoyed by Adam (and infants since then) and to exhort the reader to aspire to regain and enhance this innocence in the present.[183] He often presents the mystical path in a quasi-autobiographical vein, describing what he himself remembers from his earliest days, what he is presently experiencing, in both his fallen and his restored states, and what he hopes his readers will be able to share in. Realizing our preexistent and present identity with God, as well as recognizing that God needs human beings to complete his self-manifestation in creation, gives many of Traherne's poems hints of the mystical teachings of late medieval northern European mystics about nondual union, teaching not previously found in England.[184] There is no evidence, however, that Traherne could have had any access to late medieval German mysticism. He seems to have realized his sense of intimate oneness with God out of his own inner vision—his sense of the "I/eye" in which, as Eckhart once claimed, we can recognize our ocular identity with the divine creative "I/Eye Am." This is true "felicity," Traherne says, using one of the most frequent terms in his vocabulary.[185] Felicity is a broad term not easy to define: it is bliss, delight, and joy; it is also wholeness, a nondual union with God, and, from the point of view of salvation history, paradise.

Traherne was well educated at Oxford, and his prose works show wide reading in philosophy and theology.[186] Among recent poets, he knew Herbert and Vaughan. Like the contemporary Cambridge Platonists, with whom he shows some affinities, he was familiar with Plato and with Renaissance Neoplatonists like Marsilio Ficino and Pico della Mirandola,[187] but he also knew Aristotle and some of the Schoolmen. Traherne's poems often employ a double voice—the first-person address of one who has achieved felicity, and the "assumed voice" of someone still on the way and encouraging or advising the reader to pursue the goal.[188] In both of these voices, Traherne uses his own experience to proclaim the persona of the poet as mystic, and also, as Helen White argues, as visionary prophet.[189]

Traherne's theology has a complex account of humanity's relation to God. In *Centuries* III.43 he speaks of "man, as he is a creature of God, capable of celestial blessedness, and a subject in His kingdom: in his fourfold estate of innocency, misery, grace, and glory."[190] These four estates are not just temporally successive, but also interpenetrate in the lives of believers.[191] Traherne's thought contains a number of temporal patterns, but this four-act drama of salvation history is central.[192] The first estate is that of created innocence, the time of Adam in Eden; the second is the time of the Fall in which, due to misapprehension, we forget our heavenly destiny amid the distractions of worldly goods. The third estate is that of grace, the redemption in which we return to the joy and bliss of childhood innocence and enjoy a foretaste (and maybe more) of the beatific vision of the fourth estate. When Traherne tells his readers, "I must become a child again," he really means it, but the message is more complex than one of simple regression to chronological childhood.

The ways in which Traherne presents identity with God, and related themes such as preexistence, union, divinization, felicity, and the beatific vision, are first revealed through the perspective of the unfallen child, both Adam and all infants born of his seed. Traherne uses his own life as a model of this initial unfallenness, as well as for his account of continuing to find new levels of innocence in fulfilling our nature as partners with God in bliss and joy. While the poems of the Dobell folio (those not altered by his brother Philip) show little direct relation to Christian teaching about the incarnation and the ordinary means of salvation, such as the liturgy and the Eucharist (quite a contrast to the other Anglican poets), viewed from the wider perspective of his other writings, such as the *Centuries* and the newly discovered works, a more orthodox, if still unusual, theology emerges.[193] Traherne's views on the journey through the four estates can be clarified by a brief consideration of his underlying theology of God, world, and human nature.

The essential attribute of God for Traherne is infinity—he might be called the foremost poetic witness to divine infinity, a theme that appears over and over, both in the poems and in the prose works. The first six chapters of *The Fifth Century* summarize his teaching on divine infinity. Traherne writes:

> The infinity of God is our enjoyment, because it is the region and extent of his dominion. Barely as it comprehends infinite space, it is infinitely delightful; because it is the room and place of our treasures, the repository of our joys, and the dwelling place, yea the seat and throne, and Kingdom of our souls. But as it is the Light wherein we see, the Life that inspires us, the violence of His love, . . . it is more our treasure, and ought more abundantly to be delighted in.[194]

God's infinity is totally within us and yet also outside us (V.2). Because God is infinite, we have the capacity for insatiable imagination and desire (V.3), a defining characteristic of human nature.[195] There is a strict relationship between divine infinity and humanity: "Every man is alone the centre and circumference of it. It is all his own, and so glorious, that it is the eternal and incomprehensible essence of Deity."[196] Traherne says that space is infinite (V.5), but "God is infinitely infinite" (V.6), because infinite value is above and beyond mere quantitative infinity.[197] In *Centuries* II.80, Traherne puts the case as follows, "Because Infinite Love cannot be expressed in finite room: but must have infinite places wherein to utter and show itself," the human person is both finite and yet also infinite in his capacity for divine joy. Traherne says, "For my soul is an infinite sphere in a centre. By this you may know that you are infinitely beloved." Yet more, although few believe that the soul is infinite, on the basis of his experience of childhood, Traherne insists, "yet Infinite is the first thing that is naturally known. Bounds and limits are discerned only in a secondary manner."[198] The reciprocal relation between God and the human person means that Traherne not only can speak of both in terms of the infinite sphere but also can call both God and man an "abyss,"[199] as well as an infinite eye: "I was an inward sphere of light, / Or an interminable orb of sight."[200] These metaphors are also found in some late medieval mystics.

The other attributes of God flow from, or better, are expressions of divine infinity. In good Platonic fashion, Traherne conceives of God as self-diffusive Goodness giving itself to all things. "The face of God is goodness unto all," he says, so that "What other thing can me delight / But the blest sight / Of His eternal goodness."[201] God is also supreme actuality, or, as Traherne puts it at the end of the short treatise on God in *Centuries* V, "The essence of God therefore being all light and knowledge, love and goodness, care and providence, felicity and glory, a pure and simple Act, it is present in its operations, and by those Acts which it eternally exerteth is wholly busied in all parts and places of His dominion, perfecting and completing our bliss and happiness."[202] Further, God's diffusive goodness and actuality are the same as God's infinite love.[203] Traherne emphasizes the movement of love from God to the world and back again in a number of his poems, especially "The Circulation," where he summarizes:

> All things do first receive, that give.
>   Only 'tis God above,
> That from, and in Himself doth live,
>   Whose all-sufficient love
> Without original can flow
>   And all the joys and glories show
> Which mortal man can take delight to know.
> He is the primitive eternal spring,
> The endless ocean of each glorious thing.[204]

God's perfection is such that in divine things anticipation is the same as fulfillment. On this basis, "The Anticipation" shows how the divine nature is the source of all things, the goal to which they are directed, and the means by which they attain that end ("The end and fountain differ but in name," line 36).

Other Christian thinkers had identified infinity as the essential attribute of God (e.g., Duns Scotus), and this and the other attributes Traherne discusses were traditional. An aspect of his treatment of God that is unusual is his insistence that God needs man for the completion of his activity, infinite and perfect as it is. "The Demonstration" starts

out with the paradox of how higher things, like the sun, are better
known than lower things, which "must be cloth'd with endless glory"
before their causes and ends are evident. Hence, all created things are
gifts to us and yet they gain more value in God's eyes by our returning
them to him—"The Godhead cannot prize / The sun at all, nor yet the
skies, / Or air, or earth, or trees, or seas, / Or stars, unless the soul of
man they please." The melody of all blessed creatures is concentrated
in humanity's appreciation of God's creation: "In them He sees, and
feels, and smells, and lives, / In them affected is to whom He gives: /
In them ten thousand ways, / He all his works again enjoys."[205] God's
need for humanity, which appears in a number of poems, is recapitu-
lated in the *Centuries*, where Traherne says, "for the Glory of God is
to make us happy. Which can never be done but by giving us most
excellent natures and satisfying those natures."[206] Traherne's optimistic view of God's love even leads him to claim that God's goodness
possesses *in us* both his goodness and our own, so that our glory is
infinite and therefore, "Our Blessedness to see / Is even to the Deitie /
A Beatifick Vision!"[207]

Traherne's view of the created world flows from this optimistic,
hope-filled theology.[208] Like a good Platonist, he teaches that all things
exist eternally in the mind of God.[209] The universe, the production
of God's overflowing love, reveals the goodness and fecundity of its
Creator throughout its fabric. Traherne admires the beautiful order of
the cosmos, stressing the interrelatedness of all things and the fact that
everything was made for humanity. A negative note enters in, not from
God's intention but from human misperception. All the commonly
shared beauties of nature—sun, moon, stars, sea and land, creatures
of the earth, other humans—are meant to show God to us; but when
humans take any of these good things, or aspects of them, and fasten
on them in a possessive way, they lose sight of what they were made for
and thus fall into sin.[210] Early in *Centuries* I, Traherne has a number
of chapters on how to enjoy the world, starting with the phrase "You
never enjoy the world aright" (e.g., chap. 29: "You never enjoy the world
aright, until the Sea itself floweth in your veins"). The gist of the message is that we must enjoy all created things equally, both for their own
sakes, and as revealing their Creator. We should also enjoy them for
the sake of others: "Yet further, you never enjoy the world aright, till
you so love the beauty of enjoying it, that you are covetous and earnest
to persuade others to enjoy it."[211]

Humanity is the focus and end of God's outpouring love, the only
creatures made in God's image, as Traherne often says. He also uses

a related mystical image by talking about humans as "mirrors of eternity." [212] Like Gregory of Nyssa and some other mystics, Traherne identifies the image character primarily with man's share in divine infinity, that is, the insatiable desire we have for partaking ever more greatly in God's bliss, that is, felicity. As he says in *Centuries* III.56, "nothing but Felicity is worthy of our labour, because all other things are the means only which conduce unto it." This Anglican version of Gregory's *epektasis* is set out throughout the poems, perhaps most notably in "Insatiableness I and II."

Traherne does not give us a detailed theological anthropology. He stresses the importance of love, but he has little discussion of the nature of the will, despite his emphasis on freedom. [213] The Dobell collection has an important poem on "Love,"[214] and Traherne also wrote a short treatise on the topic, as well as a number of prayers. He was especially interested in the power of "seeing," both physical sight and what he called "thought," that is, the intellectual perception that restores fallen humans to something like the vision of God enjoyed in infancy. For Traherne, direct intuitive seeing of God and the world is a characteristic of human nature in the stage of infancy, both that of Adam and his descendants, as numerous poems show (e.g., "The Vision," "My Spirit," "An Infant Eye," "Sight," and so on). The other senses (hearing, smelling, touching, and tasting) are present but less discussed.[215] Given the loss of the infant's intuitive sight of God, fallen humans need to attain a "second naïveté" (to borrow a phrase from Paul Ricoeur),[216] that is, a fresh seeing of God by means of "thoughts," or visions of the Platonic Ideas or Forms found within the soul as reflections of their supernal existence. "Thoughts I-IV" of the Dobell manuscript, as well as "The Inference" in the Felicity poems, have much to say about this kind of seeing.

In "Thoughts I," Traherne addresses the Thoughts as, "Ye brisk and divine living things, / Ye great exemplars, and ye heavenly springs / Which I within me see." Later in the poem he describes such a "Thought" as "the substance of my mind / Transform'd, and with its object lin'd." The internal presence of the Platonic forms is also emphasized in "Thoughts II," while "Thoughts III" shows that such forms of perception are the ground for right action—"By thoughts alone the soul is made divine" (line 6). In "Thoughts IV" Traherne employs the image of the prophet Elijah rapt up to heaven in the fiery chariot (2 Kgs. 6:11–19) to show that we are already in heaven when we learn to see in this fashion (lines 1–12). The poet highlights how this mode of vision partakes of infinity—"Our blessedness, like his, is infinite," and "Eternity itself is that true light, / That doth enclose us being infinite."[217]

Traherne has a developed teaching about the relation of body and soul in our quest of God here and hereafter, an aspect of his thought that qualifies the Platonic cast to much of his mysticism. In "The Person," for instance, he addresses "Ye sacred limbs," telling them that he will give them a richer reward than what he first discovered. His praise of the limbs and parts of the body is not like those found in the false praise poems of love literature but is rather intended to reveal "the naked things," that is, the true worth of "these sacred treasures / which my great Father gave." The poet praises the body as a gift from God. The following poem, "The Estate," asks how the soul relates to the mortal body. Traherne's holistic view of human nature insists that it is in and through bodily delight that the soul finds its true service of God: "They [the senses] ought, my God, to be the pipes, / And conduits of thy praise. / Men's bodies were not made for stripes, / Nor anything but joys."[218] This rejection of asceticism reappears in "The Odour," a hymn to sensuous enjoyment. In its final stanzas Traherne proclaims, "Live to thyself; thy limbs esteem: / From Heaven they came; with money can't be bought." And later, "Talk with thyself; thyself enjoy and see: / At once the mirror and the object be."[219] This might be seen as a kind of mystical hedonism or solipsism (see below), but Traherne's defenders appeal to the poet's teaching about how the restored soul has regained a oneness with God that shows it is enjoying not *itself* but the self *in* God.

Traherne's theology undergirds the itinerary set out in his poetry, beginning with his fascination with infancy and its knowing. As Rufus Jones once said, "I know of no one who has borne louder testimony than Traherne to the divine inheritances and spiritual possibilities of the new-born child, or who has more effectively denied the fiction of total depravity."[220] Traherne's view of infancy, however, is complex and far from the views of the later Romantics. The first five poems of the Dobell collection, as well as several others, along with at least seven of the "Felicity" poems, take infancy as their theme.[221] The poem "Wonder," for example, hails the child-poet as a heavenly, preexistent being descended to earth:

> How like an angel came I down!
>   How bright are all things here!
> When first among His works I did appear

O how their glory me did crown!
The world resembled His eternity,
In which my soul did walk;
And every thing that I did see,
Did talk with me.[222]

The following piece, "Eden," speaks of the "learned and happy igno-rance" of the child, who has no knowledge of "the sloth, care, pain, and sorrow that advance / The madness and the misery / Of men." Nor does the infant know sin—all is bright and joyful. Freedom from sin is taken up at length in "Innocence," ending on the note that character-izes so much of Traherne's poetry, "I must become a child again."[223]

"The Preparative" sums up and deepens the idyllic picture of the child Adam in paradise.[224] Beginning with a description of the undif-ferentiated consciousness of the newborn, stanza 2 turns to the soul as "my only all to me," pictured (as Traherne often does) as "an inward sphere of light, / Or an interminable orb of sight," that is, "A naked simple pure intelligence." This "meditating inward eye" knew the ideas of all things (stanza 3), and, untroubled by the senses, was "Unbod-ied and devoid of care," just like the angels in heaven (stanza 4). Once again, Traherne insists that such a state was free from sin and misery (stanza 5) and in direct contact with "divine impressions" and the heav-enly light that allows the vision of felicity (stanza 6). Stanza 7 seems to address his current situation, exhorting the poet to have a mind empty of possessiveness and to become "Acquainted with the golden mean." It closes with the advice: "My soul, retire, / Get free, and so thou shalt even all admire."

Two later companion poems, "Dumbness" and "Silence," expatiate on the characteristics of the Adamic state.[225] "Dumbness" treats the prelinguistic state of the infant, who is busied only with himself and does not know or speak human words. Rather, everything is reduced to the eye, that is, to vision—"No ear, / But eyes themselves were all the hearers there." Correlatively, "Silence" praises the inward work of the "quiet silent person," who in his interiority feels his bliss, sees his "inward treasures," and gives thanks and love to God. For Traherne, this is a true state of union with God: "The world was more in me than I in it. / The King of Glory in my soul did sit. / And to Himself in me He always gave / All that He takes delight to see me have. / For so my spirit was an endless sphere, / Like God Himself, and Heaven and earth was there." The later infancy poems in the Dobell folio and in the Felicity collection mostly repeat the themes from these early verses.

The purity of the "infant-eye" did not last long, either for Adam or for Thomas Traherne. Several poems and chapters in the *Centuries* speak of the poet's life as a boy of four or five, one who is already beginning to have external experiences and to question his internal states (see "Poverty" and "Solitude," as well as *Centuries* III.16, III.23). The poem "Adam" begins: "God made man upright at the first; / Man made himself by sin accurst: / Sin is a deviation from the way / Of God." Traherne's *Christian Ethicks* contains several poems, one beginning, "Mankind is sick, the world distemper'd lies, / Oppress'd with sins and miseries. / Their sins are woes; a long corrupted train / Of poison, drawn from Adam's vein."[226] The other seventeenth-century poets we have seen were obsessed with sin; Traherne is certainly not blind to it, but his fundamental hopefulness separates him from the others, as well as from Protestant theology regarding human corruption after the Fall.

Traherne's doctrine of sin has been debated. Some have accused him of Pelagianism; others have sought to exonerate him.[227] At least in his poems and in the *Centuries* Traherne seems to be closer to Pelagius than to Augustine and the standard Western view of original sin, let alone to the theology of Calvin and the Puritans. For Traherne sin seems to come largely from two sources—the outward power of human custom present in the actions of those around us, and the inward distraction of the soul that allows itself to engage in possessiveness. Stanzas 6 to 9 of "Apostasy" provide a picture of his views. Traherne says that God did not create "the seeds of melancholy," "but only foolish men, / Grown mad with customary folly / Which doth increase their wants, so dote / As when they older grow they then / Such baubles chiefly note; / More fools at twenty than ten." Traherne admits his own fall when "Drown'd in their customs, I became / A stranger to the shining skies." His soul was "quickly murdered" (stanza 8) and he lost his vision of "all the world" by gazing on glittering tinsel things (stanza 9).[228] Like Pelagius, Traherne sees Adam's Fall primarily as a bad example, one that, like a snowball rolling downhill, gathered speed and mass throughout human history. He admits that there is a kind of internal attraction to sin inherited from Adam, but he does not explain it. Rather, as we are told in *Centuries* III.8: "our misery proceedeth ten thousand times more from the outward bondage of opinion and custom, than from any inward corruption or depravation of Nature: And that it is not our parents' loins, so much as our parents' lives, that enthralls and blinds us. Yet is all our corruption derived from Adam: inasmuch as all the evil examples and inclinations of the world arise from his sin."[229] Traherne's view of the Fall might be best described as Pre-Pelagian, close to that of some of the early Fathers of the Church.[230]

Traherne did not think that fallen humans could regain felicity on their own. Rather, he insisted on the role of the Bible, grace (though not often mentioned in the poems), and the necessity of the redemptive death of Christ. Among the Felicity poems "Dissatisfaction" expresses his disappointment with his own schooling, which he says did not teach the felicity that alone could still his insatiable desire. "Weary of all that since the Fall, / Mine eyes on earth can find, / I for a book from Heaven look / . . . . For some fair book fill'd with eternal song."[231] The answer comes in the next poem, "The Bible." Traherne starts on a high note: "That! That! There I am told / That I the son of God was made, / His image. O divine! . . ."[232] This short poem emphasizes the joyous aspect of God's word, something that Traherne found most evident in the Psalms, which he often paraphrased or imitated. The fundamental message of the Bible for believers is salvation; hence in his poems and prose writings Traherne often refers to Christ's passion, as in "Thoughts IV," where he has a vision of God's temple in heaven and all the saints:

> Men are like cherubim on either hand,
> Whose flaming love by His divine command
> Is made a sacrifice to ours: which streams
> Throughout all worlds, and fills them all with beams.
> We drink our fill, and take their beauty in,
> While Jesus's blood refines the soul from sin.
> His grievous cross is a supreme delight,
> And of all heavenly ones the greatest sight.[233]

Christ's passion and cross are especially emphasized in the first book of the *Centuries*, which also contains aspects of a cosmic Christology.[234]

Despite its anchor in salvation history, much of what Traherne has to say about the restoration to innocence in his best-known poems is couched in terms of general joy, praise, bliss, vision, felicity, union, and divinization, which do not feature many specific Christian references. Another distinctive aspect of his presentations is that the third estate, that of restoration through Christ, often has such strong references to seeing and enjoying God in true felicity that it seems that the fourth estate of glory is not only begun here below, but almost consummated. The mystical themes of felicity, glory, and the beatific vision appear throughout the poems, so a full survey would be tedious, given Traherne's repetitiveness. Here I will focus on an analysis of one poem, "My Spirit," a comprehensive, sometimes even self-subverting, poem that has been seen as the best summary of Traherne's mystical teaching.[235]

In "My Spirit," Traherne begins, as so often, with himself. He says, "My naked simple life was I. / That act so strongly shin'd / Upon the earth, the sea, the sky. / It was the substance of my mind." Then he goes on to claim "my essence was capacity," that is, an insatiable ability to encompass all things, because, "being simple like the Deity / In its own centre is a sphere / Not shut up here, but everywhere." Right from the start the reciprocity between the divine "I" and Traherne's "I" has been established. Stanza 2 expands on this identity with God, noting that the naked simple life of the soul works like God, by its own power, and not through "another engine," because it is "true and perfect act." Therefore, God is present in what we might call the spirit's transcendent capacity: "'tis all eye, all act, all sight, / And what it please can be, / not only see, / Or do. . . ." Rightly considered, the human spirit seems indistinguishable from God, an identity-in-diversity that becomes stronger as the poem proceeds. In stanza 3, the simple naked I is present and active everywhere and at all times, so that it seems that all things are the products of this mind.[236] This emphasis on the omnipresence of the mind is further explored in the fourth stanza. Unable to restrain himself, Traherne bursts out in a typical apostrophe: "O joy, O wonder, and delight! / O sacred mystery! / My soul a spirit infinite! / An image of the Deity!" The language of sphere and abyss used here (lines 77–78) is qualified by specifically Christian mystical terminology, not only of the image of God, but also of being a "son and friend of God" (line 86). The final two stanzas express a form of mystical identity, perhaps the most powerful found in Anglican mysticism (but see the "mine–thine" theme in Herbert). Stanza 6 states how the inner "orb of joy," that is, the eye of the mind, is kin to God and therefore able to "Dilate itself even in an instant, and / Like an indivisible centre stand / At once surrounding all eternity. / 'Twas not a sphere / Yet did appear / One infinite." Traherne is struggling with the inexpressible here, as can be seen by his obscure conclusion, "'Twas not a sphere, but 'twas a power / Invisible, and yet a bower." The poet's metaphor of the sphere is abandoned, but in favor of the ambiguous "power" and "bower." Paradoxically, however, the last, almost-shouted, stanza returns to the image of the sphere and the deep identity between God and the soul:

> O wondrous self! O sphere of light,
>   O sphere of joy most fair;
> O act, O power infinite;
> O subtle and unbounded air!
>   O living orb of sight!
> Thou which within me art, yet me! Thou eye,
> And temple of his whole infinity!
> O what a world art thou! A world within!

This invocation of a union of identity with God (a form of nonduality),[237] as well as the passages on divinization,[238] and those that suggest at least a foretaste (if not more) of the beatific vision enjoyed by someone who has been born again and has regained the state of innocence and felicity, are central to Traherne's mysticism. Such themes do not exhaust his mystical teaching, because there are aspects of Traherne's view of union, such as the notion of the soul as the bride of God,[239] that do not appear in "My Spirit." Nonetheless, "My Spirit" provides a good picture of Traherne's mysticism and also highlights the enthusiasm with which the poet celebrated his union with God.

To close on this note of ecstatic union, however, might suggest, as some have claimed, that Traherne was a kind of mystical solipsist, someone so absorbed in his own inner delight and identity with God that nothing else mattered.[240] Although many poems read in isolation might suggest this, Traherne, like many other mystics, insisted that inner delight and identity with God called out for loving engagement with other people. A number of poems, especially "Goodness," the piece that closes the Dobell collection, help to qualify the seeming solipsism of other verses.[241] Love for all appears at the outset of "Goodness": "The bliss of other men is my delight / (When once my principles are right): / And every soul which mine doth see / A treasure." Traherne says that, "The joys of all / On mine do fall. / And even my infinity doth seem / A drop, without them, of a mean esteem." Just as God's infinity, paradoxically, is not complete without that of the poet, so too, his infinite bliss requires sharing in the bliss of all other humans. The poem continues in stanzas 2–5 by concentrating the felicity of other humans on him: they appear "As if they were / Reflected only from them all for me, / That I a greater beauty there might see." As *his* pleasure is made more infinite, it is only at the end of the poem that attention shifts from the poet outward toward, "A choir of blessed and harmonious songs." Other poems and texts, such as "Bells,"[242] show that Traherne found a shared felicity and the necessity of active love of others as necessary expressions of one's inner felicity. Thomas Traherne may not be the finest poet among the seventeenth-century Anglicans, but his mysticism is arguably the most thoroughgoing.

Puritan Mysticism

Among those who resisted the Elizabethan Settlement and sought a "Purified, or Godly, Church" there were many concerned with finding a deeper sense of God's presence in their lives.[243] The mystical dimension of English Puritanism has often been overlooked, perhaps because of modern conceptions about the rigidity of Puritan religion—a misleading myth. H. L. Mencken's famous definition of Puritanism still reigns in the popular mind: "Puritanism is the haunting fear that someone, somewhere, may be happy." As a matter of fact, the original Puritans were not teetotalers, as is often thought, and they produced a significant literature about the delights of sexuality and marital harmony. They were also interested in the "mystical marriage" with Christ. Along with John Donne, the Puritans were among the first Christians to think about the intimate relation between marital sexuality and the soul's marriage to Christ.[244] This is not to say that the Puritans were not rigorists. If the genius of the Anglican *via media* was compromise, the Puritans, diverse as they were, were generally not compromisers, although some managed to stay in the Established Church. It is not surprising that the *Ecclesia Anglicana*, for all its tolerance, could not eventually contain its Puritan strain, which after the Restoration of Charles II moved in Separatist directions.

There were various kinds of Puritans and over the century from ca. 1570 to 1670 Puritanism went through many developments.[245] Generalizing about "Puritanism" (some have suggested "Puritanisms" would be better), as well as Puritan spirituality and mysticism, is not easy. A number of books and essays have addressed the nature of Puritanism as a spiritual movement, one that involved mystical elements, but it is perhaps only in recent decades that the mystical side of Puritanism has begun to be recovered.[246]

Like all branches of the Reformation, the Puritans were deeply biblical, insisting that the word of God was the only source for belief. Their biblicism, however, was not "fundamentalist" in the contemporary sense, because it allowed for learned interpretation, and even considerable allegory. Perhaps it might be better termed "foundationalist." The Puritans were great simplifiers, especially with regard to ritual and prayer. Thus, they preferred the Geneva Bible, an English version produced by English exiles abroad, to the Authorized Version, and they resisted using the *Book of Common Prayer*. Puritan theology was basically Calvinist, and therefore predestinarian, but it emphasized the affective and experiential side of Calvin's thought, rather than the doctrinalism of the Reformed theology that so often triumphed on the Continent. Puritans insisted on the need for conversion from sin and living according to a divine covenant. As Charles Cohen summarizes, "Puritans were a 'hotter sort' of Protestant, and what kept them bubbling was a religious sensibility bound up with conversion, an emotional confrontation with grace borne up by the Holy Spirit in the Word."[247] Piety was the center of Puritan living.

The doctrine of sanctification, centered on union with Christ achieved through the grace of the Holy Spirit, was essential to the Puritans.[248] Without neglecting the intellect, Puritanism was an affective faith, a "religion of the heart." Many Puritans spoke of the believer's mystical marriage to Christ—an aspect of Puritanism that will surprise those accustomed only to the negative stereotypes that Puritanism has labored under. Although for the Puritans life here below was understood as a difficult pilgrimage in which a disciplined life was essential, it was always divine grace, not human effort, that was essential. In cultivating inner religion, the Puritans engaged in various spiritual practices, not a few inherited from the Middle Ages. Along with private Bible reading and self-examination, programs of meditative and even contemplative prayer were used. The role of the community of saints, especially as seen in long Sabbath worship and listening to the word of God in sermons, showed the difference between the "godly" and those of lukewarm faith.[249]

The Puritan movement produced a large literature, theological and devotional. Major theologians include William Perkins (1558–1602), prominent at Cambridge and the author of an important work on predestination. Another significant figure was his student William Ames (1576–1623), whose views led to his exile to Holland, where he produced a summary of Calvinist theology, the *Medulla Theologiae (The Marrow of Theology)*, first published in 1623.[250] Other Puritans produced devotional works, among them Lewis Bayly (d. 1631), whose *The Practice of Pietie* came out around 1610, and the moderate Richard Baxter (1615–1691), the author of the popular *The Saints' Everlasting*

Rest (1650). The greatest devotional writer of Puritanism (the only one still widely read) was the layman John Bunyan (1628–1688), the author of _Grace Abounding_ (1666) and _Pilgrim's Progress_, which first came out in 1678 and has never been out of print.

Some earlier scholars have attempted to give taxonomies of Puritan mysticism, such as Jerald Brauer's distinction between the "Bridal mysticism" of someone like Francis Rous and the more widespread "Spirit mystics" of two kinds—the "Seekers," such as Henry Vane the Younger, and the "Happy Finders" like John Saltmarsh.[251] There are, however, problems that cast doubt on the usefulness of such taxonomies. The first is the fact that a number of these figures and their texts have been little studied, at least from the perspective of current views of mysticism. A second difficulty involves the extent to which the Separatists of the time of the Civil War and after (e.g., the Ranters, the Diggers, the Fifth Monarchy men, and others) are to be thought of as Puritans, and/or Puritan mystics. Many of these groups seem more millenarian and antinomian than mystical in orientation. The Quakers, begun by George Fox (1624–1691) in the 1640s and 1650s, form a special case. Fox's mysticism of inner enlightenment has affinities with Spirit-mysticism trends in some Puritans, but, given the Quaker antipathy to _all_ organized religion, it seems problematic to consider the Quakers a Puritan phenomenon, so they will not be treated in this volume of _The Presence of God_, but in the volume to come.[252] In this context, I can only look at some aspects of Puritan mysticism in select figures from across the spectrum of those identified as Puritan.

At the start, it is worth noting how indebted many Puritans were to classical mystical literature from the patristic and medieval periods. Despite their opposition to "Popery," they read and admired past mystical authors. Bernard of Clairvaux, for example, was used by all, but other mystical writers were also utilized. An example of Puritan use of classic mystics can be found in John Everard (ca. 1584?–1640), one of the early radical Puritans.[253] Everard was a problem for the Stuart kings and the conformist establishment of the English church. His sermons in _The Rending of the Vail_ were influenced by the writings of John Tauler, the _Theologia Deutsch_ (which he translated), as well as works of Sebastian Franck. He also made an English version of Nicholas of Cusa's _De visione dei_.[254] Everard's collection of sermons, _The Gospel Treasury Opened_, first printed in 1657, included a translation of the Dionysian MT. Everard is often reminiscent of Sebastian Franck, especially because of his relentless emphasis on the priority of inner religion and the birth of the Word in the depths of the soul. Freedom from the external constraints of the law (but not from its internal regulations) is emphasized, as well as deification as the goal of the Christian life. In a cycle of sermons preached in the early 1630s and found in *The Gospel Treasury*, Everard outlines six steps leading to Solomon's throne, the last of which is "Deiformity, when indeed we are no longer *men* but *gods*: mistake me not, that is, when we *act* no longer *our selves*, but God acts *in us*; that if we do *any* thing, yet we *see and feel*, and *confess* it is God *that doth it*; that if *we speak*, it is Christ *that speaks*."[255] Everard was also willing to speak about his own moments of mystical consciousness, as when in commenting on Psalm 68:25, he says that there are times "[w]hen God is not onely *in us* as he is *in all Creatures*; but when he is *there sensibly* to us, that we feel him, and see him, and *behold his presence* and glory, and so come hereby to *glorifie him* more."[256] Everard's message about interior religion and deification draws him close to some of the German Radicals.

The Puritans were fascinated with the Song of Songs and its mystical interpretation.[257] They wrote many commentaries on the book, often based on sermons preached to groups of the "godly,"[258] and also produced a number of treatises devoted to the topic of union with Christ, often employing the marriage metaphor.[259] An example of a Puritan commentary on the Song is that of Richard Sibbes (1577–1635).[260] The moderate Sibbes was one of the most prolific and widely read Puritans. A graduate of St. John's College, Cambridge, he served in a variety of posts there, as well as at St. Catherine's College. A noted preacher, Sibbes was active both in Cambridge and in London. Despite his sympathies for the "godly" and the suspicions Archbishop Laud and others had toward him, Sibbes remained within the Established Church and did not lose his positions. He published over thirty books during his lifetime, and more appeared after his death. He is one of the few Puritans whose writings are available in a modern edition.[261]

Sibbes does not figure in most lists of Puritan mystics, but a study of his reading of the Song of Songs, based on sermons and first published in 1639 with the rather disconcerting title, *Bowels Opened*, shows that there were significant mystical elements in his thought.[262] These twenty sermons treat Song of Songs 4:16 and 5:1–6:3, although Sibbes discusses other verses of what he called "a kind of pastoral . . . , a 'song of the beloved' . . . , in which [Christ] takes upon him the term and carriage, as it were, of a loving shepherd, who labours to find out for his sheep the fattest, fruitfullest, best, and sweetest pastures."[263] Sibbes advances a general reading of a somewhat political nature, interpreting the Song as an account of the true church, who is Christ's sister

by redemption in blood and Christ's spouse by marriage.[264] The fact
that he chooses a part of the Song in which the church-bride loses her
devotion to Christ and has to engage in a difficult search for him is a
perhaps less-than-subtle critique of the failure of the Stuart church to
implement true reform.[265] Sibbes has a strong doctrine of the church as
the body of Christ, or "Christ mystical," as he sometimes puts it.[266] Nevertheless, from the beginning of the commentary Sibbes is aware that
everything said of the church should also be realized in each believer:
"And therefore, as the whole church is the spouse of Christ, so is every
particular Christian; and as the whole church desires still nearer communion with Christ, so doth every particular member."[267] He argues
that there is always a "conjugal chastity in the soul of a Christian"—
"Holding firm to the covenant and marriage between Christ and it, he
keeps that inviolable. Though he may be untoward, sleepy and drowsy
[Song 5:2], yet there is always a conjugal, spouse-like affection."[268]
Like other Puritans, Sibbes does not hesitate to draw a connection
between human and divine marriage: "Therefore, the Spirit of God,
out of mercy and pity to man, would raise up his affections, by taking
comparison from earthly things, leading to higher matters, that only
deserve love, joy, delight, and admiration."[269]

The church-political aspects of Sibbes's readings often slide over into
personal appropriations, especially due to how the preacher inserts
"uses" for his theological readings. Sibbes shows acquaintance with
earlier mystics (Augustine is cited eight times; Bernard six). Although
primarily a moralist, Sibbes believes that the pious life should include
moments of direct experience of God. He often appeals to experience,
both his own and that of his readers, advising them "to justify all the
exercises of religion from an experimental taste of them and sweetness of them."[270] Tasting the "sweetness of the Lord,"[271] and enjoying
"mystical union and sweet communion" in our marriage with Christ
as portrayed in the Song of Songs is an important aspect of Sibbes's
reading.[272] At times the preacher uses erotic terms, as when he says
conversion often involves an "experience of his love to ravishment," or
when he speaks of the soul "as in a kind of ecstasy."[273] Sermon XVII
(ed., 159) contends that the love of Christ can enlarge the heart and
the tongue and even alter one's life: "This hot affection, this heavenly
fire, will so mould and alter him, that he shall be clean another man."
Sibbes's intention is to encourage his readers to aspire to the delights
of marriage to Jesus as revealed in the Song of Songs.

Sibbes's commentary, not unlike some medieval interpreters (e.g.,
William of St.-Thierry), highlights the vicissitudes of the mystical jour-

ney, that is, how experiences of delight in God's presence (both for the church and for the individual) must necessarily be followed by times of God's absence as part of the pedagogy of love that invites us to make continued progress toward God, rather than resting in false enjoyment.[274] The goal is a loving mutuality between God and the human person that Sibbes explores especially in Sermons XIX–XX, commenting on Song of Songs 6:3, "I am my beloved's, and my beloved is mine; he feedeth among the lilies." This verse was often treated in previous mystical literature but rarely in as detailed a fashion as in these two sermons.

Sibbes begins by claiming that the words of Song 6:3 "are a kind of triumphant acclamation upon all the former passages; as it were, the foot of the song" (ed., 171). After keenly feeling Christ's absence, or "forsakings" (Song 6:1-2), the bride now feels comfort from the return of the Bridegroom. By his temporary estrangements, Christ sweetens his new comings, as also shown in Song 3:1-4. "Love vents itself in broken words and sighs," says Sibbes, but here this cry of the bride expresses the union and communion between Christ and the church. Nevertheless, it also bespeaks a "mystical marriage" in which "Christ's person is ours, and our persons are his" (ed., 173). From such a union of persons comes "a communion of all other things," so that everything we have is his, and what is his is ours. Christ's love descends to us, making it possible for us to love him and to meditate on his love. Such meditation takes the form of an enumeration of the forms of mutuality found in "I am my beloved's, and my beloved is mine."[275] Again, Sibbes addresses the question of what to do when a person feels no such comfort from Christ, answering, as usual, that "His absence at length will end in a sweet discovery of himself more abundantly than before" (ed., 177). The last half of Sermon XIX addresses two questions: How Christ comes to be ours; and how we are Christ's beloved. Christ comes to be ours by the gift of the three persons of the Trinity (ed., 177-79); and we are Christ's beloved by the Father's gift, by the redeeming blood of Christ, by marriage to him, and by our own consent (ed., 179-81).

Sermon XX, less stirring than XIX, continues this line of thinking, identifying four reasons why Christ must be given to us before we can give ourselves to him. The outcry of the bride, says Sibbes, is an expression not only of love but also of the saving faith (Luther is cited) expressing the mutual dependence of justification and sanctification (183). In the "mystical body" under the action of the Spirit of Christ, "There is the same love to all as to one, and to every one, as if there were no other. He loves each one, so that every Christian may say as well as the whole church, Christ is mine, and I am Christ's" (ed., 184). All loves meet in Christ, who offers "spiritual marriage" to all who repent and turn to him. "Christ takes you not with any dowry," says Sibbes. "All that he requires is to confess your beggary and to come with emptiness. He takes us not because we are clean, but because he will purge us" (ed., 187). Hence, we must never be discouraged by our "daily infirmities" but always trust in the love of Christ. The last part of the sermon turns to the meaning of "He feedeth among the lilies," which Sibbes interprets as referring to how Christ feeds us by "his holy word and the communion of saints" (ed., 188). Here the preacher turns to church history, attacking popery and "all the school learning" for not providing the solid food of the teaching of the early church. Nonetheless, as the Good Shepherd, Christ continues to feed his flock with his word and "with his own body and blood in the sacrament." Thus, "[t]here is as sure an union and communion between Christ and the Christian soul, as there is between the food and the body, when it is once digested" (ed., 193).

The mystical marriage portrayed in the Song of Songs was popular not only among the biblical commentators, but also in Puritan treatises, both by divines and by laymen. A good example of a lay theologian is Francis Rous (ca. 1580–1659), whose *Mystical Marriage* was first published in 1631.[276] Rous was from Cornwall, studied at Oxford and at Leiden, and was active in Parliament (he sat in every parliament from 1625 to 1657).[277] He was provost of Eton College and served as a lay member of the Presbyterian Westminster Assembly of 1643. Rous began as a Presbyterian but seems to have eventually come close to the Independent Puritans. On the basis of *The Mystical Marriage*, as well as a number of other tracts,[278] especially *The Heavenly Academy* (1638), a treatise on the ascent of knowledge from its lower forms to the highest and mystical knowledge of "the celestial university,"[279] Rous has been called "one of the earliest exponents and finest examples of Puritan mysticism." [280]

Rous's education gave him an acquaintance with a good deal of theological and mystical literature. Although *The Mystical Marriage* is addressed to the general reader and does not cite sources, Rous's other works demonstrate his knowledge of many theologians, not only Augustine and Bernard but also the Dionysian writings, Aquinas, Gerson, and other late medieval mystics.[281] Rous's mysticism, however, filters these earlier traditions through the concerns of Calvinist theology, especially predestination and assurance of salvation, the two covenants, Law and Gospel, and the relation of justification and sanctification.[282] Calvin had occasionally spoken of *unio mystica*; Rous made it into a central motif of his form of Calvinism. Rous was not an academically trained theologian; *The Mystical Marriage* appeals to his own experience and is written in a heightened, almost poetic, style, to inspire his readers to seek the love of Christ through this book of "mystical and experiential Divinity."[283] Divided into nine chapters, the work summarizes the "hottest affections and spiritual lust" that at least some Puritans felt was the highest form of piety.[284] Rous does not hesitate to apply the language of human lovemaking to the soul's marriage to Christ and defends the analogy between what we know (i.e., earthly marriage) and the unknown spiritual marriage.[285] While *The Mystical Marriage* is not a formal commentary on the Song of Songs, Rous cites the biblical poem of love some twenty-three times.

Rous anchors his view of mystical union with Christ in the story of creation and salvation, as shown in chapter I. The soul's preexistence in God means that its ultimate happiness rests in him alone, but in order to have God dwell with fallen humanity the Second Person of the Trinity must become incarnate in an immediate union of God and man that makes our mediated union, or mystical marriage, possible. Rous bases his teaching about mystical marriage in the Genesis 1:26 account of humanity's creation in the image and likeness of God, a fundamental quality that is not lost through sin.[286] Thus, through Christ's intervention we are able to become one spirit with him (1 Cor. 1:17) and achieve a "blessed communion" with the Lord. As Adam had only one bride, so too the church, once married to the Law and concupiscence, has now entered into a new, second marriage with Christ, one begun in this life, but fully consummated only in heaven (chaps. II–III). There are, then, three marriages: (1) the old marriage to concupiscence, which must be rejected by entering into (2) the new marriage with Christ that prepares us for (3) the final bliss of the heavenly marriage.[287]

As we have seen with Sibbes, the border between the ecclesial and the personal readings of the mystical marriage is porous—what is said about the church is also meant to apply to each believer. Also like Sibbes, Rous is concerned with the succession of times of presence and periods of absence of the Bridegroom as portrayed in the Song of Songs and as experienced by the devout believer. The long chapter V (ed., 96–169), "The Soules estate in desertions though seeming miserable, is indeede profitable," seeks to assure the reader that, when Christ withdraws himself (Song 5:6–7), it is for the good of the beloved as a way to prepare her to profit better from when he returns.[288] Rous then turns to the "Visitations of the Husband," discussing their uses and advantages (chap. VI), as well as their signs and marks (chap. VII). He summarizes the signs and marks as follows: "For when Christ visiteth the soul, as he doth clarifie her with light, and ravish her with joy, so he doth beautifie her with holiness" (ed., 254). These visits are in the service of ever-deepening union with Christ: "In these accesses of Christ there are heights of union, and the increases of union bring with them increases of uniformity. The spirit of union is fire, & fire turns that into itself to which it is united: & the fuller and closer this union is, the more is this turning" (ed., 255). The Holy Spirit also has a role. As Christ's Spirit of power, the spiritual union given from above makes the soul fruitful (ed., 257-60). Such fruitfulness is an important issue for the Puritan mystic. Chapter IIII of *The Mystical Marriage* insists that the heavenly marriage is both "happy in pleasures and in labors of love," that is to say that the "mystical wife," like Rebekah in Genesis, seeks to please her husband by her good works, both the "service of doing," which is active, and the passive "service of suffering." The more we labor and suffer, says Rous, the greater the weight of glory that awaits us (ed., 84), because, he goes on to say, "it is utterly a fault and a loss to separate mystical divinity from practicall" (ed., 85).

The final two chapters of *The Mystical Marriage* bring the treatise to a fitting conclusion. Chapter VIII is "A collary of counsels and directions to those that are entered into the state of this blessed Marriage" (ed., 264-318). Rous advises the soul to "often go out of the body, yea out of the world by heavenly contemplations . . . " and ascend "into that upper world, where her treasure, her joy, her beloved dwelleth" (ed., 266). When the eye of the soul is made clear and piercing by faith, she can look upon Christ the Sun, who so loves "the eye of a Faith working unto love" that he cries out that he "is wounded by one of her eyes" (Song 4:9; ed., 267-68). Ever-increasing love and the desire to please Christ not the self is the law of this marital union of wills. Rous says that if we perchance offend our true Husband we should immediately repent and rekindle our love. "And having regained him," he continues, "make thyself more one with him, and increase thy communion with him. Touch him hard with thy faith, suck him strongly with thy love" (ed., 286-87). He even allows that the flesh may have some part in the sweetness of such spiritual union (ed., 294-95).

Chapter IX opens with an impassioned hymn to the Divine Lover—"Thou hast touched my soul with thy spirit, O most beloved, and virtue is gone out of thee into me, & draweth me to thee. Thy spirit is a loadstone of love" (ed., 318). Rous praises the loveliness of the Beloved, asking that his love rest in nothing short of the Divine Lover himself, "and let my spirit often be one spirit with thee in communicative & fruitive unions" (ed., 323). Such visitations increase the soul's beauty as God's image until there is a kind of fusion of human and divine love and beauty. Rous sounds almost like John of the Cross in the *Spiritual Canticle* when he prays:

> [P]ut thy own image, and beauty more and more on my soul, and then love thy own beauty in my soul, & my soul for thy own beauty, which thou hast put on her, & let my soul love thee infinitely more beauti-full, than that beauty which thou has put on my soul, and therefore infinitely more lovely than that which thou lovest in my soul. Wilt thou, my Lord, love the image and shall not the image much more love the pattern?[289]

Nevertheless, Rous insists that we should desire union not just for its pleasure but for its fruitfulness (ed., 330–32). Thus, all forms of union here below are only meant to prepare for the perpetual union and fruition of heaven. He closes the treatise by citing the cry of Revelation 22:20: "*Behold come quickly*. O hony and sweetness itself to the soul that loveth her beloved comes quickly; her consummate marriage comes quickly, her full joy, and perfect happiness comes quickly" (ed., 350).

Isaac Ambrose (1604–1664) was a non-conforming Puritan minister from Lancashire. A prolific author, Ambrose left a number of writings, several of a mystical nature. In 1640, he published two treatises, *Prima* and *Ultima*, dealing with regeneration and eschatology; more impor-tant was the subsequent work, *Media* (1650), which dealt with the spiri-tual practices of the current mid-period of life. His most popular work was *Looking unto Jesus*, first published in 1658. As a non-conformist, Ambrose was ejected from his parish during the Restoration and died not long after. Initially, he was widely read. The first edition of *The Compleat Works of Isaac Ambrose* appeared in 1674 and was reprinted several times. As with a number of the Puritan divines, however, Ambrose faded from view. Ambrose's mysticism, however, has lately been the subject of a study by Tom Schwanda,[290] who sees him as a test case for Puritan mysticism. Here I will provide only a sketch based on Schwanda's findings and *Looking unto Jesus*, the only one of Ambrose's works currently in print.[291]

More than the other Puritan mystical authors surveyed thus far, Ambrose openly appeals to his own experience of direct conscious-ness of God. From the 1640s on he began to take monthly retreats to devote himself to intense reading of the Bible and meditation. During these retreats, he had experiences of being ravished by the love of the Divine Bridegroom. Commentators like Sibbes and Rous had spoken of such raptures; Ambrose provides a personal witness. For example, *Media* for May 1640 recounts an unusual two-day experience of rapture: "[T]his day in the Evening the Lord in his mercy poured into my soul the ravishing joy of his Holy Spirit. O how sweet was the Lord unto me? I never felt such a lovely taste of Heaven before: I believe this was the *joyful sound*, the *Kisses of his mouth*, the *Sweetness of Christ*, the *Joy of his Spirit, the new wine of his kingdom*; it continued with me about two days."[292] Another example is dated to May 17, 1648, when Ambrose recounts how, during his meditations on his spiritual duties, "many a time I felt many sweet stirrings of Christ's Spirit: the Lord Jesus appeared to my soul, gave me the kisses of his mouth [Song of Songs 1:1], especially in my prayers to, and praises of his Majesty."[293]

Ambrose expresses his burning love for Jesus using erotic language drawn from the Song of Songs, as when he prays:

> O sweet Jesu, touch our souls with thy spirit . . . give us the flagons of new wine of the Kingdom, which may lift up our souls above ourselves in our loves, . . . and by an heavenly excess may be transported into an heavenly love, what we may imbrace Christ. . . . O let us desire union with thee. . . . O burn and consume whatsoever would grow one with our souls besides thee; O let the fire of thy spirit so wholly turn our soules into a spiritual fire.[294]

The language of rapture, ecstasy, and especially ravishment is frequent in Ambrose, as in this reference to another of his experiences: "This day the Lord cast one into a spiritual, heavenly, ravishing love trance; he tasted the goodnesse of God, the very sweetness of Christ, and was filled with the joys of the Spirit above measure."[295] Like other mystics, Ambrose held that such visits were foretastes of the fruition of heaven, where the highest degree of love "is a love of the glorified Saints; and in this kind of love of God, and enjoyment of ourselves in him, the soul shall be ravished with God, and be in a kinde of extasie eternally."[296] Isaac Ambrose may well be called the Puritan saint of rapture, although he is only the most expressive spokesman for a theme that was central to Puritan mysticism.[297]

Ambrose's *Looking unto Jesus*, a kind of handbook of meditation, tells the reader at the outset that "*Looking unto Jesus* is the epitome of the Christian's happiness, the quintessence of evangelical duties." Such looking, however, must not be merely intellectual—"An experimental looking unto Jesus is that my text aims at: It is not a swimming knowledge of Christ, but a hearty feeling of his inward workings; not heady notions of Christ, but hearty motions towards him, which are implied in this inward looking."[298] Such looking confirms Christ's love for us and our spousal relation to him.[299] Ambrose's manual surveys the role of Jesus throughout salvation history, from his presence in the covenants of the Old Testament (book II), through the events of his birth, life, and death on the cross (books III–V). Gradually increasing conformity to Christ is the purpose of such meditations, as well as a sense of ravishment over the Redeemer's love for us.[300] After looking to Christ in his resurrection and ascension (books VI–VII), Ambrose's work reaches its high point in our present gazing on Christ in heaven where he is now interceding for us and conveying to us "that fellowship which we have with the Father and the Son." "We cannot think," he goes on, "that there should be that oneness in equality between God and us, as between God and Christ; no, but there is a oneness in similitude, even in this life." If Christ's intercession in heaven is ours, then so is the intercession of the Holy Spirit—"Christ's intercession in heaven, and his Spirit's intercession on earth are as twins of a birth; or rather Christ's intercession in heaven breeds another intercession in the hearts of the saints."[301] Loving union is the purpose of *Looking unto Jesus*, as Ambrose shows by citing Song of Songs 6:3 toward the end of book VIII: "'My beloved is mine, and I am his,' saith the spouse."[302]

Sir Henry Vane the Younger (1613–1662) represents a distinctive form of millenarian Puritan mystical theology. His father, Henry Vane the Elder, was a wealthy member of Parliament who had moved from supporting Charles I to joining the Puritan opposition. The younger Henry briefly and unsuccessfully served as governor of the Massachusetts Bay Colony in 1636. He returned to England and served in the Long Parliament as an opponent of Archbishop Laud and also eventually of Charles I. During the Civil War and the early years of the Protectorate, Vane was second only to Cromwell among the Puritan leaders, but after a falling-out with the Protector, Vane retired to his country estates, where he wrote *The Retired Mans Meditations* (1655). After the Restoration, he was arrested, tried, and executed as a regicide in 1662. During his imprisonment he wrote *Two Treatises* (1662) and *A pilgrimage into the land of promise* (1662).

Vane was a lay theologian and mystic with a strong emphasis on Christ's dwelling in the heart and the inner working of the Holy Spirit centered on a distinctive interpretation of "mystical death" (*mors mystica*).[303] As W. Clark Gilpin has argued, the center of Vane's theological system, "was a mystical religious experience by which, as Vane himself described it, 'faith is wrought up in the soul, giving Christ an actual inhabitation and abode there, as . . . the causer and begetter of the soul into actual membership with himself, in his heavenly and spiritual human perfection.'"[304] By means of this indwelling, Vane believed that the faithful could "enter with Christ within the veyl, and are admitted into the sight and enjoyment of God in the very brightness of his glory . . . , partaking after this manner of the divine nature itself, wherein they see God face to face . . . , conversing with him, as friend speaks to friend."[305] Here Vane utilizes traditional language of mysticism concerning participation in God, but, as David Parnham has shown, Vane's view of union was developed in opposition to the apophatic, antinomian, and absorptive views of mysticism put forth by Radicals, such as Jacob Bauthumley, during and after the Civil War.[306] Vane insisted that union with God was achieved only through the mediation of Christ by means of a mystical marriage in which both bride and Celestial Bridegroom are united in love but distinct in person. As he put it in *The Retired Mans Meditations*, "the Saints by this union with Christ are not deified nor Christed, but have the place only of his *Bride and spouse.* . . . They are Heirs of God, and co-heirs with Christ, but in a weaker, inferior state of glory."[307] Vane's mysticism was one of likeness and analogy of a primarily cataphatic cast.

The Puritan leader framed his teaching on mystical marriage within an original, if at times opaque, theology that joined personal mystical piety with an apocalyptic view of history. Puritans were much concerned with God's covenant with humanity, generally distinguishing between the covenant of works made with Adam and Moses and the covenant of grace brought by Christ.[308] In *The Retired Mans Meditations* and later in his *Two Treatises* (1662), Vane recounts his pilgrimage toward union with Christ as a journey through three covenants—the natural, the legal, and the evangelical. Humanity first experienced the covenant of nature, in which natural reason illumined people to see the divine law both in creation and in their own hearts. But the natural covenant was gravely harmed by sin, so God gave humans the legal covenant, the law revealed in scripture, both in the Old Testament under the Law, and in the New Testament. Both forms of the legal covenant, however, pointed beyond themselves to the imminent "yet more glorious day of Christs second appearance and dispensation in Spirit."[309] In his later works, Vane refined his thinking about the final evangelical covenant, distinguishing two forms: that of the saints, who have already received a single portion of the Holy Spirit; and that of those favored with a double portion. Christ gives the children of the resurrection immortality insofar as "he as the giver of the Holy Ghost is of two sorts, as to the degree and measure of the Glory therof. First, Such, wherein Men and Angels are equal; And the Second, Such, wherein some Men are made in such manner Christ's Equals, the Lamb's or the Bridegroom's Wife that lies in his bosom, that they are the Angels superiours." The entry into these two stages of the evangelical covenant is by way of a mystical death following the pattern of Christ's passion, death, and entombment. The saints need to go through a period of desolation and spiritual trial, a kind of "dark night," to be brought into conformity with Christ's death. The soul's natural faculties have to fail before it can be remade and engrafted into Christ. "According to the steps and degrees of this death," said Vane, "doth the approach and increase of this higher life let it self in upon them [the saints]."[310] Vane was convinced that the saints who had received the double portion of the Holy Spirit were the two witnesses proclaimed in Revelation 11 and that they would soon begin the millennial reign of the returning Christ. In a manner reminiscent of the mystical apocalypticism of some of the late medieval followers of Joachim of Fiore and of Thomas Müntzer, Vane brought together the apocalyptic and the mystical elements of Christianity.

It would be possible to include further witnesses to Puritan mysticism, such as the Cambridge Platonist and chaplain to Oliver Cromwell, Peter Sterry (1613–1672), who has lately come in for renewed interest.[311] Another interesting figure is Edward Polhill, who wrote one of the latest, and most systematic, summaries of Puritan views of mystical union, *Christus in Corde, or The Mystical Union between Christ and the Believer* (1680).[312] Enough has been said, I hope, to show the significance of the mystical element among the Puritans. If the Puritans did not perhaps feature original mystics, or figures who influenced larger mystical traditions in the age of divided Christianity, they showed that popular conceptions of their dour religion are mistaken.

Conclusion

The fourteenth century has been rightly seen as the great age of English mysticism, but in some respects the seventeenth century does not lag far behind. In this chapter I have looked at some poets and prose authors who represented various parties of the English Reformation. The Catholic mystics who fled England and did their writing on the Continent, mostly in France and the Low Counties, will be treated in Part 3 of Volume 6. All in all, what is perhaps most remarkable about English Protestant mysticism is the succession of major poets who used their skills to try to convey aspects of consciousness of God's presence in lyric form. Some of these poets, especially Donne, Herbert, Vaughan, and Traherne, are significant figures in the canon of English poetry. They also deserve a place in the lists of mystics of the Christian tradition.

Notes

1. A general history that contains a good account of the English Reformation is MacCulloch, *The Reformation: A History*. See also Rosemary O'Day, *The Debate on the English Reformation* (London and New York: Methuen, 1986); and W. Ian P. Hazlitt, "Settlements: The British Isles," in Brady, Oberman, and Tracy, *Handbook of European History, 1400–1600*, 455–90.

2. Since the nineteenth century, some Anglicans and Episcopalians have not wanted to be called Protestant, preferring the term "Anglo-Catholic," or its equivalents. Nevertheless, for the period being considered here, the members of the *Ecclesia Anglicana* were opposed to the papacy both in ecclesiastical organization and in most doctrinal issues, as can be seen by the English rejection of the Council of Trent.

3. T. S. Eliot, "Lancelot Andrewes," in idem, *Essays Ancient & Modern* (London: Faber & Faber, 1936), 11–29; quotation from 14.

4. For a general history, see Mark D. Chapman, *Anglican Theology*, Doing Theology (London: T&T Clark, 2012).

5. For the stages in the evolution of this pillar of Anglicanism, see "Common Prayer, The Book of," in *The Oxford Dictionary of the Christian Church*, ed. F. L. Cross and E. A. Livingstone, 3rd rev. ed. (Oxford: Oxford University Press, 2005), 387–88.

6. Gordon Mursell, "Anglican Spirituality," in *The Bloomsbury Guide to Christian Spirituality*, ed. Richard Woods and Peter Tyler (London: Bloomsbury, 2012), 159–70; quotation from 168.

7. On the Thirty-Nine Articles, see the account in Chapman, *Anglican Theology*, 66–71. The text can be found in Jaroslav Pelikan and Valerie Hotchkiss, eds., *Creeds and Confessions of Faith in the Christian Tradition*, vol. 2, *The Reformation Era* (New Haven: Yale University Press, 2003), 526–40.

8. Patrick Collinson, "Puritans," in *Oxford Encyclopedia*, 3:364–70.

9. Along with the essay of Mursell on "Anglican Spirituality" noted above, see his *English Spirituality*, 2 vols. (London: SPCK, 2001). Other works include John R. H. Moorman, *The Anglican Spiritual Tradition* (Springfield, IL: Templegate Publishers, 1983); L. William Countryman, *The Poetic Imagination: An Anglican Spiritual Tradition*, Traditions of Christian Spirituality (London: Darton, Longman & Todd, 1999), as well as A. M. Allchin, "Anglican Spirituality," in *The Study of Anglicanism*, ed. Stephen Sykes and John Booty (London: SPCK, 1988), 313–25; Paul V. Marshall, "Anglican Spirituality," in Senn, *Protestant Spiritual*

Traditions, 125–64; and Richard H. Schmidt, *Glorious Companions: Five Centuries of Anglican Spirituality* (Grand Rapids: Eerdmans, 2002). From a Roman Catholic perspective, Louis Bouyer gives an account that seeks to "re-catholicize" some Anglicans (*Orthodox Spirituality and Protestant and Anglican Spirituality* [New York: Seabury Press, 1982], 104–64).

10. Allchin, "Anglican Spirituality," 353.

11. For a survey of medieval English mysticism, see McGinn, *Varieties*, part III.

12. I will not try to investigate possible mystical elements in all the major early Anglicans, including figures such as Richard Hooker and Jeremy Taylor (1613–1667).

13. A noted modern appreciation of Andrewes is T. S. Eliot, "Lancelot Andrewes," 11–29. A case for Andrewes as a mystic is made by Nicholas Lossky, *Lancelot Andrewes the Preacher (1555–1626): The Origins of the Mystical Theology of the Church of England* (Oxford: Clarendon, 1991). A. M. Allchin, who wrote the "Afterword" to the English version of this French book, concurs in declaring Andrewes a mystic. T. S. Eliot also considered Andrewes a mystic ("Lancelot Andrewes," 26–28), although he does not argue the case.

14. The most available edition is *The Private Devotions of Lancelot Andrewes (Preces Privatae)*, translated with an introduction and notes by F. E. Brightman (1903; repr., New York: Meridian Books, 1961).

15. The Oxford Tractarians helped revive interest in Andrewes. J. H. Newman published a partial version of the First Part of the *Preces Privatae* in 1840, and J. M. Neale provided a translation of the Second Part in 1844.

16. Brightman says, "But originality was scarcely the chief note of his [Andrewes] mind. He is marked rather by great, solid and readily-available learning than by great original ideas. He was scholarly, historical, inductive, rather than speculative and creative. His imagination was collective and organizing, rather than originative" ("Introduction," in *Private Devotions*, xxxix).

17. Schmidt says, "One might think of the *Devotions* as a splendid mosaic or patchwork quilt" (*Glorious Companions*, 37).

18. In some places (e.g., *Private Devotions*, 90, 214–18) Andrewes lingers over the details of Christ's death in ways reminiscent of late medieval passion piety.

19. *Private Devotions*, 187: ". . . that Christ Himself may be formed in us, that so we may be made conformable to his image, in works; his conception, in faith; his birth, in humility."

20. Andrewes refers to deification twice. In the "Second Form of Morning Prayer," he asks the Father "that we might be made partakers of the divine nature" through Christ's sacrifice (*Private Devotions*, 35, citing 2 Pet. 1:4), and the "Morning Prayer for Friday" uses the same formula (*Private Devotions*, 94).

21. A modern edition of twelve sermons is found in G. M. Story, ed., *Lancelot Andrewes Sermons* (Oxford: Clarendon, 1967). Story's introduction (xxv–lii) has a judicious evaluation of the style of the sermons. The most complete edition of Andrewes is the *Works*, ed. J. P. Wilson and J. Bliss, 11 vols. (Oxford: J. H. Parker, 1841–54).

22. Story, "Introduction," xxviii, citing Eliot's "Lancelot Andrewes." Story says that many passages in the sermons "display a virtuosity which is distracting and sometimes tedious" (xxxiii), but he concludes, "it is hard to forgive a literary taste which withholds from Andrewes a high place among English writers" (xliv).

23. Lossky, *Lancelot Andrewes the Preacher*, 336–37.

24. "Sermon 11 of the Nativitie: Christmas 1616," as found in Story, *Sermons*, 49–74; quotation at 67.

25. "Sermon 2 of the Passion: Good-Friday 1604," in Story, *Sermons*, 143–67; quotation from 166.

26. "Sermon 14 of the Resurrection: Easter 1620," in Story, *Sermons*, 192–217; quotation from 216–17.

27. The literature on John Donne is massive. For an overview, see Achsah Guibbory, ed., *The Cambridge Companion to John Donne* (Cambridge: Cambridge University Press, 2006). There is a helpful bibliography in David L. Edwards, *John Donne: Man of Flesh and Spirit* (Grand Rapids: Eerdmans, 2001). For an introduction, see Frank Kermode, *John Donne*, in *British Writers and Their Work, No. 3* (Lincoln: University of Nebraska Press, 1964).

28. Kermode, *John Donne*, 13; see also 27 and 31.

29. Peter McCullough, "Donne as Preacher," in Guiborry, *Cambridge Companion to John Donne*, 167–82. A survey of the theological content of the sermons can be found in Edwards, *John Donne*, chapter 10 (299–350). A number of works have been devoted to Donne's sermons and preaching; see, e.g., William R. Mueller, *John Donne: Preacher* (Princeton: Princeton University Press, 1962); and Gale H. Carrithers Jr., *Donne at Sermons: A Christian Existential World* (Albany: State University of New York Press, 1972).

30. The standard edition is George R. Potter and Evelyn M. Simpson, eds., *The Sermons of John Donne*, 10 vols. (Berkeley: University of California Press, 1953–62). There is a selection of eight sermons in John Booty, ed., *Selections from "Divine Poems," Sermons, "Devotions," and Prayers*, Classics of Western Spirituality (New York: Paulist Press, 1990).

31. The meditative aspect of Donne's prose and poetry has been differently evaluated, with some stressing the Catholic connection, such as Louis L. Martz, *The Poetry of Meditation: A Study in English Religious Literature of the Seventeenth Century* (New Haven: Yale University Press, 1954); and others emphasizing a Protestant background, e.g., Barbara Lewalski, *Protestant Poetics and the Seventeenth-Century Religious Lyric* (Princeton: Princeton University Press, 1979).

32. McCullough, "Donne as Preacher," 171, who quotes the text from Walton on 176.

33. Was Donne a mystic, or at least a mystical author? Interpreters differ. For arguments that Donne was a mystic, see Itrat Husain, *The Dogmatic and Mystical Theology of John Donne* (London: SPCK, 1938), chapter 7; Arthur L. Clements, *Poetry of Contemplation: John Donne, George Herbert, Henry Vaughan, and the Modern Period* (Albany: State University of New York Press, 1990), chapter 2; and Regina Mara Schwartz, *Sacramental Poetics at the Dawn of Secularism* (Stanford: Stanford University Press, 2008), chapter 5. T. S. Eliot denied that Donne was a mystic in "Donne in Our Time," in *A Garland for John Donne 1631–1931*, ed. Theodore Spencer (Gloucester, MA: Peter Smith, 1958), 8–9, 13.

34. A complete analysis of the mystical aspects of Donne's sermons would need to survey the information available in Troy D. Reeves, *An Annotated Index to the Sermons of John Donne*, 3 vols. (Salzburg: Institut für Anglistik und Amerikanistik, 1979–81). The third volume of this index lists references to many mystical terms, such as "Contemplation" (p. 53), "Ecstasies" (p. 71), "Filiation" (p. 77),

"Knowledge of God" (p. 87), "Sight of God" (p. 87), "Image of God" (p. 107), "Love" (pp. 121–23), "Sabbath" (p. 177), "Temple" (pp. 206–7), "Transfiguration" (p. 209), and "Union" (pp. 215–16).

35. The sermon was delivered on Candlemas Day (Feb. 2), probably in 1626, and can be found in *Sermons* VII:325–48.

36. "Sermon Blessed are the Pure of Heart," VII:340. For another appearance of this theme, see the first of the eight sermons preached on Psalm 32, "Sermon on 'Blessed is he whose Transgression is Forgiven'" (*Sermons* IX:256).

37. This piece is in *Sermons* VIII:219–36.

38. Donne attacked the claims of medieval Catholic visionaries like Birgitta of Sweden, in his "Sermon on Ezekiel 34:19" (*Sermons* X:145-46).

39. "Sermon For 'Now We See through a Glasse Darkly,'" in *Sermons* VIII:229. At the end of the homily (VIII:235–36), Donne analyzes how the mutuality of knowing between God and the soul in heaven also produces joint loving: "And so it shall be a knowledge so like his knowledge, as it shall produce a love, like his love, and we shall love him, as he loves us. . . . I shall know him, that is, imbrace him, adhere to him."

40. "Sermon on Psalm 89:48" (*Sermons* II:210–11).

41. "Sermon on 1 Corinthians 13:12" (*Sermons* VIII:231–32).

42. "Sermon on Psalm 32:8" (*Sermons* IX:350–70).

43. "Sermon on Psalm 32:8" (*Sermons* IX:368–69).

44. A reference to deification citing 2 Peter 1:4 is found at the end of the "Sermon For Now We see through a Glasse Darkly" (*Sermons* VIII:236). For another reference, see "Sermon Christ the Light" for Christmas 1621, in Booty, *Selections from Divine Poems*, 127, 135–36.

45. "Sermon on Gal. 4:4–5, Preached on Christmas at St. Paul's, 1625" (*Sermons* VI:334–35).

46. On dying with Christ, see "Sermon on Acts 7:60," preached at Whitehall on February 29, 1627 (*Sermons* VIII:174–91).

47. "Sermon on Hosea 3:4" (*Sermons* VII:418).

48. Schwartz, *Sacramental Poetics*, 108.

49. "Sermon on Matthew 22:30" (*Sermons* VIII:94–95).

50. "Sermon on Isaiah 50:1" (*Sermons* VII:87–88). For more on the sacrality of marriage, see "Sermon on Deuteronomy 25:5" (*Sermons* VI:81–94).

51. For Donne, as for most Christians, the soul's marriage to Christ is always based on the marriage of Christ to the church, on which he preached a notable sermon on Ephesians 5:25–27 (*Sermons* V:113–29).

52. *Sermons* III: 252–53. For other appearances of the marriage of Christ to the soul, see *Sermons* IX:10 and 248, citing 1 Corinthians 6:17 with regard to our marriage with Christ.

53. *Sermons* III:313ff., esp. 320.

54. The *Devotions* feature meditations on the progress of his physical sickness and his eventual recovery seen as the mirror image of his internal illness of sin and its overcoming through surrender to God. See Anthony Rapsa, ed., *John Donne, Devotions Upon Emergent Occasions* (New York: Oxford University Press, 1987).

55. John Donne, *Essays in Divinity*, ed. Evelyn M. Simpson (Oxford: Clarendon, 1952).

56. *Essays in Divinity*, 96.

57. What follows is not an in-depth critical analysis of these poets, nor a treatment of the abundant literature on them. What I intend is only an overview pointing to what I detect to be mystical elements in some poems.

58. Cleanth Brooks, "Henry Vaughan: Quietism and Mysticism," in *Essays in Honor of Esmond Linworth Marilla,* ed. Thomas Austin Kirby and William John Olive, Louisiana State University Studies, Humanities Series 19 (Baton Rouge: Louisiana State University Press, 1970), 3–26; quotation from 26.

59. There is an extensive literature on the metaphysical poets and their contemporaries. An older account that pays attention to their religious aspects is Helen C. White, *The Metaphysical Poets: A Study in Religious Experience* (1936; repr., New York: Collier, 1962).

60. General discussions of the relation between mysticism and poetry include Henri Bremond, *Prayer and Poetry: A Contribution to Poetical Theory* (London: Burns, Oates & Washbourne, 1927); E. I. Watkin, *Poets and Mystics* (London: Sheed & Ward, 1953), esp. chapter 1; Jacques Maritain and Raïssa Maritain, *The Situation of Poetry* (New York: Philosophical Library, 1955), chapters 1–2. See also Alois M. Haas, "Mechthild von Magdeburg: Dichtung und Mystik," in Haas, *Sermo mysticus: Studien zu Theologie und Sprache der deutschen Mystik* (Freiburg, Schweiz: Universitätsverlag, 1979), 67–103.

61. There are reflections on the mystical nature of the metaphysical poets in Anthony Low, *Love's Architecture: Devotional Modes in Seventeenth-Century English Poetry* (New York: New York University Press, 1978), esp. 197–201, in relation to Henry Vaughan. As Low puts it, "At most, mystical poems are reflections or emanations of genuine mystical experience" (200).

62. Itrat Husain, *The Mystical Element in the Metaphysical Poets of the Seventeenth Century* (London: Oliver & Boyd, 1948), 171. For more in the same vein, see 164–65, 169, 188–92. Without falling into the autobiographical trap, Arthur L. Clements (*Poetry of Contemplation*) mounts an argument for Donne, Herbert, and Vaughan as mystical poets, but his theoretical framework using W. H. Auden's four types of vision (Auden, "Introduction," in *The Protestant Mystics,* ed. Anne Freemantle [London: Weidenfield & Nicolson, 1964]) seems artificially imposed on the poets.

63. In citing Donne's poems, I will generally use *The Complete Poetry and Selected Prose of John Donne & The Complete Poetry of William Blake,* with an introduction by Robert Silliman Hillyer (New York: Modern Library, 1941).

64. In "Love's Growth" (*Complete Poetry,* 21–22), Donne says that he is speaking from his own experience, condemning poets "which have no Mistresse but their Muse."

65. Guibbory, "Erotic Poetry," in *Cambridge Companion to John Donne,* 133–47; quotation from 143. Schwartz (*Sacramental Poetics,* 89) argues that, for Donne, "physical lovemaking recapitulates the union of God and man." Clements (*Poetry of Contemplation,* chap. 2) contends that Donne's poems "display many of the distinctive characteristics of contemplative experience as a Vision of Eros" (53). Donne's attitude toward sexual love is analyzed in Irving Singer, *The Nature of Love,* vol. 2, *Courtly and Romantic* (Chicago: University of Chicago Press, 1984), 195–205.

66. For the differences between Jewish and Christian mystical views of sexuality, see Bernard McGinn, "The Language of Love in Jewish and Christian

Mysticism," in *Mysticism and Language,* ed. Steven T. Katz (New York: Oxford University Press, 1992), 202–35.

67. Anthony Low contends, "Although Donne's ideal of secular love incorporates many of the qualities, feelings and attitudes of religion, it represents an early forerunner of 'natural supernaturalism,' which cannot lead spontaneously to sacred Christian love" ("John Donne, 'The Holy Ghost Is Amorous in His Metaphors,'" in *New Perspectives on the Seventeenth-Century English Religious Lyric,* ed. John R. Roberts [Columbia: University of Missouri Press, 1994], 212).

68. "Holy Sonnet XVII" in *Complete Poetry,* 242.

69. "The Extasie" (*Complete Poetry,* 34–36). For mystical readings of this poem, see Schwartz, *Sacramental Poetics,* 111–14; and esp. Clements, *Poetry of Contemplation,* 22–45, who summarizes: "Donne's poem in effect informs us that one may discover (or, better, re-discover) one's own Godlikeness through unitive knowledge of the immanent divinity of one's human beloved as well as through unitive knowledge of the transcendent divinity of God" (38).

70. "The Canonization" (*Complete Poetry,* 8–9). "The Relique" (*Complete Poetry,* 42–43) envisages the lovers buried together as miracle-working relics when disinterred in some future age. The male lover ends by saying, "All measure, and all language, I should passe, / Should I tell what a miracle she was." For a mystical reading of the poem, see Clements, *Poetry of Contemplation,* 45–53.

71. "The Good Morrow," and "The Sunne Rising" (*Complete Poetry,* 3 and 8).

72. "The Anniversary" (*Complete Poetry,* 15–16): "All other things to their destruction draw, / Only our love hath no decay; / This, no tomorrow hath, nor yesterday, / Running, it never runs from us away, / But truly keeps his first, last, everlasting day."

73. "To His Mistris Going to Bed" (*Complete Poetry,* 84–85).

74. For surveys of Donne's devotional writings, see Helen Wilcox, "Devotional Writings," in Guibbory, *Cambridge Companion to John Donne,* 149–65; and Booty, "Introduction," in *Selections from Divine Poems,* 11–72.

75. Low, "John Donne. 'The Holy Ghost Is Amorous in His Metaphors,'" 207. Low's essay (*New Perspectives on the Seventeenth-Century English Religious Lyric,* 201–21) roots the inner conflict of Donne's sacred poems in his difficulty surrendering his male sexual persona to become "the necessarily feminine and passive recipient of God's love" (e.g., 207, 210–11, 213, 215, 221).

76. Booty, "Intoduction," 35. Wilcox maintains that an "inseparable partnership of deep devotion and intense anxiety marks Donne's devotional writings" ("Devotional Writings," 151).

77. The standard edition is *John Donne, The Divine Poems,* edited with an introduction and commentary by Helen Gardner, 2nd ed. (Oxford: Clarendon, 1978). Gardner remarks, "No poet more needs or more repays commentary than Donne" (vii).

78. Clements finds the religious poems less mystical than the erotic verses, because he judges that they do not have much on the illuminative and unitive stages of the mystical path but remain at the level of purgation (*Poetry of Contemplation,* 69–75). This illustrates the dangers of applying mystical categories to Donne that he does not employ himself.

79. Martz, *Poetry of Meditation,* 20.

80. Gardner notes, "For the *Divine Poems* are poems of faith, not of vision. Donne goes by a road which is not lit by any flashes of ecstasy" ("Introduction," xxxiv–xxxv). The emphasis on faith is true, but mysticism need not always be ecstatic.

81. Sonnet 10 [14 in some enumerations], "Batter my Heart" (Gardner ed., 11). For a reading, see Barbara Newman, "Rereading John Donne's Holy Sonnet 14," *Spiritus* 4 (2004): 84–90.

82. Sonnet 11, "Wilt thou love God" (Gardner ed., 11). On making the soul a "temple of God," see also the sermon quoted in Husain, *Dogmatic and Mystical Theology*, 124.

83. On the body as the temple of God, see "Sermon on Luke 2:29–30," preached at St. Paul's on Christmas 1626 (*Sermons* VII:291–92): "And when my soule prayes without any voice, my very body is then a Temple: And God, who knows what I am doing in these actions, erecting these Temples, he comes to them, and prospers, and blesses my devotions."

84. Christ's birth in the soul is briefly noted in the same "Sermon on Luke 2:29–30" (*Sermons* VII:280) and is discussed at length in the Christmas Sermon in *Sermons* VI:334-45.

85. "Good Friday, 1613. Riding Westward" (Gardner ed., 31). For reflections on the mystical aspects of this poem, see Malcolm Guite, *Faith, Hope and Poetry: Theology and the Poetic Imagination* (Burlington, VT: Ashgate, 2010), 113–17.

86. "A Hymne to Christ, at the Authors last going into Germany" (Gardner ed., 49).

87. For his life, see John Drury, *Music at Midnight: The Life and Poetry of George Herbert* (Chicago: University of Chicago Press, 2011), who discusses Herbert's mysticism on 4, 11, 215, 244, and 335–36.

88. On the importance of Herbert's Anglicanism, see Ilona Bell, "'Setting Foot into Divinity': George Herbert and the English Reformation," in *Essential Articles for the Study of George Herbert's Poetry*, ed. John R. Roberts (Hamden, CT: Archon Books, 1979), 63–83.

89. Walton's *Life* (ed. Tobin), 310–11 (see n. 91 below).

90. The best edition with copious annotation is Helen Wilcox, ed., *The English Poems of George Herbert* (Cambridge: Cambridge University Press, 2007). There are accessible versions in John N. Wall Jr., ed., *The Country Parson, The Temple*, Classics of Western Spirituality (New York: Paulist Press, 1981), with an "Introduction" on Herbert's spirituality; and *George Herbert. The Complete English Poems*, ed. John Tobin (New York: Penguin Books, 1991).

91. Izaak Walton's *The Life of Mr. George Herbert* is available in Tobin, *George Herbert. The Complete English Poems*, 265–314.

92. Among the studies I have found useful, see White, *Metaphysical Poets*, chapters 6–7; T. S. Eliot, *George Herbert* in *British Writers and Their Work, No. 4* (Lincoln: University of Nebraska Press, 1964); Helen Vendler, *The Poetry of George Herbert* (Cambridge, MA: Harvard University Press, 1975); Clements, *Poetry of Contemplation*, chapter 3; Robert Whalen, *The Poetry of Immanence: Sacrament in Donne and Herbert* (Toronto: University of Toronto Press, 2002); and Schwartz, *Sacramental Poetics*, chapter 6. Also helpful are the essays in Roberts, *Essential Articles for the Study of George Herbert's Poetry*.

93. For a summary of these debates, see R. V. Young, "The Presence of Grace in Seventeenth-Century Poetry," in idem, *Doctrine and Devotion in Seventeenth-*

Century Poetry: Studies in Donne, Herbert, Crashaw, and Vaughan, Studies in Renaissance Literature 2 (Cambridge: D. S. Brewer, 2000), 1–80. See also Louis L. Martz, "The Poetry of Meditation: Searching the Memory," in Roberts, *New Perspectives on the Seventeenth-Century English Religious Lyric*, 188–200.

94. Rosemund Tuve, "George Herbert and *Caritas*," *Journal of the Warburg and Courtauld Institutes* 22 (1959): 303–31.

95. Presentations of the Protestant view include William Halewood, *The Poetry of Grace: Reformation Themes in English Seventeenth-Century Poetry* (New Haven: Yale University Press, 1970); Barbara Kiefer Lewalski, *Protestant Poetics and the Seventeenth-Century Religious Lyric* (Princeton: Princeton University Press, 1979); and Richard Strier, *Love Known: Theology and Experience in George Herbert's Poetry* (Chicago: University of Chicago Press, 1983).

96. Prominent among these is Stanley Fish, "Letting Go: The Dialectic of the Self in Herbert's Poetry," in idem, *Self-Consuming Artifacts: The Experience of Seventeenth-Century Literature* (Berkeley: University of California Press, 1972), 156–223.

97. Vendler, *Poetry of George Herbert*, 3: "Herbert's apparent simplicity is deceptive."

98. Eliot, *George Herbert*, 71.

99. The catechetical nature of *The Temple* is discussed by Stanley Fish, *The Living Temple: George Herbert and Catechizing* (Berkeley: University of California Press, 1978).

100. "The Dedication" (Wilcox ed., [44–46]).

101. Once popular, "The Church Porch" has not won favor among modern critics; see Richard Strier, "Sanctifying the Aristocracy: 'Devout Humanism' in François de Sales, John Donne, and George Herbert," *Journal of Religion* 69 (1989): 36–58.

102. "Superliminare" (Wilcox ed., [85–86]): "Thou, whom former precepts have / Sprinkled and taught how to behave / Thy self in church; approach and taste / The churches mysticall repast. / Avoid profanenesse; come, not here: / Nothing but holy, pure, and cleare, / Or that which groneth to be so, / May at his peril further go." The "mystical repast" would include not only the Eucharist but also the poetic collection itself.

103. On Herbert's use of the Bible, see Chana Bloch, *Spelling the Word: George Herbert and the Bible* (Berkeley: University of California Press, 1985). Herbert devotes two poems to the importance of scripture; see "The Holy Scriptures (I) and (II)" (Wilcox ed., [207–12]).

104. On the importance of Herbert's teaching on the incarnation, see Richard E. Hughes, "George Herbert and the Incarnation," in Roberts, *Essential Articles for the Study of George Herbert's Poetry*, 52–62; and Malcolm Guite, "A Second Glance: Transfigured Vision in the Poems of John Donne and George Herbert," in idem, *Faith, Hope and Poetry*, 103–24. On the role of the Eucharist in Herbert, see Whalen, *Poetry of Immanence*, esp. chapter 6; and Schwartz, *Sacramental Poetics*, chapter 6.

105. "The Altar" (Wilcox ed., [92–94]).

106. "The Sacrifice" (252 lines) can be found in Wilcox ed., [94–110].

107. These poems start with "The Agony," then turn to another response poem, "The Sinner," before moving on to "Good Friday" (possibly two poems),

"Redemption," "Sepulchre," "Easter" (possibly two poems), and "Easter Wings." A new sequence is then launched beginning with two poems on baptism.

108. Christ's passion has an essential role in Herbert; see Julia Gatta, "George Herbert's Poetry of Transformation," in *This Sacred History. Anglican Reflections for John Booty,* ed. Donald S. Armentrout (Cambridge, MA: Cowley, 1990), 31–46, who says, "It [the cross] is the instrument of union with Christ and thus of transformation into him" (39).

109. On the structure or lack thereof in "The Church," compare White, *Metaphysical Poets,* 158–60, with Wall, *Country Parson,* 43–47. See also the essays in "Section V. The Unity of *The Temple,*" in Roberts, *Essential Articles for the Study of George Herbert's Poetry,* 328–432.

110. Many commentators touch on the spiritual/mystical dimensions of *The Temple;* see Philip Sheldrake, *Love Took My Hand: The Spirituality of George Herbert* (London: Darton, Longman & Todd, 2000); and A. L. Clements, "Theme, Tone, and Tradition in George Herbert's Poetry," in Roberts, *Essential Articles for the Study of George Herbert's Poetry,* 33–51; and idem, *Poetry of Contemplation,* chapter 3. There are a number of articles on Herbert as mystic, e.g., Robert Boenig, "George Herbert and Mysticism," *Studia Mystica* 5 (1982): 64–72; and Franz Karl Wöhrer, "The 'Sense of Presence' as a Mode of Mystical Experience in the Mystographical Poems of George Herbert (1593–1633)," in *British Literature and Spirituality: Theoretical Approaches and Transdisciplinary Readings,* ed. Franz Karl Wöhrer and John S. Bak (Zurich: LIT, 2013), 1–30.

111. "Affliction (III)" (Wilcox ed., [265–66]).

112. "Easter" (Wilcox ed., [140]): "Can there be any day but this, / Though many sunnes to shine endeavour? / We count three hundred, but we misse: / There is but one, and that one ever."

113. This goes back as far as Plato's *Symposium* 210E.

114. White says, "Practically all English religious thought of the opening years of the seventeenth century begins in a devastating sense of sin" (*Metaphysical Poets,* 169).

115. "Artillerie" (Wilcox ed. [484–87]). For a detailed analysis of this poem, see Clements, *Poetry of Contemplation,* 84–91.

116. "The Reprisall" (Wilcox ed., [116–18]).

117. "The Crosse" (Wilcox ed., [562–66]).

118. For remarks on poems of suffering, see Vendler, *Poetry of George Herbert,* 238–45.

119. "Affliction (I)" (Wilcox ed., [160–68]). The final line is capable of several readings, perhaps the best is, "Do not let me love you in the future, if I do not love you now in this time of trouble and temptation."

120. "Affliction (II)" (Wilcox ed., [223–25]).

121. See "Affliction (IV)" and "Affliction (V)" (Wilcox ed., [327–29 and 349–52]).

122. A similar position of serenity in the face of the succession of experiences of "Killing and quick'ning, bringing down to hell / And up to heaven in an hour" is found in the poem "The Flower" (Wilcox ed., [566–70]).

123. "Bitter-sweet" (Wilcox ed., [587–88]).

124. On ineffability in *The Temple,* see Robert B. Shaw, "George Herbert: The Word of God and the Words of Man," in *Ineffability: Naming the Unnamable from*

Dante to Beckett, ed. Peter S. Hawkins and Anne Howland Schotter, AMS Ars Poetica 2 (New York: AMS Press, 1984), 81–93, who treats "Prayer (I)" on 85–86.

125. For "Prayer (I)" and a discussion, see Wilcox ed., [176–81]. See also Sheldrake, *Love Took My Hand*, 89–94. Other poems on prayer include "Prayer (II)" (Wilcox ed., [371–73]), and the three poems entitled "Praise" based on the psalms.

126. "Home" and Longing" are in Wilcox ed., [383–89 and 512–18].

127. "The Glance" (Wilcox ed., [588–91]).

128. Herbert's dialogue poems include brief conversations with God ("Artillerie," "The Collar," "Dialogue," "The Pilgrimage," "A True Hymn"), as well as dialogues with a Christlike "friend" ("Love unknown") and with death ("Dialogue Anthem").

129. "The Collar" (Wilcox ed., [524–29]) directly references the collar by which we are bound to God, either a "yoke of iron" for sinners (Deut. 28:48) or a mild yoke for followers of Christ (Matt. 11:29–30). But it also signifies "the caller," that is, both God and the speaker, and "choler," the angry state of the speaker.

130. "A true Hymne" (Wilcox ed., [574–78]).

131. "Dialogue" (Wilcox ed., [407–9]).

132. On the "mine-thine" poems, see Clements, *Poetry of Contemplation*, 106–10.

133. "The Quip" (Wilcox ed., [394–96]), and "Judgement" (Wilcox ed., [653–55]).

134. "The Holdfast" (Wilcox ed., [498–500]).

135. "The Flower" (Wilcox ed., [566–70]).

136. "The Clasping of Hands" (Wilcox ed., [539–41]).

137. "Love (III)" (Wilcox ed., [658–61]). I forbear from trying to list the many insightful expositions of this poem, but note D. J. Enright's remark: "a volume of theological commentary lies behind each short phrase" ("George Herbert and the Devotional Poets," in *From Donne to Marvell*, ed. Boris Ford, Pelican Guide to English Literature 3 [Baltimore: Penguin Books, 1956], 143).

138. On Herbert's "everyday mysticism," see Sheldrake, *Love Took My Hand*, 44; and White, *Metaphysical Poets*, 182, 185–88.

139. "Aaron" (Wilcox ed., [600–603]).

140. On the inward turn of the later metaphysicals, which has sometimes been blamed on the English Civil War, see Sheldrake, *Love Took My Hand*, 67; and Enright, "George Herbert and the Devotional Poets," 153.

141. Vaughan's writings are available in L. C. Martin, ed., *The Works of Henry Vaughan*, 2nd ed. (Oxford: Clarendon, 1957). There is a collection of essays in Alan Rudrum, ed., *Essential Articles for the Study of Henry Vaughan* (Hamden, CT: Archon Books, 1987).

142. Claude J. Summers argued that the poetry of Robert Herrick and Vaughan represents a form of "Anglican Survivalism"; see "Herrick, Vaughan, and the Poetry of Anglican Survivalism," in Roberts, *New Perspectives on the Seventeenth-Century English Religious Lyric*, 46–74.

143. I will cite the *Silex Scintillans* from the edition of French Fogle, ed., *The Complete Poetry of Henry Vaughan* (Garden City, NY: Anchor Books, 1964). The first edition of the work contained seventy-six poems; the second edition reprinted these and added forty-eight more. The second edition contains "The Author's PREFACE to the following HYMNS," in which Vaughan testifies to the influence

of "the blessed man, Mr. *George Herbert*," and speaks of the need for striving for holiness of life in composing his poems: "he that desires to excel in this kinde of *Hagiography*, or holy writing, must strive (by all means) for *perfection* and true *holiness*, that a *door may be opened to him in heaven*, Rev. 4.1, and then he will be able to write (with *Hierotheus* and the holy *Herbert*) a *true Hymn*" (Fogle ed., 260).

144. On the relation of Vaughan to Herbert, see Louis L. Martz, "Henry Vaughan: The Man Within," in Rudrum, *Essential Articles for the Study of Henry Vaughan*, 99–120.

145. Among the scholars who have argued for a mystical Vaughan are White, *Metaphysical Poets*, chapters 10–11; Husain, *Mystical Element in the Metaphysical Poets*, chapters 5–6; E. C. Pettet, *Of Paradise and Light: A Study of Vaughan's* Silex Scintillans (Cambridge: Cambridge University Press, 1960); R. A. Durr, *On the Mystical Poetry of Henry Vaughan* (Cambridge, MA: Harvard University Press, 1962); Brooks, "Henry Vaughan: Quietism and Mysticism," 4–5; Clements, *Poetry of Contemplation*, chapter 4; and Anthony Low, "Henry Vaughan: Journey into Light," in idem, *Love's Architecture*, 160–207.

146. Low, "Henry Vaughan: Journey to Light," 199.

147. Edmund Blunden, *On the Poems of Henry Vaughan: Characteristics and Intimations* (London: Richard Cobden-Sanderson, 1927), 45.

148. Durr, *On the Mystical Poetry of Henry Vaughan*, 135; see also xi–xv.

149. White, *Metaphysical Poets*, 284. On the character of Vaughan's "nature" poems, see Husain, *Mystical Element in the Metaphysical Poets*, 255–61; and Clements, *Poetry of Contemplation*, 154–60. See also M. M. Mahood, "Vaughan: The Symphony of Nature," in Rudrum, *Essential Articles for the Study of Henry Vaughan*, 5–45.

150. "The Tempest" (Fogle ed., 223). For other poems in this vein, see "The Constellation," "Morning Watch," "The Check," "The Starre," "Ascension-day," "The Bird," and "The Palm-tree." Vaughan's paraphrases of the psalms concentrate on those psalms in which nature is invoked to praise God (e.g., Pss. 65, 104, 121).

151. A good deal has been written on Vaughan's use of Hermetic imagery, but it is well not to overemphasize this dimension of his poetry. Hermetic motifs appear in such poems as "Affliction," "The Favour," "The Retreate," "Cock-Crowing," "Man," and so on.

152. For poems on childhood, see "Corruption," "The Retreat," and "Childhood."

153. Linda Ching Sledge, "Typology and the Ineffable: Henry Vaughan and the 'Word in Characters,'" in Hawkins and Schotter, *Ineffability*, 95–108.

154. The poems on doctrine include "Resurrection and Immortality," "Day of Judgement," "Man's Fall and Recovery," "The Incarnation and Passion," "Peace," "The Passion," "Praise," and so on.

155. "The Search" (Fogle ed., 151–53). See the analysis of this verse and the comparable "Vanity of Spirit" in Low, "Henry Vaughan: Journey into Light," 183–90.

156. "Regeneration" (Fogle ed., 139–42). There are expositions in Durr, *On the Mystical Poetry of Henry Vaughan*, 79–99; Pettet, *Of Paradise and Light*, 101–18; Clements, *Poetry of Contemplation*, 153–55; and Low, "Henry Vaughan: Journey into Light," 191–97.

157. For example, in "Vanity of Spirit" (Fogle ed., 168) the poet's interior search leads him to try to put together the "broken letters scarce remembered" of the inner self. This effort is ultimately not successful, so he resigns himself to God, once again expressing a desire to die: "*Since in these veyls my Ecclips'd Eye / May not approach thee, (for at night / Who can have commerce with the light?) / I'le disapparell, and to buy / But one half glaunce, most gladly dye.*"

158. "Christ's Nativity" (Fogle ed., 200).

159. On the divine seed and its implications, see Durr, *On the Mystical Poetry of Henry Vaughan*, 31–60.

160. "The dwelling-place" (Fogle ed., 315).

161. "Quickness" (Fogle ed., 344–45).

162. As in "The Holy Communion" (Fogle ed., 219): "After thy blood / (Our sov'rain good,) / Had clear'd our eies, / And given us sight; / Thou dost unto thy self betroth / Our souls, and bodies both / In everlasting light."

163. In "To the Holy Bible," lines 28–36 (Fogle ed., 348–49) Vaughan lists a series of the "secret favors of the Dove," including "Fruition, union, glory, life." "The Mutinie" expresses a prayer to be knit with God (Fogle ed., 234, lines 20–28).

164. "Ascension-day" (Fogle ed., 267–68), and "Ascension-Hymn" (269–70).

165. On the importance of light in Vaughan, see White, *Metaphysical Poets*, 282–83; Husain, *Mystical Element in the Metaphysical Poets*, 214–36; and Low, "Henry Vaughan: Journey into Light."

166. "The World" (Fogle ed., 231–33). There are many commentaries on this poem; see, e.g., Clements, *Poetry of Contemplation*, 164–65; Low, "Henry Vaughan: Journey into Light," 177–79; and James D. Simmonds, "Vaughan's Masterpiece and Its Critics: 'The World' Revaluated," *Studies in English Literature 1500–1900* 2 (1962): 82–93.

167. "They are all gone into the world of light!" (Fogle ed., 270–71). For a commentary, see Pettet, *Of Paradise and Light*, 155–65.

168. Prominent among these poems of light is the wonderful "Cock-crowing" (Fogle ed., 276–77), which space precludes discussing here.

169. "The Night" (Fogle ed., 323–25). Almost everyone who has written on Vaughan comments on this poem; e.g., Durr, *On the Mystical Poetry of Henry Vaughan*, 111–22; Pettet, *Of Paradise and Light*, 138–54; Clements, *Poetry of Contemplation*, 130–50; Low, "Henry Vaughan: Journey into Light," 201–5; Brooks, "Henry Vaughan: Quietism and Mysticism," 19–25; Sledge, "Typology and the Ineffable," 102–4. See also S. Sandbank, "Henry Vaughan's Apology for Darkness," *Studies in English Literature 1500–1900* 7 (1967): 141–52.

170. Although I do not agree with Sledge's relentlessly typological reading of the poem, I think her insight that "Night is . . . Christ himself" (104) is well taken.

171. Low puts this well: "Many critics also take 'some say' as a confession that Vaughan did not experience what he writes about. Rather it suggests the difficulty of finding language to express such experience in a poem. It is also, and especially, an appropriate gesture of humble self-effacement, to avoid hubris" ("Henry Vaughan: Journey into Light," 205).

172. The *Centuries of Meditation*, written in a notebook given to Traherne by a friend, is a spiritual commonplace book addressed to the giver. The *Third Century* tells the story of Traherne's spiritual pilgrimage and provides background to the poems. The *Fifth Century* contains only ten chapters, rather than a hundred. For

an appreciation of the *Centuries*, see Louis L. Martz, *The Paradise Within: Studies in Vaughan, Traherne, and Milton* (New Haven: Yale University Press, 1964), 33–102 ("II. Thomas Traherne: Confessions of Paradise").

173. The newer literature on Traherne's theology is extensive; see Elizabeth S. Dodd, *Boundless Innocence in Thomas Traherne's Poetic Theology* (Burlington, VT: Ashgate, 2015); and also Denise Inge, *Wanting Like a God: Desire and Freedom in Thomas Traherne* (London: SCM, 2009). For a survey of Traherne and his works, see the "Introduction" in Denise Inge, *Happiness and Holiness: Thomas Traherne and His Writings* (Norwich: Canterbury Press, 2008), 1–64.

174. A recent biographical sketch is Julia Smith, "Thomas Traherne," in *The Oxford Dictionary of National Biography*, 60 vols. (Oxford: Oxford University Press, 2004), 55:205–8; also Inge, *Happiness and Holiness*, 8–14.

175. The older edition of Traherne's works is H. C. Margoliouth, ed., *Thomas Traherne. Centuries, Poems, and Thanksgivings*, 2 vols. (Oxford: Clarendon, 1958). On the basis of new discoveries, there is an expanded edition now in progress; Jan Ross, ed., *The Works of Thomas Traherne*, 6 vols. (Cambridge: D. S. Brewer, 2005–), with 5 vols. published to 2015. I will generally cite from the more accessible version of Alan Bradford, ed., Thomas Traherne, *Selected Poems and Prose* (London: Penguin Books, 1991). For the *Centuries*, I use Thomas Traherne, *Centuries* (New York: Harper & Brothers, 1960).

176. For Traherne as a mystical poet, see White, *Metaphysical Poets*, chapters 12–13; Husain, "Thomas Traherne, The Mystical Philosopher," chapter 8 in *Mystical Element in the Metaphysical Poets*, 264–300; A. L. Clements, *The Mystical Poetry of Thomas Traherne* (Cambridge, MA: Harvard University Press, 1969); Anthony Low, "Thomas Traherne: Mystical Hedonist," chapter 9 in *Love's Architecture*, 259–93; and Alison J. Sherrington, *Mystical Symbolism in the Poetry of Thomas Traherne* (St. Lucia: Queensland University Press, 1970). Less happy with a mystical identification is Barbara Kiefer Lewalski, "Thomas Traherne: Naked Truth, Transparent Words, and the Renunciation of Metaphor," in *John Donne and the Seventeenth-Century Metaphysical Poets*, ed. Harold Bloom (New York: Chelsea House, 1986), 225–41.

177. White, *Metaphysical Poets*, 332–41, contains an evaluation of Traherne's poetry testifying to its many qualities, but also honest about his limitations as a poet, such as his "obsessed repetition of a relatively narrow range of themes" (332), and a "flatness of pitch and level" (334). See also Martz, *Paradise Within*, 80, 95.

178. Clements, *Mystical Poetry*, 53–55, 75–76.

179. On Rolle's Latin style, see McGinn, *Varieties*, 344–46.

180. Sherrington devotes seven chapters of *Mystical Symbolism* to Traherne's key symbols: senses, light, water, space, child, king, and marriage. Clements identifies Traherne's seven major symbols as eye, sphere, sun, mirror, king, dwelling place, and fountain (*Mystical Poetry*, chap. 2, 35–59). Other symbols include abyss, angel, bride, friend, and vine. Dodd surveys a series of sacramental images of innocence (*Boundless Innocence*, 171–89).

181. See Clements, *Mystical Poetry*, 7–8, 61–62; seconded by Low, "Thomas Traherne," 267.

182. As quoted in Sherrington, *Mystical Symbolism*, vi. There is an edition of this work by Julia Smith, *Thomas Traherne, Select Meditations* (Manchester: Carcanet Press, 1997). (Not available to me.)

183. As Dodd has shown in her *Boundless Innocence,* the complex notion of "innocence" is a key to Traherne's thought. Rather than a simple return to paradisiacal perfection, Dodd argues that innocence is present in all the stages of salvation history as "a quality of the regenerate Christian life which is an object of celebration and lament, duty and desire, memory and imagination" (193).

184. Clements, *Mystical Poetry,* notes passages in Traherne that seem to be close to Eckhart, but many are not convincing. From a comparative perspective, James Charlton, *Non-Dualism in Eckhart, Julian of Norwich, and Traherne: A Theopoetic Reflection* (New York: Bloomsbury, 2013), puts Traherne (chap. 1) in conversation with Eckhart, Julian, and aspects of Eastern nondualism.

185. In the poem "The Author to the Critical Peruser," prefacing the Felicity collection, Traherne summarizes his literary approach, saying he will use "transparent words," without "curling metaphors," "to th'end thy soul might see / With open eyes the great felicity . . ." (Bradford ed., 79).

186. For a survey of Traherne's sources, see Inge, *Happiness and Holiness,* 15–18.

187. *Centuries* IV.74–78 (ed., 203–7) contains a partial translation of Pico's *Oration on the Dignity of Man.* References to the *Centuries* will be by book and section (e.g., IV.1).

188. Clements, *Mystical Poetry,* 61–62, 66, 153–54.

189. White, *Metaphysical Poets,* 298, 335; also Low, "Thomas Traherne," 261. In the *Centuries* III.1, Traherne emphasizes his own experience. Speaking of the "pure and virgin apprehensions" which he enjoyed in infancy and has now regained, he says, "They are unattainable by book, and therefore I will teach them by experience" (ed., 109; see also I.3 and III.3).

190. *Centuries* III.43 (ed., 133).

191. The "four estates paradigm" is emphasized in Dodd's analysis of innocence in *Boundless Innocence.*

192. Clements (*Mystical Poetry,* 61–62) divides the Dobell folio poems into three sections designated as (1) Innocence ("The Salutation" to "The Preparative"), (2) Fall ("Instruction" to "Speed"), and (3) Redemption ("The Designe" to "Goodnesse"). Lewalski ("Thomas Traherne," 227–37) uses a different three-stage meditative pattern: (1) the innocent infant, (2) the felicity proper to adults, and (3) the turn to active charity.

193. The fact that the liturgy is absent in much of the better-known poetry is offset by the liturgical meditations and prayers Traherne wrote in the manner of Lancelot Andrewes; see Jan Ross, ed., *The Works of Thomas Traherne,* vol. 4, *The Church's Year Book, Meditations and Devotions from the Resurrection to All Saints' Day* (Cambridge: D. S. Brewer, 2009).

194. *Centuries* V.2 (ed., 223). The discussion of infinity at the beginning of *Centuries* V is set up by the list of ten "strange and wonderful" infinite things given in IV.100 (ed., 219).

195. *Centuries* I.22 (ed., 11): "It is of the nobility of man's soul that he is insatiable." See also the poems "Insatiableness I and II" (Brandon ed., 146–48).

196. *Centuries* V.3 (ed., 224).

197. On the superiority of infinity of value over quantitative infinity, see *Centuries* III.21 and the poem "As in a clock" (Brandon ed., 157).

198. *Centuries* II.80–81 (ed., 94). The notion of man as an infinite sphere in a center, often found in Traherne, goes back to the characterization of God as the

infinite sphere whose center is everywhere and whose circumference is nowhere, first found in the Hermetic *Liber XXIV Philosophorum*, Axiom 2. For Traherne, the infinite sphere symbol is used of both God and the soul, as he says in "Silence": "For so my spirit was an endless sphere, / Like God Himself, and Heaven and Earth was there" (Brandon ed., 25). For the origin and background of the *Liber*, see McGinn, *Harvest*, 42–45.

199. "The Anticipation" (lines 70–71): "O what a wonderful profound abyss / Is God!" (Brandon ed., 52), while in "My Spirit" (lines 77–79), the soul is also an abyss: "A strange mysterious sphere! / A deep abyss / That sees and is / The only proper place of heavenly bliss" (Brandon ed., 28). In "Misapprehension," stanza 5 (Brandon ed., 118), the "great abyss" of the world exists within the speaker: "Of it I am th'inclusive sphere."

200. "The Preparative" (lines 15–16; Brandon ed., 11). See also "An Infant-Eye" (Brandon ed., 80–82).

201. "Goodness" (lines 5, 39–41; Brandon ed., 73–74). God's goodness is also emphasized in the *Centuries*, such as in III.16, 23, 31, 42, 53, and 99.

202. *Centuries* V.10 (ed., 228). See also *Centuries* III.63; "The Spirit," stanza 2 (Brandon ed., 26); and "The Anticipation," which says, "His essence is all act: He did, that He / All act might always be" (Brandon ed., 53).

203. God's infinite love is often discussed in the prose works; for example, *Centuries* II.39–70 (ed., 76–89) features a long discussion of the Trinitarian nature of love, as well as the passage from *The Kingdom of God*, chapter 32, given in Inge, *Holiness and Happiness*, 182–83. See also *Centuries* IV.28, 61, 66. Dodd summarizes: "The attempt to persuade the reader to love is a key feature of Traherne's theology and his poetics" (*Boundless Innocence*, 82; see also 75, 80–81).

204. "The Circulation" (lines 71–79; Brandon ed., 45–46). Other poems that discuss the circulation of love between God and man include "The Estate," "Amendment," "The Demonstration," "The Recovery," and "Another."

205. "The Demonstration," stanzas 5 and 8 (Brandon ed., 49–50).

206. *Centuries* III.39 (ed., 130).

207. "The Recovery," stanza 1 (Brandon ed., 54–55).

208. Dodd notes that the theological category of hope is perhaps more appropriate than the generic "optimism" often used to characterize Traherne's vision of the world (*Boundless Innocence*, 14, 191–92, 199).

209. For the preexistence of all things in the mind of God, see "Felicity," stanza 2 (Brandon ed., 85), and *Centuries* III.68 (ed., 146).

210. This teaching, fundamental to Traherne, can be found in *Centuries* III.7–9, 11, 30, 31, 51, and 53.

211. *Centuries* I.25–31 (ed., 13–15; quotation from chap. 31).

212. On humans as made in the image of God, see "The Bible" and "The Image" (Brandon ed. 103, 125) and numerous texts in the *Centuries*, such as I.67, 74; II.6, 68; III.13, 58–59, 61, and 74. Man as the "mirror of eternity," something also found in the Cambridge Platonists, appears in *Centuries* I.19, IV.81, as well as in a number of poems (e.g., "The Preparative," "Thoughts IV," "Sight," etc.).

213. Chapter 14 in the *Kingdom of God* is entitled "More Easily cease to live than Love" and is discussed in Inge, *Happiness and Holiness*, 181–82.

214. Love is one of the most frequent words in Traherne's vocabulary and is closely related to terms like goodness, bliss, felicity, joy, pleasure, and the like.

Along with "Love" (Brandon ed., 58–60), see "The Odour" in the Felicity collection (Brandon ed., 118–20).

215. There is a treatment in Sherrington, *Mystical Symbolism*, chapter 1, "The Senses," 7–28.

216. Ricoeur's notion of "second naïveté" is invoked by Dodd and others as a way of characterizing Traherne's thought.

217. The four "Thoughts" poems can be found in the Bradford ed., 60–62, 63–65, 66–68, and 70–73; quotation from 71.

218. "The Person," and "The Estate" can be found in the Bradford ed., 38–42.

219. "The Odour" (Bradford ed., 118–20). Traherne's "Thanksgivings for the Body," lines 427–63, a prose-poem imitation of the Psalms, emphasizes how both body and soul must necessarily share in the felicity of heaven (Bradford ed., 180–81).

220. Jones, *Spiritual Reformers in the 16th and 17th Centuries*, 327. For a discussion of the infancy poems, see chapter 3, "Innocence," in Clements, *Mystical Poetry*, 61–95.

221. The first five poems of Dobell's collection are "The Salutation," "Wonder," "Eden," "Innocence," and "The Preparative." See also "The Rapture," "Dumbness," "Silence," "Nature," and "Speed." The full title of the poems edited by Philip Traherne is *Poems of Felicity: Divine Reflections on the Native Objects of an Infant-Eye*. It includes a number of poems on infancy, such as "An Infant-Eye," "The Return," "Adam," "Apostasy," "Right Apprehension," "Sight," and "The City." See also *Centuries* III.1–5 and 11.

222. "Wonder" (Bradford ed., 4).

223. Becoming a child again is, of course, based on John 3:3, which Traherne actually cites in *Centuries* III.68. Traherne's treatment of this theme is anything but simple; see Dodd, *Boundless Innocence*, 158–60, 172–76.

224. "The Preparative" (Bradford ed., 10–12). The title may refer to the poem as preparing for the following pieces in the collection; see Clements, *Mystical Poetry*, 66–94.

225. "Dumbness" and "Silence" can be found in the Bradford ed., 21–25.

226. "Adam," and "Mankind is sick" (Bradford ed., 86, 158). Perhaps Traherne's strongest attack on sin is in the poem beginning, "Sin! / O only fatal woe," found in *Centuries* III.49 (ed., 136–37).

227. Among those who argue that Traherne has an orthodox, if attenuated, doctrine of original sin, see Clements, *Mystical Poetry*, 86–89; and Patrick Grant, "Original Sin and the Fall of Man in Thomas Traherne," *Journal of English Literary History* 38 (1971): 40–61.

228. "Apostasy" (Bradford ed., 92–93).

229. *Centuries* III.8 (ed., 114). It is difficult to square Traherne's views here with Article 9 of the *Thirty-Nine Articles*: "Original sin standeth not in the following of Adam (as the Pelagians do vainly talk), but is the fault and corruption of the nature of every man that is naturally engendered of the offspring of Adam."

230. Inge discusses sin in Traherne (*Happiness and Holiness*, 144–48). There is a more detailed account in Dodd, *Boundless Innocence*, chapter 3, who argues, on the basis of the theological writings, that sin is ultimately a failure to love (76–78).

231. "Dissatisfaction," stanza 6 (Bradford ed., 102). Traherne also speaks of his dissatisfaction at Oxford in *Centuries* III.36–45.

232. "The Bible" (Bradford ed., 103). The importance of scripture also appears in *Centuries* III.27–29, 32–35, 66, in the paraphrases of the Psalms found in 71–94, and in many of the recently discovered works.

233. "Thoughts IV" (lines 71–78; Bradford ed., 72). Inge (*Happiness and Holiness*, 174–75) includes another poem on redemptive salvation, "O Jesu God, whose own Dear Blood," from *The Kingdom of God*, chapter 11.

234. On redemption, see *Centuries* I.5 and 53. For the role of the cross and the redeeming blood of Christ, see I.53, 58–64, 75–77, 80, and 86–90. Redemption and the cross are also present in later *Centuries*; see, e.g., II.34; III.54; and IV.8. For discussions of Traherne's Christology, see Martz, *Paradise Within*, 63–67; and Dodd, *Boundless Innocence*, 120–24.

235. "My Spirit" can be found in the Bradford ed., 25–29, with comments on 324–26. For expositions, see Clements, *Mystical Poetry*, 115–34; and White, *Metaphysical Poets*, 320–21.

236. This stanza has been the subject of speculation about whether Traherne was anticipating Bishop Berkeley's Idealism, but this does not seem likely, because Traherne does not reject the independent existence of the world.

237. Other poems that speak of union with God do not always stress the language of identity so strongly; see, e.g., "Rise, noble soul," stanza 4; "Silence," lines 67–74; and "Love," stanza 4 (Bradford ed., 165–66, 25, 59–60). See also *Centuries* III.99–100 (ed., 277–78). Traherne speaks of the union and indwelling of Christ and the Holy Spirit in the soul in *Centuries* II.28, and even of an "infinite union" and "perfect indwelling" in IV.100 (ed., 180, 219).

238. For more on divinization, see "Ease" (Bradford ed., 33–34), as well as *Centuries* I.41 and IV.70–72 (ed., 20, 201–3).

239. On the soul as the bride of Christ and the use of biblical erotic language, see "The Design," stanzas 6–7; "The Recovery," stanza 4; and "Love," stanza 4 (Bradford ed., 37, 55–56, 59–60), as well as a number of texts from the prose works, such as *The Kingdom of God*, chapter 42 (Inge, *Happiness and Holiness*, 225–27).

240. For the debate over Traherne's solipsism, contrast White, *Metaphysical Poets*, who speaks of his "persistent solipsism" (300), and Clements, *Mystical Poetry*, 73–74, who argues against this view.

241. "Goodness" (Bradford ed. 73–75).

242. "Bells" (Bradford ed., 111–14). See also *Centuries* I.30 and 63 (ed., 14–15, 31).

243. For a survey of Puritanism, see John Coffey and Paul C. H. Lim, eds., *The Cambridge Companion to Puritanism* (Cambridge: Cambridge University Press, 2008).

244. Dewey D. Wallace Jr. notes: "The erotic motifs drawn from Canticles had with Protestant writers a special aspect not missed by the Puritans: married sexuality was an image of the mystical life which was not only a type or an allegory but also an experienced example of 'the improving of the creatures,' a phrase used by Puritan devotional writers to describe the finding of spiritual meanings in everyday life" (*Shapers of English Calvinism, 1660–1714: Variety, Persistence, and Transformation*, Oxford Studies in Historical Theology [Oxford and New York: Oxford University Press, 2011], 67). On Puritan sexual language, see Belden C. Lane, *Ravished by Beauty: The Surprising Legacy of Reformed Spirituality* (Oxford and New

York: Oxford University Press, 2011), 141–45. Other authors contest this, arguing that, for the Puritans, the relation between the human and the mystical marriages centered not so much on love language as on marriage as a contractual bond and the patriarchal relation of husband and wife. See Erica Longfellow, *Women and Religious Writing in Early Modern England* (Cambridge: Cambridge University Press, 2004), chapter 1, "'Blockish Adams' on Mystical Marriage'" (18–58).

245. There is a sketch in Patrick Collinson, "Puritans," *Oxford Encyclopedia,* 3:364–70, who warns, "*Puritans* was never a term of ecclesiological or confessional precision" (364). On the problem of defining Puritanism, see Randall J. Pederson, *Unity in Diversity: English Puritans and the Puritan Reformation, 1603–1689,* Brill's Series in Church History 68 (Leiden: Brill, 2014), chapter 7.

246. On Puritan spirituality in general, see Brian G. Armstrong, "Puritan Spirituality: The Tension of Bible and Experience," in *The Spirituality of Western Christendom,* vol. 2, *The Roots of the Modern Christian Tradition,* ed. E. Rozanne Elder, Cistercian Studies 55 (Kalamazoo, MI: Cistercian Publications, 1984), 229–48; Gordon S. Wakefield, "The Puritans," in *The Study of Spirituality,* ed. Cheslyn Jones, Geoffrey Wainwright, and Edward Yarnold, S.J. (New York and Oxford: Oxford University Press, 1986), 437–45; Glenn Hinson, "Puritan Spirituality," in Senn, *Protestant Spiritual Traditions,* 165–82; Richard C. Lovelace, "Puritan Spirituality I, The Anatomy of Puritan Piety: English Puritan Devotional Literature," in *Christian Spirituality III: Post-Reformation and Modern,* ed. Louis Dupré and Don E. Saliers, in collaboration with John Meyendorff, World Spirituality 18 (New York: Crossroad, 1989), 294–323; and Charles Hambrick-Stowe, "Practical Divinity and Spirituality," in Coffey and Lim, *Cambridge Companion to Puritanism,* 191–205. More extensive studies include G. F. Nuttall, *The Holy Spirit in Puritan Faith and Experience,* 2nd ed. (Chicago: University of Chicago Press, 1992); Gordon S. Wakefield, *Puritan Devotion: Its Place in the Development of Christian Piety* (London: Epworth, 1957); and Tom Schwanda, *Soul Recreation: The Contemplative-Mystical Piety of Puritanism* (Eugene, OR: Wipf & Stock, 2012). Articles on Puritan mysticism include Winthrop S. Hudson, "Mystical Religion in the Puritan Commonwealth," *Journal of Religion* 28 (1948): 51–56; Jerald Brauer, "Puritan Mysticism and the Development of Liberalism," *Church History* 19 (1950): 151–70; idem, "Types of Puritan Piety," *Church History* 56 (1987): 39–59; and Geoffrey F. Nuttall, "Puritan and Quaker Mysticism," *Theology* 78 (1975): 518–31.

247. Charles Lloyd Cohen, *God's Caress: The Psychology of Puritan Religious Experience* (New York and Oxford: Oxford University Press, 1986), 4. See esp. his "Epilogue" (271–74) on the function of conversion in the Puritan worldview.

248. Nuttall shows how "the doctrine of the Holy Spirit controlled their [i.e., the Puritans'] devotional life" (*Holy Spirit in Puritan Faith,* 134).

249. On the importance of sermons, see Lovelace, "Puritan Spirituality I," 299–302; Hambrick-Stowe, "Practical Divinity and Spirituality," 195–96; and especially Cohen, *God's Caress,* chapter 6, "Echoes of the Preacher's Call," 162–200.

250. For a sketch of Ames, see Hambrick-Stowe, "Practical Divinity and Spirituality," 192–93.

251. Brauer, "Puritan Mysticism," 152–53. Brauer lists six Puritan mystics of the seventeenth century: Francis Rous, Peter Sterry, Walter Cradock, Morgan Llwyd, John Everard, and Giles Randall (152). Hudson distinguishes between "pietistic" and "legalistic" traditions of Puritan mysticism ("Mystical Religion in

the Puritan Commonwealth"). On the historiography of Puritan mysticism, see Schwanda, "Defining Puritan Mysticism," in idem, *Soul Recreation*, 11–20.

252. Nuttall treats the two phenomena together but makes important distinctions between them ("Puritan and Quaker Mysticism").

253. Elizabeth Allen, "Everard, John (1584?–1640/41)," in *Oxford Dictionary of National Biography*, 18:782–84. There is a brief summary in Jones, *Spiritual Reformers of the 16th and 17th Centuries*, 239–52; the best account is David R. Como, *Blown by the Spirit: Puritanism and the Emergence of an Antinomian Underground in Pre-Civil-War England* (Stanford: Stanford University Press, 2004), chapter. 7.

254. On Everard's mystical sources, see Como, *Blown by the Spirit*, 225–28.

255. As cited in Como, *Blown by the Spirit*, 252. The previous five steps are (1) condemnation of our wickedness, (2) annihilation of our selves, (3) forsaking the things of the world, (4) indifference to all things, and (5) conformity to Christ.

256. Cited in Como, *Blown by the Spirit*, 263.

257. Contrary to what is often thought, Reformed thinkers studied the Song of Songs and almost universally (Sebastian Castellio was an exception) interpreted it in what we would call an allegorical way. For an introduction, see George L. Scheper, "Reformation Attitudes toward Allegory and the Song of Song," *Publications of the Modern Language Association of America* 89 (1974): 551–62. Puritan uses of the theme of spiritual marriage are treated in Schwanda, *Soul Recreation*, 54–64.

258. Puritan commentaries on the Song of Songs include George Gifford, *Fifteen Sermons upon the Song of Solomon* (1598); Thomas Brightman (d. 1607, although his Latin commentary did not appear in English until 1644); Joseph Hall, *Solomon's divine arts* (1609); Henry Finch, *An exposition of the Song of Solomon* (1615); Henry Ainsworth, *Solomon's Song of songs in English metre* (1623); Francis Quarles, *Sions sonnets sung by Solomon the king* (1627); Richard Sibbes, *Bowels Opened* (1639); John Cotton, *A brief exposition of the whole book of Canticles* (1642); John Collinges, *The spouses hidden glory* (1646); Edmund Hall, *Manus testium movens* (1651); John Robotham, *An exposition of the whole book of Solomon's Song* (1652); William Guild, *Loves entercourse between the Lamb and his bride* (1658); and James Dunham, *Clavis Cantici* (1668). Not all of these commentaries were mystical. For a discussion of some seventeenth-century religious writers on the Song, see Longfellow, "'Blockish Adams' on Mystical Marriage," chapter 1 in eadem, *Women and Religious Writing*, 18–58. On the political use of the Song, see Elizabeth Clarke, *Politics, Religion and the Songs of Songs in Seventeenth-Century England* (London: Palgrave Macmillan, 2011).

259. Puritan treatises on union with Christ include James Baillie, *Spiritual Marriage, the union between Christ and the Church* (1627); Francis Rous, *The Mystical Marriage* (1631); Thomas Hooker, *The Soul's Exaltation* (1638); Benjamin King, *The Marriage of the Lamb* (1640); Joseph Hall, *Christ mystical* (1647); Thomas Goodwin, *The Heart of Christ* (1651); Isaac Ambrose, *Media* (1650), and *Looking unto Jesus* (1658); John Brinsley, *Mystical Implantation* (1652); Thomas Watson, *Christs loveliness* (1657); John Owen, *Of Communion with God the Father, Sonne, and Holy Ghost* (1657); Rowland Stedman, *The Mystical Union of Believers with Christ* (1668); Edward Pearse, *The Best Match* (1673); Edward Polhill, *Christus in Corde* (1680); and Thomas Lye, *The True Believers Union with Christ Jesus* (ca. 1685).

260. Mark E. Dever, "Sibbes, Richard (1577?–1635)," in *Oxford Dictionary of*

National Biography, 50:486–88. More detail can be found in Dever, *Richard Sibbes: Puritanism and Calvinism in Late Elizabethan and Early Stuart England* (Macon, GA: Mercer University Press, 2000).

261. Alexander B. Grosart, ed., *Works of Richard Sibbes*, 7 vols. (1862–64; repr., Carlisle, PA: Banner of Truth Trust, 1983).

262. *Bowels Opened; or, Expository Sermons on Canticles IV.16, V. VI*, in Grosart, *Works of Richard Sibbes*, 2:2–195. The title comes from Song of Songs 5:4, "My bowels were moved. . . ." The same volume includes two sermons preached on Song of Songs 1:2 under the title *The Spouse, her Earnest Desire after Christ* (2:197–208). Longfellow discusses Sibbes's commentary in *Women and Religious Writing*, 41–47.

263. *Bowels Opened*, Sermon XX (ed., 188).

264. *Bowels Opened*, Sermon II (ed., 22-24).

265. Examples of political readings can be found in Sermon III (ed., 43–45) on the bride's sleep (Song 5:2), and the reading of the "watchmen" of Song 5:6–7 in Sermon XI (ed., 118–19). On the political dimensions, see Longfellow, *Women and Religious Writing*; as well as Clarke, *Politics, Religion, and the Song of Songs*, 62–65.

266. *Bowels Opened*, Sermon VII (ed., 81): "Then, because the church is Christ mystical, it is near to him; and, in a manner, as near as that sacred body of his, both making up one Christ mystical" (see also 135, 154).

267. *Bowels Opened*, Sermon I (ed., 7).

268. *Bowels Opened*, Sermon V (ed., 58). For more on our marriage to Christ, see the extended discussion in Sermon XV on why all things are ours because of our marriage to Christ who is Lord of all (ed., 142–45). At times Sibbes speaks of this marriage as one of friendship with Christ (e.g., Sermon VI, ed., 70).

269. *Bowels Opened*, Sermon I (ed., 6). There is a longer defense of the divine condescension in using earthly marriage to describe spiritual marriage in *The Spouse* (ed., 200).

270. *Bowels Opened*, Sermon XVIII (ed., 164). For other appeals to the need for personal experience, see, e.g., 55, 105, 107, 117, 167, 172, and 185.

271. Tasting the "sweetness" of the Lord is a frequent motif; see, e.g., Sermon I (ed., 22), as well as 33–34, 107, 164, etc.

272. *Bowels Opened*, Sermon II (ed., 23): "True riches are the heavenly graces; true nobility is to be born of God, to be the sister and spouse of Christ; true pleasures are those of the Spirit, which endure for ever, and will stand by us when all comforts fail. That mystical union and sweet communion is set down with such variety of expression, to shew *that whatsoever is scattered in the creature severally is in him entirely*." References to union and communion are frequent; see, e.g., 77, 102, 135, 161, 173–74, 177, 193, etc.

273. *Bowels Opened*, Sermon XI (ed., 117), and Sermon XII (ed., 126).

274. This is how Sibbes interprets the withdrawal of the Bridegroom in Song 5:6 in Sermons IX–XI (ed., 100–121), as well as the brief treatment of Song 3:1–4 in Sermon XIX (ed., 172–73).

275. Sibbes discusses seven aspects of the mutuality between Christ and the soul: mutual propriety, mutual love, mutual familiarity, mutual likeness, mutual care, mutual complacency, and the courage that goes with it (Sermon XIX, ed., 174–76).

276. I will use Rous, *The Mysticall Marriage: Experimental Discoveries of the heavenly Marriage betweene a Soule and her Saviour* (London: William Jones, 1631).

277. On Rous and his mysticism, see Jerald C. Brauer, "Francis Rous, Puritan Mystic, 1579-1659: An Introduction to the Study of the Mystical Element in Puritanism" (PhD diss., University of Chicago, 1948); Longfellow, *Women and Religious Writing*, 47–50; Clarke, *Politics, Religion, and the Song of Songs*, 50–60; and Pederson, *Unity in Diversity*, chapter 4, "Francis Rous," 153–209.

278. For a discussion of Rous's writings, see Pederson, *Unity in Diversity*, 178–95.

279. *The Heavenly Academy* describes a four-step mystical ladder to the heavenly learning of the School of Christ (see Pederson, *Unity in Diversity*, 186–89). The first step is to desire God; the second is to deny human "wit and wisdom" and all self-reliance. In the third step we attain conformity with God in the friendship and "marriage-love" between God and the soul. The fourth is "conversing with God, and diligent coming to his School."

280. Brauer, "Francis Rous," 48. Clarke comments, "What Rous has done is to reconceptualise the entire Gospel in terms of the marriage between Christ and the soul" (*Politics, Religion, and the Song of Songs*, 54).

281. Pederson discusses Rous's sources in *Unity in Diversity*, 157, 160, 169, 182, and 189–90.

282. For a survey of Rous's theology, Pederson, *Unity in Diversity*, 195–208.

283. Rous's desire to have his book included among the works on "mystical and experiential Divinity" is found in his preface (ed., A4r). For the appeal for personal experience, see, e.g., 52–53, 85–86, the whole of chapter VII, and 271–72.

284. *The Mystical Marriage*, chapter I (ed., 12–13): "And accordingly fasten on him, not thine Eye only, but thy mightiest love, and hottest affections. Looke on him so, that thou mayest lust after him, for here it is a sin, not to look that thou mayest lust, and not to lust having looked" (see also 272). Strong erotic language is found throughout *The Mystical Marriage*, such as the appeal to "inebriating sweetnesse," "extasie and ravishment," and "a kind of excesse" in chapter III (ed., 48–49; cf. 140, 173–74, 320, 329–30, and 346). Chapter V (ed., 113–14) makes much of the kisses and embraces featured in the Song of Songs, while chapter VI (ed., 174–75) speaks of the whispering of mysteries by the Bridegroom to his beloved on the bed of love, and later advises the soul: "If thou want any thing now ask it, for in these heates of love, thy husband will deny thee nothing" (ed., 184).

285. *The Mystical Marriage*, chapter III (ed., 54–55).

286. The stress on *imago dei* anthropology in the text connects Rous to important mystical traditions; see *The Mystical Marriage*, 26–28, 59, 256–57, 259, 265, 324–25. Rous uses another anthropological mystical theme when he speaks of the soul as the temple of God (e.g., ed., A2v, 179, and 186).

287. The contrast between the old marriage and the new marriage is set out especially in chapter II (ed., 17–42) and in chapter VIII (ed., 280–87). On the heavenly marriage, see 224–25 and 344–51.

288. Rous discusses six reasons why the desertions are profitable: (1) By present desertions we learn how to prevent desertions in the future. (2) Desertions help us to realize how we may have offended Christ. (3) Desertions prevent pride. (4) A husband must try the truth of a bride's love. (5) Desertions teach patience. And (6) desertions and desolations draw our attention from earth to heaven.

289. *The Mystical Marriage*, chapter IX (ed., 324–25). The passage I have in mind is John of the Cross, *Spiritual Canticle*, stanza 36.5.

290. Schwanda, *Soul Recreation*; see also Schwanda, "'Hearts Sweetly Refreshed': Puritan Spiritual Practices Then and Now," *Journal of Spiritual Formation and Soul Care* 3 (2010): 21–41.

291. Isaac Ambrose, *Looking unto Jesus, as Carrying on the Great Work of Man's Salvation, or a View of the Everlasting Gospel* in *Works of Isaac Ambrose* (repr., London: Forgotten Books, 2015). This is a photomechanical reprint of the 1815 abridgment by Rev. Robert Cox.

292. Ambrose, *Media* (1650), 71, as quoted in Schwanda, *Soul Recreation*, 178.

293. Ambrose, *Media* (1650), 74, cited in Schwanda, 84, who collects a number of similar passages.

294. Ambrose, *Media* (1650), 265; see Schwanda, 147 (see also 70).

295. Ambrose, *Media* (1657), 183. Schwanda discusses Ambrose's language of excess, noting that ravishment appears over ninety times in his writings ("The Rhetoric of Ravishment: The Language of Delight and Enjoyment," chapter 5 in *Soul Recreation*, 163–96, esp. 177n81).

296. Ambrose, *Ultima* (1657), 221, as cited in Schwanda, 194.

297. See Gordon Rupp, "A Devotion of Rapture in English Puritanism," in *Reformation Conformity and Dissent: Essays in Honour of Geoffrey Nuttall*, ed. R. Buick Knox (London: Epworth, 1977), 115-31, who does not, however, mention Ambrose.

298. *Looking unto Jesus* II, Explanation (ed., 6).

299. *Looking unto Jesus* II, 6 (ed., 12).

300. On the need for growing conformity with Christ, see *Looking unto Jesus*, 124, 133-35, 180-83, 224-27, etc. Ambrose also incorporates our growing ravishment over the gifts given us through Christ's life and death (e.g., 175-77).

301. *Looking unto Jesus*, book VIII (ed., 245–46).

302. *Looking unto Jesus*, book VIII.ii.4 (ed., 250).

303. David Parnham, *Sir Henry Vane, Theologian: A Study in Seventeenth-Century Religious and Political Discourse* (Madison, NJ: Teaneck University Press, 1997). On Vane's mysticism, see Parnham, chapter 3, "Approaches to Theological Utterance," esp. 71, 76, 84-91, and 100-102. See also W. Clark Gilpin, "Sir Henry Vane: Mystical Piety in the Puritan Revolution," in *Death, Ecstasy, and Otherworldly Journeys*, ed. John J. Collins and Michael Fishbane (Albany: State University of New York Press, 1995), 361-80.

304. Gilpin, "Sir Henry Vane," 363, quoting Vane's *The Retired Mans Meditations* (London, 1655), 223.

305. Vane, *The Retired Mans Meditations*, 128, as cited in Gilpin, "Sir Henry Vane," 367.

306. Parnham, *Sir Henry Vane*, 84-91 and 100-102. On Bauthumley, see Christopher Hill, *The World Turned Upside Down: Radical Ideas during the English Revolution* (New York: Penguin, 1975), 219-20.

307. On the mystical marriage, see *The Retired Mans Meditations*, 73, 76, 123, 334, 395-96, 409-10, and 423-24. Quotations in Parnham, 87.

308. For an account of the two covenants, see Cohen, *God's Caress*, chapter 2.

309. On the three covenants, see *The Retired Mans Meditations*, 128, 133, 195-96, and 208, as well as *Two Treatises*, 20-38.

310. On the mystical death, see *The Retired Mans Meditations*, 289-91, 296-97, 301, 305; quotations from Gilpin, "Sir Henry Vane," 367.

311. On Sterry's mysticism, see Dewey D. Wallace Jr., "Peter Sterry, Calvinist Mystic," in idem, *Shapers of English Calvinism, 1660–1714: Variety, Persistence, and Transformation* (Oxford and New York: Oxford University Press, 2011), 51–85. The "Preface" to Sterry's *A Discourse of the Freedom of the Will* is available in Charles Taliaferro and Alison J. Teply, eds., *Cambridge Platonist Spirituality*, Classics of Western Spirituality (New York: Paulist Press, 2004), 178–86. Again, for reasons of space, I have elected not to go into the issue of how far the Cambridge Platonists may be said to represent a distinct movement in the story of English mysticism.

312. Polhill (1622-1694) was a conforming Puritan layman who served as justice of the peace in Burwash, Sussex. His *Christus in corde*, first published in London in 1680, was reprinted in 1788, and revised and abridged in 1842. This edition was reprinted several times in the nineteenth and twentieth centuries.

Conclusion

THIS BOOK IS ONLY PART 1 OF VOLUME 6 of *The Presence of God*, but since this part surveys a distinctive chapter in the history of Western mysticism, a few concluding remarks are in order. As mentioned in the preface and in more detail in the introduction, the book was written with a partly polemical purpose, that is, to argue against those Protestant theologians (and their Catholic sympathizers) who contend that the Protestant branch of Christianity was not favorable to mysticism and therefore had few, if any, important mystics. Protestants who were seen as mystics, such as the Lutheran layman Jacob Boehme, were shunted to the margins, if not condemned as heretical. This view seems increasingly outmoded, as many Protestant scholars of the past century have demonstrated. This is not to say that there is a consensus among Protestant theologians and historians about the contours and the importance of Protestant mysticism, at least as a general category. There are also controversies about individual figures. The most important of these is the debate about Martin Luther. Is the great Reformer to be thought of as a mystic, if of an unusual type, as many Luther scholars are becoming inclined to say? Or, as I have argued in agreement with Heiko A. Oberman, is it more accurate to think of Luther as having a *sic et non* relationship to mysticism, that is, utilization in some ways but rejection in others?

There is more agreement that a mysticism of deep interiority was vital to at least some of the Radical Reformers, though there is some disagreement over which Radicals should be called mystics, as well as the characteristics of Radical mysticism. These thinkers frequently used the resources of late medieval

299

Germanic mysticism, especially John Tauler, the *Theologia Deutsch*, and even Eckhart in some cases. I have tried to suggest that in their stress to find the inner light of the Holy Spirit, as well as their embracing of mystical "releasement" (*Gelassenheit*), these mystics learned much from their German predecessors at the same time that they went further in the direction of a thorough anti-institutionalism not shared by mainline medieval mystics. There would be little disagreement that Johann Arndt can be called a mystic, and one who had a long-lasting and widespread impact on later Protestant religious traditions. As noted in the pages devoted to him above, it may be useful to think of Arndt as a "catholic mystic," one much in harmony with the broad patristic and medieval tradition, but definitely independent of contemporaneous Counter-Reformation Roman Catholicism. Jacob Boehme, of course, remains a problematic figure, both for the murky power of his thought and for the difficulties involved in determining his place in the Christian mystical tradition. For all the originality of his works, even with their theosophical coloring, Boehme, I think, needs to be seen within the tradition of Luther and the Lutheran communion, although not that of seventeenth-century Lutheran orthodoxy.

The *Ecclesia Anglicana* was a special development of the Reformation, an attempt at a typically English "middle way" between Roman Catholicism, with its bishops, high liturgy, and traditional theology, and the rigorous evangelical thought and polity not of Luther but of Calvin and the Geneva tradition. The English Reform developed in the midst of the tension between those who agreed with the Anglican Settlement and the Puritans who desired further Reform. Many of the heirs of the Puritans eventually became "Separatists," who moved outside the established church. What is perhaps most interesting is that both sides of the contentious English Reformation produced considerable mystical literature. Those who agreed with the Settlement were notable for expressing their mysticism primarily in poetry rather than prose—some of the finest mystical poetry of the Christian tradition. The Puritans, surprisingly for their negative reputation, often wrote about their ecstasies and erotic contact with Jesus in language that reminds one of some of the more excessive medieval mystics.

I do not claim to have treated all the Protestants of the period 1500–1650 who might be thought of as mystics in some way, but I hope to have presented an account of some major figures who demonstrate that Protestant mysticism is not a false category. The basic message, or balance sheet, of Protestant mysticism is still under review. It is clear, though, that a significant aspect of Protestant mysticism is its variety.

Like the medieval mystics who preceded them, as well as Catholic mystics of the sixteenth and seventeenth centuries, one size does not fit all. The rich variety among the Protestant religious thinkers who sought deeper and transforming contact with God is a good reason for affirming that Protestant mysticism is a necessary category, even as we are only beginning to realize how complex it really is.

Bibliography

SECTION I. SOURCES

1. ISAAC AMBROSE

Texts

Looking unto Jesus, as Carrying on the Great Work of Man's Salvation, or a View of the Everlasting Gospel. In *Works of Isaac Ambrose.* Reprint. London: Forgotten Books, 2015.
Media, The Middle Things in Reference to the First and Last Things. . . . London, 1650.

2. LANCELOT ANDREWES

Texts

Lancelot Andrewes Works. Edited by J. P. Wilson and J. Bliss. 11 vols. Oxford: J. H. Parker, 1841–54.
The Private Devotions of Lancelot Andrewes (Preces Privatae). Translated by F. E. Brightman. 1903. Reprint. New York: Meridian Books, 1961.
Sermons. Selected and edited by G. M. Story. Oxford: Clarendon, 1967.

3. JOHANN ARNDT

Texts

Herrn Johann Arndts Sechs Bücher vom Wahren Christenthum . . . Nebst dem Paradies-Gärtlein. 7th ed. Hof: Johann Christoph Leidenfrost, 1753.

Translations

True Christianity. Translated by Peter Erb. Classics of Western Spirituality. New York: Paulist Press, 1979.

4. BERNARD OF CLAIRVAUX

Texts

Sancti Bernardi Opera. Edited by Jean Leclercq et al. 9 vols. Rome: Editiones Cistercienses, 1957–98.

5. JACOB BOEHME

Texts

Aurora. (Morgen Röte im auffgang, 1612) and Fundamental Report (Gründlicher Bericht, Mysterium Pansophicum, 1620). Edited and translated by Andrew Weeks. Leiden: Brill, 2013.
Jacob Böhme Werke. Edited by Ferdinand van Ingen. Vol. 1. Frankfurt-am-Main: Deutscher Klassiker Verlag, 1997.
Sämtliche Schriften. Edited by August Faust and Will-Erich Peuckert. 11 vols. Stuttgart: Frommann-Holzboog, 1955–60.

Translations

The Forty Questions of the Soul. Translated by John Sparrow. Kila, MT: Kessinger, n.d.
Genius of the Transcendent: Mystical Writings of Jakob Boehme. Edited by Michael L. Birkel and Jeff Bach. Boston and London: Shambala, 2010.
Mysterium Magnum, or An Exposition of the First Book of Moses called Genesis. Translated by John Sparrow. 2 vols. Kila, MT: Kessinger, n.d.
Of the Incarnation of Jesus Christ by Jacob Böhme. Translated by John Rolleston Earle. London: Constable, 1934.
Six Theosophical Points and Other Writings by Jacob Boehme. Translated by John Rolleston Earle. Ann Arbor: University of Michigan Press, 1958.
The Way to Christ. Translated by Peter Erb. Classics of Western Spirituality. New York: Paulist Press, 1978.

6. JOHN CALVIN

Texts

Ioannis Calvini opera quae supersunt omnia. Edited by Wilhelm Baum et al. 59 vols. Brunswick: C, A. Schwetschke, 1863–1900.

Translations

Commentary on the Epistles of Paul the Apostle to the Corinthians. Translated by John Pringle. 2 vols. Grand Rapids: Baker Book House, 1984.

Institutes of the Christian Religion. Edited and translated by John T. McNeill and Ford Lewis Battles. 2 vols. Library of Christian Classics 20–21. Philadelphia: Westminster, 1959.

Treatises against the Anabaptists and against the Libertines. Translated by Benjamin Wirt Farley. Grand Rapids: Baker Book House, 1982.

Writings on Pastoral Piety. Edited and translated by Elsie Anne McKee. Classics of Western Spirituality. New York: Paulist Press, 2001.

7. HANS DENCK

Texts

Hans Denck Schriften. Edited by Georg Baring and Walter Fellmann. 3 vols. Gütersloh: Bertelsmann, 1955–60.

Translations

Selected Writings of Hans Denck. Edited and translated by E. J. Furcha. Pittsburgh: Pickwick, 1975. Reissued in an expanded form as *Selected Writings of Hans Denck 1500–1527,* edited and translated by E. J. Furcha. Lewiston, NY: Edwin Mellen, 1989.

8. JOHN DONNE

Texts

The Complete Poetry and Selected Prose of John Donne & The Complete Poetry of William Blake. Introduction by Robert Silliman Hillyer. New York: Modern Library, 1941.

Devotions upon Emergent Occasions. Edited by Anthony Rapsa. New York: Oxford University Press, 1987.

The Divine Poems. Edited by Helen Gardner. 2nd ed. Oxford: Clarendon, 1978.

Essays in Divinity. Edited by Evelyn M. Simpson. Oxford: Clarendon, 1952.

Selections from Divine Poems, Sermons, Devotions, and Prayers. Edited by John Booty. Classics of Western Spirituality. New York: Paulist Press, 1990.

The Sermons of John Donne. Edited by George R. Potter and Evelyn M. Simpson. 10 vols. Berkeley and Los Angeles: University of California Press, 1953–62.

9. SEBASTIAN FRANCK

Texts

Declaration. In *Beiträge zur Geschichte der Mystik in der Reformationszeit*, 137–77. Edited by Alfred Hegler and Walther Köhler. Archiv für Reformationsgeschichte Ergänzungsband 1. Berlin: C. A. Schwetschke, 1906.

Sämtliche Werke: Kritische Ausgabe mit Kommentar. Edited by Peter Klaus Knauer. Bern: Peter Lang, 1992–.

Sebastian Francks lateinischen Paraphrase der Deutschen Theologie und seine holländisch erhaltenen Traktate. Edited by Alfred Hegler. Tübingen: G. Schnürlen, 1901.

Translations

280 Paradoxes or Wondrous Sayings. Translated by E. J. Furcha. Lewiston, NY: Edwin Mellen, 1986.

Paradoxa. Translated by Heinrich Ziegler. Jena: Eugen Dietrichs, 1909.

10. JOHANN GERHARD

Translations

Meditations. In *Seventeenth-Century Lutheran Meditations and Hymns.* Translated by Eric Lund. Classics of Western Spirituality. New York: Paulist Press, 2011.

11. GEORGE HERBERT

Texts

The Complete English Poems. Edited by John Tobin. New York: Penguin Books, 1991.

The Country Parson. The Temple. Edited by John N. Wall Jr. Classics of Western Spirituality. New York: Paulist Press, 1981.

The English Poems of George Herbert. Edited by Helen Wilcox. Cambridge: Cambridge University Press, 2007.

12. ANDREAS KARLSTADT

Texts

Was gesagt ist / Sich gelassen / und das wort gelassenheit bedeüt / und wa es in hailiger geschrift begriffen. 1523.

Translations

The Essential Carlstadt. Fifteen Tracts by Andreas Bodenstein (Carlstadt) from Karlstadt. Translated by E. J. Furcha. Classics of the Radical Reformation 8. Scottdale, PA: Herald Press, 1995.
Karlstadt's Battle with Luther: Documents in a Liberal-Radical Debate. Edited by Ronald J. Sider. Philadelphia: Fortress, 1978.

13. MARTIN LUTHER

Texts

Archiv zur Weimarer Ausgabe der Werke Martin Luthers. Edited by Gerhard Hammer. 2 vols. Cologne: Böhlau, 1981.
D. Martin Luthers Werke: Kritische Gesamtausgabe. 120 vols. Weimar: H. Böhlau, 1883–2009.
Lateinisch-Deutsche Studienausgabe. Edited by Johannes Schilling. 3 vols. Leipzig: Evangelische Verlagsanstalt, 2006.
Luthers Werke im Auswahl. Vol. 5, *Der junge Luther.* Edited by Erich Vogelsang. Berlin, 1933.

Translations

Luther's Spirituality. Edited and translated by Philip D. W. Krey and Peter D. S. Krey. Classics of Western Spirituality. New York: Paulist Press, 2007.
Luther's Works. Editor-in-Chief, Jaroslav Pelikan. 60 vols. St. Louis: Concordia, 1955–86.
The Theologica Germanica of Martin Luther. Edited and translated by Bengt Hoffman. Classics of Western Spirituality. New York: Paulist Press, 1980.
Three Treatises. Translated by W. A. Lambert. 2nd rev. ed. Philadelphia: Fortress, 1970.

14. THOMAS MÜNTZER

Texts

"Fürstenpredigt." In *Politische Schriften.* Edited by Carl Hinrichs. Halle: Niemeyer, 1950.
Schriften und Briefe: Kritische Gesamtausgabe. Edited by Günther Franz. Quellen und Forschungen zur Reformationsgeschichte 33. Gütersloh: Gerd Mohn, 1968.

Translations

Revelation and Revolution: Basic Writings of Thomas Müntzer. Translated by Michael G. Baylor. Bethlehem, PA: Lehigh University Press, 1993.

15. EDWARD POLHILL

Texts

Christus in Corde, or the mystical union between Christ and Believers. . . . London: Thomas Cockerill, 1680.

16. FRANCIS ROUS

Texts

The Heavenly Academie. London, 1638.
The Mysticall Marriage: Experimental Discoveries of the heavenly Marriage betweene a Soule and her Saviour. London: William Jones, 1631.

17. RICHARD SIBBES

Texts

Works of Richard Sibbes. Edited by Alexander B. Grosart. 7 vols. 1862–64. Reprint. Carlisle, PA: Banner of Truth Trust, 1983.

18. PETER STERRY

Texts

Preface to A Discourse of the Will. In *Cambridge Platonist Spirituality,* edited by Charles Taliaferro and Alison J. Teply. Classics of Western Spirituality. New York: Paulist Press, 2004.

19. JOHANNES TAULER

Texts

Johannis Tauleri des seligen lerers Predig. Basel: Adam Petri, 1522.
Die Predigten Taulers. Edited by Ferdinand Vetter. 1910. Reprint. Frankfurt am Main: Weidmann, 1968.

20. THOMAS TRAHERNE

Texts

Centuries. New York: Harper & Brothers, 1960.

Centuries, Poems, and Thanksgivings. Edited by H. C. Margoliouth. 2 vols. Oxford: Clarendon, 1958.

Selected Poems and Prose. Edited by Alan Bradford. London: Penguin Books, 1991.

Select Meditations. Edited by Julia Smith. Manchester: Carcanet Press, 1997.

The Works of Thomas Traherne. Edited by Jan Ross. 6 vols. Cambridge: D. S. Brewer, 2005–.

21. HENRY VANE, THE YOUNGER

Texts

The Retired Mans Meditations. London, 1655.

22. HENRY VAUGHAN

Texts

The Complete Poetry of Henry Vaughan. Edited by French Fogle. Garden City, NY: Anchor Books, 1964.

The Works of Henry Vaughan. Edited by L. C. Martin. 2nd ed. Oxford: Clarendon, 1957.

23. JOHANN VON STAUPITZ

Translations

Eternal Predestination and its Execution in Time. In *Forerunners of the Reformation: The Shape of Late Medieval Thought,* edited by Heiko A. Oberman, 175–203. New York: Holt, Reinhart & Winston, 1966.

24. VALENTIN WEIGEL

Texts

Sämtliche Schriften. Edited by Horst Pfefferl. 15 vols. Stuttgart-Bad Canstatt: frommann-holzboog, 1996–2016.

Translations

Valentin Weigel: Selected Spiritual Writings. Edited and translated by Andrew Weeks. New York: Paulist Press, 2003.

SECTION II. SECONDARY WORKS

Alberigo, Giuseppe. "'Réforme' en tant critère de l'Histoire de l'Église." *Revue d'Histoire Ecclésiastique* 76 (1981): 72–81.

Allchin, A. M. "Anglican Spirituality." In *The Study of Anglicanism,* edited by Stephen Sykes and John Booty, 313–25. London: SPCK, 1988.

Allen, Elizabeth. "Everard, John (1584?–1640/41)." In *The Oxford Dictionary of National Biography,* 18:782–84. 60 vols. Oxford: Oxford University Press, 2004.

Allers, Rudolph. "Microcosmos from Anaximandros to Paracelsus." *Traditio* 2 (1944): 319–409.

Anderson, Luke. "The *Imago Dei* Theme in John Calvin and Bernard of Clairvaux." In *Calvinus Sacrae Scripturae Professor / Calvin as Professor of Sacred Scripture,* edited by Wilhelm H. Neusner, 178–98. Grand Rapids: Eerdmans, 1994.

Andersson, Bo. "Jacob Böhme's polemischer Konflikt mit Gregorius Richter." In *Offenbarung und Episteme: Zur europäischen Wirkung Jacob Böhmes im 17. und 18. Jahrhundert,* edited by Willhelm Kühlmann and Friedrich Vollhardt, 33–46. Frühe Neuzeit 173. Berlin: Walter de Gruyter, 2012.

Appel, Helmut. *Anfechtung und Trost im Spätmittelalter und bei Luther.* Leipzig: M. Heinsius, 1938.

Armstrong, Brian G. "Puritan Spirituality: The Tension of Bible and Experience." In *The Spirituality of Western Christendom.* Vol. 2, *The Roots of the Modern Christian Tradition,* edited by E. Rozanne Elder, 229–48. Cistercian Studies 55. Kalamazoo, MI: Cistercian Publications, 1984.

Asendorf, Ulrich. "Die Einbettung der Theosis in die Theologie Martin Luthers." In *Luther und Theosis: Vergöttlichung als Thema der abendländische Theologie,* edited by Simo Peura and Antti Raunio, 85–102. Erlangen: Martin-Luther-Verlag, 1990.

Auden, W. H. "Introduction." In *The Protestant Mystics,* edited by Anne Freemantle, 3–40. London: Weidenfield & Nicolson, 1964.

Bagchi, David, and David C. Steinmetz, eds. *The Cambridge Companion to Reformation Theology.* Cambridge: Cambridge University Press, 2004.

Baring, Georg. *Bibliographie der Ausgaben der "Theologia Deutsch" (1516–1961): Ein Beitrag zur Lutherbibliographie.* Baden-Baden: Heitz, 1963.

——. "Valentin Weigel und die 'Deutsche Theologie.'" *Archiv für Reformationsgeschichte* 55 (1964): 5–16.

Bast, Robert J., ed. *The Reformation of Faith in the Context of Late Medieval Theology and Piety: Essays by Berndt Hamm.* Leiden: Brill, 2004.

Battles, Ford Lewis. "True Piety according to Calvin." In Battles, *Interpreting John Calvin,* 289–306. Grand Rapids: Baker Book House, 1996.

Bauman, Clarence. *The Spiritual Legacy of Hans Denck: Interpretation and Translation of Key Texts.* Studies in Medieval and Reformation Thought 47. Leiden: Brill, 1991.

Bell, Ilona. "'Setting Foot into Divinity': George Herbert and the English Reformation." In *Essential Articles for the Study of George Herbert's Poetry,* edited by John R. Roberts, 63–83. Hamden, CT: Archon Books, 1979.

Bell, Theo. *DIVUS BERNHARDUS: Bernard von Clairvaux in Martin Luthers Schriften.* Mainz: Philipp von Zabern, 1993.

Berdyaev, Nicholas. "Unground and Freedom." In *Six Theosophical Points and Other Writings by Jacob Boehme,* translated by John Rolleston Earle, v–xxxvii. Ann Arbor: University of Michigan Press, 1958.

Bireley, Robert. *The Refashioning of Catholicism, 1450–1700: A Reassessment of the Counter-Reformation.* European History in Perspective. Washington, DC: Catholic University of America Press, 1999.

Blaumeiser, Hubertus. *Martin Luthers Kreuzestheologie: Schlüssel zu seiner Deutung von Mensch und Wirklichkeit; Eine Untersuchung anhand der Operationes in Psalmos, 1519–1521,* Konfessionskundliche und kontroverstheologische Studien 60. Paderborn: Bonifatius, 1995.

Bloch, Chana. *Spelling the Word: George Herbert and the Bible.* Berkeley: University of California Press, 1985.

Blunden, Edmund. *On the Poems of Henry Vaughan: Characteristics and Intimations.* London: Richard Cobden-Sanderson, 1927.

Boenig, Robert. "George Herbert and Mysticism." *Studia Mystica* 5 (1982): 64–72.

Bornkamm, Heinrich. *Luther und Böhme.* Bonn: A. Marcus and E. Weber, 1925.

Bossy, John. *Christianity in the West, 1400–1700.* Oxford and New York: Oxford University Press, 1987.

Bouwsma, William J. *John Calvin: A Sixteenth-Century Portrait.* Oxford and New York: Oxford University Press, 1988.

——. "Renaissance and Reformation: An Essay in Their Affinities and Connections." In *Luther and the Dawn of the Modern Era: Papers for the Fourth International Congress for Luther Research,* ed. Heiko A. Oberman, 127–49. Studies in the History of Christian Thought 8. Leiden: Brill, 1974.

———. "The Spirituality of John Calvin." In *Christian Spirituality II: High Middle Ages and Reformation,* edited by Jill Raitt, in collaboration with Bernard McGinn and John Meyendorff, 318–33. World Spirituality 17. New York: Crossroad, 1987.

Bouyer, Louis. *Orthodox Spirituality and Protestant and Anglican Spirituality.* New York: Seabury Press, 1982.

Braaten, Carl E., and Robert W. Jensen, eds. *Union with Christ: The New Finnish Interpretation of Luther.* Grand Rapids: Eerdmans, 1998.

Brady, Thomas A., Jr., Heiko A. Oberman, and James D. Tracy, eds. *Handbook of European History, 1400–1600: Late Middle Ages, Renaissance, and Reformation.* 2 vols. Grand Rapids: Eerdmans, 1996.

———. "The German Reformation between Late Middle Ages and Early Modernity." In *Die deutsche Reformation zwischen Spätmittelalter und Früher Neuzeit,* edited by Thomas A. Brady and Elisabeth Müller-Luckner, VII–XX. Munich: R. Oldenbourg, 2001.

Brauer, Jerald. "Francis Rous, Puritan Mystic, 1579–1659: An Introduction to the Study of the Mystical Element in Puritanism." PhD dissertation, University of Chicago, 1948.

———. "Puritan Mysticism and the Development of Liberalism." *Church History* 19 (1950): 151–70.

———. "Types of Puritan Piety." *Church History* 56 (1987): 39–59.

Braw, Christian. *Bücher im Staube: Die Theologie Johann Arndts in ihrem Verhältnis zur Mystik.* Studies in Medieval and Reformation Thought 39. Leiden: Brill, 1986.

Bremond, Henri. *Prayer and Poetry: A Contribution to Poetical Theory.* London: Burns, Oates & Washbourne, 1927.

Brooks, Cleanth. "Henry Vaughan: Quietism and Mysticism." In *Essays in Honor of Esmond Linworth Marilla,* edited by Thomas Austin Kirby and William John Olive, 3–26. Louisiana State University Studies, Humanities Series 19. Baton Rouge: Louisiana State University Press, 1970.

Bubenheimer, Ulrich. "Bodenstein von Karlstadt, Andreas." In *The Oxford Encyclopedia of the Reformation,* edited by Hans J. Hillerbrand, 1:178–80. 4 vols. New York and Oxford: Oxford University Press, 1996.

———. "Karlstadtrezeption von der Reformation bis zum Pietismus im Spiegel der Schriften Karlstadts zur Gelassenheit." In *Andreas Bodenstein von Karlstadt (1486–1541): Ein Theologe der frühen Reformation; Beiträge eines Arbeitsgesprächs vom 24.–25. November 1995 in Wittenberg,* edited by Sigrid Looss and Markus Matthias, 25–71. Themata Leucoreana. Wittenberg: Hans Lufft, 1998.

Canlis, Julie. *Calvin's Ladder: A Spiritual Theology of Ascent and Ascension.* Grand Rapids: Eerdmans, 2010.

Carrithers, Gale H., Jr. *Donne at Sermons: A Christian Existential World.* Albany: State University of New York Press, 1972.

Casteigt, Julie. *Connaissance et verité chez Maître Eckhart: Seul le juste connaît la justice.* Paris: Vrin, 2006.

Chapman, Mark D. *Anglican Theology.* Doing Theology. London: T&T Clark, 2012.

Charlton, James. *Non-Dualism in Eckhart, Julian of Norwich, and Traherne: A Theopoetic Reflection.* New York: Bloomsbury, 2013.

Clarke, Elizabeth. *Politics, Religion and the Songs of Songs in Seventeenth-Century England.* London: Palgrave Macmillan, 2011.

Clements, Arthur L. *The Mystical Poetry of Thomas Traherne.* Cambridge, MA: Harvard University Press, 1969.

———. *Poetry of Contemplation: John Donne, George Herbert, Henry Vaughan, and the Modern Period.* Albany: State University of New York Press, 1990.

———. "Theme, Tone, and Tradition in George Herbert's Poetry." In *Essential Articles for the Study of George Herbert's Poetry,* edited by John R. Roberts, 33–51. Hamden, CT: Archon Books, 1979.

Coffey, John, and Paul C. H. Lim, eds. *The Cambridge Companion to Puritanism.* Cambridge: Cambridge University Press, 2008.

Cohen, Charles Lloyd. *God's Caress: The Psychology of Puritan Religious Experience.* New York and Oxford: Oxford University Press, 1986.

Collinson, Patrick. "Puritans." In *The Oxford Encyclopedia of the Reformation,* edited by Hans J. Hillerbrand, 3:364–70. 4 vols. New York and Oxford: Oxford University Press, 1996.

Colloque Boehme. *Jacob Boehme ou l'obscure lumière de la connaissance mystique: Hommage à Jacob Boehme dans le cadre du Centre d'études et de recherches interdisciplinaires de Chantilly.* Bibliothèque d'histoire de la philosophie. Paris: Vrin, 1979.

Como, David R. *Blown by the Spirit: Puritanism and the Emergence of an Antinomian Underground in Pre-Civil-War England.* Stanford: Stanford University Press, 2004.

"Common Prayer, The Book of." In *The Oxford Dictionary of the Christian Church,* edited by F. L. Cross and E. A. Livingstone, 387–88. 3rd rev. ed. Oxford: Oxford University Press, 2005.

Countryman, L. William. *The Poetic Imagination: An Anglican Spiritual Tradition.* Traditions of Christian Spirituality. London: Darton, Longman & Todd, 1999.

Courcelle, Pierre. *Les Confessions de Saint Augustin dans la tradition littéraire: Antécedents et postérité*. Paris: Études Augustiniennes, 1963.

Cristiani, Léon. "Luther et saint Augustin." In *Augustinus Magister*, 2:1029–33. 3 vols. Paris: Études Augustiniennes, 1954–55.

Dammaschke, Marion, and Günter Vogler. *Thomas Müntzer Bibliography (1519–2012)*. Bibliotheca bibliographica Aureliana 233, Bibliotheca Dissidentium 28. Baden-Baden: Valentin Koerner, 2013.

Dejung, Christoph. "Sebastian Franck." In *Bibliotheca Dissidentium*, 7:39–119. Baden-Baden: Valentin Koerner, 1986.

Delumeau, Jean. *Catholicism between Luther and Voltaire: A New View of the Counter-Reformation*. London: Burns & Oates, 1977.

DeMolen, Richard, ed. *Religious Orders of the Catholic Reformation: In Honor of John C. Olin on His Seventy-Fifth Birthday*. New York: Fordham University Press, 1994.

Dever, Mark E. *Richard Sibbes: Puritanism and Calvinism in Late Elizabethan and Early Stuart England*. Macon, GA: Mercer University Press, 2000.

———. "Sibbes, Richard (1577?–1635)." In *The Oxford Dictionary of National Biography*, 50:486–88. 60 vols. Oxford: Oxford University Press, 2004.

Dipple, Jeffrey. "The Spiritual Anabaptists." In *A Companion to Anabaptism and Spiritualism, 1521–1700*, edited by John D. Roth and James M. Stayer, 257–71. Brill's Companions to the Christian Tradition 6. Leiden: Brill, 2007.

"Divinisation." In *Dictionnaire de spiritualité: Ascétique et mystique, doctrine et histoire*, edited by Marcel Viller et al., 3:1370–1459. 17 vols. Paris: Beauchesne, 1937–97.

Dodd, Elizabeth S. *Boundless Innocence in Thomas Traherne's Poetic Theology*. Burlington, VT: Ashgate, 2015.

Drury, John. *Music at Midnight: The Life and Poetry of George Herbert*. Chicago: University of Chicago Press, 2011.

Duffy, Eamon. *The Stripping of the Altars: Traditional Religion in England, 1400–1580*. New Haven and London: Yale University Press, 1992.

Durr, R. A. *On the Mystical Poetry of Henry Vaughan*. Cambridge, MA: Harvard University Press, 1962.

Ebeling, Gerhard. "Luther and the Beginning of the Modern Age." In *Luther and the Dawn of the Modern Era: Papers for the Fourth International Congress for Luther Research*, ed. Heiko A. Oberman, 11–39. Studies in the History of Christian Thought 8. Leiden: Brill, 1974.

Edwards, David L. *John Donne: Man of Flesh and Spirit*. Grand Rapids: Eerdmans, 2001.

Edwards, Mark U., Jr. *Luther and the False Brethren.* Stanford: Stanford University Press, 1975.

Eliot, T. S. "Donne in Our Time." In *A Garland for John Donne 1631–1931,* edited by Theodore Spencer, 8–9, 13. Gloucester, MA: Peter Smith, 1958.

———. *George Herbert.* In *British Writers and Their Work, No. 4.* Lincoln: University of Nebraska Press, 1964.

———. "Lancelot Andrewes." In Eliot, *Essays Ancient & Modern,* 11–29. London: Faber & Faber, 1936.

Enright, D. J. "George Herbert and the Devotional Poets." In *From Donne to Marvell,* edited by Boris Ford, 142–59. Pelican Guide to English Literature 3. Baltimore: Penguin Books, 1956.

Erb, Peter. "Anabaptist Spirituality." In *Protestant Spiritual Traditions,* edited by Frank C. Senn, 86–124. New York: Paulist Press, 1986.

Erikson, Erik. *Young Man Luther: A Study in Psychoanalysis and History.* New York: W. W. Norton, 1958.

Evener, Vincent M. "'Enemies of the Cross': Suffering, Salvation, and Truth in Sixteenth-Century Religious Controversy." PhD dissertation, University of Chicago, 2014.

Evennett, H. Outram. *The Spirit of the Counter-Reformation.* Cambridge: Cambridge University Press, 1968.

Faivre, Antoine. "Théosophie." *Dictionnaire de spiritualité: Ascétique et mystique, doctrine et histoire,* edited by Marcel Viller et al., 15:548–62. 17 vols. Paris: Beauchesne, 1937–97.

Fasolt, Constantin. "Hegel's Ghost: Europe, the Reformation, and the Middle Ages." *Viator* 39 (2008): 345–86.

Febvre, Lucien. "The Origins of the French Reformation: A Badly-Put Question?" In *A New Kind of History from the Writings of Lucien Febvre,* edited by Peter Burke, 44–107. New York: Harper & Row, 1973.

Fischer, Hermann. "Protestantismus." In *Theologische Realenzyklopädie: Studienausgabe,* edited by Gerhard Krause and Gerhard Müller, 27:542–51. 36 vols. Berlin: Walter de Gruyter, 1993–2006.

Fish, Stanley. "Letting Go: The Dialectic of the Self in Herbert's Poetry." In idem, *Self-Consuming Artifacts: The Experience of Seventeenth-Century Literature,* 156–223. Berkeley: University of California Press, 1972.

———. *The Living Temple: George Herbert and Catechizing.* Berkeley: University of California Press, 1978.

Flogaus, Reinhard. *Theosis bei Palamas und Luther: Ein Beitrag zum ökumenischen Gespräch.* Forschungen zur systematischen und ökumenischen Theologie 78. Göttingen: Vandenhoeck & Ruprecht, 1997.

Froehlich, Karlfried. "Pseudo-Dionysius and the Reformation of the Sixteenth Century." In "Introduction" to *Pseudo-Dionysius: The Complete Works*, edited and translated by Colm Luibhead, 33–46. Classics of Western Spirituality. New York: Paulist Press, 1987.

Ganoczy, Alexandre. *The Young Calvin*. Philadelphia: Westminster, 1987.

Gatta, Julia. "George Herbert's Poetry of Transformation." In *This Sacred History: Anglican Reflections for John Booty*, edited by Donald S. Armentrout, 31–46. Cambridge, MA: Cowley, 1990.

Gauger, Andreas. *Jacob Böhme und das Wesen seiner Mystik*. Berlin: Weissensee, 1999.

George, Timothy. "The Spirituality of the Radical Reformation." In *Christian Spirituality II: High Middle Ages and Reformation*, edited by Jill Raitt, in collaboration with Bernard McGinn and John Meyendorff, 334–71. World Spirituality 17. New York: Crossroad, 1987.

Gerrish, Brian A. *Grace and Gratitude: The Eucharistic Theology of John Calvin*. Minneapolis: Fortress, 1993.

———. "'To the Unknown God': Luther and Calvin on the Hiddenness of God." *Journal of Religion* 53 (1973): 263–92.

Geyer, Hermann. *Verborgene Weisheit: Johann Arndts "Vier Bücher vom Wahren Christentum" als Programm einer spiritualistisch-hermetischen Theologie*. 3 vols. Arbeiten zur Kirchengeschichte 80. Berlin: Walter de Gruyter, 2001.

Gilpin, W. Clark. "Sir Henry Vane: Mystical Piety in the Puritan Revolution." In *Death, Ecstasy, and Otherworldly Journeys*, edited by John J. Collins and Michael Fishbane, 361–80. Albany: State Univesity of New York Press, 1995.

Gnädinger, Louise. *Johannes Tauler: Lebenswelt und mystische Lehre*. Munich: C. H. Beck, 1993.

Goertz, Hans-Jürgen. "Karlstadt, Müntzer and the Reformation of the Commoners." In *A Companion to Anabaptism and Spiritualism, 1521–1700*, edited by John D. Roth and James M. Stayer, 1–44. Brill's Companions to the Christian Tradition 6. Leiden: Brill, 2007.

———. *Thomas Müntzer: Apocalyptic, Mystic, and Revolutionary*. Edinburgh: T&T Clark, 1993.

———, ed. *Profiles of Radical Reformers: Biographical Sketches from Thomas Müntzer to Paracelsus*. Kitchener, ON: Herald Press, 1982.

Goldhammer, Kurt. "Lichtsymbolik in philosophischer Weltanschauung, Mystik und Theosophie vom 15. bis zum 17. Jahrhundert." *Studium Generale* 13 (1960): 670–82.

Gorceix, Bernard. *La mystique de Valentin Weigel*. Paris: Université de Paris, 1972.

Gordon, Bruce. *John Calvin's "Institutes of the Christian Religion": A Biography.* Princeton: Princeton University Press, 2015.

Grant, Patrick. "Original Sin and the Fall of Man in Thomas Traherne." *Journal of English Literary History* 38 (1971): 40–61.

Gregory, Brad S. *Salvation at Stake: Christian Martyrdom in the Early Modern Period.* Cambridge, MA: Harvard University Press, 1999.

———. *The Unintended Reformation: How a Religious Reformation Secularized Society.* Cambridge, MA: Belknap Press of Harvard University Press, 2012.

Gritsch, Eric W. "Thomas Müntzer and Luther: A Tragedy of Errors." In *Radical Tendencies in the Reformation: Divergent Perspectives,* edited by Hans J. Hillerbrand, 55–83. Sixteenth Century Essays and Studies 9. Ann Arbor, MI: Edwards Brothers, 1988.

Gross, Jules. *The Divinization of the Christian according to the Greek Fathers.* Anaheim, CA: A & C Press, 2002.

Grosse, Sven. "Der junge Luther und die Mystik: Ein Beitrag zur Frage nach dem Werden der reformatorischen Theologie." In *Gottes Nähe unmittelbar erfahren,* edited by Berndt Hamm and Volker Leppin, 187–235. Tübingen: Mohr Siebeck, 2007.

Gruebner, Birgit. *Gott und die Lebendigkeit in der Natur: Eine Interpretation des Dritten und Vierten Buches von Johann Arndts "Wahrem Christentum."* Arbeiten zur Theologiegeschichte 4. Rheinbach: CMZ, 1998.

Gründler, Otto. "John Calvin: Ingrafting in Christ." In *The Spirituality of Western Christendom,* edited by E. Rozanne Elder, 169–87. Cistercian Studies 30. Kalamazoo, MI: Cistercian Publications, 1976.

Grunsky, Hans. *Jacob Böhme.* Stuttgart: Frommann, 1956.

Guibbory, Achsah, ed. *The Cambridge Companion to John Donne.* Cambridge: Cambridge University Press, 2006.

———. "Erotic Poetry." In *The Cambridge Companion to John Donne,* edited by Achsah Guibbory, 133–47. Cambridge: Cambridge University Press, 2006.

Guite, Malcolm. *Faith, Hope and Poetry: Theology and the Poetic Imagination.* Burlington, VT: Ashgate, 2010.

Haas, Alois M. "Erfahrung und Sprache in Böhme's *Aurora.*" In *Gott, Natur und Mensch in der Sicht Jacob Böhmes und seiner Rezeption,* edited by Jan Garewicz and Alois M. Haas, 1–21. Wolfenbütteler Arbeiten zur Barockforschung 24. Wiesbaden: Harrassowitz, 1994.

———. *Der Kampf um den Heiligen Geist: Luther und die Schwärmer.* Freiburg, Schweiz: Universitätsverlag, 1997.

———. "Luther und die Mystik." *Deutsche Vierteljahrsschrift für Literaturwissenschaft und Geistesgeschichte* 60 (1986): 177–207.

———. "Mechthild von Magdeburg: Dichtung und Mystik." In Haas, *Sermo mysticus: Studien zu Theologie und Sprache der deutschen Mystik*, 67–103. Freiburg, Schweiz: Universitätsverlag, 1979.

Hageman, Howard G. "Reformed Spirituality." In *Protestant Spiritual Traditions*, edited by Frank C. Senn, 55–79. New York: Paulist Press, 1986.

Halewood, William. *The Poetry of Grace: Reformation Themes in English Seventeenth-Century Poetry*. New Haven: Yale University Press, 1970.

Hambrick-Stowe, Charles. "Practical Divinity and Spirituality." In *The Cambridge Companion to Puritanism*, edited by John Coffey and Paul C. H. Lim, 191–205. Cambridge: Cambridge University Press, 2008.

Hamel, Adolf. *Der junge Luther und Augustin*. 2 vols. Gütersloh: C. Bertelsmann, 1934.

Hamm, Berndt. *The Early Luther: Stages in a Reformation Reorientation*. Grand Rapids: Eerdmans, 2014.

———. "How Innovative Was the Reformation?" In *The Reformation of Faith in the Context of Late Medieval Theology and Piety: Essays by Berndt Hamm*, edited by Robert J. Bast, 254–72. Studies in the History of Christian Thought 110. Leiden: Brill, 2004.

———. "Johann Arndts Wortverständnis: Ein Beitrag zu dem Anfängen des Pietismus." In *Pietismus und Neuzeit*. Vol. 8, *Der radikale Pietismus*, 43–73. Göttingen: Vandenhoeck & Ruprecht, 1982.

———. "Wie mystisch war der Glaube Luthers?" In *Gottes Nähe unmittelbar erfahren*, edited by Berndt Hamm and Volker Leppin, 187–235. Tübingen: Mohr Siebeck, 2007.

Hamm, Berndt, and Volker Leppin, eds. *Gottes Nähe unmittelbar erfahren*. Tübingen: Mohr Siebeck, 2007.

Harnack, Adolph. *History of Dogma*. 8 vols. New York: Dover, 1961.

Hayden-Roy, Patrick. "Franck, Sebastian." In *The Oxford Encyclopedia of the Reformation*, edited by Hans J. Hillerbrand, 2:134–35. 4 vols. New York and Oxford: Oxford University Press, 1996.

Hazlitt, Ian P. "Settlements: The British Isles." In *Handbook of European History, 1400–1600: Late Middle Ages, Renaissance, and Reformation*, edited by Thomas A. Brady Jr., Heiko A. Oberman, and James D. Tracy, 2:455–90. 2 vols. Grand Rapids: Eerdmans, 1996.

Hegel, G. W. F. *The Philosophy of History*. New York: Dover, 1956.

Hegler, Alfred. *Geist und Schrift bei Sebastian Franck*. Freiburg im Breisgau: J. C. B. Mohr, 1892.

Hendrix, Scott H., ed. and trans. *Early Protestant Spirituality*. Classics of Western Spirituality. New York: Paulist Press, 2009.

———. *Ecclesia in via: Ecclesiological Developments in the Medieval Psalms Exegesis and the Dictata super Psalterium (1513–1515) of Martin Luther.*

Studies in Medieval and Reformation Thought 8. Leiden: Brill, 1974.

——. "Luther." In *The Cambridge Companion to Reformation Theology*, edited by David Bagchi and David C. Steinmetz, 39–56. Cambridge: Cambridge University Press, 2004.

Hessayon, Ariel, and Sarah Apetrei, eds. *An Introduction to Jacob Boehme: Four Centuries of Thought and Reception.* Routledge Studies in Religion 31. New York and London: Routledge, 2014.

Hill, Christopher. *The World Turned Upside Down: Radical Ideas during the English Revolution.* New York: Penguin, 1975.

Hillerbrand, Hans J. "The Lonely Individualist: *Sebastian Franck*." In Hillerbrand, *A Fellowship of Discontent*," pp. 31–64. New York: Harper & Row, 1967.

——, ed. *Radical Tendencies in the Reformation: Divergent Perspectives.* Sixteenth Century Essays and Studies 9. Ann Arbor, MI: Edwards Brothers, 1988.

Holl, Karl. *Gesammelte Aufsätze zur Kirchengeschichte.* 3 vols. Tübingen: Mohr, 1923–63.

Höss, Irmgard. "Althamer, Andreas." In *The Oxford Encyclopedia of the Reformation*, edited by Hans J. Hillerbrand, 1:21. 4 vols. New York and Oxford: Oxford University Press, 1996.

Hsia, R. Po-chia, ed. *The Cambridge History of Christianity.* Vol. 6, *Christianity: Reform and Expansion, 1500–1660.* Cambridge: Cambridge University Press, 2007.

Hudon, William V., ed. and trans. *Theatine Spirituality: Selected Writings.* Classics of Western Spirituality. New York: Paulist Press, 1996.

Hudson, Winthrop S. "Mystical Religion in the Puritan Commonwealth." *Journal of Religion* 28 (1948): 51–56.

Hughes, Richard. "George Herbert and the Incarnation." In *Essential Articles for the Study of George Herbert's Poetry*, edited by John R. Roberts, 52–62. Hamden, CT: Archon Books, 1979.

Husain, Itrat. *The Dogmatic and Mystical Theology of John Donne.* London: SPCK, 1938.

——. *The Mystical Element in the Metaphysical Poets of the Seventeenth Century.* London: Oliver & Boyd, 1948.

Inge, Denise. *Happiness and Holiness: Thomas Traherne and His Writings.* Norwich: Canterbury Press, 2008.

——. *Wanting Like a God: Desire and Freedom in Thomas Traherne.* London: SCM Press, 2009.

Iserloh, Erwin. "Luther's Christ-Mysticism." In *Catholic Scholars Dialogue with Luther*, edited by Jared Wicks, 37–58. Chicago: Loyola University Press, 1970.

Jannell, Pierre. *The Catholic Reformation*. Milwaukee: Bruce, 1949.

Jedin, Hubert. *Geschichte des Konzils von Trient*. 4 vols. Freiburg im Breisgau: Herder, 1949–75.

———. *Katholische Reformation oder Gegenreformation? Ein Versuch zur Klärung der Begriffe nebst einer Jubiläumsbetrachtung über das Trienter Konzil*. Lucerne: Josef Stocker, 1946.

Jones, Rufus M. *Spiritual Reformers in the 16ᵗʰ and 17ᵗʰ Centuries*. London: Macmillan, 1928.

Keller, Carl-A. *Calvin Mystique: Au coeur de la pensée du Réformateur*. Geneva: Labor et Fides, 2001.

Kermode, Frank. *John Donne*. In *British Writers and Their Work, No. 3*. Lincoln: University of Nebraska Press, 1964.

Klassen, Walter. *Living at the End of the Ages: Apocalyptic Expectation in the Radical Reformation*. Lanham, MD: University Press of America, 1992.

Kleinedam, Erich. "Ursprung und Gegenstand der Theologie bei Bernhard von Clairvaux und Martin Luther." In *Dienst der Vermittlung: Festschrift zum 25-jährigen Bestehen d. Philosoph.-Theol. Studiums in Priesterseminar Erfurt*, edited by Wilhelm Ernst, Konrad Feiereis, and Fritz Hoffmann, 221–47. Erfurter theologische Studien 37. Leipzig: St. Benno, 1977.

Koepp, Wilhelm. *Johann Arndt: Eine Untersuchung über die Mystik im Luthertum*. Berlin: Protestantische Schriftenvertrieb, 1912.

———. *Johann Arndt und sein "Wahres Christentum": Lutherisches Bekenntnis und Oekumene*. Aufsätze und Vorträge zur Theologie und Religionswissenschaft 7. Berlin: Evangelische Verlaganstalt, 1959.

Kolb, Robert. "Confessional Lutheran Theology." In *The Cambridge Companion to Reformation Theology*, edited by David Bagchi and David C. Steinmentz, 68–79. Cambridge: Cambridge University Press, 2004.

———. "Lutheranism, Theology." In *The Oxford Encyclopedia of the Reformation*, edited by Hans J. Hillerbrand, 2:470–73. 4 vols. New York and Oxford: Oxford University Press, 1996.

Kolfhaus, Wolfgang. *Christusgemeinschaft bei Johannes Calvin*. Neukirchen: Buchhandlung des Erziehungsverein, 1938.

Kouri, E. I., ed. *Politics and Society in Reformation Europe*. London: Macmillan, 1987.

Koyré, Alexandre. *Mystiques, Spirituels, Alchimistes du XVI siècle allemande*. Paris: Librarie Armand Colin, 1955.

———. *La philosophie de Jacob Boehme*. Paris: Vrin, 1929. Reprint, 1968.

Kühlmann, Wilhelm, and Friedrich Vollhardt, eds. *Offenbarung und Episteme: Zur europäischen Wirkung Jakob Böhmes im 17. und 18. Jahrhundert*. Frühe Neuzeit 173. Berlin: Walter de Gruyter, 2012.

Lane, Belden C. *Ravished by Beauty: The Surprising Legacy of Reformed Spirituality.* Oxford and New York: Oxford University Press, 2011.

Langer, Otto. "Inneres Wort und inwohnender Christus: Zum mystischen Spiritualismus Sebastian Francks und seiner Implikation." In *Sebastian Franck (1499–1542)*, edited by Jan-Dirk Müller, 55–69. Wolfenbütteler Forschungen 56. Wiesbaden: Harrassowitz, 1993.

Laube, Adolf. "Radicalism as a Research Problem in the History of the Early Reformation." In *Radical Tendencies in the Reformation: Divergent Perspectives*, edited by Hans J. Hillerbrand, 9–23. Sixteenth Century Essays and Studies 9. Ann Arbor, MI: Edwards Brothers, 1988.

Lehmann, Hartmut. "Lutheranism in the Seventeenth Century." In *The Cambridge History of Christianity.* Vol. 6, *Christianity: Reform and Expansion, 1500–1660*, edited by R. Po-chia Hsia, 56–72. Cambridge: Cambridge University Press, 2007.

Leppin, Volker. "Mystik." In *Luther Handbuch*, edited by Albrecht Beutel, 57–61. Tübingen: Mohr Siebeck, 2003.

———. "'omnem vitam fidelium penitentiam esse voluit': Zur Aufnahme mystischer Traditionen in Luthers erster Ablassthese." *Archiv für Reformationsgeschichte* 93 (2002): 7–25.

———. "Transformationen spätmittelalterliche Mystik bei Luther." In *Gottes Nähe unmittelbar erfahren: Mystik im Mittelalter und bei Martin Luther*, edited by Berndt Hamm and Volker Leppin, 165–85. Tübingen: Mohr Siebeck, 2007.

Lewalski, Barbara Kiefer. *Protestant Poetics and the Seventeenth-Century Religious Lyric.* Princeton: Princeton University Press, 1979.

———. "Thomas Traherne: Naked Truth, Transparent Words, and the Renunciation of Metaphor." In *John Donne and the Seventeenth-Century Metaphysical Poets*, edited by Harold Bloom, 225–41. New York: Chelsea House, 1986.

Liechty, Daniel, ed. and trans. *Early Anabaptist Spirituality.* Classics of Western Spirituality. New York: Paulist Press, 1994.

Lienhard, Marc. "Luther and the Beginnings of the Reformation." In *Christian Spirituality II: High Middle Ages and Reformation*, edited by Jill Raitt, in collaboration with Bernard McGinn and John Meyendorff, 268–99. World Spirituality 17. New York: Crossroad, 1987.

Lohse, Bernhard. "Luther und Bernard von Clairvaux." In *Bernhard von Clairvaux: Rezeption und Wirkung im Mittelalter und in der Neuzeit*, edited by Kaspar Elm, 271–303. Wolfenbütteler Mittelalter-Studien 6. Wiesbaden: Harrassowitz, 1994.

Longfellow, Erica. *Women and Religious Writing in Early Modern England.* Cambridge: Cambridge University Press, 2004.

Looss, Sigrid. "Radical Views of the Early Andreas Karlstadt (1520–1525)." In *Radical Tendencies in the Reformation: Divergent Perspec-*

tives, edited by Hans J. Hillerbrand, 43–53. Sixteenth Century Essays and Studies 9. Ann Arbor, MI: Edwards Brothers, 1988.

Lossky, Nicholas. *Lancelot Andrewes the Preacher (1555–1626): The Origins of the Mystical Theology of the Church of England.* Oxford: Clarendon, 1991.

Lovelace, Richard C. "Puritan Spirituality I, The Anatomy of Puritan Piety: English Puritan Devotional Literature." In *Christian Spirituality III: Post-Reformation and Modern,* edited by Louis Dupré and Don E. Saliers, in collaboration with John Meyendorff, 294–323. World Spirituality 18. New York: Crossroad, 1989.

Low, Anthony. "John Donne, 'The Holy Ghost Is Amorous in His Metaphors.'" In *New Perspectives on the Seventeenth-Century English Religious Lyric,* edited by John R. Roberts, 201–21. Columbia: University of Missouri Press, 1994.

———. *Love's Architecture: Devotional Modes in Seventeenth-Century English Poetry.* New York: New York University Press, 1978.

Lund, Eric, ed. *Seventeenth-Century Lutheran Meditations and Hymns.* Classics of Western Spirituality. New York: Paulist Press, 2011.

MacCulloch, Diarmaid. *The Reformation: A History.* New York: Penguin Books, 2003.

Mahood, M. M. "Vaughan: The Symphony of Nature." In *Essential Articles for the Study of Henry Vaughan,* edited by Alan Rudrum, 5–45. Hamden, CT: Archon Books, 1987.

Malysz, Piotr. "Luther and Dionysius: Beyond Mere Negations." In *Re-Thinking Dionysius the Areopagite,* edited by Sarah Coakley and Charles M. Stang, 149–62. Directions in Modern Theology. Oxford: Wiley-Blackwell, 2009.

Maritain, Jacques, and Raïssa Maritain. *The Situation of Poetry.* New York: Philosophical Library, 1955.

Marshall, Paul V. "Anglican Spirituality." In *Protestant Spiritual Traditions,* edited by Frank C. Senn, 125–64. New York: Paulist Press, 1986.

Marty, Martin. *Martin Luther.* New York: Viking Penguin, 2004.

Martz, Louis L. *The Paradise Within: Studies in Vaughan, Traherne, and Milton.* New Haven: Yale University Press, 1964.

———. *The Poetry of Meditation: A Study in English Religious Literature of the Seventeenth Century.* New Haven: Yale University Press, 1954.

———. "The Poetry of Meditation: Searching the Memory." In *New Perspectives on the Seventeenth-Century English Religious Lyric,* edited by John R. Roberts, 188–200. Columbia: University of Missouri Press, 1994.

———. "Henry Vaughan: The Man Within." In *Essential Articles for the*

Study of Henry Vaughan, edited by Alan Rudrum, 99–120. Hamden, CT: Archon Books, 1987.

McCullough, Peter. "Donne as Preacher." In *The Cambridge Companion to John Donne*, edited by Achsah Guibbory, 167–82. Cambridge: Cambridge University Press, 2006.

McGinn, Bernard. "The Abyss of Love." In *The Joy of Learning and the Love of God: Studies in Honor of Jean Leclercq*, edited by E. Rozanne Elder, 95–120. Cistercian Studies 160. Kalamazoo, MI: Cistercian Publications, 1995.

———. "Apocalypticism and Mysticism: Aspects of the History of Their Interaction." *Zeitsprünge: Forschungen zur Frühen Neuzeit* 3 (1999): 292–315.

———. "The Language of Love in Jewish and Christian Mysticism." In *Mysticism and Language*, edited by Steven T. Katz, 202–35. New York: Oxford University Press, 1992.

———. "Lost in the Abyss: The Function of Abyss Language in Medieval Mysticism." *Franciscan Studies* 73 (2014): 373–89.

———. *The Mystical Thought of Meister Eckhart: The Man from Whom God Hid Nothing.* Edward Cadbury Lectures 2000–2001. New York: Crossroad, 2001.

———. *"Vere tu es Deus absconditus*: The Hidden God in Luther and Some Mystics." In *Silence and the Word of God: Negative Theology and Incarnation*, edited by Oliver Davies and Denys Turner, 94–114. Cambridge: Cambridge University Press, 2002.

McLaughlin, R. Emmet. "The Radical Reformation." In *The Cambridge History of Christianity.* Vol. 6, *Christianity: Reform and Expansion, 1500–1660*, edited by R. Po-chia Hsia, 37–55. Cambridge: Cambridge University Press, 2007.

———. "Sebastian Franck and Caspar Schwenkfeld: Two Spiritualist *Viae.*" In *Sebastian Franck (1499–1542)*, edited by Jan-Dirk Müller, 71–86. Wolfenbütteler Forschungen 56. Wiesbaden: Harrassowitz, 1993.

———. "Spiritualism." In *The Oxford Encyclopedia of the Reformation*, edited by Hans J. Hillerbrand, 4:105–7. 4 vols. New York and Oxford: Oxford University Press, 1996.

———. "Spiritualism: Schwenkfeld and Franck and Their Early Modern Resonances." In *A Companion to Anabaptism and Spiritualism, 1521–1700*, edited by John D. Roth and James M. Stayer, 119–61. Brill's Companions to the Christian Tradition 6. Leiden: Brill, 2007.

Midelfort, H. C. Erik. "Madness and the Millennium at Münster, 1534–1535." In *Fearful Hope: Approaching the New Millennium*, edited by Christopher Kleinhenz and Fannie J. LeMoine, 115–34. Madison: University of Wisconsin Press, 1999.

Miller, Arlene A. "The Theologies of Luther and Boehme in the Light of their *Genesis* Commentaries." *Harvard Theological Review* 63 (1970): 261–303.

Moeller, Bernd, ed. *Die frühe Reformation in Deutschland als Umbruch.* Heidelberg: Gütersloh, 1998.

———. *Die Reformation und das Mittelalter: Kirchenhistorische Aufsätze,* ed. Joannes Schilling. Göttingen: Vandenhoeck & Ruprecht, 1991.

———. "Tauler und Luther." In *La mystique rhénane: Colloque de Strasbourg, 16–19 mai 1961,* 157–67. Paris: Presses universitaires de France, 1963.

Moorman, John R. H. *The Anglican Spiritual Tradition.* Springfield, IL: Templegate, 1983.

Moynihan, Robert. "The Development of the 'Pseudo-Joachim' Commentary 'Super Hieremiam': New Manuscript Evidence." *Mélanges de l'école française de Rome: Moyen Age–Temps Modernes* 98 (1986): 109–42.

Mueller, William R. *John Donne: Preacher.* Princeton: Princeton University Press, 1962.

Müller, Jan-Dirk, ed. *Sebastian Franck (1499–1542).* Wolfenbütteler Forschungen 56. Wiesbaden: Harrassowitz, 1993.

Mullett, Michael A. *The Catholic Reformation.* London and New York: Routledge, 1999.

Mursell, Gordon. "Anglican Spirituality." In *The Bloomsbury Guide to Christian Spirituality,* edited by Richard Woods and Peter Tyler, 159–70. London: Bloomsbury, 2012.

———. *English Spirituality.* 2 vols. London: SPCK, 2001.

Nestingen, James Arne. "Gnesio-Lutherans." In *The Oxford Encyclopedia of the Reformation,* edited by Hans J. Hillerbrand, 2:177–80. 4 vols. New York and Oxford: Oxford University Press, 1996.

Neuser, Wilhelm H., ed. *Calvinus Sacrae Scripturae Professor / Calvin as Professor of Holy Scripture.* Grand Rapids: Eerdmans, 1994.

Newman, Barbara. "Rereading John Donne's Holy Sonnet 14." *Spiritus* 4 (2004): 84–90.

Niesel, Wilhelm. *Reformed Symbolics.* Edinburgh: Oliver & Boyd, 1962.

Nipperday, Thomas. "The Reformation and the Modern World." In *Politics and Society in Reformation Europe: Essays for Sir Geoffrey Elton on His Sixty-fifth Birthday,* edited by E. I. Kouri and Tom Scott, 535–52. London: Macmillan, 1987.

Nischan, Bodo. "Osiander, Lucas II." In *The Oxford Encyclopedia of the Reformation,* edited by Hans J. Hillerbrand, 3:185. 4 vols. New York and Oxford: Oxford University Press, 1996.

North, John D. "Microcosm and Macrocosm in Paracelsus." In *Neue Beiträge zur Paracelsus-Forschung,* edited by Peter Dilg and Hartmut

Rudolph, 41–58. Hohenheimer Protokolle 47. Stuttgart: Akademie der Diözese Rottenburg-Stuttgart, 1995.

Nuttall, G. F. *The Holy Spirit in Puritan Faith and Experience*. Chicago: University of Chicago Press, 1992.

——. "Puritan and Quaker Mysticism." *Theology* 78 (1975): 518–31.

Oakley, Francis. *The Conciliarist Tradition: Constitutionalism in the Catholic Church*. Oxford: Oxford University Press, 2003.

Oberman, Heiko A. "The Augustinian Renaissance of the Later Middle Ages." In Oberman, *Masters of the Reformation: The Emergence of a New Intellectual Climate in Europe*, 64–110. Cambridge: Cambridge University Press, 1981.

——. *The Dawn of the Reformation: Essays in Late Medieval and Early Reformation Thought*. Edinburgh: T&T Clark, 1986.

——. *Forerunners of the Reformation*. New York: Holt, Reinhart & Winston, 1966.

——. *The Harvest of Medieval Theology: Gabriel Biel and Late Medieval Nominalism*. Cambridge, MA: Harvard University Press, 1963.

——. "The Long Fifteenth Century: In Search of Its Profile." In *Die deutsche Reformation zwischen Spätmittelalter und Früher Neuzeit*, edited by Thomas A. Brady and Elisabeth Müller-Luckner, 1–18. Munich: R. Oldenbourg, 2001.

——, ed. *Luther and the Dawn of the Modern Era*. Leiden: Brill, 1974.

——. *Luther: Man between God and the Devil*. New Haven: Yale University Press, 1989.

——. "The Pursuit of Happiness: Calvin between Humanism and Reformation." In *Humanity and Divinity in Renaissance and Reformation: Essays in Honor of Charles Trinkaus*, edited by John W. O'Malley, Thomas M. Izbicki, and Gerald Christianson, 251–83. Studies in the History of Christian Thought 51. Leiden: Brill, 1993.

——. *The Reformation: Roots and Ramifications*. Grand Rapids: Eerdmans, 1994.

——. "*Simul Gemitus et Raptus:* Luther and Mysticism." In *The Reformation in Medieval Perspective*, edited by Steven E. Ozment, 219–51. Chicago: Quadrangle Books, 1971.

Oberman, Heiko, and Wolfgang Böhme, eds. *Von Eckhart bis Luther: Über mystischen Glauben*. Karlsruhe: Evangelische Akademie: Baden, 1981.

O'Day, Rosemary. *The Debate on the English Reformation*. London and New York: Methuen, 1986.

Olin, John C. *The Catholic Reformation: Savonarola to Ignatius Loyola*. New York: Harper & Row, 1969.

O'Malley, John W. *The First Jesuits*. Cambridge, MA: Harvard University Press, 1993.

——. *Trent and All That: Renaming Catholicism in the Early Modern Era.* Cambridge, MA: Harvard University Press, 2000.

——. *Trent: What Happened at the Council.* Cambridge, MA: Harvard University Press, 2013.

O'Regan, Cyril. *Gnostic Apocalypse: Jacob Boehme's Haunted Narrative.* Albany: State University of New York Press, 2002.

Otto, Henrik. *Vor- und frühreformatorische Tauler-Rezeption: Annotationen in Drucken des späten 15. und frühen 16. Jahrhunderts.* Quellen und Forschungen zur Reformationsgeschichte 75. Gütersloh: Gütersloher Verlagshaus, 2003.

Ozment, Steven. *The Age of Reform (1250–1550): An Intellectual and Religious History of Late Medieval and Reformation Europe.* New Haven and London: Yale University Press, 1980.

——. "An Aid to Luther's Marginal Comments on Johannes Tauler's Sermons." *Harvard Theological Review* 63 (1970): 305–11.

——. "Eckhart and Luther: German Mysticism and Protestantism." *The Thomist* 42 (1978): 259–80.

——. *Homo Spiritualis: A Comparative Study of the Anthropology of Johannes Tauler, Jean Gerson, and Martin Luther (1509–16) in the Context of Their Theological Thought.* Studies in Medieval and Reformation Thought 6. Leiden: Brill, 1969.

——. *Mysticism and Dissent: Religious Ideology and Social Protest in the Sixteenth Century.* New Haven: Yale University Press, 1973.

Packull, Werner O. "Hans Denck: Fugitive from Dogmatism." In *Profiles of Radical Reformers: Biographical Sketches from Thomas Müntzer to Paracelsus,* edited by Hans-Jürgen Goertz, 62–71. Kitchener, ON: Herald Press, 1982.

——. "An Introduction to Anabaptist Theology." In *The Cambridge Companion to Reformation Theology,* edited by David Bagchi and David C. Steinmentz, 194–214. Cambridge: Cambridge University Press, 2004.

——. *Mysticism and the Early South German-Austrian Anabaptist Movement, 1525–1531.* Scottdale, PA: Herald Press, 1977.

Parker, Geoffrey, ed. *The Thirty Years' War.* 2nd ed. London and New York: Routledge, 1987.

Parnham, David. *Sir Henry Vane, Theologian: A Study in Seventeenth-Century Religious and Political Discourse.* Madison, NJ: Teaneck University Press, 1997.

Pater, Calvin Augustine. *Karlstadt as the Father of the Baptist Movements: The Emergence of Lay Protestantism.* Toronto: University of Toronto Press, 1984.

Pederson, Randall J. *Unity in Diversity: English Puritans and the Puritan*

Reformation, 1603–1689. Brill's Series in Church History 68. Leiden: Brill, 2014.

Peinze, Ulrike. "'From Fiery Source to Divine Light': The Theological Anthropology of Jacob Boehme." Unpublished paper.

Pektas, Virginie. *Mystique et philosophie: Grunt, Abgrunt et Urgrund chez Maître Eckhart et Jacob Böhme.* Bochumer Studien zur Philosophie 45. Amsterdam: B. R. Grüner, 2006.

Pelikan, Jaroslav, and Valerie Hotchkiss, eds. *Creeds and Confessions of Faith in the Christian Tradition.* Vol. 2, *The Reformation Era.* New Haven: Yale University Press, 2003.

Penman, Leigh T. I. "Böhme's Student and Mentor: The Leignitz Physician Balthasar Walther (c. 1558–c. 1630)." In *Offenbarung und Episteme: Zur europäischen Wirkung Jakob Böhmes im 17. und 18. Jahrhundert,* edited by Willhelm Kühlmann and Friedrich Vollhardt, 47–65. Frühe Neuzeit 173. Berlin: Walter de Gruyter, 2012.

Pesch, Hermann Otto. "Existential and Sapiential Theology—the Theological Confrontation between Luther and Thomas Aquinas." In *Catholic Scholars Dialogue with Luther,* edited by Jared Wicks, 59–81. Chicago: Loyola University Press, 1970.

Pettet, E. C. *Of Paradise and Light: A Study of Vaughan's* Silex Scintillans. Cambridge: Cambridge University Press, 1960.

Peura, Simo. *Mehr als ein Mensch? Der Vergöttlichung als Thema der Theologie Martin Luthers von 1513 bis 1519.* Mainz: Institut für Europäische Geschichte, 1994.

Peura, Simo, and Antti Raunio, eds. *Luther und Theosis: Vergöttlichung als Thema der abendländische Theologie.* Erlangen: Martin-Luther-Verlag, 1990.

Posset, Franz. "*Divus Bernhardus*: Saint Bernard as Spiritual and Theological Mentor of the Reformer Martin Luther." In *Bernardus Magister: Papers Presented at the Nonacentenary Celebration of the Birth of Saint Bernard of Clairvaux, Kalamazoo, Michigan, Sponsored by the Institute of Cistercian Studies,* edited by John R. Sommerfeldt, 517–32. Cistercian Studies 135. Kalamazoo, MI: Cistercian Publications, 1992.

Preus, Robert D. *The Theology of Post-Reformation Lutheranism.* 2 vols. St. Louis: Concordia, 1970–72.

Reeves, Troy D. *An Annotated Index to the Sermons of John Donne.* 3 vols. Salzburg: Institut für Anglistik und Amerikanistik, 1979–81.

Repgen, Konrad. "Reform." In *The Oxford Encyclopedia of the Reformation,* edited by Hans J. Hillerbrand, 3:392–95. 4 vols. New York and Oxford: Oxford University Press, 1996.

Richard, Lucien Joseph. *The Spirituality of John Calvin*. Atlanta: John Knox, 1974.

Ritschl, Albrecht. *Geschichte des Pietismus*. 3 vols. Bonn: A. Marcus, 1880–86.

Roberts, John R., ed. *Essential Articles for the Study of George Herbert's Poetry*. Hamden, CT: Archon Books, 1979.

Rorem, Paul. "Martin Luther's Christocentric Critique of Pseudo-Dionysian Spirituality." *Lutheran Quarterly* 11 (1997): 291–307.

Roth, John D., and James M. Stayer, eds. *A Companion to Anabaptism and Spiritualism, 1521–1700*. Brill's Companions to the Christian Tradition 6. Leiden: Brill, 2007.

Rudrum, Alan, ed. *Essential Articles for the Study of Henry Vaughan*. Hamden, CT: Archon Books, 1987.

Rupp, Gordon. "Andrew Karlstadt: The Reformer as Puritan." In Rupp, *Patterns of Reformation*, 49–153. London: Epworth, 1969.

———. "A Devotion of Rapture in English Puritanism." In *Reformation Conformity and Dissent: Essays in Honour of Geoffrey Nuttall*, edited by R. Buick Knox, 115–31. London: Epworth, 1977.

———. "The Gospel according to Thomas Müntzer." In Rupp, *Patterns of Reformation*, 251–304. London: Epworth, 1969.

Saak, Erik L. "Luther, Martin." In *The Oxford Guide to the Historical Reception of Augustine*, edited by Karla Pohlmann et al., 3:1341–45. 3 vols. Oxford: Oxford University Press, 2013.

Sandbank, S. "Henry Vaughan's Apology for Darkness." *Studies in English Literature 1500–1900* 7 (1967): 141–52.

Scheper, George L. "Reformation Attitudes toward Allegory and the Song of Songs." *Publications of the Modern Language Association of America* 89 (1974): 551–62.

Schilling, Heinz. "Confessional Europe." In *Handbook of European History, 1400–1600: Late Middle Ages, Renaissance, and Reformation*, edited by Thomas A. Brady Jr., Heiko A. Oberman, and James D. Tracy, 2:641–81. 2 vols. Grand Rapids: Eerdmans, 1996.

———. "Reformation—Umbruch oder Gipfelpunkt eines Temps des Réformes?" In *Die frühe Reformation in Deutschland als Umbruch*, edited by Bernd Moeller, 13–34. Heidelberg: Gütersloh, 1998.

Schmidt, Martin. "Arndt, Johann (1555–1621)." In *Theologische Realenzyklopädie: Studienausgabe*, 4:121–29. 36 vols. Berlin: Walter de Gruyter, 1993–2006.

Schmidt, Richard H. *Glorious Companions: Five Centuries of Anglican Spirituality*. Grand Rapids: Eerdmans, 2002.

Schoeller Reisch, Donata. *Enthöhter Gott–vertiefter Mensch: Zur Bedeutung der Demut, ausgehend von Meister Eckhart und Jakob Böhme*. Alber-Reihe Philosophie. Munich: Karl Alber, 2009.

Schoeps, Hans Joachim. *Vom himmlischen Fleisch Christi: Eine dogmengeschichtliche Untersuchung.* Tübingen: J. C. B. Mohr, 1951.

Schreiner, Susan E. *Are You Alone Wise? The Search for Certainty in the Early Modern Era.* New York: Oxford University Press, 2011.

Schulitz, John. *Jakob Böhme und die Kabbalah: Eine vergleichende Werkanalyse.* Frankfurt am Main: P. Lang, 1993.

Schwanda, Tom. "'Hearts Sweetly Refreshed': Puritan Spiritual Practices Then and Now." *Journal of Spiritual Formation and Soul Care* 3 (2010): 21–41.

——. *Soul Recreation: The Contemplative-Mystical Piety of Puritanism.* Eugene, OR: Wipf & Stock, 2012.

Schwartz, Regina Mara. *Sacramental Poetics at the Dawn of Secularism.* Stanford: Stanford University Press, 2008.

Schwarz, Reinhard. "Mystische Glaube: Die Brautmystik Martin Luthers." In *Von Eckhart bis Luther: Über mystischen Glauben,* edited by Heiko A. Oberman and Wolfgang Böhme, 20–32. Karlsruhe: Evangelische Akademie Baden, 1981.

——. "Thomas Müntzer und die Mystik." In *Die Theologie Thomas Müntzer: Untersuchungen zu seiner Entwicklung und Lehre,* edited by Siegfried Bräuer and Helmar Junghans, 283–301. Göttingen: Vandenhoeck & Ruprecht, 1989.

Schwarz, Reinhold. "Martin Luther (1483–1546)." In *Grosse Mystiker: Leben und Wirken,* edited by Gerhard Ruhbach, and Josef Sudbrack, 185–201. Munich: C. H. Beck, 1984.

Schweitzer, Albert. *The Mysticism of Paul the Apostle.* London: A. & C. Black, 1931.

Seebas, Gottfried. "Osiander, Andreas." In *The Oxford Encyclopedia of the Reformation,* edited by Hans J. Hillerbrand, 3:183–85. 4 vols. New York and Oxford: Oxford University Press, 1996.

Senn, Frank C., ed. *Protestant Spiritual Traditions.* New York: Paulist Press, 1986.

Shaw, Robert B. "George Herbert: The Word of God and the Words of Man." In *Ineffability: Naming the Unnamable from Dante to Beckett,* edited by Peter S. Hawkins and Anne Howland Schotter, 81–93. AMS Ars Poetica 2. New York: AMS Press, 1984.

Sheldrake, Philip. *Love Took My Hand: The Spirituality of George Herbert.* London: Darton, Longman & Todd, 2000.

Sherrington, Alison J. *Mystical Symbolism in the Poetry of Thomas Traherne.* St. Lucia: Queensland University Press, 1970.

Sider, Ronald J. "Andreas Bodenstein von Karlstadt: Between Liberal and Radical." In *Profiles of Radical Reformers: Biographical Sketches from Thomas Müntzer to Paracelsus,* edited by Hans-Jürgen Goertz, 45–53. Kitchener, ON: Herald Press, 1982.

——. *Andreas Bodenstein von Karlstadt: The Development of His Thought, 1517–1525.* Studies in Medieval and Reformation Thought 11. Leiden: Brill, 1974.

——, ed. *Karlstadt's Battle with Luther: Documents in a Liberal–Radical Debate.* Philadelphia: Fortress, 1978.

Simmonds, James D. "Vaughan's Masterpiece and Its Critics: 'The World' Revaluated." *Studies in English Literature 1500–1900* 2 (1962): 82–93.

Singer, Irving. *The Nature of Love.* Vol. 2, *Courtly and Romantic.* Chicago: University of Chicago Press, 1984.

Sledge, Linda Ching. "Typology and the Ineffable: Henry Vaughan and the 'Word in Characters.'" In *Ineffability: Naming the Unnamable from Dante to Beckett,* edited by Peter S. Hawkins and Anne Howland Schotter, 95–108. AMS Ars Poetica 2. New York: AMS Press, 1994.

Smirin, M. M. *Die Volksreformation des Thomas Müntzers und der Grosse Bauernkrieg.* Berlin: Dietz, 1956.

Smith, Julia. "Thomas Traherne." *The Oxford Dictionary of National Biography,* 55:205-8. 60 vols. Oxford: Oxford University Press, 2004.

Stayer, James M. "Introduction: Radicalism and Dissent—A Provisional Assessment." In *Radikalität und Dissent im 16. Jahrhundert / Radicalism and Dissent in the Sixteenth Century,* edited by Hans-Jürgen Goertz and James M. Stayer, 9–25. Zeitschrift für historische Forschung, Beiheft 27. Berlin: Duncker & Humblot, 2002.

——. "The Radical Reformation." In *Handbook of European History, 1400–1600: Late Middle Ages, Renaissance, and Reformation,* edited by Thomas A. Brady Jr., Heiko A. Oberman, and James D. Tracy, 2:249–82. 2 vols. Grand Rapids: Eerdmans, 1996.

——. "The Significance of Anabaptism and Anabaptist Research." In *Radikalität und Dissent im 16. Jahrhundert / Radicalism and Dissent in the Sixteenth Century,* edited by Hans-Jürgen Goertz and James M. Stayer, 77–85. Zeitschrift für historische Forschung, Beiheft 27. Berlin: Duncker & Humblot, 2002.

Steinmetz, David C. "Andreas Bodenstein von Carlstadt." In Steinmetz, *Reformers in the Wings: From Geiler von Kaysersberg to Theodore Beza,* 123–30. 2nd ed. Oxford: Oxford University Press, 2001.

——. *Luther and Staupitz: An Essay in the Intellectual Origins of the Protestant Reformation.* Duke Monographs in Medieval and Renaissance Studies 4. Durham, NC: Duke University Press, 1980.

——. *Misericordia Dei: The Theology of Johannes von Staupitz in Its Late Medieval Setting.* Studies in Medieval and Reformation Thought 4. Leiden: Brill, 1968.

———. "The Theology of John Calvin." In *The Cambridge Companion to Reformation Theology*, edited by David Bagchi and David C. Steinmetz, 113–29. Cambridge: Cambridge University Press, 2004.

Steinmetz, Max. "Thomas Müntzer und die Mystik: Quellenkritische Bemerkungen." In *Bauer, Reich, und Reformation: Festschrift für Günther Franz zum 80. Geburtstag am 23 Mai 1982*, edited by Peter Blickle, 148–59. Stuttgart: Ulmer, 1982.

Strauss, Gerald. "Ideas of *Reformatio* and *Renovatio* from the Middle Ages to the Reformation." In *Handbook of European History 1400–1600: Late Middle Ages, Renaissance, and Reformation*, edited by Thomas A. Brady Jr., Heiko A. Oberman, and James D. Tracy, 2:1–30. 2 vols. Grand Rapids: Eerdmans, 1996.

Strier, Richard. *Love Known: Theology and Experience in George Herbert's Poetry*. Chicago: University of Chicago Press, 1983.

———. "Sanctifying the Aristocracy: 'Devout Humanism' in François de Sales, John Donne, and George Herbert." *Journal of Religion* 69 (1989): 36–58.

Summers, Claude J. "Herrick, Vaughan, and the Poetry of Anglican Survivalism." In *New Perspectives on the Seventeenth-Century English Religious Lyric*, edited by John R. Roberts, 46–74. Columbia: University of Missouri Press, 1994.

Taliaferro, Charles, and Alison J. Teply, eds. *Cambridge Platonist Spirituality*. Classics of Western Spirituality. New York: Paulist Press, 2004.

Tamburello, Dennis E. *Union with Christ: John Calvin and the Mysticism of St. Bernard*. Louisville: Westminster John Knox, 1994.

Tavard, George. "Medieval Piety in Luther's *Commentary on the Magnificat*." In *Ad fontes Lutheri: Toward the Recovery of the Real Luther; Essays in Honor of Kenneth Hagen's Sixty-Fifth Birthday*, edited by Timothy Maschke, Franz Posset, and Joan Skocir, 281–301. Milwaukee: Marquette University Press, 2001.

Troeltsch, Ernst. "Die Bedeutung des Protestantismus für die Entstehung der modernen Welt." *Historische Zeitschrift* 97 (1906): 1–66.

———. *Protestantism and Progress: A Historical Study of the Relation of Protestantism to the Modern World*. Boston: Beacon Press, 1958.

Tuve, Rosemund. "George Herbert and *Caritas*." *Journal of the Warburg and Courtauld Institutes* 22 (1959): 303–31.

Urban, Hugh B. "Mysticism and Imagination in the 16th and 17th Centuries: A Comparison of Ignatius Loyola and Jacob Boehme." Unpublished paper.

Vendler, Helen. *The Poetry of George Herbert*. Cambridge, MA: Harvard University Press, 1975.

Versluis, Arthur. "The Mystery of Boehme's 'Ungrund.'" *Studies in Spirituality* 11 (2001): 205–11.

———. *Wisdom's Children: A Christian Esoteric Tradition.* Albany: State University of New York Press, 1999.

Vogelsang, Erich. "Luther und die Mystik." *Luther Jahrbuch* (1937): 32–53.

———. "Die Unio mystica bei Luther." *Archiv für Reformationsgeschichte* 35 (1938): 63–80.

Vogler, Günter. *Thomas Müntzer.* Berlin: Dietz, 1989.

Völker, Ludwig. "'Gelassenheit': Zur Enstehung des Wortes in der Sprache Meister Eckharts und seiner Überlieferung in der nacheckhartischen Mystik bis Jacob Böhme." In *'Getempert und Gemischet': Für Wolfgang Mohr zum 65. Geburtstag von seiner Tübinger Schülern,* edited by Franz Hundsnurcher and Ulrich Müller, 281–312. Göppingen: Alfred Kümmerle, 1972.

Wakefield, Gordon S. "The Puritans." In *The Study of Spirituality,* edited by Cheslyn Jones, Geoffrey Wainwright, and Edward Yarnold, S.J., 437–45. New York and Oxford: Oxford University Press, 1986.

Wallace, Dewey D., Jr. *Shapers of English Calvinism, 1660–1714: Variety, Persistence, and Transformation.* Oxford Studies in Historical Theology. Oxford and New York: Oxford University Press, 2011.

Wallmann, Johannes. "Johann Arndt (1555–1621)." In *The Pietist Theologians: An Introduction to Theology in the Seventeenth and Eighteenth Centuries,* edited by Carter Lindberg, 21–37. The Great Theologians. Oxford: Blackwell, 2005.

———. "Johann Arndt und die protestantische Frömmigkeit: Zur Rezeption der mittelalterlichen Mystik im Luthertum." In *Frömmigkeit in der frühen Neuzeit: Studien zur religiösen Literatur des 17. Jahrhunderts in Deutschland,* edited by Dieter Breuer, 50–74. Chloe 2. Amsterdam: Rodopi, 1984.

Walsh, David. *The Mysticism of Innerworldly Fulfullment: A Study of Jacob Boehme.* Gainesville: University Presses of Florida, 1983.

Ward, W. Reginald, and Richard P. Heitzenrater, eds. *The Works of John Wesley.* Vol. 19, *Journals and Diaries II (1738–43).* Nashville: Abingdon, 1990.

Watkin, E. I. *Poets and Mystics.* London: Sheed & Ward, 1953.

Weber, Edmund. *Johann Arndts Vier Bücher vom Wahren Christentum als Beitrag zur protestantischen Irenik des 17. Jahrhundert: Eine quellenkritische Untersuchung.* Marburg/Lahn: Elwert, 1969.

Webster, Charles. *Paracelsus: Medicine, Magic, and Mission at the End of Time.* New Haven: Yale University Press, 2009.

Weeks, Andrew. *Boehme: An Intellectual Biography of the Seventeenth-Century Philosopher and Mystic.* Albany: State University of New York Press, 1991.

———. *German Mysticism from Hildegard of Bingen to Ludwig Wittgenstein.* Albany: State University of New York Press, 1993.

———. "Meister Eckhart and Valentin Weigel." In *A Companion to Meister Eckhart,* edited by Jeremiah M. Hackett, 607–27. Brill's Companions to the Christian Tradition 36. Leiden: Brill, 2013.

———. *Paracelsus: Speculative Theory and the Crisis of the Early Reformation.* Albany: State University of New York Press, 1997.

———. *Valentin Weigel (1533–1588): German Religious Dissenter, Speculative Theorist, and Advocate of Tolerance.* Albany: State University of New York Press, 2000.

Weigelt, Horst. "Campanus, Johannes." In *The Oxford Encyclopedia of the Reformation,* edited by Hans J. Hillerbrand, 1:249–50. 4 vols. New York and Oxford: Oxford University Press, 1996.

Whalen, Robert. *The Poetry of Immanence: Sacrament in Donne and Herbert.* Toronto: University of Toronto Press, 2002.

White, Helen C. *The Metaphysical Poets: A Study in Religious Experience.* 1936. Reprint, New York: Collier, 1962.

Wicks, Jared. "Luther (Martin)." In *Dictionnaire de spiritualité: Ascétique et mystique, doctrine et histoire,* edited by Marcel Viller et al., 9:1206–43. 17 vols. Paris: Beauchesne, 1937–97.

———. *Man Yearning for Grace: Luther's Early Spiritual Teaching.* Washington, DC: Corpus Books, 1968.

Wilcox, Helen. "Devotional Writings." In *The Cambridge Companion to John Donne,* edited by Achsah Guibbory, 149–65. Cambridge: Cambridge University Press, 2006.

Williams, George Hunston. *The Radical Reformation.* 3rd ed. Sixteenth Century Essays and Studies 15. Ann Arbor, MI: Edwards Brothers, 1992.

Williams, George, and Angel M. Mergal, eds. *Spiritual and Anabaptist Writers: Documents Illustrative of the Radical Reformation.* Library of Christian Classics 25. Philadelphia: Westminster, 1957.

Willis-Watkins, D. "The Unio Mystica and the Assurance of Faith according to Calvin." In *Calvin: Erbe und Auftrag; Festschrift für Wilhelm Heinrich Neuser zum 65. Geburtstag,* 77–84. Kampen: Kok, 1991.

Wöhrer, Franz Karl. "The 'Sense of Presence' as a Mode of Mystical Experience in the Mystographical Poems of George Herbert (1593–1633)." In *British Literature and Spirituality: Theoretical Approaches and Transdisciplinary Readings,* edited by Franz Karl Wöhrer and John S. Bak, 1–30. Zurich: LIT, 2013.

Wollgast, Siegfried. *Der deutsche Pantheismus der 16. Jahrhundert: Sebastian Franck und seine Wirkungen auf die Entwicklung der pantheistischen Philosophie in Deutschland.* Berlin: Deutscher Verlag der Wissenschaften, 1972.

Wriedt, Markus. "Mystik und Protestantismus—ein Widerspruch? In *Mystik: Religion der Zukunft – Zukunft der Religion?,* 67–87. Leipzig: Evangelische Verlagsanstalt, 2003.

Young, R. V. "The Presence of Grace in Seventeenth-Century Poetry." In idem, *Doctrine and Devotion in Seventeenth-Century Poetry: Studies in Donne, Herbert, Crashaw, and Vaughan,* 1–80. Studies in Renaissance Literature 2. Cambridge: D. S. Brewer, 2000.

Zeller, Winfried. "Der ferne Weg des Geistes: Zur Würdigung Valentin Weigels." In Zeller, *Theologie und Frömmigkeit: Gesammelte Aufsätze,* edited by Bernd Jaspert, 2:89–102. 2 vols. Marburg: Elwert, 1971-78.

———. "Luthertum und Mystik." In Zeller, *Theologie und Frömmigkeit: Gesammelte Aufsätze,* edited by Bernd Jaspert, 2:35–54. 2 vols. Marburg: Elwert, 1971–78.

———. "Meister Eckhart bei Valentin Weigel." In Zeller, *Theologie und Frömmigkeit: Gesammelte Aufsätze,* edited by Bernd Jaspert, 2:56–88. 2 vols. Marburg: Elwert, 1971–78.

———. "Protestantische Frömmigkeit im 17. Jahrhundert." In Zeller, *Theologie und Frömmigkeit: Gesammelte Aufsätze,* edited by Bernd Jaspert, 1:85–116. 2 vols. Marburg: Elwert, 1971–78.

Zur Mühlen, Karl-Heinz. *Nos extra nos: Luthers Theologie zwischen Mystik und Scholastik.* Beiträge zur historischen Theologie 46. Tübingen: Mohr Siebeck, 1972.

Index of Subjects

Index of Names

Index of Scripture References (Vg)